FEMINIST JUDGMENTS: IMMIGRATION LAW OPINIONS REWRITTEN

This volume, part of the Feminist Judgment Series, shows how feminist legal theory along with critical race theory and intersectional modes of critique might transform immigration law. Here, a diverse collection of scholars and lawyers bring critical feminist, race, and intersectional insights to Supreme Court opinions. Feminist reasoning values the perspectives of outsiders, exposes the deep-rooted bias in the legal opinions of courts, and illuminates the effects of ostensibly neutral policies that create and maintain oppression and hierarchy. One by one, the chapters reimagine the norms that drive immigration policies and practices. In place of discrimination and subordination, the authors demand welcome and equality. Where current law omits the voice and stories of noncitizens, the authors center their lives and experiences. Collectively, they reveal how a feminist vision of immigration law could center a commitment to equality and justice and foster a country where diverse newcomers readily flourish with dignity.

Kathleen Kim, Associate Dean for Equity & Inclusion, Professor of Law, and William M. Rains Fellow, Loyola Marymount University, Loyola Law School Los Angeles.

Kevin Lapp, Associate Dean for Faculty and Professor of Law, Loyola Marymount University, Loyola Law School Los Angeles.

Jennifer J. Lee, Associate Professor of Law and Director of the Social Justice Lawyering Clinic, Sheller Center for Social Justice, Temple University Beasley School of Law.

Feminist Judgments Series Editors

Bridget J. Crawford
Elisabeth Haub School of Law at Pace University

Kathryn M. Stanchi
University of Nevada, Las Vegas William S. Boyd School of Law

Linda L. Berger
University of Nevada, Las Vegas William S. Boyd School of Law

Advisory Panel for Feminist Judgments Series

Kathryn Abrams, Herma Hill Kay Distinguished Professor of Law, University of California, Berkeley, School of Law

Katharine T. Bartlett, A. Kenneth Pye Professor Emerita of Law, Duke University School of Law

Mary Anne Case, Arnold I. Shure Professor of Law, The University of Chicago Law School

April L. Cherry, Professor of Law, Cleveland-Marshall College of Law

Margaret E. Johnson, Professor of Law, University of Baltimore School of Law

Sonia Katyal, Roger J. Traynor Distinguished Professor of Law, University of California, Berkeley, School of Law

Nancy Leong, Professor of Law and William M. Beaney Memorial Research Chair, University of Denver Sturm College of Law

Rachel Moran, Distinguished Professor of Emeritus of Law, University of California, Irvine School of Law

Angela Onwuachi-Willig, Dean and Ryan Roth Gallo & Ernest J. Gallo Professor of Law, Boston University School of Law

Nancy D. Polikoff, Professor of Law Emerita, American University Washington College of Law

Daniel B. Rodriguez, Harold Washington Professor, Northwestern University Pritzker School of Law

Susan Deller Ross, Professor of Law, Georgetown University Law Center

Dean Spade, Professor of Law, Seattle University School of Law

Robin L. West, Frederick J. Haas Professor of Law and Philosophy Emeritus, Georgetown University Law Center

Verna L. Williams, Chief Executive Officer, Equal Justice Works

Feminist Judgments: Immigration Law Opinions Rewritten

Edited by

KATHLEEN KIM
LMU Loyola Law School Los Angeles

KEVIN LAPP
LMU Loyola Law School Los Angeles

JENNIFER J. LEE
Temple University Beasley School of Law

CAMBRIDGE
UNIVERSITY PRESS

Shaftesbury Road, Cambridge CB2 8EA, United Kingdom

One Liberty Plaza, 20th Floor, New York, NY 10006, USA

477 Williamstown Road, Port Melbourne, VIC 3207, Australia

314–321, 3rd Floor, Plot 3, Splendor Forum, Jasola District Centre, New Delhi – 110025, India

103 Penang Road, #05–06/07, Visioncrest Commercial, Singapore 238467

Cambridge University Press is part of Cambridge University Press & Assessment, a department of the University of Cambridge.

We share the University's mission to contribute to society through the pursuit of education, learning and research at the highest international levels of excellence.

www.cambridge.org
Information on this title: www.cambridge.org/9781009198936

DOI: 10.1017/9781009198950

First published 2024

A catalogue record for this publication is available from the British Library

A Cataloging-in-Publication data record for this book is available from the Library of Congress

ISBN 978-1-009-19893-6 Hardback
ISBN 978-1-009-19894-3 Paperback

This book is dedicated to our parents and our partners.

Contents

Advisory Panel for Feminist Judgments: Immigration Law Opinions Rewritten

Sameer Ashar, Associate Dean for Equity Initiatives and Clinical Professor of Law, University of California Irvine School of Law

Angela Banks, Charles J. Merriam Distinguished Professor of Law, Arizona State University Sandra Day O'Connor College of Law

Richard Boswell, Professor of Law, University of California Hastings School of Law

Jennifer Chacón, Professor of Law, Stanford Law School

Marielena Hincapié, Executive Director, National Immigration Law Center (NILC)

Kevin R. Johnson, Dean and Mabie-Apallas Professor of Public Interest Law, and Professor of Chicana/o Studies, University of California Davis School of Law

Nancy Morawetz, Professor of Clinical Law, New York University School of Law

Hiroshi Motomura, Susan Westerberg Prager Distinguished Professor of Law, Faculty Co-Director of the Center for Immigration Law and Policy, University of California Los Angeles School of Law

Juliet Stumpf, Robert E. Jones Professor of Advocacy and Ethics, Lewis & Clark Law School

Michael Wishnie, William O. Douglas Clinical Professor of Law and Counselor to the Dean, Yale Law School

Notes on Contributors

Ahilan Arulanantham, Professor from Practice and Faculty Co-Director of the Center for Immigration Law and Policy, University of California Los Angeles School of Law and Senior Counsel, American Civil Liberties Union of Southern California.

Raymond Audain. Adjunct Professor of Clinical Law, New York University School of Law and Senior Counsel, Legal Defense Fund.

Sabrina Balgamwalla. Assistant Professor of Law and Director of the Asylum and Immigration Law Clinic, Wayne State University Law School.

Kristina M. Campbell is Professor of Law, University of the District of Columbia David A. Clarke School of Law.

Stacy Caplow, Associate Dean of Experiential Education, Professor of Law, and Co-Director of the Safe Harbor Project, Brooklyn Law School.

Stewart Chang, Associate Dean for Academic Affairs and Professor of Law, University of Nevada, Las Vegas William S. Boyd School of Law.

Gabriel J. Chin, Edward L. Barrett Jr. Chair of Law, Martin Luther King Jr. Professor of Law, and Director of Clinical Legal Education, University of California Davis School of Law.

Erin Corcoran, Associate Teaching Professor, University of Notre Dame Keough School of Global Affairs.

Julie Dahlstrom, Clinical Associate Professor of Law and Director of the Immigrants' Rights and Human Trafficking Program, Boston University School of Law.

Stella Burch Elias, Professor of Law and Chancellor William Gardiner Hammond Fellow in Law, University of Iowa College of Law.

Maryellen Fullerton, Suzanne J. and Norman Miles Professor of Law, Brooklyn Law School.

Ruben J. Garcia, Professor of Law and Co-Director of the Workplace Law Program, University of Nevada, Las Vegas William S. Boyd School of Law.

Kati Griffith, Jean McKelvey-Alice Grant Professor and Stephen H. Weiss Junior Fellow, Cornell Law School.

Nicole Hallett, Associate Clinical Professor of Law and Director of the Immigrants' Rights Clinic, University of Chicago Law School.

Lindsay M. Harris, Associate Dean of Clinical and Experiential Programs, Professor of Law, and Director of the Immigration and Human Rights Clinic, University of the District of Columbia David A. Clarke School of Law.

Julia Hernández, Associate Professor of Law, City University of New York School of Law.

Kevin R. Johnson, Dean, Mabie-Apallas Professor of Public Interest Law, and Professor of Chicana/o Studies, University of California Davis School of Law.

Joy Kanwar, Associate Professor of Legal Writing, Brooklyn Law School.

Kathleen Kim, Associate Dean for Equity and Inclusion, Professor of Law, and William M. Raines Fellow, Loyola Marymount University, Loyola Law School Los Angeles.

Annie Lai, Clinical Professor of Law, Co-Associate Dean for Experiential Education, and Co-Director of the Immigrant Rights Clinic, University of California Irvine School of Law.

Kevin Lapp, Associate Dean for Faculty, Professor of Law, Loyola Marymount University, Loyola Law School Los Angeles.

Eunice C. Lee, Associate Professor of Law, University of Arizona James E. Rogers College of Law.

Jennifer J. Lee, Associate Professor of Law and Director of the Social Justice Lawyering Clinic, Sheller Center for Social Justice, Temple University Beasley School of Law.

Jennifer Lee Koh, Professor of Law and Co-Director of the Nootbaar Institute for Law, Religion, and Ethics, Pepperdine Caruso School of Law.

H. Marissa Montes, Associate Clinical Professor of Law and Director of the Loyola Immigrant Justice Clinic, Loyola Marymount University, Loyola Law School Los Angeles.

Michael A. Olivas (Emeritus), William B. Bates Distinguished Chair in Law and Director of the Institute for Higher Education Law & Governance, University of Houston Law Center.

Jaya Ramji-Nogales, Associate Dean for Research and I. Herman Stern Research Professor of Law, Temple University Beasley School of Law.

Rachel E. Rosenbloom, Assoicate Dean for Experiential Education and Professor of Law, Northeastern University School of Law.

Sarah Schendel, Associate Professor of Law, Suffolk University Law School.

Sarah Sherman-Stokes, Clinical Associate Professor and Associate Director of the Immigrants' Rights and Human Trafficking Clinic, Boston University School of Law.

Shoba Sivaprasad Wadhia, Associate Dean for Diversity, Equity, and Inclusion, Samuel Weiss Faculty Scholar, Clinical Professor of Law, and Director of the Center for Immigrants' Rights Clinic, Penn State Law.

Jonathan Weinberg, Associate Dean for Research and Professor of Law, Wayne State University Law School.

Patricia Winograd, Associate Clinical Professor of Law, Loyola Marymount University, Loyola Law School Los Angeles.

Acknowledgments

The editors would like to give special thanks to the artist, Ben Sakoguchi, who generously donated the image of his painting, *Sobre la tierra de los libres (O'er the land of the free)* which adorns the cover of this book. The authors who contributed chapters of this book would like to thank the following: KT Albiston, Farrin Anello, Jennifer Araujo, Christopher Beauchamp, Susan Bibler Coutin, Richard Boswell, Dana Brakman Reiser, Sucheng Chan, James Cho, Karen Clarke, Andy Coan, Margaret Colgate Love, Maria Esther Cortes de Vizcarra, Adam Cox, Susan Craddock, Marissa Cunha, Pooja Dadhania, Jean Davis, Michael Alan Dressler Jr., Joshua English, Brian Flaherty, Kelly Folkers, Amanda Frost, Jennifer Hanna, Laura Hyun Yi Kang, Lady Idos, Stephen Kang, BK Katzmann, Jonathan J. Koehler, Alina Krauff, Kristin Kuraishi, Erika Lee, Karen J. Leong, Jessica Litman, Eithne Luibheid, Servando Martinez, Hiroshi Motomura, Karen Musalo, Laura Nader, Luke Nelson, Aihwa Ong, Leilani O' Sullivan, George Peffer, Charlie Perkins, Sara Perkins, Jean Pfaelzer, Christian Rabin, Sunna Rabin-Lai, Carmen Ramirez de Arellano, Carrie Rosenbaum, Rachel E. Rosenbloom, Jim Silk, Mia Stefanou, Kate Steiker-Ginzberg, Jane Stoever, Angela Stolzfus, Michael Tan, Angela Termini, Andrew Urban, Christine M. Venter, Mike Wishnie, Stephen Yale-Loehr, Eric Yap, the late Stuart Creighton Miller and Judy Yung. In addition, they thank the California State Archives and all the immigrants who have trusted them with their stories.

Table of Cases

1

Introduction

Kathleen Kim, Kevin Lapp, and Jennifer J. Lee

U.S. immigration law is a complex system of rules, regulations, and practices involving multiple agencies and actors. Understanding the U.S. immigration system requires not only knowledge of the vast body of immigration law judicial opinions but also familiarity with the historical, political, and social context surrounding such opinions. The overt and implicit biases that pervade immigration law and influence the actors in the immigration system inflict all manner of harms on noncitizens, their families, and their communities. Moreover, the system's rampant discrimination and intentional subordination of noncitizens undermine the country's commitment to equality and justice for all.

This is not a story confined to the nativist nineteenth century. Recent public revelations have exposed persistent draconian immigration practices, such as migrant family separation, the exclusion and removal of asylees and refugees to unsafe countries of origin, and prolonged mandatory detention in deplorable conditions. While the Trump administration's anti-immigrant rhetoric grabbed headlines, the preceding Obama administration deported record-breaking numbers of noncitizens. The Biden administration continues some of the harsh policies of its predecessors, underscoring the fiction that a new presidential administration can "fix" this country's immigration system.

The inhumane federal regulation of immigration perseveres, justified by a canon of U.S. Supreme Court jurisprudence that authorizes the exclusion of foreigners for virtually any reason, including the pretexts of national security, health and public safety, and the protection of American jobs. This case law establishes and sustains an immigration regime that denies noncitizens the promise of welcome in a land of supposed opportunity. For immigrants already in the United States, the Court has no reservations about making rules about their treatment that would be unacceptable if applied to U.S. citizens. Noncitizens confront diminished access to legal protections in the workplace, detention settings, and immigration court proceedings, to name a few. Only in rare cases has the Supreme Court held that noncitizens in certain settings, such as undocumented children in public schools or immigrants facing criminal prosecution, were entitled to constitutional rights. As a result, the dominant immigration law paradigm favors government sovereignty – through the exercise of detention, deportation, and exclusion – to determine who belongs in our national community and what rights they hold while here.

This book envisions a different kind of immigration jurisprudence. A feminist version of immigration law could foster a country where diverse newcomers readily flourish with dignity. Given the human suffering caused by the immigration system, it is time to reconsider the norms that drive immigration policies and practices. Feminist reasoning values the perspectives of outsiders, exposes the deeprooted bias in the legal opinions of courts, and illuminates the effects of ostensibly neutral policies that create and maintain oppression and hierarchy. This book seeks to add depth and social relevance to U.S. Supreme Court immigration law decisions while prioritizing critical feminist and race concerns in the redesign of immigration law.

In the spirit of the original volume, *Feminist Judgments: Rewritten Opinions of the United States Supreme Court* (Cambridge University Press, 2016), we asked authors to rewrite foundational Supreme Court immigration opinions and present reimagined doctrinal and normative perspectives through a feminist lens. These new opinions confront and tear down the troubling pillars of existing immigration doctrine and lay a new foundation, grounded in a feminist vision of justice. Their approaches are as diverse as they are inspirational. The rewritten opinions shed new light on judicial decision-making by resisting dominant paradigms. The related commentaries consider the historical, social, and political circumstances in which the original opinions were decided.

This volume began with several conversations with the founding editors of the series in which they passed on to us the process and goals of the *Feminist Judgments* project. These conversations provided a conceptual, yet flexible, framework that helped us to assemble a diverse advisory panel of widely recognized immigration scholars, with whom we consulted on the selection of the U.S. Supreme Court immigration opinions featured in this volume. We finalized a list of fourteen opinions far reaching in their implications for noncitizens.

Collectively, this volume undertakes an analytic approach that we call critical immigration legal theory.[1] At their core, the chapters interrogate the ways in which immigration law constructs and sustains subclasses of people based on gender, race, class, and other historically oppressed identities. In so doing, they employ a variety of feminist approaches that embrace anti-subordination theory, are intersectional and anti-essentialist, and closely align with critical race theory. In particular, this critical study of immigration law elucidates the current doctrine's role in reifying white patriarchy via the regulation of noncitizens. If the approaches collected

---

[1]   Kathleen Kim, Kevin Lapp, & Jennifer J. Lee, *Critical Immigration Legal Theory* (Aug. 20, 2022) (unpublished manuscript) (on file with authors).

here were integrated in future judicial opinions and discussions on immigration policy, they could help to bring this country's immigration system in harmony with a multicultural democracy.

SUPREME COURT IMMIGRATION JURISPRUDENCE

The U.S. Supreme Court immigration opinions examined and rewritten in this volume are well known in the canon of immigration jurisprudence. They represent a thoughtful and thorough curation of Supreme Court opinions from the early foundations of immigration law to twenty-first century developments in immigration law addressing the rights of immigrants in deportation proceedings or detention, state versus federal immigration regulation, and the rights of undocumented workers and children. These opinions also tackle the interaction of immigration law with other areas such as criminal law, education law, labor law, and administrative law.

The dominant immigration law paradigm of federal supremacy and noncitizen subordination emerged from a line of Supreme Court decisions that began in 1875, wherein the Court pronounced immigration policy and regulation to be an exclusive function of federal governmental control.[2] The timing of these foundational immigration opinions coincided with the end of Reconstruction. Post-Civil War efforts to fully realize the citizenship and rights of newly freed slaves faced a swift and strong backlash. White supremacy succeeded in abruptly ending Reconstruction and fed new energy into xenophobic attacks against Chinese, other Asian migrants, and Mexican migrants, who had filled the U.S. demand for low to no cost labor following the formal end of chattel slavery. Indeed, the long-term residence of a growing number of Chinese laborers prompted this country's first immigration laws, meant to exclude and remove Chinese and Asian migrants along explicit gendered and racialized terms.[3] The Page Act, enacted in 1875, prohibited the entry of migrants from China "and other oriental countries." It rendered Asian women as prostitutes, inherently immoral and debase, and therefore unfit to enter the United States. The law portrayed Asian men as taking jobs away from white Americans and, like Asian women, inherently criminal and unable to assimilate to white America.

Such xenophobia continued well into the 1920s, when the Court denied citizenship to Asian immigrants on the basis that they could not readily integrate with Europeans to be considered "free white persons" under the Naturalization Act.[4] The Undesirable Aliens Act of 1929 criminalized illegal reentry for the purpose of expelling Mexican agricultural workers in the United States after the growing season and harvest. Supreme Court opinions addressing these laws deliberately

---

[2] Chy Lung v. Freeman, 92 U.S. 275, 280 (1875).
[3] Nishimura Ekiu v. United States, 142 U.S. 651, 659–60 (1892); United States v. Wong Kim Ark, 169 U.S. 649, 653 (1898); MAE NGAI, THE CHINESE QUESTION: THE GOLD RUSHES AND GLOBAL POLITICS 149–50 (2021).
[4] United States v. Bhagat Singh Thind, 261 U.S. 204, 214–15 (1923).

reinforced white patriarchal supremacy by defending government efforts to eliminate the migration and integration of non-white persons.

The Supreme Court upheld the validity of exclusionary immigration restrictions like the Page Act, the Chinese Exclusion Acts, and others, through what
became known as the plenary power doctrine. This doctrine designates the political branches of the federal government as having exclusive authority to regulate
immigration. It commands that neither states nor the judiciary may interfere in
the authority of Congress and the Executive over immigration matters. This power
was not explicitly enumerated anywhere in the Constitution. Rather, the Court
justified the plenary power doctrine by inferring extraconstitutional principles that
invoked the inherent power of a sovereign nation to protect its borders in the name
of national security.

Via the plenary power doctrine, the Court granted the federal government unfettered discretion in determining immigration enforcement priorities and practices.
Following World War II, the government deployed that power to uphold legislation
and immigration agency decisions that targeted Communists. In a series of cases,
the Court held that excluding noncitizens from entry to the United States without
a hearing, and without ever disclosing the basis for the decision to exclude, did not
violate the Constitution.[5] Rather, the Court concluded that "[w]hatever the procedure authorized by Congress is, it is due process as far as an alien denied entry is
concerned." At the same time, it made it clear that discrimination against noncitizens in favor of citizens did not violate the Constitution.[6]

Beginning in the 1980s, federal immigration law increasingly criminalized migration by prohibiting the employment of undocumented workers, expanding the
grounds for deporting longstanding lawful permanent residents ("green card" holders), and creating mandatory detention for certain immigrants subject to removal.[7]
The resources devoted to surveilling the border and enforcing immigration laws in
the country's interior vastly expanded. At the same time, immigration enforcement
became increasingly punitive through the expanded use of immigrant detention
and a militarization of border security.[8]

U.S. Supreme Court jurisprudence endorsed this enforcement regime over
the rights of immigrant children, families, and workers. The Court, for example,
refused to consider whether the government had violated the equal protection
doctrine by racially discriminating against Black Haitian asylees in the 1980s who

---

[5] United States ex. rel. Knauff v. Shaughnessy, 338 U.S. 537, 546–47 (1950); Shaughnessy v. United
States ex. rel. Mezei, 345 U.S. 206, 214–15 (1953), Kleindienst v. Mandel, 408 U.S. 753, 769 (1972).

[6] Mathews v. Diaz, 426 U.S. 67, 80 (1976).

[7] Immigration Reform and Control Act of 1986, Pub. L. No. 99-603, 100 Stat. 3359; Anti-Drug Abuse Act
of 1988, Pub. L. No. 100-690, 102 Stat. 4181; Illegal Immigration Reform and Immigrant Responsibility
Act of 1996, Pub. L. No. 104-208, 110 Stat. 3009; Antiterrorism and Effective Death Penalty Act of 1996,
Pub. L. No. 104-132, 110 Stat. 1214.

[8] ADAM GOODMAN, THE DEPORTATION MACHINE: AMERICA'S LONG HISTORY OF EXPELLING
IMMIGRANTS 167–68 (2020).

fled persecution by the authoritarian Duvalier government. The Haitian asylum seekers were immediately incarcerated, a sudden reversal of longstanding policy that had allowed all immigrants seeking asylum to await disposition of their asylum claims inside the United States. The Court, however, found the government's actions nondiscriminatory.[9] In another case, the Court refused to scrutinize the government's detention of children. It declined to consider the best interest of the child when detaining unaccompanied children fleeing persecution from Central America in the 1980s and 1990s.[10] The Court also held that immigration enforcement goals superseded the labor organizing rights of undocumented workers under the National Labor Relations Act. An undocumented worker who suffered illegal retaliation by his employer for exercising his labor rights could not recover full labor remedies because his employment violated federal immigration law.[11]

Notwithstanding the Supreme Court's typical deference to the federal government's plenary power, the Court has recognized limited constitutional rights of noncitizens in narrow circumstances. These include the procedural due process rights of a long-time lawful permanent resident with significant ties to the United States[12] and the Sixth Amendment's guarantee that noncitizen criminal defendants receive effective assistance of counsel, including guidance on the immigration consequences of certain plea deals.[13] Other decisions have found that undocumented children have the right to attend public school under the Equal Protection Clause,[14] and that substantive due process requires that detained immigrants must receive a bond hearing every six months if there is no country to which they can be deported in the foreseeable future.[15]

While it is difficult to discern a unifying rationale for the constitutional protections afforded by these seemingly outlier cases, their influence has been limited to the circumstances under which they arose. The Court, for example, has declined to further recognize the substantive due process rights of detained immigrants awaiting their deportation.[16] For immigrants subjected to prolonged detention during the pendency of their deportation hearings, the Court has held that federal immigration law did not require periodic six-month bond hearings.[17] Moreover, undocumented immigrants as a class have not succeeded in gaining equal protection rights except for children in public schools.[18]

---

[9] Jean v. Nelson, 472 U.S. 846, 854–55 (1985).
[10] Reno v. Flores, 507 U.S. 292, 315 (1993).
[11] Hoffman Plastic Compounds, Inc. v. NLRB, 535 U.S. 137, 151–52 (2002).
[12] Landon v. Plasencia, 459 U.S. 21, 34 (1982).
[13] Padilla v. Kentucky, 559 U.S. 356, 374 (2010).
[14] Plyler v. Doe, 457 U.S. 202, 221–22 (1982).
[15] Zadvydas v. Davis, 533 U.S. 678, 701 (2001).
[16] Demore v. Kim, 538 U.S. 510, 527–28 (2003).
[17] Jennings v. Rodriguez, 138 S. Ct. 830, 844 (2018).
[18] Hiroshi Motomura, *The Rights of Others: Legal Claims and Immigration Outside the Law*, 59 Duke L.J. 1723, 1734 (2010).

Curiously, the plenary power doctrine has strengthened federal preemption challenges to invalidate state anti-immigrant policies that obstruct federal jurisdiction
over immigration. In 1984, California's enactment of Proposition 187, which denied
access to public services by undocumented immigrants, triggered a wave of similar
anti-immigrant efforts by states and localities.[19] Thereafter, multiple states and localities enacted anti-immigrant laws purportedly in response to the perceived failure
of the federal government to control unauthorized migration. These laws, such as
Arizona's S.B. 1070 enacted in 2010, were designed to create inhospitable living conditions for immigrants to encourage their self-deportation.[20] Relying on the plenary
power doctrine, the Supreme Court invalidated Arizona's infamous "show me your
papers" mandate that sought to criminalize undocumented status.[21] It found that
such state efforts unconstitutionally preempted exclusive federal jurisdiction over
the enforcement of immigration law.[22]

The Court's deference to the political branches on immigration matters legiti-
mizes an immigration regime that, because of politics and noncitizens' lack of a
right to vote, enables the othering of noncitizens. Today, the plenary power doctrine
remains alive and well in U.S. Supreme Court decisions that address immigration
matters. In the 2018 case, *Trump* v. *Hawaii*, the Court recited the plenary power doctrine in upholding the constitutionality of the Trump administration's third attempt
at an Executive Order, which had been initially premised on prohibiting the entry
of immigrants from Muslim-majority countries.[23] The overt discriminatory intent
of the Executive Order to ban noncitizens based on their race, national origin, and
religion would have drawn heightened judicial scrutiny under the equal protection
doctrine in non-immigration matters. Yet the Court reiterated:

> For more than a century, this Court has recognized that the admission and exclu-
> sion of foreign nationals is a fundamental sovereign attribute exercised by the gov-
> ernment's political departments largely immune from judicial control. Because
> decisions in these matters may implicate relations with foreign powers, or involve
> classifications defined in the light of changing political and economic circum-
> stances, such judgments are frequently of a character more appropriate to either
> the Legislature or the Executive.

Consequently, the immigration system continues to maintain a racialized hierarchy that determines who gets in and is allowed to remain, while inflicting serious
harms by separating families, incarcerating immigrants in deplorable conditions,
and exploiting undocumented workers. In a recent decision addressing the Trump
administration's rescission of the Deferred Action for Childhood Arrivals (DACA)

---

[19] 1994 Cal. Legis. Serv. Proposition 187.
[20] S.B. 1070, 49th Leg., 2d Reg. Sess. (Ariz. 2010).
[21] Arizona v. United States, 567 U.S. 387, 416 (2012).
[22] Kerry Abrams, *Plenary Power Preemption*, 99 Va. L. Rev. 601, 610 (2013).
[23] Trump v. Hawaii, 138 S. Ct. 2392, 2418–20 (2018).

program, the Court declined to consider plaintiffs' claims of discrimination.[24] DACA provided deportation relief for hundreds of thousands of young immigrants brought to the United States as children. While the Court reinstated the program on procedural grounds, it refused to contend with the ample evidence of explicit racial animus that may have motivated DACA's revocation.

The Court's avoidance of the racialized ways in which the federal government discriminates against noncitizens of color is emblematic of its treatment of immigration matters generally. Rather than invalidate the subordination of noncitizens, the Court has strengthened an immigration enforcement system that deprives noncitizens of protections against arrest, detention, and deportation. Consequently, social and political movements for immigrants' rights often look well beyond the courts for reimagining the immigration law system.

FEMINIST JUDGMENTS

Confronted with this canon of U.S. Supreme Court opinions, we asked contributing authors to reimagine these opinions through a feminist lens, broadly conceived. Although bound by the precedent and facts that informed the original Supreme Court cases, authors were free to reach different outcomes. Some authors chose to draft a new majority opinion reaching a new result. Others penned a concurrence to address issues ignored by the majority. A few drafted a new dissent. Accompanying each rewritten opinion is a commentary that contextualizes the original opinion and discusses the interventions raised by the rewrite. As a result, this volume engages an innovative analytical approach that highlights the interventions that critical feminist reasoning can bring to reshape the current immigration legal regime.

A. Contributing Authors

To encourage maximum inclusivity in our roster of contributing authors for this volume, we publicized an open solicitation. We reviewed submissions from interested authors and selected those with a variety of backgrounds who endeavored to apply critical perspectives to the designated cases.

The contributing authors bring considerable knowledge and insight to each opinion addressed in this volume. The authors are experts in immigration law and other substantive legal areas, such as criminal law, workplace rights, administrative law, critical race theory, and civil rights. They represent a diverse range of prominent legal voices in the field of immigration law. They include law professors who teach immigration law and run legal clinics that work directly with immigrants and their communities. Others are from outside the academy and at the forefront of the fight

---

[24] Dep't of Homeland Sec. v. Regents of Univ. of Cal., 140 S. Ct. 1891, 1915–16 (2020).

for immigrant rights. Indeed, some authors served as counsel or filed amicus briefs in the cases included here. These authors have grappled with the opinions in this volume as legal advocates and thought leaders, whose incisive analyses bring a new vision to these U.S. Supreme Court immigration law opinions.

B. *Critical Approaches*

While we refrained from asking authors to adopt a specific feminist theoretical framework, the chapters in this volume collectively embody critical immigration legal theory. They reach beyond basic doctrinal knowledge of immigration law to contest the fundamental presumptions that the immigration system makes about who belongs in our national community. Notwithstanding their diversity, the authors share some common approaches in the feminist rewriting of their opinions. Many opinions apply a feminist anti-subordination framework by illuminating how entrenched systems of power maintain a structural hierarchy over noncitizens. Others engage in feminist storytelling by focusing on the lived experiences of diverse noncitizens whose lives lay at the heart of the legal decisions decided in their name. Some embrace feminist anti-essentialism by considering the social, historical, and political context of such opinions not only to contest immigrant stereotyping but also to wrestle with the inherent complexities of each situation. These approaches closely align with other critical theories, such as critical race theory, by exposing and challenging deep-rooted biases in immigration law based on race, class, and gender.

Like other critical theories, critical immigration legal theory also has a praxis dimension that aims to transform the immigration system.[25] Given the background of these authors as movement lawyers, clinicians, activists, and immigrants themselves, their chapters reflect the practice of those actively seeking a better world. Some opinions fundamentally expand the scope of noncitizen rights to enter and remain in the United States. Other opinions identify the collateral consequences of seemingly "immigrant friendly" opinions that result in further subordinating noncitizens by reinforcing stereotypes. Still others replace immigration enforcement concerns with communal values such as inclusivity, equity, and relational bonds. As many of the authors are engaged in the fight for immigrant rights, they have become intimately familiar with their clients' interactions within the immigration law system.[26] Bolstered by such experience, the commentaries and rewritten opinions provide space for reimagining how the law can and should resist the structural determinism of the Supreme Court's immigration law jurisprudence.

---

[25] *See* RICHARD DELGADO & JEAN STEFANCIC, CRITICAL RACE THEORY: AN INTRODUCTION 3 (3d ed. 2017).

[26] *See* Wendy A. Bach & Sameer M. Ashar, *Critical Theory and Clinical Stance*, 26 CLINICAL L. REV. 81, 91 (2019).

1. Anti-Subordination

Most of the opinions in this volume undertake an anti-subordination examination of immigration jurisprudence, which contends with the ways in which immigration law structurally oppresses noncitizens of color. Feminist legal theory is rooted in a commitment not just to equality, but to anti-subordination. Anti-subordination feminism recognizes the social oppression of certain groups.[27] According to this framing, "it is inappropriate for certain groups in society to have subordinated status because of their lack of power in society as a whole."[28] As such, the concept of power is central to an anti-subordination critique. There is arguably no greater power than the power to make and enforce law. For much of U.S. history, that power was exclusively held by white men in the role of legislators, judges, and law enforcers. As law makers and enforcers who lived middle or upper class lives, they enshrined their own supremacy and codified, or imposed through the exercise of their power, the subordination of women, people of color, the poor, and outsiders.

This subordination was often intentional and explicit, but not always. Feminist scholars realize that at first glance, many laws appear neutral and can be justified by reasonable concerns. Upon closer scrutiny, however, those same laws may reveal sexist, racist, classist, or other repugnant motivations and embody powerful mechanisms of discrimination and devaluation. Critical race theorists have similarly argued about the shortcomings of facially neutral laws that have had a devastating impact on the economic, political, and social lives of Black people and other people of color.[29]

Immigration law maintains a racialized and gendered regime premised on white patriarchal supremacy that subordinates noncitizens of color and constrains their ability to enter, remain in, and become full political members of, the United States. Other marginalized identities exacerbate this subordination. Undocumented immigrants, for example, lack political membership as well as lawful status in the country. Undocumented immigrants of color who are women, LGBTQ+ and in poverty experience additional axes of systemic inequality.

The subordination of noncitizens results from blindness or acquiescence to the traditional power structure that dominates cases involving noncitizens. For over a century, the U.S. Supreme Court has accepted this. The Court upheld the constitutionality of explicit anti-Chinese immigration laws by granting the Executive and Congress with virtually unfettered power to govern the entry and removal of

---

[27] Kathryn M. Stanchi, Linda L. Berger & Bridget Crawford, *Introduction to the U.S. Feminist Judgments Project, in* FEMINIST JUDGMENTS: REWRITTEN OPINIONS OF THE UNITED STATES SUPREME COURT 3, 19 (2016).

[28] Ruth Colker, *Anti-Subordination Above All: Sex, Race, and Equal Protection*, 61 N.Y.U. L. REV. 1003, 1007 (1986).

[29] Kimberlé Williams Crenshaw, *Race, Reform, and Retrenchment: Transformation and Legitimation in Antidiscrimination Law*, 101 HARV. L. REV. 1331, 1378 (1988).

noncitizens. Further, facially neutral immigration regulations make it difficult to challenge the discriminatory impact of such rules. Prior to the Immigration and Nationality Act (INA) of 1965, for example, the United States had explicit racial quotas for immigration admissions. The INA of 1965 supplanted those racial quotas with seemingly neutral immigration admission criteria. Yet today's immigration system still enables a racialized hierarchy that prevents the legal admission of certain immigrants from India, China, Mexico, Central America, and the Philippines. Immigration policies and practices disproportionately harm noncitizens of color. Approximately ninety-five percent of deportees are Latino.[30] And although only seven percent of noncitizens in the United States are Black, they comprise twenty percent of those facing deportation based on criminal grounds.[31] Without proof of intentional discrimination, the law of equal protection does not generally provide redress. Even when there is evidence of discriminatory intent, such as with the Trump Administration's travel ban targeting Muslim immigrants, the Court has chosen to ignore it in the immigration context.

Given this history of structural racism, it is not surprising that anti-subordination analysis is prominent throughout the rewritten opinions in this volume. In *Chy Lung v. Freeman*, the first case in U.S. history with a Chinese plaintiff, Professor Stewart Chang rewrites the majority opinion to reject the overt racism of a California immigration statute that discriminated against Chinese and Asian women on equal protection grounds, rather than deferring to the federal government's plenary power over immigration. Professor Jonathan Weinberg rewrites the majority opinion in *Wong Kim Ark*, to uplift the Fourteenth Amendment's anti-subordination promise of territorial birthright citizenship to the children of the formally enslaved to the U.S. born children of noncitizens of color. Professor Joy Kanwar's dissent in *United States v. Thind* critiques the ways in which the immigration system explicitly maintained white supremacy through its naturalization regime. Professor Shoba Sivaprasad Wadhia's concurrence in *Plyler v. Doe* and Professor Kati Griffith's majority opinion in *Hoffman Plastic v. NLRB*, focus on recognizing and remedying the subordination of undocumented immigrants in the context of education or the workplace. Professor Marissa Montes's dissent in *Padilla v. Kentucky* demands that the obligations of criminal defense counsel under the Sixth Amendment take into account the racism, classism, sexism and overall discrimination that plague our criminal system. These authors highlight the ways in which race is intertwined with the subordination of immigrants.

---

[30] *Detention, Deportation, and Devastation: The Disproportionate Effect of Deportations on the Latino Community*, MEXICAN AM. LEGAL DEF. & EDUC. FUND (May 2014), www.maldef.org/assets/pdf/DDD_050614.pdf.

[31] Juliana Morgan-Trostle et al., *The State of Black Immigrants, Part II: Black Immigrants in the Mass Criminalization System*, BLACK ALL. FOR JUST IMMIGRATION & N.Y.U. L. IMMIGRANT RTS. CLINIC (Sept. 28, 2016), https://nyf.issuelab.org/resource/the-state-of-black-immigrants-part-ii-black-immigrants-in-the-mass-criminalization-system.html.

Other authors use an anti-subordination approach to expose the discriminatory animus motivating ostensibly neutral legislation. Professor Annie Lai's concurrence in *Arizona v. United States*, Professor Jennifer Lee Koh's majority opinion in *DHS v. Regents*, and Professor Julia Hernández's majority opinion in *Reno v. Flores* call out the discriminatory intent behind the pretext of neutral government action concerning noncitizens. These authors show how a jurisprudence that recognizes and rejects such discrimination results in a different and more protective legal regime for noncitizens.

2. Storytelling

Another common approach within this volume is the practice of centering the humanity and the stories of the people impacted by the law. As the original volume in this Feminist Judgment series explained, "[b]ecause of the centrality of story to law, feminists and other critical legal scholars have embraced narrative as a distinctive method of subverting and disrupting the dominant legal discourse."[32] Law's alleged neutrality hides that it is premised on the perspectives of the powerful while excluding those who are relatively powerless. This feminist narrative method focuses on the experiences of outsiders while empowering both those telling and listening to stories by virtue of its opposition to dominant legal discourse.

The storytelling focus harkens back to the original "consciousness-building" aim of women telling their stories of discrimination and subordination in the 1970s. Feminist theory underlines the value of claiming knowledge based on these experiential lessons.[33] Real stories of real people legitimize the truth by grounding its explication in individual experiences. The recent #MeToo movement met resistance to the breadth of sexual harassment and violence with proof in the undeniable volume of individual stories.

Critical race theorists too appreciate outsider storytelling to counter "the bundle of presuppositions, received wisdoms, and shared understandings against a background of which legal and political discourse takes place."[34] They argue that those who have different history and experience with oppression are better able to assess the "law's master narratives."[35] Prioritizing the voices of those who are actually oppressed leads to different legal results.[36] A focus on the effects of harm, for example, can illuminate particular values and suggest solutions.[37] Centering the stories of named individuals, therefore, can force reconsideration of the concrete impact of abstract principles like due process, equity, and dignity.

---

[32] Stanchi et al., *supra* note 27, at 15–16.
[33] Kathryn Abrams, *Hearing the Call of Stories*, 79 CAL. L. REV. 971, 983–84 (1991).
[34] Richard Delgado, *Storytelling for Oppositionists and Others: A Plea for Narrative*, 87 MICH. L. REV. 2411, 2413 (1989).
[35] DELGADO & STEFANCIC, *supra* note 25, at 11.
[36] Mari J. Matsuda, *Looking to the Bottom: Critical Legal Studies and Reparations*, 22 HARV. C.R.-C.L. L. REV. 323, 325–26 (1987).
[37] Mari J. Matsuda, *Public Response to Racist Speech: Considering the Victim's Story*, 87 MICH. L. REV. 2320, 2325–26 (1989).

In this volume, the storytelling approach helps to humanize immigrants who are so often characterized as the other – as "aliens" who are strangers or foreigners. Their lived experiences help to promote understanding of the harms done to them and the circumstances that led to their entanglement with immigration enforcement. Conditions that may increase noncitizens' susceptibility to immigration violations – thus triggering enforcement efforts to exclude, detain, or deport – include humanitarian needs to flee persecution, reunification with U.S. family members, or the necessity to earn a subsistence wage. These narratives of immigrants about why they came and what their lives are like in the United States are essential to subverting the dominant immigration enforcement discourse.

In their feminist judgments, several authors incorporate the stories and voices of the individuals impacted by the law to return to the immigrant litigants their humanity and self-determination. Storytelling appears throughout many of the feminist judgments, including Professor Joy Kanwar's dissenting opinion in *United States v. Thind*, Professors Stacy Caplow's and Maryellen Fullerton's concurrence in *Zadvydas v. Davis*, and Professor Erin Corcoran's dissent in *Landon v. Plasencia*. Professor Jennifer Lee Koh's majority opinion in *DHS v. Regents* and Professor Julia Hernandez's majority opinion in *Reno v. Flores* tell the stories of immigrant youth that are notably absent from the original opinions that decide their future fate of whether they can remain in the United States and be detained by the government. Professor Patricia Winograd's rewritten majority opinion in *Jean v. Nelson* names the litigants and details how they struggled to flee persecution in Haiti, only to encounter racialized abuses by immigration enforcement as Black persons in the United States. In her *Arizona v. U.S.* opinion, Professor Annie Lai introduces Kris Kobach, the architect of Arizona's anti-immigrant legislation whose name is not mentioned in the Supreme Court opinion, to lay bare the source of the racial animus at the center of the law. Professors Sarah Sherman-Stokes and Sarah Schendel celebrate the device of class actions in their *Rodriguez v. Jennings* opinion for allowing the less powerful and often unseen to make their stories visible. And while class actions are defined by the commonality of claims among a group of people, they emphasize that such claims are, at heart, full of unique stories of individual claimants.

3. Anti-Essentialism and Intersectionality

Another theme within this volume is anti-essentialism, which rejects stereotypes of immigrants as a monolithic group by providing broader historical, social, and political context. In feminist legal theory, anti-essentialism challenges the notion that "there is a fixed and identifiable 'essence' that characterizes a certain set of human beings, such as women."[38] It teaches the value in recognizing the unique qualities

---

[38] Stanchi et al., *supra* note 27, at 21.

of difference and the danger of universals.[39] Rather than rely on a foreordained definition, prescription, or generalization, anti-essentialism requires attention to specific context and the lived lives of immigrants.[40]

U.S. Supreme Court immigration jurisprudence reinforces an essentialist account of immigrants as "aliens," inassimilable outsiders who seek to exploit the resources and threaten the public safety of the United States. Inflammatory anti-immigrant rhetoric magnifies this outsider stereotype that depicts immigrants as criminals and invaders bent on conquering and pillaging rather than contributing and integrating in U.S. society.[41] Undocumented immigrants are labeled as "illegal aliens," whose very existence and identity are characterized by illegality.[42] The federal government's largesse ultimately determines whether these noncitizens have sufficient desirable or deserving equities to enter and remain in the United States.

The authors of the rewritten opinions fought against the stereotyped identities of noncitizens in the immigration law jurisprudence by adding varying social, historical, and political contexts missing from the original Supreme Court opinions. Professor Julia Hernandez's majority opinion in *Reno v. Flores* and Professors Stacy Caplow's and Maryellen Fullerton's concurrence in *Zadvydas v. Davis* highlight the ways in which war, ethnic strife, and dissolution of nations, including the United States' involvement in such situations, create refugees or stateless individuals. Rejecting the inherent criminality of undocumented immigrants, Professor Shoba Sivaprasad Wadhia's concurrence in *Plyler v. Doe* explains the contextual circumstances surrounding why undocumented parents enter the United States unlawfully and how they, along with their children, are here to stay. The rewritten opinions of *Plyler* and *Zadvydas* also explicitly push back on the stereotyping of noncitizens as invaders, pillagers, and criminals by replacing the pejorative terminology of "alien" or "illegal alien" with new language to describe the noncitizens before the Court.

A related theme found in the rewritten opinions is intersectionality. Originating from Black feminist criticism, intersectionality rejects a single-axis framework of treating race and gender as mutually exclusive that is dominant in antidiscrimination law, feminist theory, and antiracist politics.[43] Rather, intersectionality moves beyond a singular experience to reveal the interaction of coexisting identities

---

[39] Nancy Levit, *Feminism for Men: Legal Ideology and the Construction of Maleness*, 43 UCLA L. Rev. 1037, 1053 (1996).

[40] Katharine T. Bartlett, *Feminist Legal Methods*, 103 Harv. L. Rev. 829, 851 (1990); Delgado & Stefancic, *supra* note 25, at 11.

[41] Leo R. Chavez, The Latino Threat: Constructing Immigrants, Citizens, and the Nation 23–25 (2d ed. 2013); Ediberto Román, Those Damned Immigrants: America's Hysteria Over Undocumented Immigration 17–18 (2013).

[42] Susan Bibler Coutin, *Contesting Criminality: Illegal Immigration and the Spatialization of Legality*, 9 Theoretical Criminology 5, 7 (2005).

[43] Kimberlé Crenshaw, *Demarginalizing the Intersection of Race and Sex: A Black Feminist Critique of Antidiscrimination Doctrine, Feminist Theory and Antiracist Politics*, 1 U. Chi. Legal F. 139, 139 (1989).

including gender, race, class, and sexual orientation. The intersectionality of these identities produces distinct lived experiences and differences in individual and institutionalized privilege and discrimination.[44]

The immigration system exercises control over individual noncitizens in distinctive ways such that intersectional identities compound discrimination against noncitizens. For example, the grounds for deporting noncitizens from the United States, particularly those with a criminal record, are wide in scope. Beyond the mandatory detention of some noncitizens (e.g., those labeled as "aggravated felons"), government actors frequently incarcerate immigrants who are arrested as a matter of course.[45] Structural factors also heighten immigrant vulnerability to immigration enforcement such as subordination based on gender, race, national origin, religion, linguistic isolation, and/or socioeconomic status. For example, those who engage in enforcement racially profile immigrants.[46] Poorer noncitizens are more likely to be detained because they are unable to afford the high costs of bonds to be released from detention, or they are denied admission to the United States because they are deemed to be "public charges" who will utilize public benefits.

A few rewritten opinions shed new light on how different noncitizens experience marginalization due to the intersection of multiple oppressed identities. Professor Stella Burch Elias' opinion in *Ekiu v. U.S.* considers Ms. Ekiu's individual circumstances as a Japanese woman who sought legal admission to the United States as the spouse of a legal resident, and scrutinizes Ms. Ekiu's treatment by immigration authorities. Ms. Ekiu, determined to be a "public charge" by immigration officials, was immediately detained and deprived of procedural due process including a hearing in her language in which she could present her case. Professor Stewart Chang's majority opinion in *Chy Lung v. Freeman*, appreciates the gendered racism experienced by the plaintiff and those similarly situated – Chinese women immigrants seeking entry to the United States and therefore presumed to be sex workers.

CONCLUSION

Through Supreme Court opinions rewritten from a feminist perspective, this book reimagines the norms that drive immigration policies and practices. In place of frequent and intentional discrimination and subordination, the authors here demand welcome and equality. Where current law omits the voice and stories of noncitizens, the authors here center their lives and experiences. Collectively, they demonstrate the transformative possibility of incorporating feminist approaches and methods to judicial decision-making.

---

[44] Angela P. Harris, *Race and Essentialism in Feminist Legal Theory*, 42 STAN. L. REV. 581, 588 (1990).
[45] Denise Gilman, *To Loose the Bonds: The Deceptive Promise of Freedom from Pretrial Immigration Detention*, 92 IND. L.J. 157, 167 (2016).
[46] Kevin R. Johnson, *The Case against Racial Profiling in Immigration Enforcement*, 78 WASH. U. L. Q. 675, 697–702 (2000).

2

Commentary on *Chy Lung v. Freeman*, 92 U.S. 275 (1875)

Julie Dahlstrom

Although often an overlooked Supreme Court decision, *Chy Lung v. Freeman* played a significant role in contributing to the growth of federal immigration power that took root in the so-called Chinese Exclusion cases of the late nineteenth century.[1] In *Chy Lung*, the Supreme Court struck down a patently racist and gendered California law that had allowed officials to exclude Chinese female passengers found to be "lewd" and "debauched" from entering into the United States.[2] In the decision, Justice Samuel Miller, writing for the unanimous Supreme Court, expressed grave concerns about state corruption and the abuse of power at the border.[3] In particular, Justice Miller worried that this California law granted officials excessive power to label any Chinese woman "lewd" and prevent them entry into the United States. To mitigate these concerns, the Court held that the federal government, not the states, should retain the exclusive power to make laws related to immigration and foreign relations. Over a century later, the *Chy Lung* decision still provides an important window into how immigration officials have historically exercised discretion at the intersections of race and gender. Indeed, the *Chy Lung* decision exemplified how the Supreme Court could have – but did not – respond to similarly discriminatory federal exclusion laws aimed at Chinese immigrants.[4]

Professor Stewart Chang's feminist opinion provides a different vision of *Chy Lung*, one firmly grounded in the application of the Fourteenth Amendment and the Civil Rights Act of 1870.[5] Professor Chang artfully explores how the Court might have fully acknowledged the realities of race, gender, and class that animated the California law. The feminist judgment provides a constitutional and statutory framework grounded in equal protection and due process, which, unlike the Court's

---

[1]   Chy Lung v. Freeman, 92 U.S. 275 (1875); *see, e.g.,* Gerald Neuman, The Lost Century of American Immigration Law, 93 COLUM. L. REV. 1833, 1887 (1993).

[2]   Chy Lung, 92 U.S. at 277.

[3]   *Id.* at 280.

[4]   Immigration Act of 1882, 22 Stat. 214 (Aug. 3, 1882); Chae Chan Ping v. United States, 130 U.S. 581 (1889).

[5]   U.S. Const. amend. XIV; Civil Rights Act of 1870, ch. 114, §§ 16–17, 16 Stat. 140, 144.

approach, offers more enduring solutions for immigrant litigants at the border, and indeed in deportation cases as well. Ultimately, the Court failed to adopt Professor Chang's reasoning. Thus, the real legacy of *Chy Lung* and its progeny, sadly, is one of rising federal immigration power, extreme judicial deference, and persistent anti-Chinese racism: forces that would continue to sustain harsh immigration measures at the border and within the United States.

BACKGROUND

Chinese immigration was a key tool to maintain white supremacy after the Civil War. As slavery came to an end, wealthy white southerners faced a shortage of workers and turned to Chinese immigrants, whom they believed would offer a cheaper source of labor to exploit.[6] At the same time, the Burlingame-Seward Treaty of 1868 opened up new pathways for labor migration from China to the United States. The Treaty provided that Chinese immigrants would enjoy "the same privileges, immunities, and exemptions in respect to travel or residence" and encouraged Chinese workers to immigrate.[7]

However, the words of the Burlingame-Seward Treaty stood in stark contrast to the realities of violence and oppression that most Chinese immigrants found upon entry. In California, for example, many Chinese laborers faced rampant discrimination, exploitation, and violence. California legislators were openly hostile toward Chinese immigrants, using racist rhetoric to support discriminatory legislation. They argued that Chinese immigrants could not assimilate, took jobs from white laborers, and were a race of "heathens and slaves."[8] Legislators passed a series of measures, including the foreign miners' tax, commutation tax, and the police tax, all aimed at Chinese workers.[9] Meanwhile, the anti-Chinese movement uniquely targeted Chinese women. Legislators further portrayed Chinese women as a threat to Victorian-era attitudes about sexuality. They often cast Chinese women as "prostitutes," pointing to practices of polygamy, prostitution, adultery, and domestic servitude as evidence of deviance and "immorality."[10]

---

[6] Mae Ngai, *Racism Has Always Been Part of the Asian American Experience*, THE ATLANTIC (Apr. 21, 2021); ANDREW GYORY, CLOSING THE GATE: RACE, POLITICS, AND THE CHINESE EXCLUSION ACT 39 (1998); Kathleen Kim, *The Thirteenth Amendment and Human Trafficking: Lessons and Limitations*, 36 GA. ST. U. L. REV. 1005, 1009 (2020).

[7] Treaty of Peace, Amity, and Commerce (Burlingame-Seward Treaty), China-U.S., art. VI, July 28, 1868, 16 Stat. 739; *see* Paul Yin, *The Narratives of Chinese-American Litigation during the Chinese Exclusion Era*, 19 ASIAN AM. L. J. 145, 147 (2012).

[8] Ngai, *supra* note 6 ("Governor John Bigler, facing a tight race for reelection, made an incendiary speech before the state legislature, claiming that the Chinese, a race of heathens and slaves, were invading the state and threatening its society of free producers.").

[9] CHARLES J. MCCLAIN, IN SEARCH OF EQUALITY: THE CHINESE STRUGGLE AGAINST DISCRIMINATION IN NINETEENTH-CENTURY AMERICA 47 (1994).

[10] Kerry Abrams, *Polygamy, Prostitution, and the Federalization of Immigration Law*, 105 COLUM. L. REV. 641, 643–47 (2005). As scholars have pointed out, the term "prostitute" is often pejorative

In the face of anti-Chinese discrimination and violence, some Chinese immigrants returned to China; others developed alliances to creatively use the press, politics, and the courts to challenge these discriminatory measures.[11] San Francisco became an important site of resistance. As laborers completed construction of the Central Pacific Railroad, thousands relocated to San Francisco, where they found jobs in the "boot and shoe, woolens, cigar and tobacco, and sewing industries."[12] By 1870, San Francisco was the home to approximately a quarter of the Chinese immigrant population in California. At the same time, Chinese laborers, disproportionately men, sparked a demand for female migration and a bustling market for commercial sex. According to one estimate, 23.4 percent of Chinese women in San Francisco by 1860 were involved in commercial sex.[13]

The expanding commercial sex industry gave rise to concerns about Chinese "slavery." Popular understandings of human trafficking, at the time, were quite nascent. Human trafficking was not yet defined in federal or international law, and no legal protections existed for immigrant victims of trafficking. As a result, survivors of sex trafficking who entered the United States often found themselves at the mercy of immigration officials and subject to unbridled, harsh discretion with no viable immigration avenues.

To be sure, not all Chinese female immigrants in the sex industry were victims of sex trafficking. From 1849 to 1854, many Chinese women were self-employed. However, from 1854 to 1925, the commercial sex trade became more organized and dangerous, with a complex network of Chinese procurers, importers, and brothel owners profiting from migration of Chinese women. Many importers were connected to secret criminal gangs, called Tongs, and ran major smuggling and trafficking routes from Hong Kong to San Francisco. Luring and kidnapping were common practices.

Tongs also benefited from poor economic conditions in China and the low status of women. In the patrilineal and patriarchal Chinese culture of the nineteenth century, practices like infanticide, abandonment, and sale of female children were common. Poor families often sold daughters to work in the commercial sex industry or as bonded domestic servants, adopted children, mistresses, or wives. As a result of these practices, many young Chinese women were brought to the United States based on false promises or with debt. Faced with few economic

---

because it is a status-based noun, equating a person with a crime, and it promotes stigmatization and alienation. *See* Anita Bernstein, *Working Sex Words*, 24 MICH. J. GENDER L. 221, 228 (2017). In this chapter, the term is used when a direct quotation from a source or to refer to the crime of "prostitution." Otherwise, the term "commercial sex" is used to refer to sex in exchange for something of value.

[11] Yin, *supra* note 7, at 148; MCCLAIN, *supra* note 9, at 54; BETH LEW-WILLIAMS, THE CHINESE MUST GO: VIOLENCE, EXCLUSION, AND THE MAKING OF THE ALIEN IN AMERICA 95 (2018).

[12] RONALD TAKAKI, A DIFFERENT MIRROR: A HISTORY OF MULTICULTURAL AMERICA 198 (1993).

[13] SUCHENG CHAN, THIS BITTERSWEET SOIL 59 (1986); Lucie Cheng Hirata, *Free, Indentured, Enslaved: Chinese Prostitutes in Nineteenth-Century America*, 5 WOMEN LATIN AM. 2, 23 (1979).

opportunities, some were "exploited, abused, and some kept in a state of virtual enslavement by their masters."[14]

In California and elsewhere, instead of devising affirmative rights and protections for potential victims, legislators tended to stigmatize and blame Chinese women. California legislators particularly targeted Chinese women for exclusion and punishment. In 1866, the California legislature declared all Chinese "houses of ill fame" nuisances.[15] They invalidated leases to brothels and made it a misdemeanor offense for landlords to lease properties as brothels. In 1870, California legislators enacted a law, permitting the government to charge any woman found to be a "prostitute" with a misdemeanor punishable by imprisonment and hefty fines.[16] In 1873, this law was then combined with a provision of the California Political Code, which added "lewd" and "debauched" women to a broad class of persons, who were barred entry into the United States.[17] The law also permitted state immigration officials to determine – in their broad discretion – if a woman was "lewd" or "debauched" – terms left undefined as if self-evident. And, if they could not pay a $500 bond, the women were subject to exclusion from the United States. Thus, Chinese women, especially those with little financial resources, were often caught in a web of punitive, discriminatory laws with little legal recourse.

THE ORIGINAL OPINION

Against this fractious political and legal landscape, twenty-two Chinese women arrived at a U.S. port of entry on August 24, 1874. These women undertook a thirty-day voyage from Hong Kong to San Francisco.[18] They travelled with more than 500 Chinese passengers via the steamship *Japan*, owned by the Pacific Mail Steamship Company. When the steamship docked in San Francisco, Rudolph Norwin Piotrowski, the commissioner of immigration and an immigrant himself, boarded the vessel.[19] He then subjected the Chinese women to a humiliating interrogation about their marital status, children, and relatives in the United States.[20] Finding their responses "perfectly not satisfactory," he determined that they were "lewd," detained the women, and ordered them sent back to Hong Kong.[21]

---

[14] Hirata at 6.

[15] Act of Mar. 31, 1866, ch. 505, 1866 Cal. Stat. 641–42. The legislation, entitled "An Act for the Suppression of Chinese Houses of Ill Fame," initially targeted Chinese women.

[16] Act of Mar. 18, 1870, ch. 230, 1870 Cal. Stat. 330, 330–31.

[17] Cal. Pol. Code § 2952, as amended.

[18] Paul A. Kramer, *The Case of the 22 Lewd Chinese Women*, SLATE (Apr. 23, 2012).

[19] Transcript of Record at 4, Chy Lung v. Freeman, 92 U.S. 275 (1875) [hereinafter Transcript of Record].

[20] *Id.* at 6–7 ("The questions which I gave them were generally where they were married; if they had any relatives or companions when they came here; or why&by [sic] what means they came.").

[21] Chy Lung, 92 U.S. at 276–277.

One day later, an individual – accounts differ as to whether he was a wealthy merchant or a perpetrator of human trafficking[22] – hired Leander Quint, an attorney and former judge, to file a writ of habeas corpus in the California District Court. The writ was filed on behalf of one of the detained Chinese women, Ah Fook. In the writ, the petitioner asserted that Ah Fook was entitled to land and reside in California under the Burlingame-Seward Treaty and the U.S. Constitution.[23]

In the animated four-day trial that followed, the government and counsel for the twenty-two women offered strident arguments on prominent issues of the day, ranging from the balance of state and federal power, the perils of discretion, Chinese "slavery," and women's rights.[24] The women testified, denying any involvement in commercial sex. Meanwhile, state witnesses, lacking any direct evidence that the women were "lewd" or "debauched," pointed to the women's clothing, consisting of handkerchiefs on their heads and bright colored silk-embroidered garments, to justify their suspicions. In response, Judge Robert F. Morrison ultimately upheld the California statute, finding it a permissible exercise of state police power.[25] The petitioners then filed a writ to the Supreme Court of California, which sustained the District Court's judgment.

Subsequently, one of the Chinese women, Ah Fong, filed a writ of habeas corpus in the federal Circuit Court for the District of California where Supreme Court Justice Stephen Field sat as a lower court judge. Justice Field, in *In re Ah Fong*,[26] struck down the California statute, finding the California law to be an overly broad exercise of police power, contrary to the Burlingame-Seward Treaty and in violation of the exclusive federal power over intercourse with federal nations. Significantly, Justice Field held that the statute violated the Fourteenth Amendment and the Civil Rights Act of 1870. This decision was reportedly the first case to articulate such a robust vision of statutory and constitutional protections for noncitizens.

---

[22] Newspaper accounts raise questions about the identity of the person who filed the writ. *See* McClain, *supra* note 9, at 57 n.59. The *Examiner*, a newspaper, described two Chinese people, Ah You and Tom Poy, who made the application for the writ. *Id.* (citing Examiner, Aug. 25, 1874, p. 3, col. 4). In contrast, *The Daily Alta*, a local newspaper, referenced Ah Lung, who was reportedly a perpetrator of trafficking, as filing it. *Id.* (citing Daily Alta, Aug. 26, 1874, p. 1, col. 3). The trial transcript references Chy Lung as filing the writ, and *The San Francisco Daily Union* called Chy Lung the "owner of twenty-two Chinese women brought to San Francisco." Transcript of Record, *supra* note 19, at 1; *Sacramento Daily Union*, Jan. 15, 1878, vol. 1, no. 1. Chy Lung also happens to be a well-known mercantile company in San Francisco, described as the "the richest merchants of San Francisco, wholesale dealers in teas, general groceries and dry goods." However, it is unknown whether the firm had a role in the litigation or anyone with commercial or other interests in the trafficking or smuggling of Chinese women funded or participated in the litigation effort. McClain, *supra* note 9, at 57 n.59; *Our Chinese Visitors: Who They Are, What They Have Come For, and Where They Are*, N.Y. Times 2 (Aug. 13, 1869).

[23] Sucheng Chan, Entry Denied: Exclusion and the Chinese community in America, 1882–1943 100 (1991) [hereinafter Chan, Entry Denied].

[24] Transcript of Record, *supra* note 19, at 4.

[25] Kramer, *supra* note 18.

[26] In re Ah Fong, 1 F. Cas. 213 (C.C.D. Cal. 1874).

Justice Field was particularly disturbed by the excesses of state power. He pointed to how the California statute distinguished in "sweeping" terms "persons widely variant in character." While the state retained certain powers, including the right to self-defense, Justice Field found that the right to control immigration resided solely with the federal government. While the state could permissibly engage in "vigorous enforcement" of laws, it could not unilaterally discriminatorily exclude Chinese women.

Justice Field also affirmed that the protections of the Fourteenth Amendment applied to any *person*, rather than only to U.S. citizens. Field proclaimed that, "[d]iscriminating and partial legislation, favoring particular persons, or against particular persons of the same class, is now prohibited." He acknowledged the reality of rampant discrimination against Chinese immigrants. Furthermore, Field, in a novel move, applied the Civil Rights Act of 1870, a federal statute that applied to a discriminatory tax or charge, to state action. He found that the bond requirement in the California statute imposed an undue burden on Chinese immigrants and that this provision could be interpreted as a "charge" under the Civil Rights Act of 1870. As it unequally burdened Chinese women, Field held that it violated federal law.[27]

As Field issued the oral opinion, Field ended his reading by suggesting that the government file a writ of error to the Supreme Court. The government, however, failed to appeal or even submit a brief in *Chy Lung*. Eventually, the petitioner filed a writ, and two years later, the court issued a decision. In 1875, Justice Samuel Miller, writing for the unanimous Supreme Court in *Chy Lung*, struck down the California law.[28] But, he employed strikingly different reasoning than Justice Field.

Justice Miller expressed grave concerns about state corruption and abuse of power. The Court observed the growing power of state officials, like Piotrowski, who, armed with the California law, can "compel them to submit to systematic extortion of the grossest kind." Justice Miller found that the California law was a recipe for discretionary excesses. By allowing the commissioner to label any young woman as "lewd" if they had improper manners, Justice Miller observed that the California law granted vast, unfettered power to state immigration officials. As a result, the Court found that the federal government, not the states, had the exclusive power to make laws related to immigration and foreign relations. Justice Miller notably remained silent on the application of the Fourteenth Amendment or the Civil Rights Act of 1870.[29] In doing so, he failed to consider the federal government's constitutional obligation to ensure the equal protection of laws, and the potential for the federal government to engage in discriminatory excesses against immigrants of the kind he condemned as state abuse of power. In fact, this is precisely what occurred.

[27] *Id.*
[28] Chy Lung, 92 U.S. at 281. While Justice Miller identifies the petitioner as Chy Lung, it is believed that Chy Lung might have been a perpetrator of trafficking or a wealthy merchant who had taken an interest in the litigation. CHAN, ENTRY DENIED, *supra* note 23, at 104 n.31.
[29] Chy Lung, 92 U.S. at 278–80.

THE FEMINIST JUDGMENT

Professor Chang, writing as Justice Miller, alters the majority opinion by reviving Justice Field's analysis in *In re Ah Fong*. Chang relies on the Fourteenth Amendment and the Civil Rights Act of 1870 to find that the California statute impermissibly discriminates against Chinese women on the basis of their national origin and sex. He resurrects the history of Section 16 of the Civil Rights Act to support a wide-ranging interpretation of the federal statute to protect against anti-Chinese discrimination at the border. As Chang notes, the Chinese community in San Francisco mobilized to pass Section 16 to address discriminatory anti-Chinese legislation in California.[30] Indeed, Senator Stewart of Nevada had introduced the legislation to extend civil rights not only to Chinese immigrants, but to *all persons*. While Section 16 centered on economic legislation, like the miner's tax or police tax,[31] Chang persuasively argues that this provision should apply to the California law because the California bond amounts to a "charge" under federal law.

Chang also reengages with then-existing precedent to support a more expansive vision of the Fourteenth Amendment, one that would offer more generous protections for Chinese women against discriminatory state action. While the Supreme Court in the *Slaughterhouse Cases* (1873) adopted a very limited interpretation of the Fourteenth Amendment, Chang applies the dissent's approach to equal protection. In a dissenting opinion of the *Slaughterhouse Cases*, Justice Field reads the Fourteenth Amendment's promises of equal protection and due process to apply to *all* persons, regardless of citizenship. Chang applies Field's analysis and then expands it to reach discrimination on the basis of sex, an approach which the Supreme Court would not adopt until nearly a century later.

Chang also artfully brings to the foreground the social, economic, and cultural backdrop that brought about the anti-Chinese California legislation. He describes how the Burlingame-Seward Treaty was negotiated to benefit American white industrialists, many of whom were former plantation owners who would benefit from the "steady flow of low-cost Chinese immigrant labor" to meet labor shortages. As the railroads were completed, white public opinion embraced anti-Chinese racism, viewing the Chinese as a "threat to domestic labor" and pushing expeditiously for discriminatory laws to effectuate their exclusion and expulsion. Chang also shows how the California law in question was tied to earlier efforts to tax the Chinese, limit Chinese immigration, and restrict their ability to testify or effectively challenge discriminatory laws. Thus, he argues that the California law in *Chy* Lung should be viewed alongside these other calculated efforts to discriminate against Chinese immigrants.

---

[30] McClain, *supra* note 9, at 565–67. Chinese leaders remained focused on three primary injustices, first the miner's tax that violated the Burlingame-Seward Treaty, second the commutation tax, and third the ban on Chinese testimony in U.S. courts. *Id.* at 565.

[31] *Id.* at 566.

The Chang opinion also highlights how concerns about Chinese "slavery" in the late nineteenth century did little to protect or assist potential victims. The California law in *Chy Lung* failed to protect Chinese women who were victims of trafficking. Instead, it targeted potential victims with exclusion, casting them back into the hands of perpetrators. The California law, moreover, did nothing to address the "men who might be traffickers." It also failed to provide potential victims of human trafficking with protection from deportation or potential "redress." Such affirmative protections would not emerge for another hundred years, when Congress defined trafficking in the Trafficking Victims Protection Act of 2000.[32]

CONCLUSION

Had Professor Chang's reasoning been accepted in 1875, it would have strengthened the constitutional rights of Chinese immigrants against both state and federal action. Instead, the *Chy Lung* decision ultimately set the stage for the rise of federal immigration power and increasingly harsh gendered and racialized enforcement measures aimed at Chinese immigrants. Almost immediately, Congress passed the Page Act, which permitted federal immigration officials to exclude noncitizens who enter "for lewd and immoral purposes."[33] The law would ultimately expand the federal government's power to exclude Chinese women based on mere suspicion of involvement in commercial sex.[34] Congress then passed the Immigration Act of 1882, the first race-based federal exclusion law, which significantly restricted the entry of all Chinese laborers.[35] The Supreme Court upheld the constitutionality of the Act in *Chae Chan Ping* in 1889.[36] Thus, while the decision in *Chy Lung* called out the harms of official discretion, it did little to change the realities of persistent anti-Chinese discrimination that would remain embedded in federal immigration law.

Still, the *Chy Lung* case offers important lessons about resistance. *Chy Lung* was ultimately a victory for the twenty-two women detained. It marked the first win by a Chinese litigant before the Supreme Court. While it would not put an end to anti-Chinese racism or violence, it was one victory that would punctuate a decades-long struggle by Chinese immigrants for the right to remain, immigrate, and live safely in the United States.

---

[32] *See* TVPA, Pub. L. No. 106–386, § 102(b)(2), 115 Stat. 1464 (2000). In the TVPA, Congress recognized that immigrant victims often "are repeatedly punished more harshly than the traffickers themselves," and established the "T visa," a special immigration protection for trafficking survivors. TVPA, Preamble.

[33] Ch. 141, 18 Stat. pt. 3, 477–487. Some believe that the law was drafted with Field's decision in *Ah Fong* in mind. *See* McCLAIN, *supra* note 9, at 62 n. 83.

[34] Ngai, *supra* note 6.

[35] Immigration Act of 1882, 22 Stat. 214 (Aug. 3, 1882).

[36] Chan Chae Ping v. United States, 130 U.S. 581 (1889).

CHY LUNG v. FREEMAN, 92 U.S. 275 (1875)

Justice Stewart Chang, delivered the opinion of the court.

On August 24, 1874, following a 30-day voyage from Hong Kong, the steamship *Japan* landed in the port of San Francisco, carrying approximately 600 Chinese passengers, including 89 women.

Pursuant to Section 2952 of Chapter 1, Article 7, of the Political Code of California, the commissioner of immigration for the State of California, Rudolph Piotrowski, boarded the *Japan* and through interpreters, interviewed all of these eighty-nine women to ascertain whether any of them were "lunatic, deaf, dumb, blind, crippled or infirm, and [] not accompanied by relatives who are able and willing to support [them], or [are] likely to become permanently a public charge, or [have] been a pauper in any other country, or [are], from sickness or disease, existing either at the time of sailing from the port of departure, or at the time of [their] arrival in this state, a public charge, or likely to become so, or is a convicted criminal, or a lewd or debauched woman." After interviewing the women, Piotrowski found that the testimony of twenty-two of the eighty-nine, specifically those who were travelling unaccompanied, were "perfectly not satisfactory" and declared that they were lewd, debauched, or abandoned women. The statute then stipulates that upon such a finding by the commissioner, that:

a. no person who shall belong to either class, or who possesses any of the infirmities or vices specified herein, shall be permitted to land in this state,

b. unless the master, owner, or consignee of said vessel shall give a joint and several bond to the people of the state of California, in the penal sum of five hundred dollars, in gold coin of the United States,

c. conditioned to indemnify and save harmless every county, city and county, town and city of this state, against all costs and expenses which may be by them necessarily incurred for the relief, support, medical care, or any expense whatever, resulting from the infirmities or vices herein referred to, of the persons named in said bonds, within two years from the date of said bonds;

d. and if the master, owner, or consignee of said vessel shall fail or refuse to execute the bond herein required to be executed, they are required to retain such persons on board of said vessel until said vessel shall leave the port, and then convey said passengers from this state;

e. and if said master, owner, or consignee shall fail or refuse to perform the duty and service last herein enjoined, or shall permit said passengers to escape from said vessel and land in this state, they shall forfeit to the state the sum of five hundred dollars, in gold coin of the United States, for each passenger so escaped, to be recovered by suit at law.

Thus, as authorized under the statute, Piotrowski prohibited the captain of the steamship, John Freeman, from allowing those twenty-two women to disembark, unless he or the consignee of the vessel posted $500 bonds for the women. When Captain Freeman and the owner of the vessel both refused to pay the bonds, Piotrowski ordered that the twenty-two women remain detained onboard the *Japan* and to be returned to Hong Kong when the steamship was next to sail.

These twenty-two women applied for a writ of habeas corpus to the District Court of California to protest their detention, first denying that they were lewd or debauched women, but also alleging that the statute under which they were being held was an unlawful contravention of the Burlingame-Seward Treaty between the United State and China and was a violation of their rights under the Constitution of the United States.

The District Court ruled against the women, making the factual finding that they were lewd and reaching the legal conclusion that the statute legitimately sought to preserve the "well-being and safety" of the state of California. The women then appealed to the Supreme Court of California under another writ of habeas corpus, but additionally requested that they be remanded to the custody of the sheriff of the city and county of San Francisco given that they were in imminent danger of being forcibly removed against their will since the steamship on which they were being held was about to depart. The Supreme Court of California granted their application and remanded them to the custody of coroner of the city and county of San Francisco, but ultimately sustained the ruling of the District Court, denied their application to be discharged, and ordered that they be returned to the *Japan* to await transport back to Asia. Since that time, however, the *Japan* had sailed from the port of San Francisco, not set to return for possibly three months, and in addition, Captain Freeman had been discharged from his service with the steamship company. Thus, the twenty-two women were ordered to remain in the custody of the coroner.

The women next appealed to the Circuit Court for the District of California for their release for the same reasons they alleged before, that the law violated federal treaty law and the U.S. Constitution. Because the case involved citizens of a foreign nation having treaty relations with the United States, the federal court was permitted to decide the case notwithstanding the prior orders of the state courts. This time, Justice Field, riding circuit in San Francisco, found the statute an overly broad exercise of police power that contravened federal powers over commerce and foreign relations as well as protections provided to foreign aliens in the Civil Rights Act of 1870. Accordingly, Justice Field issued a writ of habeas corpus and ordered the release of the twenty-two women from the custody of the coroner.

Contrary to the state court decisions, Justice Field did not find the California statute to be a valid exercise of police power. As Justice Field explains in the decision, *In re Ah Fong*, the ability of the state to exercise measures against the increase in crime, pauperism, and the spread of infectious disease is properly within the valid exercise of police power, except when it conflicts with the Constitution or an established principle of law. Whereas during the era of slavery, the courts had recognized the ability of Southern states to exclude free black persons from their borders, the Civil War and the subsequent amendments to the Constitution had ensured that, according to Justice Field, "no such power would be asserted, or if asserted, allowed, in any federal court." 1 F. Cas. 213, 217 (1874). The power of the state to police foreigners should not extend to the ability to exclude them; the exclusionary power resides with the federal government.

Justice Field did not stop there. He enumerated additional reasons that invalidated the law. According to Justice Field, the California statute directly conflicted with the Burlingame Treaty by imposing restrictions that were not part of the federal treaty between the United States and China and thus interfered with the federal power to intercourse with foreign nations. Significantly, Justice Field highlighted the applicability of the Fourteenth Amendment and subsequent federal legislation, specifically the Civil Rights Act of 1870, which prohibited the imposition of special taxes or charges on individuals immigrating to the United States.

Despite the favorable ruling by the Circuit Court, Chy Lung, one of the twenty-two detained women, brought a writ of error to this Court against the judgment issued by the Supreme Court of California, for the purpose, we presume, of testing the constitutionality of the California statute under which she was held prisoner.

We agree with Justice Field's holding in *Ah Fong* that the California statute is an impermissibly broad exercise of state police power that violates both the Burlingame Treaty and the Civil Rights Act of 1870. We also address the question of whether, even absent the existence of a conflicting federal treaty or federal legislation, the California statute is fundamentally repugnant to the Constitution of the United States under the recently ratified Fourteenth Amendment. We hold that it is.

Section 16 of the Civil Rights Act of 1870 states clearly that "no tax or charge shall be imposed or enforced by any state upon any person immigrating thereto from a foreign country which is not equally imposed or enforced upon every person immigrating to such state from any other foreign country, and any law of any state in conflict with this provision is hereby declared null and void." 16 Stat. 144 (1870). The California law violates the equal protection principles of this provision on several levels. First, the statute applies only to immigrants arriving by vessel, whereas those who travel by land from British possessions to the north or Mexico to the south, or over plains by railway, are exempt from having the charge assessed against them. Second, the California law targets only women and does not allow for a charge to be levied against potentially lewd or debauched men, yet another unequal application based on gender. Therefore, as the statute on its face was not equally imposed or enforced against all immigrants, but rather targets only a select few, it directly violates the Civil Rights Act of 1870.

The anti-tax provision in Section 16 of the Civil Rights Act of 1870, demonstrates that Congress intended to extend protections for immigrants beyond the simple federal jurisdictional question queried in *People v. Downer*, 7 Cal. 169 (1857), and *Lin Sing v. Washburn*, 20 Cal. 534 (1862), which invalidated California laws levying special taxes targeting Chinese immigrants. In *Downer*, the Supreme Court of California struck down a California law imposing a $50.00 tax on all persons arriving by sea who were ineligible for citizenship, the majority of whom were Chinese, because it infringed upon the federal commerce power. *Downer* referred to the *Passenger Cases, Smith v. Turner (Passenger Cases)*, 48 U.S. 282 (1849), as controlling authority, where the Supreme Court struck down head taxes imposed by New York and Massachusetts on foreign passengers arriving to those states. According to the Supreme Court majority in the *Passenger Cases*, taxes on foreigners arriving in the country were commercial in nature and thus infringed upon federal commerce power. In *Lin Sing*, the Supreme Court of California invalidated a California law imposing a $2.50 head tax on Asiatic immigrants residing in the state because it trespassed upon federal power over foreign commerce. *Lin Sing* cited as precedent, *Brown v. Maryland*, 25 U.S. 419 (1827), where the Supreme Court struck down a law establishing licensure requirements for importers to sell goods in Maryland because it interfered with federal power over foreign commerce. Justice Field applied similar reasoning in *Ah Fong*, as he also cited the *Passenger Cases* and spoke extensively on the ways in which the California statute allowing the detention of the twenty-two women constituted state interference with federal commerce with foreign nations. While Justice Field might be correct in noting that the California law excluding the Chinese women infringes upon powers typically exercised by the federal government, the paramount question here is whether the California law transgresses the protections Congress intended to make with the Civil Rights Act of 1870 and the specific constitutional protections that it was designed to enforce. An established line of case precedent invalidates discriminatory taxes against immigrants – *Brown v. Maryland*, the *Passenger Cases, Downer*, and *Lin Sing*. Yet importantly, Congress chose to codify these prohibitions in Section 16 of the Civil Rights Act of 1870 using the principles of equal protection established by the Fourteenth Amendment.

The Civil Rights Act of 1870 was specifically designed to enforce the Fifteenth Amendment, which prohibits any state from denying the right to vote based on race, color, or previous conditions of servitude. This legislation was a direct response to attempts by white vigilante groups to harass and intimidate black voters to dissuade them from voting. Nested within this Act are Sections 16 and 17 that confer protections to foreign aliens. At first glance, the inclusion of these provisions may seem peculiar, given that noncitizens are ineligible to vote. Yet Section 16 of the Civil Rights Act of 1870 stands for the broader principle of rights enjoyed by citizens as well as "all persons within the jurisdiction of the United States," including rights "to make and enforce contracts, to sue, be parties, give evidence, and to the full and equal benefit of all laws and proceedings for the security of person and property as is enjoyed by white citizens." Section 16 is, in fact, a codification of a bill initially introduced in January 1870 by Senator William Stewart of Nevada, specifically to address concerns raised by the Chinese community in San Francisco before a Congressional delegation in July 1868:

Be it enacted …. That all persons within the jurisdiction of the United States, Indians not taxed or excepted, shall have the same right in every State and Territory in the United States to make and enforce contracts, to sue, be parties, give evidence, and to the full and equal benefit of all laws and proceedings for the security of person and property as is enjoyed by white citizens, and shall be subject to like punishments, pains, penalties, taxes, licenses, and exactions of every kind and none other, any law, statute, ordinance, regulations, or custom to the contrary notwithstanding. No tax or charge shall be imposed or enforced by any State upon any person emigrating thereto from a foreign country which is not equally imposed and enforced upon every person emigrating to such State from any other foreign country, and any law of any State in conflict with this provision is hereby declared null and void. S. 365, 41st Cong., 2d Sess., Cong. Globe 1536 (1869–70).

Reiterating the identical protections enumerated in Section 1 of the Civil Rights Act of 1866 that pertained only to citizens, it is evident that Congress intended with Section 16 of the Civil Rights Act of 1870 to apply the Fourteenth Amendment principle of equal protection universally to citizens and noncitizens alike.

Further, even if the California statute that allowed the detention of the twenty-two women had been facially neutral, its application has proven to be unequal. Of the eighty-nine female passengers immigrating to the United States aboard the *Japan*, only twenty-two were singled out for examination because of their race. Officials suspected they were prostitutes simply because of they were Chinese. Had the appellant and her twenty-one companions been the white subjects of the Queen of Great Britain, for instance, they undoubtedly would have avoided scrutiny. There are likely as many if not more sex workers of white European than Asian Chinese descent practicing their profession in California. Yet, a white sex worker from London or Paris would have slipped by undetected because her race was not the intended target of the law. Moreover, if a primary purpose of the statute was to eliminate the forced prostitution of women, then it defies logic to inspect only Asian women, who comprise such a small fraction of the general population.

The history of the statute in question confirms the discriminatory exclusion of Chinese and other Asians through anti-prostitution legislation. The California legislature began targeting Chinese using anti-prostitution legislation when it passed on March 21, 1866 "An Act for the Suppression of Chinese Houses of Ill Fame." This law was followed by a variation of the law that is the subject of this case, which was passed on March 18, 1870 as "An Act to Prevent the Kidnapping and Importation of Mongolian, Chinese and Japanese Females, for Criminal or Demoralizing Purposes." Under this Act, if a passenger of a vessel was an Asiatic female, she was required to present evidence that she was immigrating voluntarily and that she was a "good person of correct habits and good character." If she was unable to do so, the captain of the vessel she was on could be charged with a misdemeanor punishable by a $1,000 to $5,000 fine or two to twelve months imprisonment. During the 1873–74 legislative session, this Act merged into its present form as the provision of the California Political Code that governed immigration, which added lewd or debauched women as one of the classifications of individuals to whom monetary bonds could be attached prior to disembarkation. This is the law that we are evaluating today. An 1874 amendment removed race and ethnicity from the law so that it appeared facially neutral and broadly applicable. Coincidentally in 1874, the word "Chinese" was excised from the 1866 Act for the Suppression of Chinese Houses of Ill Fame so that it also became race neutral. Until 1874, however, the California legislature specifically targeted the Chinese. And the current application of the law, regardless of its neutral text, shows that Chinese women continue to experience unequal treatment under the law and thus, unlawful discrimination.

As Justice Field rightly notes in *Ah Fong*, the California statute violates federal treaty law and also implicate the constitutional principle of equal protection. Article V of the Burlingame-Seward Treaty recognizes the "mutual advantage of the free migration and emigration of their citizens and subjects respectively from one country to the other." This treaty between the United States and China acknowledges the right of citizens of both countries to freely immigrate to the other nation as either temporary visitors or as permanent residents. It states that citizens of either country shall enjoy reciprocal privileges, immunities, and exemptions while visiting or residing in the other nation.

Negotiated during the construction of the transcontinental railroad, the treaty was heavily backed by American industrialists who owned the companies charged with its construction. One of the primary purposes of the Burlingame Treaty was to ensure a steady flow of low-cost Chinese immigrant labor to meet labor shortages that had delayed construction until the railroad companies began to import Chinese laborers. Thus, for decades since the treaty was signed, primarily men have been able to take advantage of the privileges of immigration from China to the United States under this treaty due to their ability to meet the demand for physical labor. This has created an extreme gender imbalance among the Chinese population living in the United States, distinct from other populations residing in the United States. The 1870 census indicates that a mere 7.2 percent of the Chinese population in the United States are women. The disproportionately high number of Chinese men residing in the United States as compared to very small number of Chinese women is not due to cultural factors as some have suggested, but by the practicalities of labor demand that facilitated immigration in the years following the negotiation of the treaty.

Now that the railroads are complete and there is no longer practical demand for low-cost immigrant labor from China, public opinion has shifted against these immigrants from China who are now seen as a threat to domestic labor, and there has been a political push for their exclusion. The California statute we are currently evaluating is the first instance of legislation that has come from this animosity toward the Chinese people and seeks to prevent their immigration into the state. Though public sentiment has changed, the treaty nevertheless remains in place and in effect.

While the Burlingame Treaty facilitated the entry of primarily Chinese male laborers to build the railroads, the treaty itself did not impose gender-based limitations on those seeking to enter the United States. Had it stated a gender-based limitation, it would be rendered invalid under the current equal protection guarantees of the U.S. Constitution. The California statute nonetheless sets out to create a distinction based on gender, as no man, even a notoriously lewd or debauched man, would be subject to scrutiny, the demand of bond, or exclusion under the statute. Ironically, the law does not provide for government enforcement of male perpetrators of forced prostitution, presumably the primary offenders of the vice that the law purportedly regulates. Forced prostitution of women cannot be eradicated without prosecuting the men who are often the purveyors of such crimes. In this respect, if eliminating the evils of prostitution and sale of women is the motivation for the law, then scrutiny of the women alone and not any men who might be responsible for their capture and subjugation makes no logical sense. By targeting only women for exclusion, the California law treats women differently than men, in contravention of the Burlingame Treaty, and also in violation of the equal protections afforded by the Fourteenth Amendment.

The targeting of Chinese women for exclusion also denies the entire Chinese population in the United States, the same protections enjoyed by other racial communities present. Those rights include the right to marry and form families. There is an increasing trend among the Western states and territories prohibiting the intermarriage of Chinese with whites. Nevada passed such an ordinance in 1861, Nev. Terr. Laws ch. 32, sec. 1, 3; Idaho in 1864, Idaho Terr. Gen. Laws at 604; Arizona in 1865, Ariz. Terr. Laws ch. 30, secs, 3, 4, 5; and Oregon in 1866, Ore. Laws at 10, secs. 1–2. More states are likely to follow suit. The combination of these anti-miscegenation statutes with laws excluding Chinese women from entering the country effectively consigns Chinese men in the United States to lives of perpetual bachelorhood. Anti-miscegenation laws prohibit Chinese men from entering into interracial marriages, while exclusionary immigration laws prevent the possibility of Chinese men forming families with newly arriving Chinese women. These legal barriers to marriage could lead to the eradication of the currently residing Chinese population in one generation. If nothing else, this constitutes a denial of a right to liberty, if not the right to life itself. The right to marriage and procreation is not merely a benefit that the state should provide to all individuals equally, but it is a fundamental right that must be rigorously protected by the state. In this respect, the California statute goes far beyond improper discrimination against a group of individuals based on race, by also trampling upon a fundamental right to liberty that the state is obligated to protect.

The question remains, however, whether this is a correct construal of the protections conferred to noncitizen immigrants within the relatively recently adopted Fourteenth Amendment, as there is little case precedent interpreting this issue. It is our conclusion that it is.

The most significant decision by this Court interpreting the protections afforded by the Fourteenth Amendment has been in the *Slaughterhouse Cases*, 83 U.S. 36 (1873), which also dealt with a state regulation pertaining to public health and welfare. In *Slaughterhouse*, the Court upheld a Louisiana law requiring that all butchering in the city of New Orleans be performed in an area south of the city owned by one private company, thereby creating a de facto monopoly. Justice Miller, writing for the majority, reasoned that the law was a legitimate exercise of the state's police power to protect public health and welfare. The Court concluded that the butchers, who argued that their constitutional right to make a living was threatened by the Louisiana regulation, had no claim under the Fourteenth Amendment. In interpreting the privileges and immunities clause of the Fourteenth Amendment, Justice Miller stated that it only applied to rights related to national citizenship, which were extremely limited. The right to earn a living, though fundamental, was not inherently a right of national citizenship but of state citizenship. Such rights were in the purview of state governments to protect and secure. According to Justice Miller, the privileges and immunities of national citizenship, with which the Fourteenth Amendment was exclusively concerned, was not constrained by the Louisiana legislation.

Justice Miller further suggested that the drafters of the Fourteenth Amendment intended to protect former slaves and no one else, stating "we doubt very much whether any action of a State not directed by way of discrimination against the negroes as a class, or on account of their race, will ever be held to come within the purview of this provision." This view was applied in another case *Bradwell v. Illinois*, 83 U.S. 130 (1873), decided by the Court the same day as *Slaughterhouse*. Myra Bradwell was denied admission to the bar of Illinois on the ground that she was a woman. The Illinois Supreme Court ruled that the law intended to allow only men and not women to practice law in Illinois. Like the Louisiana butchers, Bradwell also challenged the constitutionality of this restriction under the Fourteenth Amendment. As in *Slaughterhouse*, the Court in *Bradwell* held that the privileges and immunities clause did not apply to her because the right to earn a living was not a right of national citizenship but of state citizenship. It summarily dismissed her equal protection argument by reference to *Slaughterhouse*.

The *Slaughterhouse* Court's determination that the Fourteenth Amendment applied solely to former slaves contradicts a straightforward reading of the text, which explicitly declares constitutional protections not only for citizens, but for "any person." This is clarified by the concluding clause of the Fourteenth Amendment which guarantees due process and equal protection to "any person." As Justice Field established in *Ah Fong*, "Equality of privilege is the constitutional right of all citizens, and equality of protection is the constitutional right of all persons." Accordingly, equal protection and due process as delineated in the Fourteenth Amendment are universal principles that transcend differences between national and state citizenship, or citizenship at all.

In the present case we are dealing not with citizens of the United States nor of any individual state, but with noncitizen immigrants whom the Constitution protects. In *Slaughterhouse*, Justice Miller recognized the potential for additional protected classifications of individuals, saying of the Thirteenth Amendment "if Mexican peonage or the Chinese coolie labor system shall develop slavery of the Mexican or Chinese race within our territory, this amendment may safely be trusted to make it void. And so if other rights are assailed by the States which properly and necessarily fall within the protection of these articles, that protection will apply, though the party interested may not be of African descent."[37] We conclude that constitutional protections do indeed extend to Chinese immigrants.

Justice Field's dissent in *Slaughterhouse* proposed that the Fourteenth Amendment's protections extended beyond former slaves to apply to all people. The first clause of the Fourteenth Amendment defines citizenship in a manner that rectifies the misguided *Dred Scott* decision that permitted individual states to make that determination. The Fourteenth Amendment confirms that national citizenship is conferred on the basis of birthright and naturalization rather than inconsistent rules specific to individual states. According to Justice Field's *Slaughterhouse* dissent, the first portion of the Fourteenth Amendment establishes the primacy of federal citizenship above state citizenship, so that all free citizens, including but not exclusive to newly emancipated slaves, were to enjoy equal protection against state interference of their rights. Quoting Justice Washington in *Corfield v. Coryell*, 6 F. Cas. 546 (1823), Justice Field asserted that these rights included the natural and inalienable rights that belong to citizens of all free governments, such as "protection by the government, the enjoyment of life and liberty, with the right to acquire and possess property of every kind, and to pursue and obtain happiness and safety."

The *Slaughterhouse* opinions confine their analyses to the rights of citizens. As such, it is only a partial analysis of the Fourteenth Amendment. In its totality, however, the Fourteenth Amendment expressly states broader reach. Significantly, the final clause of the Fourteenth Amendment makes clear that its equal protection guarantee applies to "any person" regardless of citizenship status. All persons found within a state, regardless of whether they are citizens of that state, another state, or even the nation, possess rights of due process and equal protection of the laws. No state can deprive any person of a fundamental right without due process, which reasonably infers that fundamental rights exist outside of those defined by the individual state. In this regard, all persons within the territorial jurisdiction of the United States are to be treated equally. All persons must be accorded the same protections under the law enjoyed by others in the state. Thus, the state cannot deprive any individual of their fundamental rights, and also has an affirmative duty to protect those rights for all individuals equally under the law.

---

[37] Slaughterhouse Cases, 83 U.S. 36, at 72 (1873).

A handful of California cases challenging the constitutionality of laws prohibiting the Chinese from testifying in court against white persons provides more guidance on the meaning of equal protection under the law. Before passage of the Fourteenth Amendment, California law permitted the exclusion of the testimony of a Chinese man in a criminal case against a white man. *People v. Hall*, 4 Cal 399 (1854). After the Fourteenth Amendment was enacted, the constitutionality of testimonial exclusions based on race was revisited in *People v. Washington*, 36 Cal. 658 (1869). In that case, a mulatto defendant challenged his conviction because it relied on the testimony of Chinese witnesses. The case invoked a California statute that stipulated "no Indian or person having one half or more of Indian blood, or Mongolian, or Chinese, shall be permitted to give evidence in favor or against any white person." The defendant argued that the statute violated his right to equal protection of the law. If the defendant was white, the Chinese witnesses would have been excluded from testifying against him.

Ultimately, the *Washington* court struck down the California statute pursuant to the Civil Rights Act of 1866. The court noted the potential applicability of the Fourteenth Amendment, stating "The Fourteenth Amendment goes one step further than the Civil Rights Act, and after declaring who are citizens of the United States, and securing them in the enjoyment of their privileges and immunities, contains a provision applicable to all persons, whether citizens or not, in these words: 'Nor shall any State deprive any person of life, liberty or property without due process of law, nor deny to any person within its jurisdiction the equal protection of the laws.'" *People v. Washington*, 36 Cal. 658, at 671–72 (1869). Indeed, the Fourteenth Amendment was intended to constitutionally enshrine the protections of the Civil Rights Act of 1866 to all persons and to make it immune from possible repeal or alteration by future Congresses.

A year later, the Supreme Court of California in *People v. Brady*, 40 Cal. 198 (1870), overturned *People v. Washington*, ruling that the prohibition of Chinese from testifying against white defendants was still valid. Because the Civil Rights Act of 1866 established equal protection for citizens alone, Chinese witnesses were not covered by the Act. Further, the full constitutional force of the Fourteenth Amendment's equal protection guarantee to all persons had not yet been realized. The *Brady* court reasoned that the exclusion of testimony by Chinese witnesses against white defendants did not raise equal protection concerns. The court considered the heightened vulnerability of Chinese victims of crime against white assailants who might enjoy impunity because of the statute's prohibition of Chinese witnesses. Yet, the court concluded that Chinese persons, like white persons, were subject to and protected by the same criminal laws. The testimonial exclusion of Chinese witnesses against white defendants did not disturb the equal application of criminal laws' prohibitions and protections. The court found that the ability to testify as a witness was not a right connected to the right to protection, but a privilege which the officer conducting a prosecution may invoke or not at his discretion. The statute was challenged again in *People v. McGuire*, 45 Cal. 56 (1872). In *McGuire*, the Supreme Court of California recognized that Section 16 of the Civil Rights Act of 1870 would eventually repeal the Chinese testamentary ban, but upheld the law and the precedent in *Brady* because the Civil Rights Act would not take effect until 1873.

Though the *Brady* court upheld the validity of the testamentary exclusion of Chinese witnesses, it also expounded on the Fourteenth Amendment concept of equal protection. The *Brady* court considered equal protection of the laws to include security against crime and the rights of victims. This is consistent with other juridical interpretations of equal protection of the laws. In *People v. Lamb*, 39 N. Y. Rep. 360 (1866), the New York Court of Appeals noted, "equality before the law is a maxim of criminal justice, and the life of the humblest and most abandoned is equally entitled to the protection of the law as that of the most cultivated, refined, or elevated." That is, a victim of a crime, no matter what their status, is entitled to have the crime prosecuted to the full extent of the law. In *Brady*, the court found that the law treats victims equally since the perpetrator of crime can be prosecuted regardless of the identity of the victim, whether they are white or Chinese.

The question remains whether the twenty-two women in the present case are being afforded equal protection under the law in this manner, and whether they are being protected against crime in the same way that other individuals are being protected. With respect to the rights of allegedly lewd women, Francis Wharton in his Treatise on the Criminal Law of the United States, suggests that even a "common strumpet … is still under the protection of the law, and may not be forced." A Treatise on the Criminal Law of the United States § 1150, 175 (1868). Amos Dean, in his Principles of Medical Jurisprudence: Designed for the Professions of Law and Medicine similarly proposed, "the crime of rape may be committed upon a virgin, a single or married woman, or even upon a prostitute. The latter being also under the protection of the law." Principles of Medical Jurisprudence 25 (1866). A rapist must be pursued and prosecuted regardless of whether the victim was a virgin or a prostitute. She is still a victim of a crime and entitled to have the crime fully prosecuted. It follows that if a prostitute is protected against rape, she too is protected against capture and enslavement as well. That means that the law should give her redress not only against a man who rapes her, but also the men who captured and forced her into prostitution.

In the present case, twenty-two women experienced unequal treatment under a California statute as well as the denial of equal protection of the law guaranteed by the Fourteenth Amendment. The legislative history of the California statute, similar to the federal Page Act of 1875, presumes that women like those in the present case are forced or coerced into prostitution. If that is the case then these women are also victims of crime. The original 1870 Act to Prevent the Kidnapping and Importation of Mongolian, Chinese and Japanese Females, for Criminal or Demoralizing Purposes stated ostensibly as its purpose the protection of not only the general public from scandal and injury, but also the prostitutes themselves who were kidnapped without their consent and against their will. Horace Page, the author of the federal Page Act which was modeled after the California law, argued that Chinese prostitutes were no more than slaves who have been captured and forced into the practice by a debased culture that is antithetical to our American system of free labor. President Ulysses Grant, in his annual message to Congress last year suggested that "the great proportion of the Chinese immigrants who come to our shores do not come voluntarily … In a worse form does this apply to Chinese women. Hardly a perceptible percentage of them perform any honorable labor, but they are brought for shameful purposes … If this evil practice can be legislated against, it will be my pleasure as well as duty to enforce any regulation to secure so desirable an end." 3 Cong. Rec. 3 (1874). If the women have indeed been kidnapped or lured to the United States for lewd and shameful purposes against their will, then excluding them from entry and instead sending them back to the place of their initial capture and enslavement does nothing to bring the evil practice to an end. If returned to their perpetrators, these women would enjoy no protection and will likely be enslaved again. Rather, if the women were to be admitted to the United States, then they may avail themselves of the protections that this country offers and possibly find redress. Turning these women away will keep them in servitude, an obvious denial of the equal protection of our laws in contravention of the Fourteenth Amendment.

On the other hand, if these twenty-two women are not being forced or coerced into prostitution, as they have been protesting all along while being misidentified as such by the whims of one commissioner, then they have been unlawfully detained against their will without due process of the law, also in contravention of the Fourteenth Amendment. Under the California law, individual passengers who might be subject to exclusion find themselves helpless in the presence of a commissioner who has been made all potent by the statute. One single commissioner is empowered under the statute to, without trial or hearing or evidence, from simple external appearances of persons whose habits he is unfamiliar, point with his finger and say to the ship's master, "These are idiots, these are paupers, these are convicted criminals, these are lewd women, and these others are debauched women. They require bond to disembark." This is an arbitrary and tyrannical power that could permit systematic extortion of the grossest kind. A wicked or obstinate commissioner could, for instance, say, "I have here a hundred blank forms of bonds, printed. I require you to fill and sign each of these for $500 in gold, and furnish me two hundred different men, residents of this State, and of sufficient means, as sureties on these bonds. I charge you five dollars in each case for preparing the bond and swearing your sureties; and I charge you seventy-five cents each for examining these passengers, and all others you have on board. If you don't do this, you are forbidden to land your passengers under a heavy penalty. But I have the power to commute with you for all this for any sum I may choose to take in cash. I am open to an offer; for you must remember that twenty percent of all I can get out of you goes into my own pocket, and the remainder into the treasury of California." Thus, the California statute permits an unreasonable, arbitrary, and capricious deprivation of liberty and property without due process of the law.

But we have thus far only considered the effect of the statute on the liberty and property rights of the owner of the vessel. The passenger herself is left completely powerless in respect to her own freedom. For even if she offers to furnish the surety on her own bond, or deposit any sum of money, the law of California takes no note of her. It is the master, owner, or consignee of the vessel alone whose bond can be accepted, even if they have no relation to the passenger and thus have no incentive to pay. As the statute places the ability of these passengers to avoid detention exclusively in the control of the commissioner and then the master, owner, or consignee of the vessel, this constitutes an unlawful deprivation of their liberty without due process of the law. Even if they are being detained because of a bona fide belief that they are in fact prostitutes, they have not been found guilty by any court or tribunal. Instead, they were found only to have given "perfectly not satisfactory" answers in an interview by a single commissioner whose only reason for even suspecting these women of prostitution was that they were unaccompanied.

Thus, we agree with Justice Field's decision in *Ah Fong* that the California statute violates federal treaty law in the Burlingame Treaty as well as federal legislation in the Civil Right of 1870. If either of these were repealed or contravened by further federal action, we find that the California statute more foundationally violates the guarantees of due process and equal protection provided by the Fourteenth Amendment of the Constitution of the United States and is therefore void.

In respect to contravening federal legislation, Justice Field in *Ah Fong* suggested that the federal government has the power to restrict immigration in a manner that the state does not, saying "if further immigration is to be stopped, recourse must be had to the federal government, where the whole power over this subject lies." Congress did engage in such action only a few short months after the *Ah Fong* decision by passing the Page Act of 1875, which was modeled under the California statute. The Page Act, among other things, prohibits the immigration of convicted criminals and prostitutes. Even though the Page Act is not the subject of our inquiry today, it seems to also stand on precarious constitutional footing. In view of our decision today that the Constitution prohibits the states from denying due process and equal protection of the laws to the Chinese women in this case, it would be unthinkable that the same Constitution would impose a lesser duty on the federal government. If other Chinese women are similarly being singled out for exclusion at the federal level under the Page Act, such practice would similarly prove to be unconstitutional as in this case.

The judgment of the Supreme Court of California is reversed, and the case remanded, with directions to make an order discharging the prisoner from custody.

3

Commentary on *Nishimura Ekiu v. United States*, 142 U.S. 651 (1892)

Eunice C. Lee

On May 7, 1891, Ms. Nishimura Ekiu arrived in San Francisco aboard the steamship *Belgic*. At age twenty-five, she had journeyed from her home country of Japan to reunite with her husband in the United States. Ms. Nishimura had the misfortunate of coming at a time of heightened fearmongering against "yellow peril"[1] and "Oriental invasion."[2] Although the immigration laws did not yet bar admission of Japanese nationals – that blanket prohibition would happen in 1924[3] – Japanese immigrants were nonetheless swept up in waves of anti-Asian sentiment. Congress had passed the Chinese Exclusion Act in 1882 and continued to further restrict Chinese immigration in the years following. In 1892, a decade after the original Exclusion Act and the same year as the Court's decision in *Nishimura Ekiu v. United States*,[4] Congress extended the ban on Chinese nationals.

The exclusion laws reflected and responded to virulent anti-Chinese sentiment of the time. Although reluctantly tolerated for providing cheap labor for railroad construction in the mid-1800s, Chinese immigrants came under increasing attack and vilification as the need for their labor diminished.[5] White Americans targeted Chinese immigrants with mob violence and lynching,[6] as well as concerted legal efforts.

The strongest anti-Chinese movement arose out of California: The Workingman's Party, founded in San Francisco in 1877 by white laborers, called for the removal of all Chinese persons from California. The Party's advocacy led to several anti-Chinese state laws as well an amendment to the California Constitution, authorizing

---

[1] *See* Erika Lee, *The "Yellow Peril" and Asian Exclusion in the Americas*, 76(4) PAC. HIST. REV. 537 (2007).

[2] Chae Chan Ping v. United States, 130 U.S. 581 (1889).

[3] *See* Immigration Act of 1924, Pub. L. 68–139, 43 Stat. 153 (1924) (prohibiting entry of all noncitizens ineligible for naturalization, which included all immigrants from Asia).

[4] 142 U.S. 651 (1892).

[5] *See* LUCY E. SALYER, LAWS HARSH AS TIGERS: CHINESE IMMIGRANTS AND THE SHAPING OF MODERN IMMIGRATION LAW 8–9 (1995).

[6] *See* BETH LEW-WILLIAMS, CHINESE MUST GO: VIOLENCE, EXCLUSION, AND THE MAKING OF THE ALIEN IN AMERICA (2021).

localities to expel Chinese residents.[7] Eventually, the Party's work helped secure the passage of the federal exclusion laws.

Yet, even before the general ban on Chinese nationals, Congress had targeted Asian women in particular. The Page Act of 1875 prohibited admission of women sex workers and made their "importation" a felony offense.[8] Horace F. Page, a Congressman from California and the named sponsor of the Act, built a platform around anti-Chinese legislation (including later sponsorship of the 1882 Exclusion Act).[9] In his speech introducing the Page Act, he called upon Congress to protect America's wives and daughters from the immorality, vice, and "deadly blight" of "Chinese prostitutes."[10]

Although legislative debates over the Page Act focused on Chinese women sex workers, the law expressly singled out Japanese women as well. The Act prohibited admission of women sex workers of all nationalities, but specifically mandated the pre-embarkation inspection of women from "China, Japan, or any Oriental country." The Act required U.S. consuls in these countries – and these countries only – to screen women for "lewd and immoral purposes." In implementing the Page Act, officials presumed nearly all Chinese women to be prostitutes and excluded them accordingly.[11]

When Ms. Nishimura arrived in San Francisco in 1891, she encountered a milieu of laws and policies that constituted her as doubly undesirable: a foreigner, racially inferior and unassimilable; and an "Oriental" woman, lewd and immoral.[12] Although the immigration inspector found her excludable as a public charge pursuant to the 1891 Immigration Act rather than under the Page Act, his disbelief in her testimony reflected gendered and racialized skepticism. Ms. Nishimura explained that she had come to the United States to reunite with her husband, consistent with the notation in her passport – but the immigration inspector refused to view her a legitimate wife. She challenged her exclusion in federal court and remained in custody at the Methodist Japanese and Chinese Mission house in San Francisco for the duration of her suit.

---

[7] *See* Cal. Const. of 1879, art. XIX. Chinese community members successfully sued to enjoin the provision. *See, e.g.*, In re Tiburcio Parrot, 1 F. 481 (C.C.D. Cal. 1880). However, that victory only prompted the Workingman's Party to push for federal legislation.

[8] Act of Mar. 3, 1875, Pub. L. 43–141, 18 Stat. 477, ch. 141 (1875).

[9] Kerry Abrams, *Polygamy, Prostitution, and the Federalization of Immigration Law*, 105(3) COLUM. L. REV. 641, 690 (2005).

[10] 3 Cong. Rec. appx. 40 (1875) (speech of Horace Page); Catherine Lee, "*Where the Danger Lies*": Race, Gender, and Chinese and Japanese Exclusion in the United States, 1870–1924, 25(2) SOCIOL. FORUM 248 (2010). An earlier California statute also targeted Chinese sex workers. That law, passed in 1866 by the California legislature and titled "An Act for the Suppression of Chinese Houses of Ill-Fame," declared Chinese prostitution to be a public nuisance and banned the issuance of leases to Chinese brothels. Act of Mar. 21, 1866, 1866 Cal. Stat. 641, ch. 505.

[11] Abrams, supra note 10, at 698.

[12] See Pooja Dadhania, *Deporting Undesirable Women*, 9 U.C. IRVINE L. REV. 53 (2018) (analyzing immigration law's long history of targeting of noncitizen women sex workers, including Chinese and Japanese women, as "undesirable").

At the time of Ms. Nishimura's arrival, immigration restrictionists had begun focusing their attention on Japanese nationals. The 1882 law almost entirely stopped immigration from China, paving the way for greater flows from other parts of Asia, particularly Japan. The Workingman's Party adopted a new slogan: "The Japs Must Go."[13] On May 4, 1891, a headline in the *Bulletin*, a prolabor San Francisco newspaper, proclaimed: UNDESIRABLES; ANOTHER PHASE IN THE IMMIGRATION FROM ASIA; JAPANESE TAKING THE PLACE OF THE CHINESE; IMPORTATION OF CONTRACT LABORERS AND WOMEN.[14] Just three days later, the *Belgic* arrived in that same port city with Ms. Nishimura onboard.

Racism and sexism against Asian women pervaded immigration law and enforcement at the turn of the twentieth century. The treatment Ms. Nishimura received from government officials reflected this, as did the Supreme Court's eventual ruling in her case. Even the decision to hold Ms. Nishimura in the Methodist mission home instead of keeping her onboard her ship, considered by the Court to be "suitable,"[15] had racist and sexist overtones. The missionaries at the home sought to "rescue" the Asian women in their care from their immoral and inferior cultures, and to inculcate them with Protestant and Victorian values.[16]

Ms. Nishimura's custody in the mission home – reflective of the racism and sexism of the era – led the Court to pronounce a novel doctrine with wide-reaching contemporary ramifications. In siding with the government, the Supreme Court established immigration's "entry fiction" – a judicial construct that treats noncitizens present on U.S. soil as outside the bounds of its territory. When individuals are "stopped at the gates," i.e., refused formal admission at a port of entry, "entry fiction" doctrine excludes them from the full protection of the U.S. Constitution with regard to immigration decisions.

Rather than cabining the fiction to the ignominious era of its pronouncement, the Court has seen fit to expand it. The fiction of nonentry now limits the rights of thousands of immigrants at our borders and ports of entry each year, including many asylum seekers.[17] The fiction applies even when Immigration and Customs

---

[13] ROGER DANIELS, ASIAN AMERICA: CHINESE AND JAPANESE IN THE UNITED STATES SINCE 1850 111 (1988).

[14] *See id.* at 112 (describing article and headline in The Bulletin).

[15] 142 U.S. at 661.

[16] See PEGGY PASCOE, RELATIONS OF RESCUE: THE SEARCH FOR FEMALE MORAL AUTHORITY IN THE AMERICAN WEST, 1874–1939 121 (1990); Laura Curry, *"Sweep All These Pests from Our Midst": The Anti-Chinese Prostitution Movement, the Criminalization of Chinese Women, and the First Federal Immigration Law*, 2(1) W. VA. U. HIST. REV. 1, 3.

[17] See Detention FY 2022 YTD, Alternatives to Detention FY 2022 YTD and Facilities FY 2022 YTD, IMMIG. & CUSTOMS ENFORCEMENT; see also Control of Communicable Diseases; Foreign Quarantine: Suspension of the Right To Introduce and Prohibition of Introduction of Persons Into United States from Designated Foreign Countries or Places for Public Health Purposes, 85 Fed. Reg. 56424 (Sept. 11, 2020); AMERICAN IMMIGRATION COUNCIL, A GUIDE TO TITLE 42 EXPULSIONS AT THE BORDER (Oct. 2021).

Enforcement (ICE) has transported these individuals hundreds of miles into the interior and detained them in prison-like facilities for months or even years. ICE's mass incarceration system primarily benefits private prison companies, which operate the vast majority of detention beds and garner over a billion taxpayer dollars each year.[18]

The far-reaching ramifications of *Nishimura Ekiu* would likely have been unimaginable to the Justices of the time. The decision pre-dated contemporary mass incarceration of immigrants and an established asylum system by almost a century. Yet the Court recently relied upon *Nishimura Ekiu* in a dramatic expansion of entry fiction. In the 2020 case of *DHS v. Thurassigiam*,[19] the Court rejected the habeas and due process claims of a Sri Lankan asylum seeker. Its reasoning compounded the errors of its earlier decision, while also failing to consider drastically different contemporary circumstances. Consequently, in other work, I have proposed the abandonment of entry fiction as a legal fiction. The current Court both misapprehends the origin of the doctrine and relies on its outdated justifications that have long since expired.[20]

THE ORIGINAL OPINION

Ms. Nishimura was one of several Japanese women aboard the *Belgic* when it landed in San Francisco. William H. Thornley, the Commissioner of Immigration for California, boarded the ship to inspect her along with other passengers. Upon questioning, Ms. Nishimura explained that she had journeyed to join her husband of two years, but Mr. Thornley disbelieved this account. He faulted her for not knowing her husband's address and deemed her excludable as "a person unable to care for herself, and liable to become a public charge." He wrote in his report, "She has $22, and is to stop at some hotel until her husband calls for her."[21]

The relevant law had passed only two months prior. The Immigration Act of 1891 prohibited admission of "[a]ll idiots, insane persons, paupers or persons likely to become a public charge" (among others).[22] It also established the office of the superintendent of immigration within the Treasury Department.[23]

On May 13, 1891, Ms. Nishimura brought a habeas corpus suit in federal court. Rather than keeping her aboard the ship, the U.S. government agreed with her attorney that she would remain in the custody of the Methodist Episcopal Japanese and Chinese Mission boarding home in the City of San Francisco.

---

[18] Eunice Cho, *More of the Same: Private Prison Corporations and Immigration Detention Under the Biden Administration*, ACLU.ORG (Oct. 5, 2021).

[19] 140 S. Ct. 1959 (2020).

[20] *See* Eunice Lee, *The End of Entry Fiction*, 99 N. C. L. REV. 565 (2021).

[21] 142 U.S. at 651.

[22] An Act in Amendment to the Various Acts Relative to Immigration and the Importation of Aliens under Contract or Agreement to Perform Labor, Pub. L. 51–551, 26 Stat. 1084, c. 551, §1 (1891).

[23] *Id.* § 7.

On May 14, 1891, the Secretary of Treasury appointed John L. Hatch as inspector of immigration at the port of San Francisco. Mr. Hatch adopted the findings and conclusions of Mr. Thornley verbatim in his own report, deeming Ms. Nishimura excludable as a public charge.

In her hearing before the circuit court, Ms. Nishimura argued that the Immigration Act of 1891 deprived her of liberty without due process of law under the Fifth Amendment.[24] She also contended that her right to habeas corpus mandated review of the legality of her detention, including an inquiry into the facts. Finally, she offered to introduce new evidence on her right to land. The circuit court rejected Ms. Nishimura's arguments and proffer of evidence, holding that the decision of Mr. Hatch was lawful, final, and unreviewable.

The Supreme Court granted Ms. Nishimura's petition for certiorari but ultimately affirmed the court below. Justice Gray penned the near-unanimous decision. After confirming its appellate jurisdiction to hear the appeal, the majority decision opened by stating that "inherent in sovereignty and essential to self-preservation" is the power of the federal government to "forbid the entrance of foreigners within its dominion, or to admit them only in such cases and upon such conditions as it may see fit." This power, the Court emphasized, "belongs to the political department of the government."[25]

Importantly, the Court agreed that Ms. Nishimura had a clear right to habeas review of her exclusion by the federal court: "[a]n alien immigrant, prevented from landing by any such officer claiming authority to do so under an act of congress, and thereby restrained of his liberty, is doubtless entitled to a writ of *habeas corpus* to ascertain whether the restraint is lawful."[26] But the Court shied away from full constitutional review, reasoning that:

> It is not within the province of the judiciary to order that foreigners who have never been naturalized, nor acquired any domicile or residence within the United States, nor even been admitted into the country pursuant to law, shall be permitted to enter, in opposition to the constitutional and lawful measures of the legislative and executive branches of the national government. *As to such persons, the decisions of executive or administrative officers, acting within powers expressly conferred by congress, are due process of law.*[27]

Deeming executive decisions authorized by Congress "due process of law" reflected a drastic abdication of the judiciary's role. Rather than protecting individual rights against executive and Congressional overreach, the Court simply stepped aside. It did so even though the action at issue had enormous impact on the lives and liberty of people subject to governmental coercion. Under the majority's analysis, the

---

[24] U.S. Const. amend. V.
[25] 142 U.S. at 659.
[26] *Id.* at 660.
[27] *Id.* (emphasis added).

Constitution faded out of view – subsumed by statute and executive action, rather than serving as a check against them.

The fact that the immigration action here concerned *exclusion* – and not deportation – would prove key to the majority decision. Immigration officers never formally admitted Ms. Nishimura, and she was brought onto U.S. territory in government custody. In other words, she did not effect a technical immigration "entry," which entails either formal admission or a crossing onto territory free from restraint:[28] The fact of her physical presence on U.S. soil at the time of her lawsuit did not constitute an entry, and thus did not confer constitutional or statutory protections. The Court explained:

> Putting her in the mission-house as a more suitable place than the steam-ship, pending the decision of the question of her right to land, and keeping her there, by agreement between her attorney and the attorney for the United States, until final judgment upon the writ of *habeas corpus*, left her in the same position, so far as regarded her right to land in the United States, as if she never had been removed from the steam-ship.[29]

The Court here emphasized the "suitable" nature of the mission house, as well as her custody there pursuant to her own agreement.[30] As noted the mission home was not a jail, but rather a boarding house in the city center of San Francisco, offering shelter, food, clothing, transportation, and social services to its residents. This infers a humanitarian impulse underpinning entry fiction in statute and doctrine. Later cases reaffirming the fiction also reflect a desire to benefit individuals by minimizing detention in harsh condition on ships or in detention centers.[31] In this specific context, the Court assimilated Ms. Nishimura's constitutional status to that of a person outside the United States despite her presence within it – pronouncing immigration's entry fiction.

A little over a decade later, in a 1903 case also involving a young Japanese woman, the Court would recognize due process principles for entrants. The petitioner, Kaoru Yamataya, had made a landing in the United States; just four days later, an immigration inspector deemed her wrongly admitted and found her excludable as a public charge. The fact of formal entry made all the difference in her case. The Court in *Yamataya v. Fisher* declined to extend the reasoning in *Nishimura Ekiu* to recent entrants. Rather than accepting executive decisions pursuant to federal statute as "due process of law" in and of themselves, it explained that the government could not deport the petitioner absent a hearing: "[n]o such arbitrary power can exist where the principles involved in due process of law are recognized."[32] But for Ms. Nishimura, a technical non-entrant present in San Francisco, due process protections against governmental power did not apply.

---

[28] *See in re* Z-, 20 I. & N. Dec. 707, 707–08 (B.I.A. 1993); *in re* Patel, 20 I. & N. Dec. 368 (B.I.A. 1991).
[29] 142 U.S. at 661.
[30] *See* Lee, supra note 19, at 587–97; *see also* Leng May Ma v. Barber, 57 U.S. 185 (1958).
[31] *See* ESTHER CRAIN, THE GILDED AGE IN NEW YORK, 1870–1910 (2016).
[32] Yamataya v. Fisher, 189 U.S. 86, 101 (1903).

THE FEMINIST JUDGMENT

Professor Stella Burch Elias, writing as Justice Elias, concurring in part and dissenting in part, would grant habeas relief to Ms. Nishimura. At the outset of her opinion, she recounts the facts presented to the Court with far more care and concern than the majority.[33] She casts a skeptical eye on the Court's characterization of Ms. Nishimura's inspection by Mr. Thornley as "careful," noting that "the record is silent as to Ms. Nishimura's knowledge of, or proficiency in, the English language" and "equally silent as to whether Ms. Nishimura had any access to the services of a skilled interpreter." Thus, "it is impossible to ascertain with any certainty that Mr. Thornley was able to question Ms. Nishimura effectively or that Ms. Nishimura was able to respond knowingly or appropriately to Mr. Thornley's questions." Similarly, she observes that the record did not clarify whether Mr. Hatch ever met with the petitioner, "or whether he gave her any opportunity at all to present her case in any meaningful way."

Professor Elias concurs with the majority that the federal courts have jurisdiction to review Ms. Nishimura's challenge to her exclusion. As she notes, English common law has long recognized the availability of the writ of habeas to all persons detained by the government, including foreign subjects; and Article I of the U.S. Constitution enshrines this "fundamental and longstanding" right.[34] Thus, she agrees with the majority that noncitizens arriving at our shores and prevented entry have the right to seek habeas relief with regard to their exclusion.

In the remainder of her opinion, Professor Elias diverges significantly from the holdings and reasoning of the majority. First, she disagrees that the statutory framework of the Immigration Act of 1891 divests federal courts of full judicial review of exclusion decisions. The majority emphasized Section 8 of the Act which provides that: "all decisions by the inspection officers or their assistants touching the right of any alien to land, when adverse to such right, shall be final, unless appeal[ed] … to the superintendent of immigration, whose action shall be subject to review by the secretary of treasury." Professor Elias, however, points out that Section 13 of the Act instructs federal circuit and district courts to remain "invested with full and concurrent jurisdiction of all causes, civil and criminal, arising under any provisions of this act." This language permits – indeed, requires – federal courts to review the exclusion decisions of executive officers.

In Section IV of her opinion, Elias sets forth her most salient and important dispute with the majority, regarding due process rights in immigration proceedings. In this section, she deviates from not only the majority decision but also the Court's prior plenary power doctrine decisions.[35] Rather than deferring to the political

---

[33] Angela Harris, *Compassion and Critique*, 1 COLUM. J. RACE L. 326 (2012).
[34] U.S. Const. art. I, § 9 cl. 2.
[35] *See* Chae Chan Ping, 130 U.S. 581 (1889); Fong Yue Ting, 149 U.S. 698 (1893).

branches on immigration matters, she persuasively argues that the judiciary should engage in normal constitutional review of executive action and congressional laws. She contends that "when executive officers are actively engaged in implementing the provisions of a statute that authorizes the deprivation of a person's liberty, whether through that person's detention, exclusion, or deportation, *it is more important than ever* that the officers' behavior comports with the Due Process guarantees in our Constitution." (emphasis added).

Professor Elias unequivocally rejects the majority's statement that as to exclusion, the actions of executive officers pursuant to federal statute are due process of law. She emphasizes that government officials are not immune from "the mandates of the Constitution" or from judicial review. Thus, "[n]o officer of the United States may disregard the fundamental precept set forth in the Fifth Amendment to the Constitution of the United States that: 'No person shall be … deprived of life, liberty, or property, without due process of law.'"[36] Nor does the 1891 Act envision such a scenario: "the statute does not furnish the executive and administrative officers with unfettered and arbitrary power."

In the final section of her opinion, Professor Elias applies constitutional scrutiny to the facts of the case. She first addresses whether the immigration proceedings afforded Ms. Nishimura due process of law. She reiterates the lack of detail in the sparse, identical reports of Messrs. Hatch and Thornley and identifies several potential due process concerns. These include the record's silence on: (1) whether Ms. Nishimura received notice of the importance of her initial or subsequent interview; (2) the extent of Ms. Nishimura's English proficiency and education; (3) whether she was provided an interpreter who accurately translated questions to her; and (4) whether the officers took her testimony under oath. Elias concludes that there is simply no indication that Ms. Nishimura "was granted any opportunity at all to present her case in any meaningful way." In light of the history of the case, Elias "suspect[s] that she was not," but stops short of finding a due process violation given the record's deficiencies.

Professor Elias next considers Ms. Nishimura's treatment by the circuit court, and here, finds the record clear enough to reach a firm conclusion. She notes that although Ms. Nishimura "attempted vigorously and repeatedly to present evidence" contesting her exclusion, the lower court rejected Ms. Nishimura's proffer, wrongly deciding it had no authority to consider her claims. Elias determines that in those judicial proceedings, "Ms. Nishimura was denied her opportunity to be heard, and was therefore deprived of her liberty without due process of law."

In the last paragraph of her opinion, Professor Elias highlights the moral as well as legal failures of the lower court and government, compounded by her fellow Justices. "In denying her the opportunity to present her claims," she writes, "the immigration officials and the Circuit Court denied her humanity, failing to treat her as 'person' who could not be deprived of her liberty without due process of law."

---

[36] U.S. Const. amend. V.

Elias eloquently avers that recognizing a "person" for constitutional purposes not only gives substance to their legal claims, but also affirms that they are human. In refusing to see Ms. Nishimura as a full person, the justices in the majority rejected the common humanity they share with her.

Professor Elias acknowledges the limitations of her own perspective and role. Given the deficiencies of the record, she cannot fully know what happened to Ms. Nishimura. Even less uncertain, she notes, are the fates of the other young women who arrived with Ms. Nishimura on the *Belgic*:

> Ms. Nishimura was not alone on May 13, 1891, when the *Belgic* sailed into the Port of San Francisco. We know from Mr. Thornley's report that five other women aboard the vessel were also excluded from the United States, and in the majority's recounting of the facts of this case, their personhood is even more ephemeral than that of Ms. Nishimura. We do not know what happened to them next. We do not even know their names.

Professor Elias's insistence on seeing these women radically departs from judicial practice. The five women were not parties to the suit, and their claims were never presented to the Court. Rather than taking this as license to ignore their existence, Elias draws our attention to these women – to the lacuna of their absence, and the injustice it entails. She cannot give them names or voices, nor rectify their unconstitutional treatment, but she can recognize and acknowledge them. And this she does, concluding:

> All immigrants arriving at our borders, whatever their sex, race, nationality, or creed, are entitled to be treated humanely and justly, in accordance with due process of law. They are entitled to tell their stories and to have their voices heard. Therefore, I respectfully dissent.

Professor Elias reminds us that all immigrants who come to our shores are persons, under our Constitution and otherwise. Fictions notwithstanding, they are here.[37]

Following the majority decision, we never get to hear Ms. Nishimura's full story, nor those of the women who arrived with her. Professor Elias calls our attention to this silencing. Although she cannot speak for the women, she makes us feel their absence. Her Constitution does not discriminate on the basis of race, national origin, gender, manner of entry, or immigration status. Under her interpretation, the Due Process Clause would instead rectify government overreach reflecting these prejudices.

Professor Elias handles Ms. Nishimura's claims with fairness and an ethic of care.[38] She does not allow gendered, racialized stereotypes to color her judgment; rather, she closely scrutinizes the decisions of government officials who likely held these prejudices and who enforced laws explicitly rooted in them. She refuses to

---

[37] Kathryn Abrams, *Hearing the Call of Stories*, 79 CALIF. L. REV. 971 (1991).
[38] Carol Gilligan, *Moral Injury and the Ethic of Care: Reframing the Conversation about Differences*, 45 J. SOC. PHILOS. 89 (2014).

validate governmental action on a defective record and does not shy away from criticizing the lower court and majority for miscarriage of justice.

Elias's opinion rises above the racism and sexism of an era that viewed "Oriental" women as threats to the nation. The majority's treatment of Ms. Nishimura as a nonperson under the Constitution is deeply rooted in this historical context.[39] In the intervening century and a quarter, significant changes in law and jurisprudence might have prompted a careful Court to revisit entry fiction as pronounced in *Nishimura Ekiu*. Our immigration laws now prohibit rather than mandate discrimination on the basis of race and national origin.[40] We have an asylum system, and laws that prevent return to persecution and torture.[41] Meanwhile, in legal doctrine, over a century of due process jurisprudence has deepened the rights of individuals against governmental overreach.

Much has changed in the treatment of immigrants as well. In 1892, when the Court rendered its decision in her case, Ms. Nishimura's form of custody was a room at the Methodist mission home in San Francisco: a boarding house complete with a parlor room and dining hall.[42] The Court deemed this placement a "suitable" alternative to forcing her to stay aboard her passenger ship. Today, the Department of Homeland Security (DHS) keeps tens of thousands of noncitizens each day in immigration prisons. Immigration enforcement has also dramatically changed in scale, scope, and capability. The Treasury's immigration inspection office was nascent and tiny in Ms. Nishimura's time; in ours, Congress provided DHS with $52.81 billion in fiscal year 2022 alone, including billions for military-grade technology.[43]

The Court continues to ignore the history of racism and sexism underpinning the cases of the Chinese Exclusion Era. And it consistently fails to consider the lived reality of immigrants swept up in our enforcement and legal systems today. In *DHS v. Thuraissigiam*,[44] the Court relied on *Nishimura Ekiu* in stripping asylum seekers at the border of due process rights against removal. Justice Alito, writing for the majority, applied the fiction against a petitioner apprehended twenty-five yards north of the border, holding that his crossing did not constitute an entry for constitutional purposes. Quoting *Nishimura Ekiu*, the opinion concluded that as to Mr. Thuraissigiam, "the decisions of executive or administrative officers, acting within powers expressly conferred by Congress, are due process of law."[45] It also

---

[39] Angela Harris, *Compassion and Critique*, 1 COLUM. J. RACE L. 326 (2012).

[40] *See* 8 U.S.C. § 1152(a)(1)(A) ("[N]o person shall receive any preference or priority or be discriminated against in the issuance of an immigrant visa because of the person's race, sex, nationality, place of birth, or place of residence.").

[41] *See* 8 U.S.C. § 1158; 8 U.S.C. § 1231(b)(3); 8 C.F.R. § 208.16(c).

[42] For turn-of-the-twentieth-century photos of the San Francisco mission home from the archives of the Methodist Church, see Lee, supra note 19, at 590–92.

[43] U.S. House of Representatives, Appropriations Committee Releases Fiscal Year 2022 Homeland Security Funding Bill (June 29, 2021).

[44] 140 S. Ct. 1959 (2020).

[45] 140 S. Ct. at 1980 (quoting Nishimura Ekiu, 142 U.S. at 660).

held that he had no right under the Suspension Clause to federal court review of his legal challenge to his expedited removal order. The majority's application of entry fiction to Mr. Thurassigiam was an unprecedented expansion of the doctrine, which the Court had never before applied to border crossers. *Thurassigiam* also distorts and misunderstands the earlier decision, which had in fact reaffirmed the habeas rights of noncitizens and rested upon drastically different circumstances. Had Professor Elias's opinion been the majority in *Nishimura Ekiu*, the *Thuraissigiam* Court likely would have exercised far greater scrutiny over border officials' actions to ensure due process protections at the border. At a minimum, her opinion would have constrained the *Thuraissigiam* Court's unprecedented expansion of entry fiction.

CONCLUSION

Entry fiction stands out as a constitutional anomaly, rooted in the misconceptions and prejudices of an earlier era. Instead of cabining or rejecting the fiction, today's Supreme Court has done the opposite. Its continuous and unquestioned acceptance of *Nishimura Ekiu* ignores the drastic differences in our lives and our immigration system between 1892 and today. The Court also blindly fails to ask whether *Nishimura Ekiu*, rooted in the racism and sexism of over a century ago, was correctly decided.

The Court should ask this question and reconsider its approach. Professor Elias's feminist judgment provides a roadmap for a fairer interpretation of the Constitution. Her opinion better reflects the plain text and history of the Due Process Clause. And it honors our moral obligation to treat others as persons, in government practice and in law and jurisprudence.

For Ms. Nishimura *was* a person, and she *was* here. She endured a long and arduous voyage across the Pacific to unite with her husband. She had aspirations and dreams for life in the United States, just like all who live and have lived here, via birth or migration. The Court gave in to prejudices and status distinctions in 1892, and it continues to do so today. Professor Elias reminds us that we as a nation can do better – that we share a common humanity with all who come to our borders and shores. Our Constitution, correctly interpreted, would do the same.

NISHIMURA EKIU v. UNITED STATES, 142 U.S. 651 (1892)

Justice Stella Burch Elias, concurring in part and dissenting in part.

This action was originally instituted by the petitioner, Nishimura Ekiu, a native and subject of the Empire of Japan. The petitioner was denied entry to the United States at the Port of San Francisco and was placed in detention at the Methodist Episcopal Japanese and Chinese Mission, pending her return to her native country. She immediately filed a petition for habeas corpus, praying for release from detention. That petition was denied by the Circuit Court of the United States for the Northern District of California. Pending now before this Court is Nishimura Ekiu's appeal of the Circuit Court's denial of her petition for habeas corpus.

I FACTUAL AND PROCEDURAL BACKGROUND

On May 7, 1891, the Oriental and Occidental steamship *Belgic* arrived at the port of San Francisco. One of the passengers aboard the vessel was "Nishimura Ekiu," a twenty-five-year-old native and citizen of the Empire of Japan. Ms. Nishimura[46] was one of several young women aboard the vessel, all of whom had undertaken the lengthy and arduous 4,477 nautical-mile voyage from Yokohama, Japan, to San Francisco, California. The record before us provides only limited information about Ms. Nishimura's background before her encounter with U.S. immigration officials. But we are nonetheless able to glean some understanding of her circumstances through the reports that those officials submitted describing the questioning that she endured and her eventual detention, pending her return to Japan, in the Methodist Episcopal Church Japanese and Chinese Mission-House.

After the *Belgic* arrived in San Francisco, the Commissioner of Immigration of the State of California, Mr. William H. Thornley, boarded the vessel to inspect the arriving passengers. Mr. Thornley claimed that in so doing he was acting under instructions from, and pursuant to a contract with, Charles Foster, the Secretary of the Treasury of the United States. Mr. Thornley conducted what the majority characterizes as "a careful examination of the alien immigrants aboard the *Belgic*." It is, however, unclear from the record before us whether Mr. Thornley's examination of Ms. Nishimura was indeed "careful." As a native and subject of the Empire of Japan, Ms. Nishimura was presumably a native speaker of Japanese, and the record is silent as to Ms. Nishimura's knowledge of, or proficiency in, the English language. The record is equally silent as to whether Ms. Nishimura had any access to the services of a skilled interpreter, so it is impossible to ascertain with any certainty that Mr. Thornley was able question Ms. Nishimura effectively or that Ms. Nishimura was able to respond knowingly or appropriately to Mr. Thornley's questions.

The only contemporaneous account of the interview that Mr. Thornley conducted with Ms. Nishimura is a report, which Mr. Thornley drafted six days later, on May 13, 1891. That document, entitled "Report of alien immigrants forbidden to land under the provisions of the act of congress approved August 3, 1882, at the port of San Francisco, being passengers upon the steamer Belgic, Walker, master, which arrived May 7, 1891, from Yokohama," contains a series of brief notes about

---

[46] Although the petitioner's name appears in the record as "Nishimura Ekiu," it seems that the immigration officials, the Circuit Court, and the majority, misapprehended the petitioner's family name. Cognizant of that error, I have chosen to use the more accurate surname, Nishimura, throughout this opinion.

Ms. Nishimura. First Mr. Thornley lists her sex, "female," and her age "25." Then he notes that Ms. Nishimura's: "Passport states that she comes to San Francisco with her husband, which is not a fact." Mr. Thornley apparently questioned Ms. Nishimura further on this point, leading her to attempt to explain that she was travelling to the United States to reunite with her husband – a situation plausibly summarized in the passport notation indicating that she was traveling to San Francisco *to be* with her husband. But Mr. Thornley doubted the veracity of Ms. Nishimura's explanation, noting with suspicion that: "she has been married two years, and that her husband has been in the United States one year, but she does not know his address." Mr. Thornley was apparently skeptical that a young woman with presumably limited English language proficiency had not memorized her husband's permanent address in the United States – if indeed he had such an address at the time she sailed for San Francisco. Mr. Thornley further noted that: "She has $22, and is to stop at some hotel until her husband calls for her." Once again, Mr. Thornley doubted the plausibility of Ms. Nishimura's plan.

At the conclusion of his questioning, Mr. Thornley determined that Ms. Nishimura and five additional similarly situated young women aboard the *Belgic* were "prohibited from landing by the existing immigration laws." In his role as a contracted agent for the Secretary of the Treasury, Mr. Thornley therefore determined that, pending a final decision by the Secretary's subordinate, the Collector of the Port of San Francisco, as to the six women's right to land, he would detain them "temporarily" in the Methodist Episcopal Japanese and Chinese Mission. Mr. Thornley ordered that the women be sent to the mission-house because, according to his report, "the steamer was not a proper place to detain them, until the date of sailing."

On May 13, 1891, the same day that Mr. Thornley filed his report, Ms. Nishimura's legal counsel filed a petition for habeas corpus in the Circuit Court of the United States for the Northern District of California, seeking her release from detention in the mission-house. On the same day, Mr. Thornley responded:

> In obedience to the within writ I hereby produce the body of Nishimura Ekiu, as within directed, and return that I hold her in my custody by direction of the customs authorities of the port of San Francisco, Cal., under the provisions of the immigration act; that, by an understanding between the United States attorney and the attorney for petitioner, said party will remain in the custody of the Methodist Episcopal Japanese and Chinese Mission pending a final disposition of the writ.

The three men named in this brief response – Mr. Thornley, the District Attorney, and Ms. Nishimura's attorney – clearly came to an agreement that Ms. Nishimura would remain in detention for the pendency of her suit. Ms. Nishimura's acquiescence is, of course, implied in her attorney's participation in this "understanding," but it is impossible to ascertain the extent to which she knowingly consented to this arrangement.

Three days later, on May 16, 1891, the District Attorney of the United States intervened in the suit, arguing in opposition to the petition for habeas corpus, and insisting that the decisions of the customs and immigration officials – i.e., Mr. Thornley and the Collector of the Port of San Francisco – were final, conclusive, and nonreviewable by a court of law.

On May 14, 1891, the Secretary of the Treasury appointed John L. Hatch as Inspector of Immigration at the Port of San Francisco. And on May 16 – the same day that the District Attorney argued that federal officials' determinations about immigrants' admissibility to the United States could not be reviewed by courts – one of Mr. Hatch's first official duties was to question Ms. Nishimura.

As the majority notes, Mr. Hatch's examination of Ms. Nishimura was authorized by federal statute: "An act in amendment to the various acts relative to immigration and the importation of aliens under contract or agreement to perform labor," of March 3, 1891. Section 8 of that Act states that: "Upon the arrival by water at any place within the United States of any alien ... proper inspection officers ... shall ... go or send competent assistants on board such vessel, and there inspect all such aliens, or the inspection officers may order a temporary removal of such aliens for examination at a designated time and place, and then and there detain them until a thorough inspection is made." Where previously such inspections were carried out by state officials, like Mr. Thornley, the 1891 Act conferred this responsibility on federal officers, like Mr. Hatch. "All duties imposed and powers conferred by the second section of the act of August third, eighteen hundred and eighty-two, upon state commissioners, boards, or officers acting under contract with the secretary of the treasury, shall be performed and exercised, as occasion may arise, by the inspection officers of the United States." *Id.*

At the conclusion of his examination of Ms. Nishimura, he, too, refused to allow her to "land" in the United States. Once again, the only record that we have of Mr. Hatch's examination of Ms. Nishimura is a report that he prepared for the Collector of the Port of San Francisco, entitled: "Report of alien immigrants forbidden to land under the provisions of the act of congress approved March 3, 1891, at the port of San Francisco, being passengers upon the steamer Belgic, Walker, master, which arrived May 7, 1891, from Yokohama." As the majority astutely observes, Mr. Hatch's report was identical, "in the very words," to that submitted by Mr. Thornley, save that the date of the relevant statutory enactment was changed from August 3, 1882, to March 3, 1891. The record is silent as to the circumstances of Mr. Hatch's examination of Ms. Nishimura. We do not know when or where he met with her. We do not know whether she was afforded the assistance of an interpreter. We do not know whether Mr. Hatch took her testimony under oath, or indeed whether he gave her any opportunity at all to present her case in any meaningful way.

Two days later, on May 18, 1891, Mr. Hatch intervened in Ms. Nishimura's habeas suit. In his opposition to Ms. Nishimura's petition for habeas corpus Mr. Hatch stated that upon examination of Ms. Nishimura he found her to be "a person without means of support, without relatives or friends in the United States," and "a person unable to care for herself, and liable to become a public charge, and therefore inhibited from landing under the provisions of [the Act] of 1891, and previous acts of which said act is amendatory." Mr. Hatch insisted that his findings and decision were reviewable by the Superintendent of Immigration and the Secretary of the Treasury only, and not by the courts of the United States.

The case proceeded to a hearing before the Commissioner of the Circuit Court. At that hearing, through her counsel, Ms. Nishimura offered to introduce evidence to establish her right to land in the United States, and to rebut Mr. Hatch's claim that she was a person without means of support or relatives in the United States and therefore liable to become a public charge. She also argued that if the Act of 1891 deprived her of judicial review of the Inspector of Immigration's findings and decision, the Act was itself unconstitutional, because it deprived her of liberty without due process of law. She contended that she was entitled, under the Constitution of the United States, to petition for habeas corpus and to seek judicial review of the legality of her detention, and that the court had the right to examine the factual predicates for that detention.

The Commissioner of the Circuit Court disagreed. He excluded the evidence that Ms. Nishimura offered pertaining to her right to land, stating that it was beyond the purview of the court. He concluded that the question of her right to land in the United States had already been tried and determined by the statutorily authorized decision-maker. He stated that Mr. Hatch, as Inspector of Immigration, was entitled to decide conclusively whether Ms. Nishimura could land in the United States. Moreover, Mr. Hatch's determination that she could not land could not be reviewed by the Circuit Court. Review of Mr. Hatch's decision could be reviewed only by the Commissioner of Immigration and the Secretary of the Treasury. He therefore concluded that Ms. Nishimura was not unlawfully restrained of her liberty and was not entitled to be released from detention.

On July 24, 1891, after Ms. Nishimura had been detained at the mission-house for a subsequent two months, the Circuit Court confirmed its commissioner's report. The Court ordered that Ms. Nishimura be: "remanded by the marshal to the custody from which she has been taken, to-wit, to the custody of J. L. Hatch, immigration inspector for the port of San Francisco, to be dealt with as he may find that the law requires, upon either the present testimony before him, or that and such other as he may deem proper to take." Ms. Nishimura appeals this decision.

This case falls within the appellate jurisdiction of this Court because it involves the constitutionality of a federal statute, even though the filing of Ms. Nishimura's appeal occurred after the Act establishing Circuit Courts of Appeal took effect. Act March 3, 1891, c. 517, § 5, (26 St. 827, 828, 1115.)

II THE RIGHT TO PETITION FOR HABEAS CORPUS

In her petition for habeas corpus, Ms. Nishimura claims that she has been deprived of her liberty by officers of the United States, without due process of law. This is a grave charge, and therefore one which must be answered by those officers. It is a longstanding tenet of our laws that the writ of habeas shall run to all those detained by the organs of the state, whether those detainees are U.S. citizens or aliens.

In England, from whence our common law traditions have evolved, habeas corpus has long been available to all manner of persons detained by the Crown or otherwise subject to the sovereign's authority, including those who were not subjects of the nation. See, for example, *Somersett's Case*, 20 How. St. Tr. 1, 79–82 (K.B. 1772) (releasing an "African slave" purchased in Virginia and briefly detained on English soil pending voyage to Jamaica) or the *Case of the Hottentot Venus*, 104 Eng. Rep. 344, 344 (K.B. 1810) (reviewing the habeas petition of "native of South Africa" allegedly held against her will in England). Even those prisoners of war designated "enemy aliens" remained entitled to challenge the legality of their detention before the King's Bench by seeking habeas relief, and even though such relief was ultimately denied by the Court, searching review on the merits of the case was undertaken. See, for example, *R. v. Schiever*, 97 Eng. Rep. 551 (K.B. 1759) or *The Case of Three Spanish Sailors*, 96 Eng. Rep. 775 (C.P. 1779).

In our own nation, courts have not hesitated to exercise their jurisdiction to review habeas petitions filed by, or on behalf of, those who are not nationals of the United States. See, for example, *Ex parte D'Olivera*, 7 F. Cas. 853 (C.C.D. Mass. 1813) (Story, J., on circuit), in which Portuguese sailors imprisoned for desertion, were released from detention upon the court's ruling that American desertion laws only applied to American ships, or *Lockington's Case*, in which the Pennsylvania Supreme Court considered the habeas petition of an Englishman imprisoned as an enemy alien during the War of 1812. 9 Bright (N.P.) 269 (Pa. 1813).

This fundamental and longstanding common law principle is so significant that it is enshrined in the U.S. Constitution itself, which states that the writ of habeas corpus may only be suspended when public safety requires it in the event of rebellion or invasion. U.S. Const., Art. I, § 9, cl. 2 ("[t]he Privilege of the Writ of Habeas Corpus shall not be suspended, unless when in Cases of Rebellion or Invasion the public Safety may require it."). The Habeas Corpus Act of 1867 does not diminish the fundamental right of detainees to seek habeas relief, nor does it preclude this Court from reviewing whether a noncitizen has been detained by agents and officers of the federal government in violation of her due process rights.

Here, the majority acknowledges this clear and settled principle of law: "An alien immigrant, prevented from landing by any such officer claiming authority to do so under an act of congress, and thereby restrained of his liberty, is doubtless entitled to a writ of habeas corpus to ascertain whether the restraint is lawful." I concur. For this reason, I join in this part – and this part only – of the Court's opinion, before turning to the reasons why I believe that the majority has erred in its further determination of the laws governing this case, and in its ultimate conclusion that Ms. Nishimura's detention was lawful.

III THE IMMIGRATION ACT OF 1891

In the United States, as the majority explains, the power "to forbid the entrance of foreigners within its dominions, or to admit them" is vested in the "political depart-ment" of the "national government," which "may be exercised either through trea-ties made by the president and senate, or through statutes enacted by congress." Congress has passed a series of statutory enactments to control migration, and those acts have granted decision-making powers with respect to the admission or exclusion of immigrants arriving at our borders to the Secretary of the Treasury, to Collectors of Customs, and to Inspectors acting under their authority. See Acts of March 3, 1875, c. 141, (18 St. 477;) August 3, 1882, c. 376, (22 St. 214;) February 23, 1887, c. 220, (24 St. 414;) October 19, 1888, c. 1210, (25 St. 566).

The Immigration Act of 1891 is the most recent legislative enactment pertaining to the admission and exclusion of arriving immigrants. The various provisions of this statute are purported to provide the basis for the ongoing detention and pending exclusion of Ms. Nishimura. Section 1 of the Act of 1891 provides that:

> The following classes of aliens shall be excluded from admission into the United States, in accordance with the existing acts regulating immigration, other than those concerning Chinese laborers: All idiots, insane persons, paupers or persons likely to become a public charge, persons suffering from a loathsome or a danger-ous contagious disease, persons who have been convicted of a felony or other infa-mous crime or misdemeanor involving moral turpitude,' etc.'

Ms. Nishimura was excluded from admission on the basis that Mr. Hatch and Mr. Thornley believed that she was impoverished and friendless and therefore "likely to become a public charge."

Section 7 of the Act of 1891 creates the office of Superintendent of Immigration:

> Who shall be an officer in the treasury department, under the control and supervi-sion of the secretary of the treasury, to whom he shall make annual reports in writ-ing of the transactions of his office, together with such special reports in writing as the secretary of the treasury shall require.

And Section 8 of the Act sets forth the duties of the immigration inspectors, including Mr. Hatch, who are employed by the office of the Superintendent of Immigration:

> Upon the arrival by water at any place within the United States of any alien immi-grants it shall be the duty of the commanding officer and the agents of the steam or sailing vessel by which they came to report the name, nationality, last resi-dence, and destination of every such alien, before any of them are landed, to the proper inspection officers, who shall thereupon go or send competent assistants on board such vessel, and there inspect all such aliens, or the inspection officers may order a temporary removal of such aliens for examination at a designated time and place, and then and there detain them until a thorough inspection is made. But such removal shall not be considered a landing during the pendency of such

examination.... The inspection officers and their assistants shall have power to administer oaths, and to take and consider testimony touching the right of any such aliens to enter the United States, all of which shall be entered of record. During such inspection, after temporary removal, the superintendent shall cause such aliens to be properly housed, fed, and cared for, and also, in his discretion, such as are delayed in proceeding to their destination after inspection.

This Section of the Act further states that:

All decisions made by the inspection officers or their assistants touching the right of any alien to land, when adverse to such right, shall be final, unless appeal be taken to the superintendent of immigration, whose action shall be subject to review by the secretary of the treasury.

This provision, referring to the process for internal review of the inspection officers' decisions, apparently forms the basis of the majority's conclusion that Mr. Hatch's determination that Ms. Nishimura should be excluded at the port of entry was "final and conclusive against the petitioner's right to land in the United States." The majority therefore reaches the chilling conclusion that: "As to such persons, the decisions of executive or administrative officers, acting within powers expressly conferred by congress, are due process of law." (See, for example, *Murray's Lessee v. Hoboken Land and Improvement Co.*, 59 U.S. (18 How.) 272 (1856); and *Hilton v. Merritt*, 110 U. S. 97 (1884)).

I believe, however, that such a conclusion goes too far. The majority misapprehends the scope and finality of the powers of the Superintendent of Immigration and his inspection officers, as set forth in this Act. This is made explicit in Section 13 of the Act which provides that, notwithstanding the enumerated powers of the immigration inspectors, the circuit and district courts of the United States remain: "Invested with full and concurrent jurisdiction of all causes, civil and criminal, arising under any of the provisions of this act," from the date that it entered into effect, April 1, 1891. 26 St. 1084–1086. Moreover, and more importantly, the majority misapprehends the fundamental guarantees within the Due Process Clause of the Fifth Amendment to the Constitution of the United States.

IV DUE PROCESS IN IMMIGRATION PROCEEDINGS

This Court has established that the power to admit or exclude noncitizens arriving at our nation's ports of entry is entrusted to the political branches of the federal government, and that executive officers serving in the Department of the Treasury may be charged with the enforcement of our immigration laws at our borders. See, for example, *The Head Money Cases*, 112 U.S. 580 (1884), *Ping v. United States*, 130 U.S. 581 (1889). However, we have never held previously, and should not now hold, that administrative officers undertaking such duties are unburdened by the restraints that our Constitution imposes on actions by the government of the United States. Indeed,

when executive officers are actively engaged in implementing the provisions of a statute that authorizes the deprivation of a person's liberty, whether through that person's
detention, exclusion, or deportation, it is more important than ever that the officers'
behavior comports with the Due Process guarantees in our Constitution.

No officer of the United States may disregard the fundamental precept set forth in
the Fifth Amendment to the Constitution of the United States that: "No person shall
be ... deprived of life, liberty, or property, without due process of law." Immigrants
arriving at our ports who are subject to custody determinations by our officers are
"persons" within the meaning of this Clause, and, therefore, they may not be deprived
of their liberty and placed in detention without the benefit of "due process of law."
In the case of an arriving immigrant, who faces exclusion or detention at the border,
"due process of law" need not mean a trial before a court of law – such a requirement would arguably be both impractical and unfeasible. See *Den ex dem. Murray v.
Hoboken Land & Imp. Co.*, 59 U.S. 272 (1855) (providing for summary actions against
revenue officers, rather than full trials, in the interests of expediency). But it should
mean that all individuals, be they citizens or aliens, will have the opportunity upon
arrival in the United States to be given notice that an immigration inspector will
examine them to ascertain their admissibility. It should also mean that, during that
examination, the arriving individual will have a meaningful opportunity to be heard.

The majority's assertion that insofar as arriving noncitizens are concerned, "the
decisions of executive or administrative officers ... are due process of law" flies in
the face of the guarantees of the Fifth Amendment. Executive or administrative
officers are not immune from the mandates of the Constitution. They do not enjoy
absolute powers, immune from judicial review, to determine for themselves how
much process is due. They may not arbitrarily detain a person, take her into their
custody, confine her in isolation for months, and then ship her to a foreign land,
without giving her an opportunity to be fully heard upon the questions involving her
rights to enter and reside in the United States.

The majority suggests that the Immigration Act of 1891 authorizes immigration
officers to disregard the Due Process guarantees found within the Constitution, but
this is manifestly not the case. Indeed, allowing an arriving alien to fully present her
case for admission is wholly consistent with both the Due Process Clause and the
provisions in the Immigration Act of 1891. Section 8 of the Act, after all, empowers
immigration inspectors "to administer oaths, and to take and consider testimony
touching the right of any such aliens to enter the United States, all of which shall
be entered of record." The very existence of this statutory provision illustrates that
Congress contemplated a searching inquiry by executive officers into arriving immigrants' personal circumstances and a meaningful opportunity for those immigrants
to present their own case for admission.

The majority further suggests that the Immigration Act of 1891 precludes this
Court from reviewing the decisions and actions of immigration inspectors, such as
Mr. Hatch. Once again, the text of the statute itself belies this assertion. Section 13

of the Act provides that the circuit and district courts of the United States remain: "Invested with full and concurrent jurisdiction of all causes, civil and criminal, arising under any of the provisions of this act." Under the plain language of the statute, review of petitions for habeas corpus, such as that filed by Ms. Nishimura, therefore fall firmly within the jurisdiction of the courts of the United States. And indeed, it is fortunate that they do, for if the Immigration Act were to strip the courts of their jurisdiction, then it would, as the petitioner has argued, call into question the constitutionality of the statute itself. But we need not reach that potentially thorny question, because the statute does not furnish the executive and administrative officers with unfettered and arbitrary powers, nor does it make their actions immune from judicial review.

Having established that this Court has jurisdiction to consider Ms. Nishimura's petition for habeas corpus, and that this Court has the authority, under the Constitution of the United States and the Immigration Act of 1891, to determine whether Ms. Nishimura has been deprived of her liberty without due process of law, I now turn to the facts of her case, as set forth in the record before the Court.

V APPLICATION OF THE LAW TO THE FACTS OF THIS CASE

It is hard to ascertain, based on the scant record before the Court, whether Ms. Nishimura was afforded due process of law before being confined to the Methodist Episcopal Japanese and Chinese Mission, pending her return to her native country. It is, however, apparent, that she was denied the opportunity to be heard when she sought review of that detention by the Circuit Court.

There are just two documents in the record describing immigration officials' examinations of Ms. Nishimura, namely Mr. Thornley's "Report of alien immigrants forbidden to land under the provisions of the act of congress approved August 3, 1882, at the port of San Francisco, being passengers upon the steamer Belgic, Walker, master, which arrived May 7, 1891, from Yokohama" dated May 13, 1891, and Mr. Hatch's "Report of alien immigrants forbidden to land under the provisions of the act of congress approved March 3, 1891, at the port of San Francisco, being passengers upon the steamer Belgic, Walker, master, which arrived May 7, 1891, from Yokohama," dated May 16, 1891. As I previously noted, the two reports are essentially identical, with the only difference between them being the substitution of the date of the most recent statutory enactment in the title of the document. Moreover, the information contained in the reports is, at best, characterized as sparse – a simple recitation of Ms. Nishimura's name, age, sex, country of origin, the reason for her journey to the United States, the amount of money in her possession, and her immediate destination in San Francisco, followed by a conclusory statement that she and five other women were "prohibited from landing by the existing immigration laws."

There is no indication in the record that Ms. Nishimura was given notice of the import of the initial interview with Mr. Thornley, or the subsequent interview with

Mr. Hatch, nor is there any evidence that she was given a meaningful opportunity
to be heard by either of these men. The record is silent as to her educational background and English language proficiency. We do not know if she was assisted by an
interpreter during her initial examination aboard the *Belgic*, or during her questioning by Mr. Hatch, and even if she was accompanied by a translator, we have no way
of knowing if Mr. Hatch's questions and Ms. Nishimura's answers were translated
accurately. Similarly, we do not know whether the immigration officers, pursuant
to their powers under the Immigration Act took Ms. Nishimura's testimony about
her circumstances under oath, or whether she was granted any opportunity at all to
present her case in any meaningful way. I suspect that she was not, because there is
no indication in the record before us that Ms. Nishimura fully understood the grav-
ity of her situation, until she was placed in detention and retained local counsel to
represent her interests.

The record is, however, clear that as soon as Ms. Nishimura was apprised that
she would be excluded from the United States, because Mr. Hatch had determined
that she was "a person without means of support, without relatives or friends in the
United States," and "a person unable to care for herself, and liable to become a
public charge," she attempted vigorously and repeatedly to present evidence to the
contrary. She filed a petition for habeas corpus setting forth her argument that she
had been wrongfully detained. She attended a hearing before the Commissioner
of the Circuit Court and offered to present evidence in support of her contention
that she possessed means of support in the United States. She therefore, refuted that
she was liable to become a public charge. She argued that she should be offered an
opportunity to be heard, on the merits of her claim that she had the right to enter
and remain in the United States. But her petition was denied, and the evidence that
she offered to present was excluded by the Commissioner, who erroneously concluded that he did not have the authority to consider her claims. Months later, the
Circuit Court confirmed the Commissioner's ruling, affording Ms. Nishimura no
further opportunity to present her evidence or arguments. In short, Ms. Nishimura
was denied her opportunity to be heard, and was therefore deprived of her liberty
without due process of law.

We know nothing about the evidence that Ms. Nishimura wished to present
in support of her claims, and so we cannot speculate as to whether her attempt
to remain in the United States would ultimately have proven successful if it had
been fully and properly adjudicated. But, in refusing her the opportunity to present
her claims, the immigration officials and the Circuit Court denied her humanity,
failing to treat her as a "person" entitled to the protections enshrined in the Fifth
Amendment to the U.S. Constitution. Instead, they deprived her of her liberty, without due process of law. Ms. Nishimura was not alone on May 13, 1891, when the
Belgic sailed into the Port of San Francisco. We know from Mr. Thornley's report
that five other women aboard the vessel were also excluded from the United States.
In the majority's recounting of the facts of this case, their personhood is even more

ephemeral than that of Ms. Nishimura. We do not know what happened to them next. We do not even know their names. The majority's ruling in this case deprives Ms. Nishimura and her fellow passengers aboard the *Belgic* the most fundamental protections to which they are assuredly entitled, under our Constitution and our immigration laws. All immigrants arriving at our borders, whatever their sex, race, nationality, or creed, are entitled to be treated humanely and justly, in accordance with due process of law. They are entitled to tell their stories and to have their voices heard. Therefore, I respectfully dissent.

4

Commentary on *United States v. Wong Kim Ark*, 169 U.S. 649 (1898)

Rachel E. Rosenbloom

In 1898, in *United States v. Wong Kim Ark*, the Supreme Court affirmed the broad scope of the Fourteenth Amendment's Citizenship Clause in a decision that continues to serve, more than a century later, as a crucial bulwark against attempts to restrict the reach of birthright citizenship.[1] The dispute in *Wong Kim Ark* centered on the meaning of five words that sit in the middle of the first sentence of the Fourteenth Amendment: "All persons born or naturalized in the United States, and *subject to the jurisdiction thereof*, are citizens of the United States and of the State wherein they reside."[2] In its appeal, the government challenged a lower court decision that had concluded that Wong Kim Ark, the son of two Chinese immigrants, was a United States citizen based on his birth within the United States. The Solicitor General presented one question to the Court: "[W]hether a person born in the United States to parents the subjects of a foreign power is a citizen of the United States."[3] A supplementary brief filed on behalf of the government provided a clearer picture of the government's true motivation; it argued that American citizenship should be kept "sacred from the foul and corrupting taint" of the "debasing alienage" of the "obnoxious" Chinese.[4] The Court, rejecting the government's attempt to limit birthright citizenship, declared that the Fourteenth Amendment, "in clear words and in manifest intent, includes the children born within the territory of the United States of all ... persons, of whatever race or color, domiciled within the United States." It held that the Citizenship Clause "affirms the ancient and fundamental rule of citizenship by birth within the territory ... including all children

---

[1] On contemporary efforts to restrict birthright citizenship, see Robin Jacobson, *Characterizing Consent: Race, Citizenship, and the New Restrictionists*, 59 POLIT. RES. Q. 645 (2006); Marc Lacey, *Birthright Citizenship Looms as Next Immigration Battle*, N.Y. TIMES, Jan. 4, 2011, 1, Philip Bump, *Donald Trump and Scott Walker Want to Repeal Birthright Citizenship. It's Nearly Impossible*. WASHINGTON POST (Aug. 18, 2015).

[2] U.S. CONST. AMEND. XIV, § 1, cl. 1 (emphasis added).

[3] Motion to Advance at 1, United States v. Wong Kim Ark, 169 U.S. 649 (1898) (No. 132).

[4] Brief on Behalf of the Appellant at 34, 39, United States v. Wong Kim Ark, 149 U.S. 649 (1898) (No. 132).

here born of resident aliens," subject only to the three "exceptions or qualifications (as old as the rule itself) of children of foreign sovereigns or their ministers, or born on foreign ships, or of enemies within and during a hostile occupation of part of our territory" and to "the single additional exception of children of members of the Indian tribes owing direct allegiance to their several tribes."[5]

The constitutional question at issue in *Wong Kim Ark* arose within the context of the Chinese Exclusion Act[6]; Wong's citizenship status would determine whether he would be exempt from the Act's draconian provisions. In both substance and tone, *Wong Kim Ark* contrasted with many of the Court's other decisions during the Chinese Exclusion era – decisions in which the Court characterized Chinese immigrants as invading "hordes" entitled to few if any constitutional protections.[7] The decision also stood apart, in its affirmation of the Fourteenth Amendment's eradication of racial restrictions on birthright citizenship, from a line of late-nineteenth-century cases in which the Court gutted the Fourteenth Amendment of its anti-racist potential – most notoriously *Plessy v. Ferguson*,[8] decided just two years earlier.

Despite these laudable attributes, the Court's analysis in *Wong Kim Ark* leaves much to be desired. Its flaws lie not so much what the decision contains as in what it leaves out. Although lengthy and detailed, it focuses narrowly on English and American common law regarding birthright citizenship, and on a textual analysis of the Civil Rights Act of 1866 and the Fourteenth Amendment. In taking this path, the Court sidestepped the profoundly significant dynamics of race, class, gender, and sexuality that shaped debates over Chinese-American birthright citizenship. Professor Jonathan Weinberg, writing as Chief Justice Weinberg, remedies this omission, bringing a far more complex analysis to the question. The feminist judgment adds crucial historical context to *Wong Kim Ark*, as well as an incisive critique of the racism underlying the Solicitor General's position.

THE ORIGINAL OPINION

Wong Kim Ark did not set out to create a new legal precedent when he asserted his claim to birthright citizenship in 1895, challenging his exclusion from the United States with a habeas corpus petition that ultimately led, on appeal, to

---

5 United States v. Wong Kim Ark, 169 U.S. 649, 693 (1898).
6 Act of May 6, 1882, ch. 126, 22 Stat. 58. On the Chinese Exclusion Act, *see generally* LUCY SALYER, LAWS HARSH AS TIGERS: CHINESE IMMIGRANTS AND THE SHAPING OF MODERN IMMIGRATION LAW (1995) [hereinafter SALYER, LAWS HARSH AS TIGERS], 1–32; ERIKA LEE, AT AMERICA'S GATES: CHINESE IMMIGRATION DURING THE EXCLUSION ERA, 1882–1943 (2003) [hereinafter LEE, AT AMERICA'S GATES], 23–46.
7 Chae Chan Ping v. United States, 130 U.S. 581 (1889); Fong Yue Ting v. United States, 149 U.S. 698 (1893).
8 163 U.S. 537 (1896).

the Supreme Court's landmark decision. The groundwork to establish Chinese-
American birthright citizenship had in fact been laid eleven years before Wong
filed his petition, by a fourteen-year-old boy named Look Tin Sing. Look's case
was heard in San Francisco in 1884 by a panel of judges that included Supreme
Court Justice Stephen Field, riding circuit. The panel's unanimous decision,
authored by Field, held that Look, the child of Chinese immigrants, was a citizen
under the Fourteenth Amendment, and therefore could not be excluded from the
United States.[9] Field looked to the long history of territorial birthright citizenship
in English and American common law and concluded that this tradition contemplated only two narrow exceptions: children born to diplomats, "whose residence,
by a fiction of public law, is regarded as part of their own country," and children
born on a public vessel of a foreign country while within U.S. waters.[10]

In the decade following the decision, Chinese Americans seeking recognition
of their citizenship were able to rely on Look Tin Sing. Wong himself was one
of the beneficiaries of the decision, gaining admission to the United States as a
citizen upon his return from a trip to China in 1890.[11] Although Look Tin Sing was
not a Supreme Court case, its impact was considerable. It bound federal judges in
California, whose ports served as the point of disembarkation for the majority of
Chinese Americans returning from trips abroad. In addition, other federal courts
chose to follow the holding of the case.[12] And the Supreme Court itself appeared to
endorse the holding in its 1891 decision in Quock Ting v. United States. Like Look
Tin Sing, Quock Ting concerned a teenage boy of Chinese descent who claimed
to have been born in the United States. The Court's decision, authored by Justice
Field, confined itself to the question of the factual sufficiency of the evidence of
the boy's birth; it assumed, without deciding the matter, that such a showing would
establish citizenship.[13]

The driving force that propelled the issue of birthright citizenship to the Supreme
Court's attention was thus not Wong Kim Ark himself nor the network of Chinese
fraternal organizations and prominent attorneys that engineered other test cases
challenging the scope of the Chinese Exclusion Act, but rather attorneys within

---

[9] In re Look Tin Sing, 21 F. 905 (C.C.D. Cal. 1884).
[10] Id. at 906.
[11] On Wong Kim Ark himself and the litigation surrounding his citizenship claim, see AMANDA FROST,
      YOU ARE NOT AMERICAN: CITIZENSHIP STRIPPING FROM DRED SCOTT TO THE DREAMERS (2021),
      51–73; CAROL NACKENOFF AND JULIE NOVKOV, AMERICAN BY BIRTH: WONG KIM ARK AND THE
      BATTLE FOR BIRTHRIGHT CITIZENSHIP (2021); Erika Lee, Birthright Citizenship, Immigration, and
      the U.S. Constitution: The Story of United States v. Wong Kim Ark, in RACHEL F. MORAN & DEVON
      W. CARBADO eds., RACE LAW STORIES 89 (2008), 89–110; Lucy E. Salyer, Wong Kim Ark: The Contest
      over Birthright Citizenship, in DAVID A. MARTIN & PETER H. SCHUCK eds., IMMIGRATION LAW
      STORIES (2005) [hereinafter Salyer, Wong Kim Ark], 51–86; Bethany R. Berger, Birthright Citizenship
      on Trial: Elk v. Wilkins and United States v. Wong Kim Ark, 37 CARDOZO L. REV. 1185 (2016).
[12] See, e.g., Gee Fook Sing v. United States, 49 F. 146 (9th Cir. 1892); Ex parte Chin King, 35 F. 354
      (C.C.D. Or. 1888); In re Yung Sing Hee, 36 F. 437 (C.C.D. Or. 1888).
[13] Quock Ting v. United States, 140 U.S. 417, 419 (1891).

the United States Department of Justice who were eager to bring a case that would overturn *Look Tin Sing*.[14] George Collins, a San Francisco attorney who had long advocated the exclusion of Chinese Americans from birthright citizenship, was instrumental in getting the Department of Justice to pursue the case. He appeared as *amicus curiae* before the District Court, and filed a supplementary brief to the Supreme Court on which he was identified as being "of counsel" to the government. Collins was a proponent of the idea that *jus sanguinis* (citizenship by descent), rather than *jus soli* (citizenship by birth within the territory), should be deemed the basis of United States citizenship.[15]

Wong, denied entry and detained on a boat in the harbor, filed a habeas corpus petition challenging his exclusion, represented by prominent San Francisco attorney Thomas Riordan. Judge William Morrow of the Northern District of California granted the petition, concluding that Wong was a citizen based on the precedent established by *Look Tin Sing*. On March 28, 1898, the Supreme Court affirmed Judge Morrow's ruling. In a 6-2 decision, which likely would have been 6-3 had Field not retired shortly before the case was decided, the Court recognized four exceptions to birthright citizenship for those born within the territorial limits of the United States. Two of those exceptions were the ones identified by Field in *Look Tin Sing*: children born to those with diplomatic immunity and children born on foreign ships while within U.S. waters. To those, the Court added two more: children born to "enemies within and during a hostile occupation of part of our territory," and "children of members of the Indian tribes owing direct allegiance to their several tribes."[16] This final exception stemmed from the Court's 1884 decision in *Elk v. Wilkins*,[17] a case that concerned a Winnebago[18] man named John Elk, who had given up his tribal affiliation and had become a resident of Omaha, Nebraska. He sued to challenge the refusal of a local official to register him to vote. The Court concluded that Elk, born within the jurisdiction of a Native nation, was "no more 'born in the United States and subject to the jurisdiction thereof,' within the meaning of the first section of the fourteenth amendment, than the children of subjects of any foreign government born within the domain of that government[.]"[19]

---

14 On legal advocacy to challenge the Chinese Exclusion Act, see generally SALYER, LAWS HARSH AS TIGERS; LEE, AT AMERICA'S GATES. On discussions within DOJ, *see* Salyer, Wong Kim Ark, 63–67.

15 George D. Collins, *Are Persons Born within the United States Ipso Facto Citizens Thereof?* 18 AM. L. REV. 831, 834 (1884); George D. Collins, *Citizenship by Birth*, 29 AM. L. REV., 385 (1895); *Citizenship by Birth: Attorney George D. Collins Takes Issue with Justice Field*, S.F. CALL, Jun. 18, 1895, 12. *See* Salyer, Wong Kim Ark, 65–66.

16 United States v. Wong Kim Ark, 169 U.S. 649, 693 (1898).

17 Elk v. Wilkins, 112 U.S. 94 (1884).

18 Bethany R. Berger, *Birthright Citizenship on Trial: Elk v. Wilkins and United States v. Wong Kim Ark*, 37 CARDOZO L. REV. 1185, 1215 (2016) (noting that Elk was Winnebago, although that was not specified in the Supreme Court's decision) [hereinafter Berger, *Birthright Citizenship on Trial*].

19 Elk v. Wilkins, 112 U.S. at 102. Although a defeat for Elk, the case has been read as a rare affirmation of Native sovereignty from the Court. *See* Berger, *Birthright Citizenship on Trial*, 1189. On Native

The majority decision in *Wong Kim Ark*, written by Justice Horace Gray, began by noting that the Constitution did not define the term "citizen" prior to the passage of the Fourteenth Amendment.[20] It then engaged in an extensive review of English and American common law on birthright citizenship, starting with *Calvin's Case*, decided in England in 1608. It concluded that these sources supported the view that all those born within the territory were citizens, subject only to very narrow exceptions. Gray flatly rejected the theory put forth by the Solicitor General that the common law rule of citizenship by birth within the territory had been superseded by the rule that citizenship of a child followed that of a parent; he noted that in 1789, continental European law in fact favored *jus soli*, and that "[t]he later modifications of the rule in Europe rest upon the constitutions, laws, or ordinances of the various countries, and have no important bearing upon the interpretation and effect of the constitution of the United States." As further ground for rejecting *jus sanguinis* as the default rule, Gray cited the fact that citizenship by descent for children born abroad to U.S. citizens had always been governed by statute and included numerous exceptions.[21]

Gray then considered what was perhaps the Solicitor General's strongest argument: the narrower reading of the Citizenship Clause that the Court appeared to adopt in the *Slaughter-House Cases*.[22] In that decision, in 1873, the Court had commented that children of "citizens or subjects of foreign States born within the United States" were not "subject to the jurisdiction" of the United States. In *Wong Kim Ark*, Gray dismissed this language as mere dictum. On the contrary, he found, it was "beyond doubt [prior to the Civil War] that all white persons, at least, born within the sovereignty of the United States, whether children of citizens or of foreigners, excepting only children of ambassadors or public ministers of a foreign government, were native-born citizens of the United States" – a principle that the Civil Rights Act of 1866 and the Fourteenth Amendment extended across racial lines.[23]

Turning to the heart of the case, Gray parsed the meaning of the phrase "subject to the jurisdiction thereof" in the Citizenship Clause. He cited three reasons for construing the phrase broadly. First, a ruling that immigrants residing in the United States are not subject to the jurisdiction of the United States would create chaos:

> When private individuals of one nation spread themselves through another as business or caprice may direct, mingling indiscriminately with the inhabitants of that other, or when merchant vessels enter for the purposes of trade, it would be

---

sovereignty and U.S. citizenship, *see generally* Robert B. Porter, *Demise of the Ongwehoweh and the Rise of the Native Americans: Redressing the Genocidal Act of Forcing American Citizenship upon Indigenous Peoples*, 15 HARV. BLACKLETTER L. J. 107 (1999); Kevin Bruyneel, *Challenging American Boundaries: Indigenous People and the 'Gift' of U.S. Citizenship*, 18 STUD. AM. POLIT. DEV. 30 (2004).

[20] Wong Kim Ark, 169 U.S. at 654.
[21] *Id.* at 656–67, 672–74.
[22] 83 U.S. (16 Wall.) 36 (1873).
[23] Wong Kim Ark, 169 U.S. at 678–79, 675.

obviously inconvenient and dangerous to society, and would subject the laws to continual infraction, and the government to degradation, if such individuals or merchants did not owe temporary and local allegiance, and were not amenable to the jurisdiction of the country.[24]

Second, the federal naturalization statute required applicants for citizenship to have resided for a certain time "within the limits and under the jurisdiction of the United States," a phrase that would not make sense if immigrants were not subject to the nation's jurisdiction.[25] And lastly, the final clause of Section 1 of the 14th Amendment prohibits a state from "deny[ing] to any person within its jurisdiction the equal protection of the law," and the Court had previously held in *Yick Wo v. Hopkins* that Chinese immigrants were "persons" within the jurisdiction of a state for purposes of equal protection.[26] It would be unreasonable, Gray concluded, to interpret the word "jurisdiction" as being used in two different ways within the same section of the same amendment. The decision proclaimed the Citizenship Clause to be "affirmative and declaratory, intended to ally doubts and to settle controversies which had arisen, and not to impose any new restrictions upon citizenship."[27] It also noted the havoc that would result from a ruling that would "deny citizenship to thousands of persons of English, Scotch, Irish, German, or other European parentage, who have always been considered and treated as citizens of the United States."[28]

Finally, Gray considered the relationship between constitutional birthright citizenship and naturalization, which was then – and remained until 1952 – subject to explicit racial restrictions.[29] The decision noted that the naturalization statute, which had limited naturalization to "free, white person[s]" when originally enacted in 1790,[30] was broadened in 1870 – a full two years after the ratification of the Fourteenth Amendment – to include persons "of African nativity … [or] African descent."[31] Yet no one doubted, Gray observed, that Black people born in the United States were citizens under the Fourteenth Amendment from the moment that the amendment was ratified, despite the fact that some of them, between 1868 and 1870, were born to parents who were ineligible to naturalize. By the same token, he concluded, the fact that Chinese immigrants were barred from naturalizing had no bearing on the birthright citizenship of their U.S.-born children.[32]

---

[24] *Id.* at 685–86, quoting The Schooner Exchange v. McFadden, 7 Cranch. 116, 144 (1812).
[25] *Id.* at 686–87.
[26] *Id.* at 694–95, citing Yick Wo v. Hopkins, 118 U.S. 356 (1886).
[27] *Id.* at 688.
[28] *Id.* at 694.
[29] *See generally* IAN HANEY LÓPEZ, WHITE BY LAW: THE LEGAL CONSTRUCTION OF RACE Rev'd 2d Ed. (2006).
[30] Act of March 26, 1790, ch. 3, 1 Stat. 103.
[31] Act of July 14, 1870, ch. 255, § 7, 16 Stat. 254.
[32] Wong Kim Ark, 169 U.S. at 701–02.

In dissent, Chief Justice Fuller and Justice Harlan characterized the English common law doctrine of birthright citizenship as a relic of feudalism and argued that the framers of the Constitution had no intention "to adhere to the principles derived from regal government, which they had just assisted in overthrowing."[33] The dissent allowed that "all persons born in a country are presumptively citizens thereof," but argued that in the United States, as distinct from England, the presumption could be rebutted in cases such as births during temporary or accidental sojourns. The dissenters leaned heavily on the reading of the Citizenship Clause offered by the Court in the *Slaughter-House Cases*. They also relied on *Elk v. Wilkins*, in which the Court commented that in order to be born a citizen, one needed to be born "not merely subject in some respect or degree to the jurisdiction of the United States, but completely subject to their political jurisdiction, and owing them direct and immediate allegiance."[34] In the dissent's view, this language supported the conclusion that a child born to parents who were subjects of the Chinese emperor did not become a citizen merely by "accident of birth."[35]

THE FEMINIST JUDGMENT

The feminist judgment, authored by Chief Justice Jonathan Weinberg, reaches the same conclusion as the original majority opinion: that Wong Kim Ark is a citizen under the Fourteenth Amendment. However, Professor Weinberg adds two key elements that are lacking in the original. First, his judgment squarely confronts the racist underpinnings of both the Solicitor General's arguments and the exclusion laws that shaped Chinese immigration. Second, it approaches the question of Chinese American birthright citizenship within a sophisticated analysis of the race, gender and class dynamics of Chinese exclusion, highlighting lawmakers' assumptions about Chinese women's morality; the class bias that permeated the Chinese Exclusion Act, including its application to Chinese women; and the ways in which federal and state laws affecting Chinese immigrants created majority-male "bachelor societies" in which Chinese men often performed labor that was viewed as feminine.

The feminist judgment begins by addressing the racist foundations of the brief on behalf of the government filed by George Collins. While distinct from the official brief of the Solicitor General, the Collins brief was styled as a brief "on behalf of the appellant" and Collins was identified as being "of counsel" to the government; moreover, the brief was co-signed by Solicitor General Holmes Conrad.[36] The feminist judgment calls out the brief's reference to Chinese people as "obnoxious"; its

---

[33] *Id.* at 707–09 (Fuller, C.J., dissenting).
[34] *Id.* at 718, 724 (quoting Elk v. Wilkins, 112 U.S. 94, 102 (1884)).
[35] *Id.* at 731.
[36] Brief on Behalf of the Appellant at 1, 39, United States v. Wong Kim Ark, 149 U.S. 649 (1898) (No. 132).

statement that there "should be some honor and dignity in American citizenship that would be sacred from the foul and corrupting taint of a debasing alienage"; and its argument that the inclusion of Chinese Americans within the scope of American birthright citizenship – with the attendant implications regarding eligibility to the presidency – would render "American citizenship ... not worth having." These aspects of the government's position, which went unmentioned in the original opinion, take center stage in the feminist judgment, which contextualizes the remarks within the extensive history of racist lawmaking and anti-Chinese mob violence in the decades leading up to *Wong Kim Ark*.[37]

Next, the feminist judgment provides an insightful historical analysis of the policies that shaped Chinese immigrant communities like the one into which Wong was born. These communities, it notes, were shaped by white attitudes that "are the product of beliefs about Chinese women's propensities and morality, Chinese men's failure to protect female virtue, Chinese men's conformance to the rules for proper masculine behavior, and the nature of Chinese families." Professor Weinberg provides a history of public attitudes linking Chinese women to sex work and of legislative efforts to prevent their immigration, culminating in the Page Act of 1875, which barred the entry of any Asian woman coming to the United States for "lewd or immoral purposes."[38] He notes that laws limiting the immigration of Chinese men came later, in the 1880s; the Page Act, along with social mores in China that discouraged women from emigrating, resulted in Chinese immigrant communities in which men far outnumbered women and often took on occupations, such as laundry and cooking, that were deemed to be women's work.[39]

The gender imbalance within Chinese immigrant communities, combined with state laws that prohibited intermarriage, made it very difficult for Chinese men to start families in the United States. As the feminist judgment observes, "U.S. law ... did its best, to ensure that people like Mr. Wong would not exist." Yet as it further observes, this endeavor did not entirely succeed, in part because of loopholes that allowed the wives and daughters of affluent Chinese merchants to immigrate. While describing the inhumanity of the laws that shaped Chinese immigrant communities, Professor Weinberg simultaneously recognizes the persistence of those Chinese women who managed to create lives in the United States in the face of those laws:

> Chinese women are here in this country, and all along have formed families and raised children on U.S. soil. They have done so notwithstanding the best efforts of government actors and the larger public to interfere with their entry and to pretend

---

[37] On anti-Chinese violence, *see generally*, BETH LEW-WILLIAMS, THE CHINESE MUST GO: VIOLENCE, EXCLUSION, AND THE MAKING OF THE ALIEN IN AMERICA (2018).

[38] *See generally* Kerry Abrams, *Polygamy, Prostitution, and the Federalization of Immigration Law*, 105 COLUMBIA L. REV. 641 (2005).

[39] On the exclusion of Chinese women, see generally, Sucheng Chan, "The Exclusion of Chinese Women, 1870–1943," in SUCHEN CHAN, ed., ENTRY DENIED: EXCLUSION AND THE CHINESE COMMUNITY IN AMERICA, 1882–1943 (1991).

that they did not exist. They have done so notwithstanding the best efforts of government actors and the larger public to pretend that 'debauched' Chinese women
lack the capacity to love, to join together in families, and to nurture children as
men and women of other races do.

This section of the feminist judgment closes with an unequivocal rejection of the
Solicitor General's arguments, in particular as they were expressed in the Collins
brief: "To the extent that [these arguments] are based on the racial inferiority
of the Chinese, we reject them," it proclaims. "To the extent that they are based
on the notion that Chinese persons, born in this country, are unfit for citizenship
because they (if men) are feminized, or (if women) are debauched and immoral,
or because American law has restricted the opportunities of Chinese men to marry,
or because their occupational choices do not conform to the dominant understanding in this society of the separate spheres of men and women, we reject that as well."

Only after this rebuke does the feminist judgment turn to a more traditional
doctrinal analysis of the Citizenship Clause. In this latter portion of the judgment,
the analysis follows the general contours of the original opinion, with a review of
English and American common law and the debates on the Civil Rights Act of
1866 and the Fourteenth Amendment. Like the original decision, the feminist
judgment rejects the Solicitor General's attempt to impose a rule of *jus sanguinis*,
finding it to be a novel proposition in light of the extent to which American courts
had applied the rule of territorial birthright citizenship since the founding of the
republic. While the two analyses overlap somewhat in substance, they differ significantly in tone, with the feminist judgment maintaining its uncompromising
condemnation of the racism of the government's position. Drawing a direct line
between the *Dred Scott* decision and the Solicitor General's position in *Wong
Kim Ark*, it proclaims, "We … cannot ignore the racism in the bones of these
briefs …. Citizenship rules that allocate citizenship on the basis of descent inherently perpetuate racial division. That is their nature – they allocate citizenship
to one group of people, and deny it to another, based on who their parents and
ancestors were."

Professor Weinberg ends by contrasting the racial restrictions that were embodied in the naturalization statute with the broad scope of citizenship under the
Fourteenth Amendment. Unlike the original opinion, in which the naturalization
statute is mentioned only to make a point about the application of birthright citizenship, the feminist judgment takes the opportunity to forcefully condemn the statute.
"That racist exclusion is a stain upon us," it states in closing. "But its saving grace is
that the harm it perpetuates exists for only a single generation. After that, we are all
Americans."

In ending on this note, Professor Weinberg points us toward what is generally
hailed as the most significant aspect of the Citizenship Clause: its anti-caste potential. As legal scholar Cristina Rodriguez has written, "The Citizenship Clause,
read in historical and textual context, represents our constitutional reset button. It

places all people, regardless of ancestry, on equal terms at birth, with a legal status that cannot be denied them."[40] *Wong Kim Ark,* as the decision that cemented an expansive reading of the Citizenship Clause, is often viewed in the same light, as an embodiment of the most noble, anti-caste impulses of a Court that proved all too willing, in *Plessy* and other cases, to lend its weight to racial caste systems.[41] However, the contrasts between the original decision and the feminist judgment provide an opportunity to reflect on the extent to which the original decision deserves such accolades.

On a doctrinal level, there is no question that the Court's broad reading of the Citizenship Clause in *Wong Kim Ark* has proven to be a potent tool. The decision may not have done anything to end the harsh immigration laws that excluded Chinese immigrants in the late nineteenth century and that were later broadened to encompass immigrants from all over Asia.[42] Nor did it do anything to block the proliferation of alienage laws that created pervasive forms of state-sanctioned discrimination against those who were not U.S. citizens and particularly against those who were racially barred from naturalizing.[43] However, it did significantly blunt the impact of these laws, shielding the next generation from their direct effects.

Yet while providing a valuable legal principle, the Court failed to deliver the reckoning with caste that was so urgently needed. The decision did not grapple with the legacy of *Dred Scott* or with the unfolding horrors of Jim Crow, of the Chinese exclusion laws, or of the genocide and dispossession of Native peoples (carried out in part, ironically, through the *imposition* of U.S. citizenship).[44] It did not condemn the racial exclusions embodied in the naturalization laws, or any other aspect of the American legal architecture of racial subordination. The result was a holding that has proven to be both hugely important and at the same time incomplete in

---

[40]   Cristina M. Rodriguez, *The Citizenship Clause, Original Meaning, and the Egalitarian Unity of the Fourteenth Amendment,* 11 U. Pa. J. Const. L. 1363, 1165 (2009).

[41]   On the limits of the Court's anti-caste impulses within the context of birthright citizenship, *see* Sam Erman, Almost Citizens: Puerto Rico, the Constitution, and Empire (2018) (exploring the Court's unwillingness to extend birthright citizenship to residents of America's expanding overseas empire).

[42]   On Asian exclusion, see generally Erika Lee, The Making of Asian America: A History (2015), 89–173.

[43]   On alienage laws, see generally, Linda Bosniak, The Citizen and the Alien: Dilemmas of Contemporary Membership (2006). On the proliferation of "alien land laws" in the United States in the early twentieth century, see Keith Aoki, *No Right to Own?: The Early Twentieth-Century "Alien Land Laws" As a Prelude to Internment,* 40 B.C. L. Rev. 37 (1998).

[44]   *See* Stephen Kantrowitz, *White Supremacy, Settler Colonialism, and the Two Citizenships of the Fourteenth Amendment,* 10 J. Civ. War Era 29 (2020); Bethany R. Berger, *Birthright Citizenship on Trial: Elk v. Wilkins and United States v. Wong Kim Ark,* 37 Cardozo L. Rev. 1185, 1189 (2016); Robert B. Porter, *Demise of the Ongwehoweh and the Rise of the Native Americans: Redressing the Genocidal Act of Forcing American Citizenship upon Indigenous Peoples,* 15 Harv. Blackletter L. J. 107 (1999).

its reach. Even an expansive reading of the Citizenship Clause goes only so far on its own, in eradicating caste. That lesson was already abundantly clear in the 1890s, with the citizenship status of African Americans and of white women having been firmly settled but having utterly failed to translate into full citizenship rights.[45] For the direct beneficiaries of the *Wong Kim Ark* holding – Asian Americans and other descendants of non-white immigrants – that lesson has repeated itself in many ways since the case was decided, from the "repatriation" to Mexico of Mexican Americans in the 1930s[46] to the mass incarceration of Japanese Americans in the 1940s[47] to the experiences of U.S. citizens caught up in contemporary systems of mass detention and deportation.[48] Describing this phenomenon, historian Mae Ngai has coined the term "alien citizen" to describe

> an American citizen by virtue of her birth in the United States but whose citizen-ship is suspect, if not denied, on account of the racialized identity of her immigrant ancestry. In this construction, the foreignness of non-European peoples is deemed unalterable, making nationality a kind of racial trait. Alienage, then, becomes a permanent condition, passed from generation to generation, adhering even to the native-born citizen.[49]

There is no question that *Wong Kim Ark* deserves it status as a landmark decision. Yet in providing a racially inclusive doctrine of birthright citizenship without con-fronting systems of racial oppression, it fell far short of what it could have done to advance the cause of abolishing caste in the United States. The feminist judgment allows us to glimpse what an alternative path might have looked like.

UNITED STATES v. WONG KIM ARK, 169 U.S. 649 (1898)

Justice Jonathan Weinberg delivered the opinion of the Court.

On July 28, 1868, this Nation adopted the fourteenth amendment to our Constitution, providing that "[a]ll persons born … in the United States and subject to the jurisdiction thereof, are citizens of the United States." 15 Stat. 708–11. On the

---

[45] On the evolving significance of citizenship status and its relationship to race and gender, *see generally* KUNAL PARKER, MAKING FOREIGNERS: IMMIGRATION AND CITIZENSHIP LAW IN AMERICA, 1600–2000 (2015).

[46] *See generally* FRANCISCO E. BALDERRAMA AND RAYMOND RODRIGUEZ, DECADE OF BETRAYAL: MEXICAN REPATRIATION IN THE 1930S (1995).

[47] *See generally* Roger Daniels, Sandra C. Taylor, Harry H.L. Kitano and Leonard J. Arrington, JAPANESE AMERICANS: FROM RELOCATION TO REDRESS. Rev'd 2 ed (1991); ERIKA LEE, THE MAKING OF ASIAN AMERICA, 211–51 (2016).

[48] *See generally* Rachel E. Rosenbloom, *The Citizenship Line: Rethinking Immigration Exceptionalism*, 54 B.C. L. REV. 1965 (2013); Jacqueline Stevens, *U.S. Government Unlawfully Detaining and Deporting U.S. Citizens as Aliens*, 18 VA. J. SOC. POL'Y & L. 606 (2011).

[49] Mae M. Ngai, *Birthright Citizenship and the Alien Citizen*, 75 FORDHAM L. REV. 2521, 2521 (2007).

very same day, the United States concluded a treaty recognizing the "free migration" of Chinese to this country "for purposes of curiosity, trade, or as permanent residents." *Burlingame-Seward Treaty*, art. V. Wong Li Ping and Wee Lee migrated to the United States pursuant to that treaty's invitation, and made a home at 751 Sacramento Street in San Francisco. In 1873, at that address, Wee Lee gave birth to a son, named Wong Kim Ark. The question before the Court today is whether the younger Mr. Wong, by the terms of the fourteenth amendment, is a citizen of the United States. We hold that he is.

I BACKGROUND

Solicitor General Holmes Conrad and Mr. George Collins (who is identified in his brief as "of counsel" to the United States) each offer argument in opposition to Mr. Wong's citizenship. We will begin with Mr. Collins's striking claim that there "should be some honor and dignity in American citizenship that would be sacred from the foul and corrupting taint of a debasing alienage." While the Solicitor General is more restrained, suggesting only that the Chinese have characteristics that "seem[] to preclude" them from citizenship, Mr. Collins straightforwardly refers to the Chinese as "obnoxious." Recognizing a Chinese person as a U.S. citizen and thus eligible to the Presidency, he continues, would mark a degenerate departure from the ideals of America's founders; "surely in that case American citizenship is not worth having."

This argument is familiar. We recall the Congressional debate over the Naturalization Act of 1870, in which Congress rejected language that would have allowed persons born in China to naturalize as U.S. citizens. Senator Stewart of Nevada painted any law allowing such naturalization as disastrous; the Chinese, he said, were incapable of honest and intelligent citizenship. *See Cong. Globe*, 41st Cong., 2d Sess. 5150 (July 4, 1870). Senator Williams of Oregon referred to the Chinese as "benighted and groveling pagans," whose "besotted ignorance is only equaled by their moral debasement." Allowing them to gain citizenship through naturalization, he continued, would sacrifice American pride and glory to Chinese "[i]gnorance, idolatry, immorality, vice, disease and prostitution." *Id.* at 5157 (July 4, 1870).

Legislation hostile to the Chinese has not been limited to that concerning citizenship. Congress in 1882 enacted the Chinese Exclusion Act, almost entirely banning new migration from China to this country. *See* Chinese Exclusion Act of 1882, Pub. L. No. 47-126, 22. Stat. 58. Senator Miller of California urged the necessity of that law in part by describing the Chinese as "utterly unfit for and incapable of free or self-government." 13 *Cong. Rec.* 1484 (1882). Since that time, Congress has shut down Chinese migration with ever-higher fences and walls. *See* Act of Sept. 13, 1888, Chap. 1015, 25 Stat. 476; Scott Act, ch. 1064, 25 Stat. 504 (1888). The Chinese are the only ethnic or national group whose entry the U.S. government has seen fit to restrict that way.

All this has taken place alongside horrific racism and violence directed in this country against Chinese members of our community. Chinese persons have been the targets of mass violence throughout the Pacific Northwest in cases too numerous to mention. The burning of Seattle's Chinatown in 1885, and the consequent expulsion of Chinese from Seattle and Tacoma, provides only a single example.

We cannot address the arguments in this case outside of that larger context. The contours of Chinese communal settlement in the United States – and thus Mr. Wong's very existence – have been shaped by white American attitudes toward the Chinese. Those attitudes are the product of racism, to be sure, but not only of racism. More specifically, they are the product of beliefs about Chinese women's propensities and morality, Chinese men's failure to protect female virtue, Chinese men's conformance to the rules for proper masculine behavior, and the nature of Chinese families. Those attitudes have molded United States law, which has in turn shaped the ability of Chinese people to move to, and form families in, this country. At the same time, white American understandings of appropriate behavior for Chinese men and women, and of whether Chinese persons have behaved in a role appropriate to their sex, have driven lawmakers' attitudes regarding the suitability of people of Chinese ancestry for citizenship.

A starting point: Hysteria over perceived Chinese female immorality and promiscuity has long driven U.S. policymakers' attitudes to the Chinese migration. Our government's officials have seen most Chinese women presumptively as prostitutes. That belief has given form to our immigration law. As early as 1875, or even before, laws seeking to bar the entry of Chinese prostitutes had the effect of hindering the migration of women from China. It is in part by virtue of those laws that there is today in this country only one Chinese woman in residence for every twenty Chinese men.

Lawmakers' assumptions about the immorality of Chinese women have had different effects on women of different economic classes. U.S. law had an unambiguous suppressive effect on migration by women of the laboring class. By contrast, white judges' assumptions about the proper roles of men and women – and about the role of the husband as master of the family unit, with a right to unimpeded and uninterrupted connubial access to his wife – have had an opposite effect in connection with migration of certain women of China's middle and upper classes, allowing their entry into the United States even when the statutory text has seemed to forbid it.

U.S. law has helped cement in place an undesirable situation in which Chinese laborers in this country have overwhelmingly been single men, without wives or children. Some businesses and some American policymakers have welcomed this. But others have seen a threat, and have seen Chinese men in the United States – ill-positioned to marry, and not conforming to white America's dominant understanding of the separate spheres to be occupied by men and women – as on that basis feminized and unfit for citizenship. Imagining Chinese women in the

United States as either prostitutes or absent, they have denied the very existence of Chinese children born in this country. For all that, Chinese women have been here in this country all along, forming families and raising children on United States soil.

II A. GENDERED RACISM AGAINST CHINESE PERSONS

White people's associations of Chinese women with prostitution are of long standing. Horace Greeley penned an editorial in 1854 in which he explained (notwithstanding, insofar as appears, never actually having met a Chinese person) that "every [Chinese] female is a prostitute of the basest order." *New York Tribune*, Sept. 29, 1854. As Chinese migrants came to California from the 1850s through to less than a decade ago, most of that state – and indeed much of the nation – was caught up in a hysteria about Chinese women and prostitution. Thus, in President Grant's 1874 State of the Union address, he declaimed that "[h]ardly a perceptible percentage of [Chinese women] perform any honorable labor, but they are brought for shameful purposes, to the disgrace of the communities where they are settled and to the great demoralization of the youth of those localities."

Contemporary testimony before federal and California legislative bodies overflows with expressions of disgust and fear regarding Chinese prostitution, which witnesses identified as the source of noxious disease and the corruption of innocent white boys. An eminent doctor testified that he had seen white boys as young as eight years old who had patronized Chinese prostitutes and contracted syphilis. Nowhere else in the world were there so many boys with venereal disease, and nearly all of them gotten it because they had "been with Chinawomen." The Chinese prostitutes' prices were low, he explained, and they did not care that they were consorting with children. *Chinese Immigration: Its Social, Moral and Political Effect, Report to the California State Senate of its Special Committee on Chinese Immigration* 25–27 (1878) (testimony of Dr. H.H. Toland).

Senator Cornelius Cole (R-Calif.) in 1870 described Chinese women in the United States as "the most undesirable of population, who spread disease and moral death among our white" citizenry.

The Workingman's Party of California, with the support of San Francisco's then-mayor and board of health, penned a statement in 1880 charging that from Chinese houses of prostitution there was infusing "an incurable and hereditary curse, ultimately destroying whole nations through the instrumentality of Chinese prostitutes, who, in diseasing our young men, implant into them the germs of leprosy and other loathsome, constitutional and hereditary disorders." An 1885 report of a special committee to the San Francisco Board of Supervisors agreed that Chinese prostitution was "the source of the most terrible pollution of the blood of the younger and rising generations" and "destined to be the source of contamination and hereditary diseases among those who come after us too frightful to contemplate" – although it did add as another "count[] in the indictment against the [Chinese] race" that there were white prostitutes in Chinatown as well. *Report of Special Committee to the Board of Supervisors of San Francisco* (1885), at 14–15. We could multiply these examples many times over.

Chinese prostitutes' white customers, in these testimonies, are routinely constructed as young boys, innocent victims to be protected. Thus the patronage of Chinese prostitutes by white customers is characterized as a heinous offense and source of contagion on the part of the Chinese women (and their procurers), while the patronage of white prostitutes by Chinese customers is simultaneously seen as a heinous offense on the part of Chinese men against white womanhood.

The trafficking of Chinese women for prostitution was real. But that hardly explains the degree to which that activity seized the public imagination, or to which Chinese prostitution specifically was seen as the downfall of American white Christendom. As San Francisco's health officer Dr. John Meares explained, Chinese women were not the chief source of syphilis contagion – "we have plenty of prostitution outside of the Chinese." *Report of the Joint Special Committee to Investigate Chinese Immigration*, 44th Cong. 2d Sess. No. 689 (1877), at 141 (testimony of Dr. Meares); see also id. at 457 (testimony of Rev. Loomis) (the activities of "the fallen women of other nationalities" went far beyond "anything to be seen in the Chinese quarter"). *Cf.* "Editorial: Sanitary Condition of San Francisco," 1 *Medico-Legal Journal* #2 (Oct. 1878), at 19 (those politicians who raise "a great hue and cry over the sanitary condition" of Chinatown ignore the city's "ten thousand other pest-holes").

Nor was it the case that, as many claimed in these testimonies, nearly every Chinese woman in this country was a prostitute. The Rev. A.W. Loomis charged that "nearly all Chinese women in San Francisco are a disgrace to their nation." A.W. Loomis, "Chinese Women in California," *Overland Monthly* (April 1869). The Rev. Otis Gibson, in an 1877 book, estimated that there were 2,600 Chinese women in San Francisco who were "enslaved prostitutes," as compared to only 120 in "respectable families." Otis Gibson, *The Chinese in America* 59 (1877). But reports from the subsequent census tell another story: they suggest that the number of those engaged in prostitution in 1880, out of a total population in excess of two thousand women, was under 500. The figures from the 1870 census are somewhat different, to be sure, but there is substantial reason to doubt their accuracy.

B. *Anti-Chinese State and Federal Laws*

California politicians were quick to respond to the threat that Chinese women were said to pose. After the state legislature failed in its efforts simply to ban the entry of all Chinese into the state, *see Lin Sing v. Washburn*, 20 Cal. 534 (1862), it set its sights on women specifically. Thus, in 1866, the California legislature enacted *An Act for the Suppression of Chinese Houses of Ill Fame*, Cal. Stats, 1865–66, ch. 505, at 641. That law declared premises "used by Chinese women for the purposes of common prostitution" to be public nuisances, and made it a crime for the owner of property to allow it to be used for such a purpose. The law did not, for its first eight years, apply to prostitution engaged in by non-Chinese. *See* Cal. Stats., 1873–74, ch. 76, at 84 (subsequent amendment). The brothels continued in existence notwithstanding the law.

California politicians next turned to immigration law as a more powerful tool. A bill introduced in Congress by California's Senator Williams would have barred the entry of "any Chinese woman not accompanied by her husband or father." *Cong. Globe*, 41st Cong., 2d Sess. 299 (Dec. 22, 1869). That bill failed, though, and in its wake the state legislature enacted *An Act to Prevent the Kidnapping and Importation of Mongolian, Chinese, and Japanese Females, for Criminal or Demoralizing Purposes*, Cal. Stats., 1869–70, ch. 230, at 330 (Mar. 18, 1870). That statute barred the entry of any East Asian woman into California absent evidence satisfactory to the state commissioner of immigration that she was not being trafficked and was "a person of correct habits and good character."

An 1872 legislative codification, and an 1874 amendment, rewrote that law. The result was a California statute giving the state commissioner of immigration wide discretion to demand a heavy bond from ship captains before a ship could land any of several disfavored classes of persons, including "lewd or debauched wom[e]n." Cal. Stat., 1873–74 Code Amendments, Political Code § 70, at 39–40. Because captains had no incentive to pay such bonds, the effect was to bar those classes of immigrants altogether. State authorities sought to enforce that provision aggressively against incoming Chinese.

Upon federal-court challenge, though, Justice Field (sitting as Circuit Justice) held the state law unconstitutional. He noted his lack of respect for "that discriminating virtue which is shocked when a frail child of China is landed on our shores, and yet allows the bedizened and painted harlot of other countries to parade our streets … without censure." *In re Ah Fong*, 1 F. Cas. 213, 217, 218 (1874). We upheld that ruling on federalism grounds. *Chy Lung v. Freeman*, 92 U.S. 275, 278, 281 (1875).

This ruling proved only a temporary setback, though, for those seeking to limit the immigration of Chinese women. With the situation plain that Chinese women's migration could be restricted only at the federal level, Rep. Horace Page introduced a bill in Congress to do just that. Representative Page pronounced that he sought "to place a dividing line between vice and virtue … send[ing] the brazen harlot who openly flaunts her wickedness in the faces of our wives and daughters back to her native country," so that we were no longer China's "cess-pool." 43rd Cong., 2d Sess., Cong. Rec. App. 44 (Feb. 10, 1875).

Congress swiftly enacted the Page bill. That law required U.S. diplomatic authorities in "China, Japan, or any Oriental country" to examine every woman seeking to depart for the United States, and to allow the woman's passage only upon a determination that she had not "entered into a contract or agreement for a term of service within the United States, for lewd and immoral purposes." At the end of the trip, customs inspectors in the United States could inspect arriving ships and forbid the entry of any woman deemed "imported for the purposes of prostitution." The statute made it a five-year felony for any person knowingly and willingly to bring women to the United States for that purpose. Page Act of 1875, Pub. L. 43–141, 18 Stat. 477 (1875).

The Page Act sharply changed the environment of Chinese women's immigration to the United States. Under procedures put in place immediately after its enactment by David Bailey, the American consul in Hong Kong, each Chinese woman seeking to emigrate had to submit an official "declaration of purpose in emigration and personal morality," along with a processing fee (or bribe). The consulate shared that document with the elite Hong Kong businessmen's association and the British colonial government, both of which then investigated the underlying facts. The woman would be questioned repeatedly as to her plans, her marriage status, her sexual history, and her morality. Consul Bailey considered himself to have the authority to reject an application on mere suspicion of immorality, and he exercised that authority liberally. (In this, perhaps he was informed by the view encapsulated by the contemporary testimony of J.P.M. Fraser, a veteran of the British consular service in Canton, that "respectable Chinese women [do not] leave China." *See Chinese Immigration: Its Social, Moral and Political Effect, Report to the California State Senate of its Special Committee on Chinese Immigration, supra*, at 151.)

If a woman were cleared to go, she would receive a certificate attesting that she had been determined to be of "good moral character." Out of concern that a Chinese women might gain certification notwithstanding her dishonest nature, and then surreptitiously pass along her documents to another woman who was even less worthy, the consulate relied on cutting-edge identification technology: It had a photograph made for each successful applicant, and affixed it to her papers. *See id.* at 218–19 (testimony of Giles Gray). That way, any substitution might be detected.

The recent testimony of Frederick Bee (who represented the interests of the Chinese government in San Francisco from 1878 to 1882) in the case of *In re Wah Ah Chin* explains the next step in the process, at least during Bee's tenure. The Hong Kong consulate supplied Bee with duplicates of the women's photographs and paperwork, including a summary of the information they had given when questioned in China. Armed with those materials, he would question the women anew when their ship arrived in San Francisco. If their photographs or answers did not match, they would be returned to their home country.

The Page Act procedures demonstrate the degree to which U.S. government officials saw Chinese female immigration, and Chinese female sexuality, as threatening. To migrate to the United States, a Chinese woman had to run a fearsome gauntlet of repeated interrogation in controlled settings, together with multiple third-party investigations. She had to satisfy demands for details of her life relating to her sexual history and virtue. She would be subjected to an unprecedented new system of documentary control, including the innovative use of photographs as a means of identification, and officials' cross-checking files as a safeguard against the falsehoods they expected her to provide. All of this applied only to women. No comparable paperwork was required of men. Although there was statutory authority before 1882 for customs inspectors to return some East Asian men arriving in the United States in violation of law, that authority wasn't exercised. Bee testified in 1882 that he had never in his four-year tenure returned a male.

The effect of Page Act examination and exclusion, moreover, was not limited to the statute's putative targets. The prospect of being put through this process, along with its indiscriminate nature, discouraged the migration of women from China more generally. The result? The overall movement of women from China to the United States dropped sharply beginning in 1875. It appears that in the period 1870–75, more than five hundred Chinese women arrived in the United States every year; from 1876 through the passage of the Exclusion Act in 1882, that annual number dropped to less than two hundred. During that same period, the male population surged; indeed, the increases in the Chinese male population on the U.S. Pacific Coast in 1875 and 1876 were greater than in any prior year since the 1852 Gold Rush.

There are many reasons why Chinese men in this country have come to outnumber women vastly. For migrant populations to be predominantly male in an initial period of labor migration is not unusual. It is said that Chinese women are less free to leave home and sojourn abroad than their male counterparts, because of family restraints including a married women's obligation to her parents-in-law. It is said that dominant Chinese social mores see women as properly confined to the home, where their sexuality can be properly regulated, rather than wandering out into the public sphere – much less travelling across oceans to other nations, insulated from social control.

These considerations help explain the fact in 1870, before the period of legislative restriction, Chinese women were scarcely more than seven percent of the total Chinese population in this country. *See* 1870 Census, Table XXII. But just at the point when one might have expected the number of Chinese women in the United States to increase more generously, as the Chinese settlement here grew and matured, legal restrictions choked that off. It is by virtue of United States law that the gap between the male and female Chinese populations in this country, since 1875, has not only persisted but increased. In the most recent census, two years before passage of the Exclusion Act, the fraction of Chinese people in this country who were women dropped to less than five percent.

C. *Effect of Anti-Chinese Laws on Chinese Integration*

The Page Act regime, along with earlier California law, helped limit the ability of Chinese migrants to form families in the United States. U.S. law, in other words, did its best to ensure that people like Mr. Wong would not exist. White people's imagining of the disease and degradation emanating from contact with Chinese women led to the Page Act, which in turn legally suppressed the migration of Chinese women, which in turn contributed to a gender imbalance that has crippled Chinese family and communal life in this country on an ongoing basis.

And yet Mr. Wong does exist, as do many other persons of Chinese ancestry born in this country. United States law was only incompletely successful in suppressing Chinese settlement. That lack of complete success can be attributed, in part, to the force of sexual stereotypes running in the other direction. It's worth remembering that some Chinese women have migrated to the United States all along. This group has included not only the trafficked sex workers who loomed so large in the public imagination, but also a significant number of upper- and middle-class merchants' wives and daughters. As representatives of the San Francisco Chinese business community wrote in a memorial to President Grant in 1876, "a few hundred" of those wealthier adult women were then in the city – "all chaste, pure, keepers-at-home, not known on the public street." They were the mothers, the authors estimated, of at least a few hundred – perhaps as many as a thousand – Chinese children born in the U.S. Lee Ming How et al., "Memorial to President Grant" (1876); *see also Report of the Joint Special Committee to Investigate Chinese Immigration, supra,* at 446 (testimony of Rev. Loomis).

Six years later, the 1882 Chinese Exclusion Act barred any new migration to the United States of men and women of the Chinese laboring classes, but it maintained current law allowing Chinese merchants to come here – and at that point judicial musing on the proper roles of the two sexes demanded that the law preserve as well the free entry of merchants' wives.

This wasn't an obvious result; there was no support in statutory or treaty text for allowing the entry of Chinese women into this country. The statutory text seemed to bar the admission of any Chinese person other than holders of so-called "Section Six certificates," along with their body and household servants. Those certificates could only be issued to "teachers, students [or] merchants," and judges thought it obvious that "Chinese women are not teachers, students, or merchants." *In re Chung Toy Ho & Wong Choy Sin,* 42 F. 398, 399 (D. Ore. 1890).

But at the same time, merchants' wives were plainly members of the Chinese elite, not the lower-class laborers whom courts saw the restrictive laws as targeting. More to the point, could it really be that the lawmakers contemplated allowing a Chinese merchant to bring his servants, but to bar his wife and children? On the contrary, one judge reasoned, "the domicile of the wife and children is that of the husband and father." The natural order of things demanded that a Chinese merchant migrating to the United States be able to "bring with him, and have with him, his wife and children. The company of the one, and the care and custody of the other, are his by natural right …." *Id.* at 399–400; *see also In re Tung Yeong,* 19 F. 184, 189 (D. Cal. 1884).

The courts thus saw it as clear that Chinese merchant wives could continue to enter the United States, attached to their merchant husbands. Their reasoning echoed treatise-writers' explanation for why, it has been said, married women cannot engage in binding contracts – because "[t]he right of the husband to the person of his wife [is] guarded by the law with the utmost solicitude." If a woman could bind herself in contract, then "she would be liable to be arrested, taken in execution, and confined in a prison; and then the husband would be deprived of the company of his wife, which the law will not abide." Tapping Reeve, *The Law of Baron and Femme* 182 (3d ed. 1862).

The upshot? In the case of lower-class Chinese women, stereotypes about women's immorality led to a suppression of their migration. But in the case of upper class Chinese women, stereotypes about their proper sexual service to their husbands led to judges' easing their migration. Chinese women of the middle and upper classes – such as Mr. Wong's mother Wee Lee – were able to come to the United States to live both before and after the 1882 statute. Because of their class background and their signifiers of respectability (often including bound feet), they were less likely to be labeled as prostitutes and thus barred under the Page Act. *Cf. In re Lum Lin Ying*, 59 F. 682, 683 (D. Ore. 1894) (noting and rejecting "whispered suggestions" that the putative merchant wife seeking admission was actually a prostitute).

Merchants' wives were not the only Chinese women raising families in this country. Some women without that class background came prior to 1882 as part of the general migration, notwithstanding legal barriers, and married (or joined husbands). A large number of poorer women were trafficked – and while mortality among indentured prostitutes was substantial, some survived or escaped their terms of service and married. *See Chinese Immigration: Its Social, Moral and Political Effect, Report to the California State Senate of its Special Committee on Chinese Immigration, supra*, at 112 (testimony of George Duffield); Albert S. Evans, *A la California: Sketches of Life in the Golden State* 276 (1873). Other women who came to this country as indentured household servants were able eventually to live independent lives. All classes of these women had daughters, who swelled the ranks of Chinese women present here. There is reason to think, though, that a majority of adult Chinese women in the United States today are women of the middle and upper classes, here by virtue of the law's solicitude for a husband's "marital right." Reeve, *supra*; *see* Sui Sin Far (Edith Eaton), "The Chinese Woman in America," 6 *Land of Sunshine* #2 (Jan. 1897), at 59.

Chinese women are here in this country, and all along have formed families and raised children on U.S. soil. They have done so notwithstanding the best efforts of government actors and the larger public to interfere with their entry and to pretend that they did not exist. They have done so notwithstanding the best efforts of government actors and the larger public to pretend that "debauched" Chinese women lack the capacity to love, to join together in families, and to nurture children as men and women of other races do.

D. *Anti-Chinese Laws Prevent Chinese Family Formation*

American policymakers have tended to ignore the smaller number of middle- and upper-class Chinese who are resident in the United States, not infrequently as part

of families with children. Instead, they focus their attention on Chinese labor-
ers, whom they see as a "bachelor society of serfs." J.C. Holbrook, "Chinadom in
California," *Hutching's California Magazine* (Sept. 1859). When Senate Judiciary
Chair Lyman Trumbull pointed out in 1870 that there were hundreds of U.S.-born
Chinese children being raised in San Francisco families, the response of Nevada's
Senator Stewart was simply to deny that it could be true. *See Cong. Globe*, 41st
Cong., 2d Sess. 5173 (July 4, 1870).

To a very great extent, Chinese laborers in this country have indeed been a bachelor society – single men without wives or children. That state of affairs, though,
though did not happen of itself; U.S. law was written in such a way as to help ensure
it. It is hardly unreasonable to believe that that might have been one of the Page
Act's goals. Our learned colleague Judge Lorenzo Sawyer, formerly Chief Justice
of the California Supreme Court and currently sitting on the federal bench in
California, put the matter succinctly in a letter a few years ago to the eminent historian Hubert Bancroft. Chinese laborers, he explained, were useful: "their industry,
their economy, their frugality and perseverance" is a "great advantage to the country." And yet, he continued, their presence was undesirable given "the dissimilarity
of races." So how might that dilemma be bridged?

The answer, Sawyer explained, is plain: "If they would never bring their women
here and never multiply and we would never have more than we can make useful" –
if they "don't come here to stay" – then their temporary migration would be an
advantage to the Nation. There's reason to be concerned about the possibility of the
Chinese abandoning the idea of temporary labor migration, "get[ting] over the idea
that they must go back." At that point, "they will begin to multiply here and that
is where the danger lies." But that danger can be averted: "When the Chinaman
comes here and don't bring his wife here, sooner or later he dies like a worn out
steam engine; he is simply a machine, and don't leave two or three or half dozen
children to fill his place."

We do not share the views of our learned colleague, but we are indebted to him
for the clarity with which he expressed them. Suppressing the migration of Chinese
women to this country did more than free white men and women from the perceived baleful effects of white men having sex with Chinese women for money. It
also helped ensure that Chinese (male) workers could be housed more cheaply, in
crowded and substandard housing. It avoided workers' pressing for higher wages to
support homes including children and adults with unpaid childcare responsibilities.
And it offered the promise of avoiding a permanent ethnically Chinese population
in the United States.

Senator John Conness made a related point in 1866: "This portion of our population," he explained, "namely, the children of Mongolian parentage born in
California, is very small indeed, and never promises to be large." The Chinese come
to the United States only temporarily, and then return. "[T]hey do not bring their
females to our country but in very limited numbers, and rarely ever in connection

with families," so that "it is only in exceptional cases that they have had children." *Cong. Globe*, 39th Cong., 1st Sess. 2891 (May 30, 1866); *see also id*. at 1757 (Sen. Trumbull). He made this argument in support of the fourteenth amendment's enactment; he explained that Americans need not fear Chinese citizenship, because Chinese women and Chinese families were barely to be found in this country.

In addition to law's helping to block the presence of non-merchant-class Chinese women on American shores, law has limited Chinese men's familial options in other ways as well. An 1880 California statute provides that the state "shall not issue a license authorizing the marriage of a white person with a ... Mongolian." An act to amend sections sixty-nine, etc., Cal. Stats., 1880 Code Amendments, Civil Code, Ch. 41, § 1 (April 6, 1880). The men making up almost all of the Chinese community in America, thus, have few opportunities for marriage within that community and even fewer outside it.

But the very considerations that made Chinese laborers' singlehood appealing from the perspective of employers and some policymakers, have made it threatening from the perspective of others. For many white observers, the fact that so many Chinese migrants are single and can work for low wages has only heightened the danger they present, and underlined their unsuitability for citizenship.

As an initial matter, critics have argued, Chinese men live so cheaply in their bunkhouses or tenements that their wages undercut those of white workers. Their costs are low because they brought "with them neither wives, families nor children" – only a few women, all of them said to be immoral, whom they "bought and sold like chattels." *Chinese Immigration*, 45th Cong., 2d. Sess., H. Rep. No. 240 (Feb. 25, 1878), at 3–4. Cameron King, president of the Anti-Chinese Union, explained to Congress that Chinese workers would, if unchecked, drive white labor out of California. This was in part because they "build no homes, have no families." White workers would be unable to compete, unless they too were to "abandon their social habits [and] renounce their wives and children." *Report of the Joint Special Committee to Investigate Chinese Immigration, supra*, at 33, 34; *see also id*. at 318–19; *Chinese Immigration: Its Social, Moral and Political Effect, Report to the California State Senate of its Special Committee on Chinese Immigration, supra*, at 49 (testimony of Mr. Duffey).

That is not the end of it, though. The unpartnered nature of Chinese men is said to do more than merely render them an economic threat. More fundamentally, it is said to make them debased and unsuitable as citizens. An 1878 report of the U.S. House Committee on Education and Labor lays out the argument: "The central idea of our system," the report explains, "is that the laborer shall possess courage self-respect, and independence. To do this he must have a home." Home, the report rhapsodizes, is the central institution of society: "Home is the mold in which society is cast. There the habits are formed which give character. There the zest and wakeful interest of living center. There the fires of patriotism are kindled. There free institutions find their source and inspiration." *Chinese Immigration, supra*, at 2.

But Chinese people in this country "have no homes. They have neither home feelings nor home interests ...." They never can have homes, because their migration consists entirely of single adult men, accepting wages too low to support home life and living in substandard, jam-packed housing. "Such a place does not deserve the name of home. No tender and loving interests cluster around it ...." As such, the Chinese in America lack "the homes, the comforts, and the appliances of personal civilization, which have always been enjoyed by the laboring classes of America, and from which springs that spirit of self-respect and manly independence" on which our political system depends. *Id.* at 2–3. Accord *Cong. Globe*, 41st Cong., 2d Sess. 5152 (July 4, 1870) (Sen. Stewart) ("they have not brought here their families; they build no houses; they have no farms").

Chinese men cannot become productive members of American society, in sum, because they have no women to civilize them. As such, they have no stake in society; they have no property to protect; they have no moral compass. And if any further proof of Chinese unsuitability were needed, their treatment of women demonstrates their lack of manhood. Chinese men have subjected women to contempt and degradation, bringing them to this country as sex-trafficked slaves. No true man could so fail to protect female virtue. *See Chinese Immigration, supra,* at 3.

Moreover, we are told that the Chinese fail to respect the proper and separate spheres of men and women, blurring the lines between what is male and what is female. Chinese men wear their hair long, in queues, and wear loose garments that white Americans see as sexually ambiguous. They have established niches in laundry service, in cooking, and as personal servants – all women's work. As Senator Henry Corbett of Oregon explained, Chinese men "supersede the servant girls, and those engaged in waiting upon tables, and in washing, and every species of employment that is pursued by the weak." *Cong. Globe,* 41st Cong., 2d Sess. 5163 (July 4, 1870).

The heads of California's Workingman's Party of California put it this way in an 1878 speech: If a white head of household seeks work, "Ah! A stout Chinaman does it cheaper. Will he get a place for his oldest boy? He cannot. His girl? Why, the Chinaman is in her place too!" The success of Chinese workers in America in performing both male and female economic roles, he speaker explained, meant that "they seem to have no sex." Nothing could have been further from the dominant white American view of an archetypal citizen.

III. A. THE FOURTEENTH AMENDMENT
AND *JUS SOLI* CITIZENSHIP

With that as background, we can return to the arguments made on behalf of the government in this case. To the extent they are based on the racial inferiority of the Chinese, we reject them. To the extent they are based on the notion that Chinese persons, born in this country, are unfit for citizenship because they (if men) are feminized, or (if women) are debauched and immoral, or because American law has restricted the opportunities of Chinese men to marry, or because their occupational choices do not conform to the dominant understanding in this society of the separate spheres of men and women, we reject that as well.

To the extent that they are based on none of those things, and must stand on their merits as theories of citizenship and explications of the words of the fourteenth amendment, they fare no better. A look at history makes that clear.

Under the British common law, a person's birth anywhere within the sovereign's territorial jurisdiction conferred the status of British subject. United States courts have held, over and over, both before and after enactment of the fourteenth amendment, that the same rule (sometimes known as *jus soli*) applies here – that citizenship attaches to all persons born within our borders, subject to our laws. *See, e.g., Inglis v. Trustees of Sailors' Snug Harbor*, 28 U.S. 99, 164 (1830) (opinion of Story, J.); *State v. Manuel*, 20 N.C. 144 (1838); *Lynch v. Clarke*, 3 N.Y. Leg. Obs. 236 (1844); *United States v. Rhodes*, 27 F. Cas. 785, 789 (1866) (Swayne, J., sitting as Circuit Justice); *United States v. Elm*, 25 F. Cas. 1006, 1006–07 (N.D.N.Y 1877); *In re Look Tin Sing*, 21 F. 905 (D. Calif. 905 (1884) (Field, J., sitting as Circuit Justice).

Even when some in this country brought forward the benighted proposition that free Black persons born here should not enjoy citizenship, they made no fundamental challenge to the *jus soli* rule. They did not endorse the claim that Mr. Collins puts forward here: that (male) parentage should displace place of birth as the source of American citizenship. Instead, courts in Southern states developed a new exception to *jus soli*, under which a state's systematically depriving a class of people of the rights and privileges of citizenship meant that members of the disfavored class could not, "in the proper sense of the term," be deemed citizens. *Amy v. Smith*, 1 Little 326, 333 (Ky. 1822). Chief Justice Taney in *Dred Scott v. Sandford*, 60 U.S. 393 (1857), developed a simpler rule – that no person could be a citizen if that person were Black. But Chief Justice Taney too saw his rule as an exception to the generally applicable principle of *jus soli*. *See id.* at 415, 417 (explaining that a person born outside the United States must be naturalized to become a citizen, and that naturalization is by its nature inapplicable to persons born inside the United States). And the fourteenth amendment has now sent those both of those evil doctrines to the grave.

In short, the principle that a person's birth in the United States, subject to United States law, makes him or her a United States citizen has long been well-understood by legal experts and the public at large. No party contests this. As the Solicitor General puts it, until 1885 "the opinions of the Attorneys-General, the decisions of the Federal and State courts, and … the rulings of the State Department all concurred in the view that birth in the United States conferred citizenship" by virtue of the common-law rule.

In 1866, Congress for the first time sought to fix the bounds of U.S. birthright citizenship in statute. It enacted the Civil Rights Act of 1866, which begins with the words "[A]ll persons born in the United States and not subject to any foreign power, excluding Indians not taxed, are hereby declared to be citizens of the United States." The parties in this case agree that that statutory language and the fourteenth amendment guarantee are coextensive – that the words "not subject to any foreign power" in the Civil Rights Act have the same meaning as "subject to the jurisdiction thereof" in the constitutional text.

There is plain evidence of the intent of the Civil Rights Act's drafters. Senate Judiciary Chair Lyman Trumbull, who introduced the bill, explained that its language carried forward existing law, and that "children who are born here of parents who have not been naturalized are citizens." Chinese persons born in this country, he continued, "[u]ndoubtedly" were citizens on that basis. *Cong Globe*, 39th Cong. 1st. Sess. 498 (Jan. 30, 1866); *see also id.* at 1757 (Apr. 4, 1866) ("even the infant child of a foreigner born in this land is a citizen of the United States long before his father"). President Johnson, in the message accompanying his (overridden) veto, made the same point: He criticized the enacted bill on the ground that it made citizens of the U.S.-born children of Chinese migrants. *Cong. Globe*, 39th Cong., 1st Sess. 1679 (Mar. 27, 1876) ("Every individual of [the Chinese race], born in the United States, is by this bill made a citizen of the United States.").

In the congressional debate later that year over the fourteenth amendment, proponents of the new provision stated explicitly that their new constitutional language incorporated the same rule: Citizenship derived from a person's being "born within the limits of the United States and subject to their laws." *Id.* at 2765 (May 23, 1866) (Sen. Howard). The phrase "subject to the jurisdiction" in the constitutional text, they explained, required that the individual at birth be subject to U.S. law – not born as a member of a Indian tribe subject to the civil and criminal jurisdiction of the tribe rather than that of the U.S. government, or into the family of a foreign ambassador. *See id.* at 2893–94 (Sen. Trumbull); *see also id.* at 2897 (Sen. Williams); *id.* at 3031–32 (Sen. Henderson). On that basis, Senator Conness explained, as far as "the children begotten of Chinese parents in California" were concerned, the fourteenth amendment "declare[s] that they shall be citizens." *Id.* at 2891.

Two years after the fourteenth amendment's enactment, when Congress debated the eligibility of people born in China to naturalize, Senators on both sides of that debate agreed that Chinese migrants' children, born in the United States, were citizens and eligible to vote. *See Cong. Globe*, 41st Cong., 2d Sess. 5159 (July 4, 1870) (Sen. Schurz); *id.* at 5173 (Sen. Stewart).

This history leaves little doubt that, under the terms of the fourteenth amendment as its drafters and enactors understood it, Mr. Wong is a United States citizen.

B. *"Dual Allegiance" Cannot Overcome Birthright Citizenship*

The briefs supporting the United States, however, argue that this long-held understanding of American citizenship has been incorrect since the beginning. They contend that the United States in 1776 should be understood to have thrown off the British common-law rule. Under that law, birth within the King's domain meant that a subject owed allegiance to the King, a personal obligation traceable to the divine right to rule. The opinion of the Court of King's Bench in *Calvin's Case* explained that the relationship stemming from birth within the dominion is

> a true and faithful obedience of the subject due to his Sovereign ... an incident inseparable to every subject; for as soon as he is born he oweth by birth-right ligeance and obedience to his Sovereign .... [It] is the mutual bond and obligation between the King and his subjects, whereby subjects are called his liege subjects, because they are bound to obey and serve him; and he is called their liege lord, because he should maintain and defend him.

Calvin's Case, 77 ER 377 (1608). That law, the Solicitor General and Mr. Collins tell us, rests on the feudal principle that inhabitants of the soil can be seen as attached to it. It is essentially monarchist, and unfit to govern the question of citizenship in a republic.

The Solicitor General and Mr. Collins have different ideas as to what they imagine *was* the law in the United States after 1776. The Solicitor General suggests that the United States had no law of national citizenship until 1866; rather, only state citizenship mattered. Mr. Collins, more boldly, urges that this country at its inception adopted a new rule based on the Roman rule of descent, under which the citizenship of children of married parents follows that of the father.

But notwithstanding that disharmony, both advocates agree that the fourteenth amendment fences Mr. Wong out from citizenship. The Citizenship Clause requires that a person not only be born in the United States, but be born "subject to the jurisdiction" of the United States. That phrase, the two advocates contend, requires that a person be born fully subject to the "complete" or "political" jurisdiction of the United States. A person does not satisfy that requirement if, by virtue of international law or the law of some other nation, he can be deemed at birth to be a citizen or subject of another country. U.S.-born descendants of Chinese immigrants necessarily are subjects of China, we are told, either by virtue of that country's patrilineal law or because (as the Solicitor General's brief suggests) infant children like the young Mr. Wong inherit their fathers' nationality for reasons too obvious to articulate. Thus, they are not born fully "subject to the jurisdiction" of the United States.

Both the Solicitor General and Mr. Collins emphasize that no person can have more than a single national affiliation. Without regard to the constitutional text, if Mr. Wong's parentage renders him a subject of the Emperor of China, then that citizenship must be his only one. Otherwise, we would have to deal with what the Solicitor General describes as "the absurdity of a 'double allegiance,'" that is, dual citizenship. Mr. Collins more elaborately dismisses the notion of dual citizenship as "repulsive" and "monstrous." For a person to have more than one citizenship, he urges, is not only intolerable but impossible: "the allegiance to one country would neutralize that due the other, and there would be no allegiance to either." A person cannot "even for a moment be a citizen of two nations."

C. *The Fourteenth Amendment Confers Inclusive Birthright Citizenship*

We cannot help being struck by the novelty of these arguments. Our republic is more than a century old. In all that time, the validity in this country of the English common-law rule for citizenship has rarely been contested. The conclusion seems to us inescapable that these newly invented arguments relate not so much to a timeless zeal for democracy, as it does to the asserted inferiority of the Chinese. We have already rejected such thinking.

The challenges to Mr. Wong's citizenship are consistent with the common white conception of Chinese persons as either temporary migrant laborers or prostitutes trafficked from Chinese villages, people who in either case could not possibly have been born here as part of legitimate American families. They are consistent with the notion that Chinese men and women are neither householders nor homemakers, and thus cannot be true Americans. In this conception, Chinese persons who did not arrive in this country on a boat must have been somehow dropped from the skies, strangers, or transients like their countrymen.

But with clear eyes, we can see the reality of persons of Chinese ancestry being born into real families in real communities in the United States. The notion that Chinese migration was simply the temporary labor migration of single male workers depended on the invisibility of Chinese women, and in turn the invisibility of Chinese families producing new citizens. If Chinese women were absent, then U.S.-born children like Mr. Wong couldn't exist. If Chinese women were prostitutes, then their children would be illegitimate in any relevant sense of the word. And yet here we see Americans born and raised by mothers and fathers on American soil.

Even taken in their best light, the arguments of the Solicitor General and Mr. Collins manifest weaknesses. They are ill-fitting with the constitutional text, and ignore the intentions of those who drafted, enacted, and ratified that language. Their claim that a person with a noncitizen parent is not "subject to the jurisdiction" of the United States is contradicted by the Naturalization Act of 1790, which instructs that noncitizens, when in this country, reside "within the limits and under the jurisdiction of the United States."

The arguments of the Solicitor General and Mr. Collins would make U.S. citizenship oddly dependent on the laws of other nations – so that, in order to determine whether a person born on U.S. soil was a citizen of this country, one would first have to scrutinize the laws of other countries to see what claims those nations might make. They would render as noncitizens many thousands of persons born here, children of migrants from Europe, who have always understood themselves and been understood by others as fully American citizens.

Mr. Collins's theory that U.S. citizenship has all along passed through descent is fanciful. It has never been accepted by Congress, whose citizenship statutes have plainly contemplated *jus soli* as a default, and it was not accepted by the drafters of the fourteenth amendment. And given that Mr. Collins disclaims any argument that the fourteenth amendment altered pre-existing law, it is hardly clear when, in his estimation, the United States should be deemed to have adopted his rule. After all, no country followed that approach when our country came into existence. It had been entirely abandoned until a version of it reappeared, after our Revolution, in France's Code Napoleon.

Yet the flaws of this argument run far deeper. The Solicitor General, we should note, does seem to find Mr. Collins's approach appealing. His brief suggests magic citizenship-conferring qualities in a father's sperm, quoting Lord Mackenzie's *Roman Law* treatise for the proposition that the child becomes "a citizen, if the father was so, at the time of conception."

But we find that rule wholly unacceptable. It is predicated on the husband's legal ownership of the body of his wife, leading to the husband's heading the marital household and determining the citizenship of the children. All other contributions – those of mothers, family, and community – are negated in favor of male descent. Our law provides that an American woman who marries a noncitizen husband while continuing to reside in this country retains her U.S. citizenship. See *Shanks v. DuPont*, 28 U.S. 242 (1830). Yet the approach of the Solicitor General and Mr. Collins, in that circumstance, would elevate her husband's affiliations over not only her child's American place of birth but also over her own American citizenship.

While the traditional American *jus soli* rule accords weight and significance to the actions of Chinese women who crossed an ocean and overcame great odds to make a new home in the United States, the rule put forward here treats those women as if they did not exist, making the nationality of a child born in wedlock rest entirely on that of its father. That is an intolerable result.

We also cannot ignore the racism in the bones of these briefs. It is not a coincidence that those who champion the anti-Chinese cause are drawn to the approach of basing citizenship on bloodlines. Citizenship rules that allocate citizenship based on descent inherently perpetuate racial division. That is their nature – they allocate citizenship to one group of people, and deny it to another, based on who their parents and ancestors were. Mr. Collins makes plain that he regard that as a desirable feature. Approvingly citing *Dred Scott*, he urges that this nation was created primarily for the descendants of those individuals, residing in the United States in 1789, "who were at the time of the adoption of the Constitution recognized as citizens in the several States." We recognize that, as a historical matter, the vast bulk of those individuals traced their ancestry to somewhere in the British Isles, with Germany responsible for most of the rest.

But in selecting a *jus soli* rule for citizenship, our country has chosen another path. The *jus soli* rule embraces all those born within our borders as American citizens, regardless of background, bloodlines, or parentage. As such, it "has the effect of obliterating speedily and effectually disabilities of race, the existence of which within any community is generally an evil." *Report of a commission appointed by the Queen of Great Britain for inquiring into the laws of naturalization and allegiance* (May 21, 1868), § IV. Our strength lies in our embrace of all who migrate to our shores, and we would be mistaken to adopt a rule that narrows our family on the basis of descent or ancestry. Were we to adopt a rule of birthright citizenship for those born in the United States that allotted special rights based on (white) parentage, we would, in the words of Senator Sumner, establish "an Oligarchy inconsistent with Republican Government." *Cong. Globe*, 39th Cong., 1st Sess. 687 (Feb. 6, 1866).

Finally, the claim that our recognizing Mr. Wong's citizenship would implicate an inherently "absurd" or "monstrous" conception of dual allegiance is misguided. Our law has long recognized the United States citizenship of persons who can also claim citizenship in other nations. There is nothing new or disturbing about that. It began when Congress enacted the Naturalization Act of 1790, extending our citizenship to some "children of citizens of the United States, that may be born beyond sea." 1 Stat. 103, 104 (1790). Those individuals would have been recognized as citizens, at that time, by the countries of their births, and pursuant to this statute were recognized as citizens by the United States as well. *See, e.g., Calais v. Marshfield*, 30 Me. 511, 518 (1849) (persons granted citizenship by the Naturalization Act, as amended, "might at the same time be the subjects owing allegiance to the government of the country, in which they were born").

United States authorities have not found that prospect alarming. As President Grant's Secretary of State Hamilton Fish has put it, "[t]he child born of alien parents in the United States" is situated precisely analogously to the child of an American, satisfying statutory requirements, who is born overseas. The former is held to be a U.S. citizen notwithstanding that he may also be claimed as a citizen by some other nation, just as the latter can be claimed as a citizen both by the United States and by the country where he or she is born. *See Opinions of the Principal Officers of the Executive Departments, and Other Papers Relating to Expatriation, Naturalization, and Change of Allegiance* 17 (1873).

But more importantly, we reject the underlying premise of the "dual allegiance" argument. In its rigidity and hierarchy, this approach to citizenship apes the monarchical approach that its proponents criticize. It imagines a world of hierarchical relationships, in which one party may command, and the other must obey: ruler and subject, master and servant, parent and child, husband and wife. It emphasizes that once a person finds herself in the subordinate role, she can only serve and have loyalty to a single master.

That is not the world we choose for American law. In recognizing – as it has all along – that a person can be claimed as a citizen by more than one nation, American law properly recognizes multiplicity and the untidiness of human relationships. In the America we know, people may have multiple connections – to different governments, to different families, to different spheres of life. That is the nature, after all, of our federalism. Each of us is connected both to a state and a national government; all of us in this country have "a citizenship which owes allegiance to two sovereignties." *United States v. Cruikshank*, 923 U.S. 542, 550–51 (1875).

In our free society, our citizenship should be one of inclusion, one that recognizes community where it exists. The bonds that join us should be those of community, of sisterhood and brotherhood, rather than hierarchical subjecthood. We should not refuse, on the basis of race or parentage, to recognize our interconnections. We should not refuse to imagine that they can exist. Mr. Wong's community – his mother, his family, the larger group in which he grew up – was not supposed to exist, and yet it does, and it is part of this nation. Mr. Wong was born here and grew up here; he is part of our country, made up as it is of its overlapping communities. He has links to the nation and society in which his ancestors held membership, as does each and every one of us; we cherish those links rather than seeking to erase them. It is altogether appropriate that he be deemed a citizen of the United States.

Our law barred Mr. Wong's parents, Wong Li Ping and Wee Lee, from becoming U.S. citizens through naturalization. *See Chinese Exclusion Act*, § 14, 22 Stat. 58, 61 (1882) (no "court … shall admit Chinese to citizenship"); *In re Ah Yup*, 1 F. Cas. 223 (C.C.D. Cal. 1878) (reading U.S. naturalization statutes, as most recently amended in the Naturalization Act of 1870, 16 Stat. 254, 246, to reach the same result). That racist exclusion is a stain upon us. But its saving grace is that the harm it perpetuates exists only for a single generation. After that, we are all Americans.

IV. CONCLUSION

The decision of the district court, holding that Wong Kim Ark is a citizen of the United States, is affirmed.

5

Commentary on *United States v. Bhagat Singh Thind*, 261 U.S. 204 (1923)

Jaya Ramji-Nogales

Amidst contemporary debates on racial justice, *United States v. Bhagat Singh Thind* is a relatively obscure decision that might be discussed in a course on Race and American Law but is rarely touched on even in the survey Immigration Law course.[1] That oversight is unfortunate given the decision's role in the construction of Asian Americans as the foreign and inferior racial "other." Along with its companion case, *Ozawa v. United States*,[2] *Thind* excluded Asians from citizenship because of their race. In an era of widespread anti-Asian sentiment and violence, marked by the Chinese Exclusion Act of 1882[3] and its expansion to Indians, Japanese, and other Asians through the Immigration Act of 1917,[4] the Supreme Court chose to defer to populism and xenophobia, determining that Mr. Thind (like Mr. Ozawa before him) was not a "white person" within the meaning of the Naturalization Act of 1790.[5] Justice Sutherland's opinion demonstrates the agility and slipperiness of race as a concept, and its consequent utility in perpetuating extant power structures.[6] The continuities with subsequent immigration law and policy – and anti-Asian violence – are striking and disturbing. After briefly describing the decision, this Commentary examines those continuities and offers a critique of Justice Sutherland's opinion before discussing the opinion of Professor Joy Kanwar and the ways in which it upends the *Thind* decision.

ORIGINAL OPINION

The *Thind* case began when the Oregon Federal District Court awarded Mr. Thind a certificate of naturalization. The U.S. government filed a bill in equity to cancel that certificate, arguing that Mr. Thind was not a white person and therefore not

---

[1] United States v. Bhagat Singh Thind, 261 U.S. 204 (1923).
[2] Ozawa v. United States, 260 U.S. 178 (1922).
[3] Pub. L. No. 47-126, 22 Stat. 58 (1882).
[4] Pub. L. No. 64-301, 39 Stat. 874 (1917).
[5] Naturalization Act of 1790, Pub. L. No. 1-3, 1 Stat. 103 (1790).
[6] *See* Cheryl Harris, *Whiteness as Property*, 106 HARVARD L. REV. 1710, 1791 (1993).

eligible for naturalization.[7] This was a difficult needle for the Supreme Court to thread; just a few months prior, it had decided in *Ozawa* that "the words 'white person' are synonymous with the words 'a person of the Caucasian race,'" rejecting a test based on skin color.[8] In the eyes of the Court, this determination placed individuals born in Japan and "being of the Japanese race" squarely "outside the zone" of eligibility for citizenship. The *Ozawa* court left open a gray zone, noting that future cases falling "within the zone" of eligibility for citizenship would require a case-by-case determination. In *Thind*, the Court essentially found that being Caucasian was necessary but not sufficient to be viewed as a white person for the purposes of naturalization. Rejecting the scientific definition of Caucasian as excessively broad and its use as anachronistic, Justice Sutherland looked instead to the popular meaning of "white person" in 1790 and, defying his own critique, to the contemporary understanding of the term in 1923. This pretzel logic enabled him to determine that "a high-caste Hindu, of full Indian blood, born at Amritsar, Punjab, India" was not a "white person" for purposes of the Naturalization Act.

At the heart of the *Thind* decision is its analysis of race. Justice Sutherland's opinion demonstrates the multitude of ways in which race can be defined, enabling the concept to be put to work in service of entrenching hierarchies of power. In short, the *Thind* opinion is a paradigmatic example of populist judicial decision-making, turning as it does to the "common man's" definition of race at a time when popular perceptions were the basis for racist violence against Indians in the United States.[9]

The Court acknowledged that Caucasian is a race but argued that science classifies this category too broadly. The opinion spent some time justifying this position, first stating that a line of descent from a Caucasian ancestor is not sufficient. It explained that this common ancestor is "indefinitely remote" such that "the blond Scandinavian and the brown Hindu" have "ceased altogether to resemble one another." Acknowledging that "all mankind" has a common ancestor, the Court argued that the drafters of the 1790 Naturalization Act could not have meant to include all humans in the category of "white persons." The Court rejected ancestry as a basis for defining race, wriggling out from scientific categories by describing them as overly inclusive, and negating any claims of common humanity.

Faced with the reality that Mr. Thind could be considered Aryan as well as Caucasian, Justice Sutherland also rejected language as a grounds for defining race. He offered three reasons for this distinction. First, the Court described Aryan as a

---

[7]   The Naturalization Act of 1790 limited citizenship to "any alien, being a free white person, who shall have resided within the limits and under the jurisdiction of the United States for the term of two years." Naturalization Act of 1790, *supra* note 5. Citizenship was extended to persons of African descent and nativity in 1870. Naturalization Act of 1870, Pub. L. No. 254, 16 Stat. 254 (1870).

[8]   Ozawa, *supra* note 2, at 198.

[9]   *See generally* Vladislava Stoyanova, *Populism, Exceptionality, and the Right to Family Life of Migrants under the European Convention on Human Rights*, 10 EUR. J. LEGAL STUD. 83 (2018) (providing a theoretical framework for the concept of judicial populism).

linguistic category that does not pertain to "physical characteristics." Second, using reasoning similar to the assessment of a common ancestor, the opinion found that "a common linguistic root buried in remotely ancient soil" does not suffice to establish common racial origin. The Court made the cringe-worthy point that "millions of negroes" have learned to speak English but they "can never be classified racially with the descendants of white persons."

Finally, capitalizing on disagreement among scientists about racial categories, Justice Sutherland dispatched any claim that caste ensures racial purity or whiteness. He explained that there has been so much "intermixture of blood" between the "'Aryan' invader" and the "darkskinned Davidian" that Indians may not fit into any racial category. This analysis relied on the racial myth that high-caste Brahmins are descendants of Aryans from Central Asia and are not related to the indigenous population, particularly in the southern parts of India. Though this fiction is risible, it appeared to have been important to Mr. Thind to emphasize his "high-caste" ancestry in claiming to be a "white person."

After rejecting each of these bases for racial categorization – common ancestry, language, and racial purity – the Court turned to statutory interpretation through the framers' intent, asking who was considered white in 1790. Here, Justice Sutherland had his cake and ate it too. He explained that the congressional debates demonstrate that the words "free white persons" were intended to exclude Asians from citizenship. Yet he admitted that this debate does not enable judicial interpretation of the statute, drawing from that concession and the ambiguity of the statutory text his next move: that the Court should not at this time provide a clear definition of "white persons."

Finally, in a logical sleight-of-hand befitting Oz the Great and Terrible, Justice Sutherland leapt from that step to the conclusion that "white persons" should be interpreted according to "the understanding of the common man" or as "popularly understood." From that vantage, the outcome was obvious: Indians are not white because of their "physical group characteristics" that their descendants would "retain indefinitely." And of course, the Court was now able to put the 1917 Act to work, finding it to be "persuasive" of "the congressional attitude of opposition … toward Asiatic naturalization …, since it is not likely Congress would be willing to accept as citizens a class of persons whom it rejects as immigrants." This anachronistic understanding of congressional intent was exactly the move that Justice Sutherland decried just six pages earlier, explaining that it was "illogical to convert words of common speech used in a statute into words of scientific terminology when neither the latter nor the science for whose purposes they were coined was within the contemplation of the framers of the statute or of the people for whom it was framed." In case that logical crevasse was insufficient to leave the reader puzzled, the Court then described the decision that Indians are not "white persons" as implicating "merely racial difference," feigning that "[i]t is very far from our thought to suggest the slightest question of racial superiority or inferiority."

CONTINUITIES WITH CONTEMPORARY
IMMIGRATION LAW AND POLICY

The continuities with subsequent and contemporary immigration law and policy are numerous, from dehumanization to explicit racism, to the refutation and politicization of science, to ideological exclusion, and to retroactivity.

Justice Sutherland dehumanized Mr. Thind and the "yellow and brown races" more generally with little attention to the context or consequences. The Court failed to take into account the contemporary racial violence against Indians in the United States and the ways in which its decision would impact that deadly dynamic. The *Thind* decision had devastating ramifications for Indians in the United States, enabling the Bureau of Naturalization to begin denaturalization proceedings against them, court clerks to refuse to issue marriage licenses to Indian men who sought to marry white women, and District Attorneys to cancel contracts for land sales to Indians.[10] Unfortunately, this refusal to recognize the harms perpetrated against immigrants is paradigmatic throughout historical and contemporary immigration law; it is the rare jurist and the rarer majority opinion that describes and accounts for the violence that immigration law perpetrates against Asian Americans and other immigrants.

Another continuity with modern immigration law and policy is the explicit racism of the *Thind* decision. Though overt racism is less common in contemporary judicial opinions, it is of course now a feature of right-wing politics, while left-leaning administrations engage in anti-immigrant actions without the accompanying racist rhetoric. Justice Sutherland took pain to distinguish between the "blond Scandinavian and the brown Hindu," noting the "unmistakable and profound differences" between the two. He explained that the English, French, Germans, Italians, Scandinavians, and other Europeans "quickly merge into the mass of our population and lose the distinctive hallmarks of European origin" while those of Hindu parentage "retain indefinitely the clear evidence of their ancestry." This invidious distinction between immigrants of color and those of European descent is of course a familiar refrain in contemporary U.S. politics, reminiscent of Donald Trump's statement that the United States should not offer protections to nationals of "shithole countries" like El Salvador and Haiti and should instead accept immigrants from places like Norway.[11]

In addition to the populist method of explicit racism, Justice Sutherland's opinion utilizes the technique of refuting science to achieve political goals. He turned the Court away from deference to scientists, favoring instead a reliance on

---

[10] Sherally Munshi, *"You Will See My Family Become So American": Toward a Minor Comparativism*, 63 AM. J. COMP. L. 655, 659 (2015).

[11] Julie Hirschfeld Davis, Sheryl Gay Stolberg, & Thomas Kaplan, *Trump Alarms Lawmakers with Disparaging Words for Haiti and Africa*, N.Y. TIMES, Jan. 11, 2018, www.nytimes.com/2018/01/11/us/politics/trump-shithole-countries.html.

"unscientific men" to define race. Justice Sutherland disparaged the "science of ethnology," describing the "scientific manipulation" of the category of Caucasian, which includes not only Hindus but Polynesians and Hamites. He portrayed disagreement among scientists as demonstrative of the impossibility of determining a "proper racial division"; though he may have been correct on that particular point, his pivot to allocating definitional responsibility to the common knowledge of "unscientific men" defies logic. It is only through these logical contortions that the Court was able to determine that Mr. Thind can be Caucasian but not "a white person" as perceived at the time of the 1790 Act.

Beyond the pages of the opinion, the Supreme Court was engaging in ideological exclusion against Mr. Thind, who was politically active in the Indian resistance against British colonialism. The U.S. government had opposed Mr. Thind's application for naturalization because of his association with members of the Ghadr Party, a political party of Indian expatriates in Northern California and the Pacific Northwest that sought to overthrow British rule in India through military means. The District Court found that while Mr. Thind opposed the British occupation of India, he did not seek to end it through armed revolution. Taking into account Mr. Thind's "excellent" service in the army and the numerous attestations of his good character from U.S. citizens, the trial court approved his naturalization certificate.[12] The Supreme Court appeared instead to have capitulated to the British government's pressure to deny support to Indians in the United States who sought an end to their colonization of South Asia. Ideological exclusion through immigration law is, sadly, as American as apple pie, starting with the Alien and Sedition Acts of the 1790s and continuing through the Palmer Raids and the McCarran-Walter Act of 1952 to the current day.[13]

In addition, the *Thind* decision was applied retroactively to strip citizenship certificates from individuals of Indian descent who had previously been naturalized.[14] The practice of retroactive deportation has reappeared in subsequent immigration statutes, most notably for legal permanent residents in 1996, through the provisions of the Antiterrorism and Effective Death Penalty Act and the Illegal Immigration Reform and Immigrant Responsibility Act.[15] Despite the harsh consequences, the government's ability to upend the settled expectations of immigrants of color is not a relic of the past; it is perpetuated in statutes currently on the books.

---

[12] In re Thind, 268 F. 683, 684 (D. Or. 1920).

[13] Susan M. Akram, *Scheherezade Meets Kafka: Two Dozen Sordid Tales of Ideological Exclusion*, 14 GEO. IMMIGR. L. J. 51, 55–56 (1999); Michael Price, *Trump's Immigration Order May Violate Ideological Exclusion Rule*, BRENNAN CTR. JUSTICE (Feb. 1, 2017), www.brennancenter.org/our-work/analysis-opinion/trumps-immigration-order-may-violate-ideological-exclusion-rule

[14] *See, e.g.*, U.S. v. Khan, 1 F.2d 1006, 1008 (W.D. Pa. 1924).

[15] Nancy Morawetz, *Rethinking Retroactive Deportation Laws and the Due Process Clause*, 73 N.Y.U. L. REV. 97, 99 (1998).

THE FEMINIST JUDGMENT

Justice Sutherland's approach is ripe for feminist intervention; though feminist legal methods are diverse, one relatively common thread is the call for attentiveness to the human side of legal problems, and to our shared humanity and vulnerability.[16] Thus a feminist judgment is one that humanizes the legal subject and is cognizant of and compassionate to the real-world consequences of legal decisions. It is into this morass that Professor Kanwar, writing as Justice Kanwar, intervenes to make four important interventions through her rewritten opinion.

She begins by humanizing Mr. Thind by providing historical context as well as a detailed personal history of the human and his journey.[17] Kanwar presents an accurate and nuanced description of his journey to the United States, one that encompasses his religion and culture as well as his service in the U.S. Army. Kanwar also sets the context, describing the contemporary violence against Indians in the United States. Rather than obscuring the political underpinnings of the case against Mr. Thind, she brings them forward and debunks them. Each of these feminist methods – humanization, contextualization, and dismantling claims to neutrality that obscure political choices – serves the opinion well.[18]

Kanwar next provides a comprehensive and accurate history of racial exclusion through citizenship, describing dissenting congressional views on racial exclusion and historical harms perpetrated under the guise of race, including limited access to rights. She begins by adding complexity to the history offered by Justice Sutherland, describing Senator Sumner's effort to strike racial language from the Naturalization Act and demonstrating that congressional intent was not monolithic. Kanwar draws a crucially important parallel to the denial of full citizenship rights to African Americans, using the examples of suffrage and jury service to upend claims that racial distinctions in citizenship are anything other than invidious.

One of Kanwar's key interventions concerns the fluidity of whiteness as a concept. As she explains, the term "white person" "cannot be defined in a way that is both fixed and makes sense." Given that "white" encompasses a broad range of skin and hair colors, she explains that a color test would be impracticable. Moreover, Kanwar notes that nearly every immigrant group has been subject to anti-immigrant sentiment; in other words, the content of race as a concept shifts over time. This is why the Court struggled to define race, looking to different measures, including a

---

[16] *See, e.g.*, Martha Albertson Fineman, *The Vulnerable Subject: Anchoring Equality in the Human Condition*, 20 YALE J. L. & FEMINISM 1 (2008) (presenting a theoretical framework for the concept of vulnerability).

[17] To recount the story of Mr. Thind, the feminist judgment draws on sources published after his death, including AMANDA DE LA GARZA, DOCTORJI: THE LIFE, TEACHINGS, AND LEGACY OF DR. BHAGAT SINGH THIND (2010).

[18] RATNA KAPUR, MAKESHIFT MIGRANTS AND LAW: GENDER, BELONGING, AND POSTCOLONIAL ANXIETIES 3, 10–11, 19–23 (2010); *see also* THIS BRIDGE CALLED MY BACK: WRITINGS BY RADICAL WOMEN OF COLOR (Cherríe Moraga & Gloria Anzaldúa eds., 1983).

common person's understanding, science, precedent, and even "ocular inspection." It also struggled to situate itself in time, veering backwards and forwards between 1790 and 1923. This insight takes the Court's reasoning to its logical end: race is so malleable as to be meaningless and should as a result be removed from the statute.

Finally, Kanwar explains the work that the concept "white person" is doing in the statute and beyond: it is manipulating whiteness for exclusion through allegations of inability to assimilate. The Court's shifting definition, from scientific to populist, enabled the use of whiteness to exclude certain groups, allegedly on the basis of their "failure to assimilate" but more likely because of their anti-colonial political activities. Kanwar's interventions offer ample justification for her bold and thoughtful conclusion: the racial language in the 1790 Naturalization Act should be struck by Congress. If the Congress had eliminated racial language from the Naturalization Act in 1923, it could have prevented a range of harms that Indians suffered as a result of *Thind*. Citizenship, marriage, and land ownership would have been available not only to Indians but to all Asians, and indeed to all humans regardless of their country of origin and race.

Had the Court followed Kanwar's opinion by allowing Mr. Thind to naturalize, it could have sent an important expressive message that delegitimized political violence against Indians in the United States. This was a missed opportunity for the Court to humanize Indians and incorporate them into the fabric of American society. Had it done so, the demographic shifts playing out currently in the United States might have occurred decades earlier, which might have enabled the more effective pursuit of racial justice and dismantling of racial hierarchies. Kanwar's methods – humanization, dismantling race, and foregrounding the work that race is performing – could have led the Court to a logically sound and human-centered – dare I say feminist – outcome.

UNITED STATES v. BHAGAT SINGH THIND, 261 U.S. 204 (1923)

Justice Joy Kanwar, dissenting.

I cannot agree with my fellow Justices. While the power of this Court to shape and interpret law is mighty indeed, I feel that the majority has erred today. The Court settles upon a concept of whiteness so arbitrary that it cannot be defined, and as such, cannot be applied.

The Court's overall responsibility in this area would serve all concerned better if it would have adopted another approach. Since at least 1906, the officers in the naturalization field have looked to the federal courts for consistency on the matter of who constitutes a free white person, and over the same period, popular passions and economic insecurity have informed racial exclusions in the adjacent legislative field of immigration. This Court finally took up the question of who qualifies as a free white person for the purposes of the naturalization statute three months ago in *Ozawa v. United States*, 260 U.S. 178 (1922), and now again with a different applicant, Bhagat Singh Thind. In both cases, the Court misses the opportunity to question the category itself, and further, from a consistency standpoint, it does not even follow its own reasoning in *Ozawa* as to Mr. Thind's application.

The Court was asked to determine "whether a high-caste Hindu, a native of India, of full Indian blood, born at Amritsar, Punjab, India, is a white person within the meaning of section 2169, Revised Statutes." Justice Sutherland, penning the majority opinion, answers in the negative. Since the *Ozawa* decision, the question here really has become what the courts should do in each borderline case of a free white person seeking naturalization. Or to put a point on it, the question as only this Court can ask and answer is whether it continues to make sense to police the status of free white person for the purposes of section 2169 of the Revised Statutes. I conclude that it does not.

As the Court does today, to use the concept of "a common white person's understanding" of who is white not only serves to highlight its circular nature, but also reflects that the category contracts and expands to allow in only those immigrants that American society deems as white at a current moment in time. This is so regardless of whether the framers of the original 1790 statute would have contemplated such groups or whether such groups would have been welcomed or valued as citizens when they arrived in this country over a century later. Such a definition becomes a moving target for applicants and courts alike, one that the majority has used today to shut out naturalization of people from India, and in a larger sense, from Asia complete.

Today's decision may have far-reaching consequences, far beyond the impact on Mr. Thind alone. What happens if such a decision is applied retroactively to persons who were already naturalized and who have relied upon such a status to make a life for themselves in this country, including to marry, raise a family, buy or rent land, or start businesses? I caution this Court about the unintended – but not altogether unlikely – consequences of today's decision. Both the implication and inclination will be toward denaturalization.

I

Background

Bhagat Singh Thind was born on October 3, 1892, in the Amritsar district of Punjab, India. *In re Thind*, 268 F. 683, 683 (D. Or. 1920). This district lies in the far northwestern part of India and was part of the Sikh empire from 1749 to 1849 before being taken over by the British Raj along with the rest of India. Although we refer to all people from India as Hindus (although preferably not "Hindoos") in our day and age, Mr. Thind was raised in and continues to practice in the Sikh faith, which was founded in the late fifteenth century. Resp't Br. 15; *Who Are Sikhs?*, Berkeley

Daily Gazette (Dec. 6, 1922). Mr. Thind's contention that he is a "high-caste Hindu" makes sense for the purposes of this matter because this would accurately describe his heritage before Sikhism was established.

In 1908, Mr. Thind enrolled in Khalsa College in the Sikh holy city of Amritsar and became interested in America after reading Emerson, Whitman, Thoreau, and other Enlightenment scholars. He graduated with honors from college and decided to come to the United States to further his studies at the University of California, Berkeley. On July 4, 1913, after arriving at port in Seattle at the age of 20, Mr. Thind was admitted as an immigrant into the United States. *See In re Thind*, 268 F. at 683–84.

Around the same time, many Punjabi immigrants were coming to the west coast of the United States. *See* Girindra Mukerji, *The Hindu in America*, Overland Monthly, Apr. 1908, at 303–06. Immigrants from India arrived in smaller numbers than the Chinese and Japanese communities before them and were initially welcomed as labor to the west coast as "full-blooded Aryan" brothers. Agnes Foster Buchanan, *The West and the Hindu Invasion*, Overland Monthly, Apr. 1908, at 309. However, these communities quickly became the new "peril" to local nativist economic interests. *Id.* In 1908, the Overland Monthly observed:

> While the Chinese stood knocking at our outer doors, which had been barred and closed by legislation, their neighbors, not waiting for permission, crept stealthily past the suppliants, entered and took possession. When San Francisco awoke from her short sleep, she found herself face to face with the Japanese question, infinitely greater and more insidious in its influence than the Chinese problem had ever threatened to be, for while the yellow men had raised a labor question, their brown brothers have created an industrial one.… But unlike the other visitors, this last is a brother of our own race—a full-blooded Aryan, men of like progenitors with us. The Hindus and the Hindu Invasion is the latest racial problem with which we of the West have to deal with. *Id.*

Mr. Thind arrived at a time when other members of the Punjabi immigrant community had already faced violent retribution in the Pacific Northwest. For example, a nativist mob infamously beat Indian immigrants and destroyed their homes in Bellingham, Washington, effectively running the community out of town in 1907. *See* Werter D. Dodd, *The Hindu in the Northwest*, 13 World Today 1157 (1907). Like many Punjabis before him, Mr. Thind worked at an Oregon lumber mill, using his earnings to put himself through school. Further, Mr. Thind believed that India should be free of British rule, a cause championed by the Ghadr press, a newspaper out of San Francisco. *Exclusion of Hindus from America due to British Influence* 17–19 (Ram Chandra ed., 1916). During the Great War, he voluntarily enlisted in the U.S. Army at Camp Lewis, Washington and was honorably discharged at the end of the war in 1918. Resp't Br. 4, 34. He was the first person of the Sikh faith to wear his turban while enlisted and achieved the rank of sergeant.

In his decision below, District Court Judge Wolverton recounted his position on Mr. Thind as follows: "since his entry into this country, the applicant's deportment has been that of a good citizen, attached to the Constitution of the United States." *In re Thind*, 268 F. at 684. While he did not believe Mr. Thind favored any violence on behalf of the Ghadr cause, he noted that Mr. Thind "frankly admits, nevertheless, that he is an advocate of the principle of India for the Indians and would like to see India rid of British rule." *Id.* Judge Wolverton was convinced by the corroboration of disinterested citizens who were "most favorably impressed by his deportment, and manifestly believe in his attachment to the principles of this government." *Id.* By this account, Mr. Thind the individual, even with his ideals for an India free of British rule, should be a candidate for naturalization.

Of course, the question to the Court is whether anyone who is a "high-caste Hindu, of full Indian blood" and a native of India, including from Amritsar, Punjab, should be considered "a free white person" by the meaning of Section 2169 of the Revised Statutes. Although the question of who is considered a "free white person" under this statute has been taken up in District and Circuit Courts around the country since the late 1800s, this Court took up its first case interpreting the meaning of these words in *Ozawa* in November 1922, just three months ago. This case plays a major part in how we understand and shape this category.

II

A Brief History of Whiteness in the Naturalization Act

The Naturalization Act, originally enacted in 1790, limited naturalization to those persons in this country for two years (amended in 1795 to "five years") who could demonstrate that they were "free white" men. Ch. 3, 1 Stat. 103 (1790). At the time of enactment, the statute excluded from naturalization all persons who were enslaved,[19] those from the original native communities of this country, and women.[20]

The Act opened naturalization to everyone who was adult, male and white, regardless of whether that person had a stake in society, such as property ownership or one's own steady income. Ostensibly, this was meant to encompass every white male settler, but the reality of who was considered white once the waves of immigration began over the next century became an open question. Did the concept of white include only Anglo-Saxon Protestants, as had been in the early wave

---

[19] The 14th Amendment eventually overruled Dred Scott v. Sandford, 60 U.S. 393, 404 (1856).

[20] All married women used to have their citizenship tied to their husbands' status. Citizenship and Expatriation Act of 1907, ch. 2534, 34 Stat. 1228 (1907). While the Cable Act changed this rule for many women, it continued to revoke citizenship from women who married a specific subset of non-citizens who were ineligible to naturalize, a group primarily comprised of Asian men. Pub. L. No. 67-346, 42 Stat. 1021 (1922).

of English immigration? Or did it include Celts? Did it include all Europeans, such as the Germans and Dutch who came in the mid-nineteenth century, or the Catholic Italians and European Jews who came at the end of the century? As the country was determining who would be considered fully American for the purposes of citizenship, the expansion of democratic ideals encompassed European groups who were not in this country in measurable numbers in 1790, when the terms "free" and "white" were created within the act. See *Thind*, 261 U.S. at 213–15.

After the enactment of the 14th Amendment, Congress again took up the question of who should be able to naturalize. It ultimately revised the statute in 1870 to add "persons of African descent" and "aliens of African nativity" while leaving intact the original provision for free white persons. Ch. 254, 16 Stat. 254 (1870). Unlike those who would come to be understood as white, when citizenship came for the Black community in this country, it came piecemeal. It came only a part at a time and never whole like that accorded to immigrant men who met the definition of free and white, regardless of the latter's wealth or landowning status. Let us review, for example, the history of our cases from *Dred Scott*, 60 U.S. at 393, to *United States v. Reese*, 92 U.S. 214 (1876) and *Strauder v. West Virginia*, 100 U.S. 303 (1879).

Notably, on July 4, exactly forty-three years before Mr. Thind immigrated to this country, Senator Charles Sumner called upon Congress to strike the reference to "white" persons altogether in the debates leading up to the 1870 amendment. Cong. Globe, 41st Cong., 2d Sess. 5149. Sumner insisted that racial categories did not meet the spirit of the Declaration of Independence. *Id.* at 5155. Opponents argued that leaving out the racial language would allow Chinese immigrants to naturalize, which became the flashpoint of the debate that day. *Id.* at 5150. Senator William Stewart summarized the matter as follows: European immigrants "are of our own race … and assimilate rapidly," but "Chinese civilization is at war with ours." *Id.* at 5152. The Senate first denied, then approved, and finally rejected, Sumner's proposal. *Id.* at 5168, 5171, 5177.

It is important that we in 1923 remember Sumner's final words on that day: "Do not lose this special opportunity … [that] comes to you now unexpectedly.… Use it. Use it wisely; use it bravely; use it so that you will secure peace, harmony, and reconciliation." *Id.* at 5172. It is with hindsight that we see the historical moment – a moment when notions of inclusion and exclusion pulled in different directions. Yet Congress did not define who was considered white neither in 1790 when the act was passed, nor in the 1870 revision afterwards. This was true even when the words "free" and "white" were inadvertently left out of the act in an 1875 revision and later put back in. See *Ozawa*, 260 U.S. at 195. This leaves the term open to interpretation, and as litigants and our federal courts have been attempting to determine for decades, "what is white?" See, e.g., *Ex Parte Shahid*, 205 F. 812 (E.D.S.C. 1913).

III

The Fluidity of Whiteness

I contend that this word, as it is used in this statute, cannot be defined in a way that it is both fixed and makes sense. As Congress did not define the term, the Bureau of Immigration and Naturalization in 1906 sought that federal courts provide clarity when it asked for a uniform standard. It should have become obvious when the courts below struggled to find a standard, employing as they have the common person's understanding, scientific standard, precedent, and even "ocular inspection." It should have become further obvious when this mighty Court could not clearly articulate the role of ethnographic science as opposed to the common understanding of Caucasian between *Ozawa* and this case. More importantly, even the standard that the majority settled upon today for an "understanding of the common man" of white speaks of two formulations – one that includes those that the "fathers" (interestingly, rather than framers) understood as white in 1790 and separately, those immigrants that would be included over time. *Thind*, 261 U.S at 207, 214. These are not necessarily harmonious standards. Therein lies the problem.

I begin with the observation Mr. Thind makes that "words in a statute, other than technical terms, should be taken in their ordinary sense," and that the words white person "taken in a strictly literal sense, *constitute a very indefinite descriptions of a class of persons* where none can be said to be literally white, and those called white may be found of every shade from the lightest blonde to the most swarthy brunette." Resp't Br. 38 (emphasis added).

I note that the unanimous Court in *Ozawa* agreed with this idea that "none can be said to be literally white" and that a color test would be impracticable for the purposes of this matter:

> Manifestly the test afforded by the mere color of the skin of each individual is impracticable, as that differs greatly among persons of the same race, even among Anglo-Saxons, ranging by imperceptible gradations from the fair blond to the swarthy brunette, the latter being darker than many of the lighter hued persons of the brown or yellow races. Hence to adopt the color test alone would result in a confused overlapping of races and a gradual merging of one into the other, without any practical line of separation. *Ozawa*, 260 U.S. at 197.

The majority, however, still attempted to find that "practical line of separation." *Id.* Justice Sutherland reminds us from *Ozawa* that "[t]he intention was to confer the privilege of citizenship upon that class of persons whom the fathers knew as white, and to deny it to all who could not be so classified." *Thind*, 261 U.S. at 207 (citing *Ozawa*, 260 U.S. at 195). The trouble, of course, is that this line has been shifting over time.

Benjamin Franklin, one of our founding fathers, did not seem to welcome all persons that our majority would unquestionably include as white under the section

2169 of the Revised Statute when he asked: "Why should Pennsylvania, founded by the English, become a Colony of Aliens, who will shortly be so numerous as to Germanize us instead of our Anglifying them, and will never adopt our Language or Customs, any more than they can acquire our Complexion." Benjamin Franklin, *Observations Concerning the Increase of Mankind, Peopling of Countries, & c.* (1751).

In contrast, the majority indicates in today's decision an expanded notion of the term. These include "immigrants from Eastern, Southern and Middle Europe, among them the Slavs and the dark-eyed, swarthy people of Alpine and Mediterranean stock" who would be "received as *unquestionably akin to those already here* and readily amalgamated with them." *Thind*, 261 U.S. at 213 (emphasis added). The irony is that the people the Court names as "unquestionably akin," *id.*, were often not welcomed in practice once they actually arrived here. Active "homegrown" political movements countered immigrant labor and political participation, organizing to keep new immigrants – even those who looked white – from naturalizing.[21]

When a term is so vague, its application cannot lead to consistent results. Here, I contend that the word "white" is undefinable. The term changes based on who is considered white at the time. Immigrants from Germany, Italy, Eastern Europe, and Ireland all successfully became "white" over time, but were part of the wave of immigrants who were not immediately – or consistently – categorized as such upon coming to the United States. When such a term has a great import for life and liberty, this Court must tread carefully in addressing such an undefinable term.

IV

Inconsistency with Ozawa

Today, the majority chooses to draw a line based on an arbitrary distinction. Mr. Thind argues that as a high-caste Hindu from Punjab, he is of the Caucasian race. Resp't Br. 2–3. He notes that "[a]s ordinarily used everywhere in the United States, one would scarcely fail to understand that the party employing the words 'white persons' would intend a person of the Caucasian race." Resp't Br. 38–39. It may be to Mr. Thind's great surprise that this Court ruled against his naturalization when this Court in *Ozawa* held that the applicant, a person of Japanese origin who lived in the United States continuously for twenty-eight years and raised his family here, could not be eligible for naturalization because he was not a "Caucasian." *Ozawa*, 260 U.S. at 189, 198.

---

[21] A growing eugenics movement aims to purify the white race, referring to "southern Italians, Mediterraneans and Jews" as unassimilable people who could destroy the "Aryan race." Madison Grant, *The Passing of the Great Race*, (1917). A counter-movement claims that race and identity are culturally determined rather than biologically ordained. *See, e.g.*, Franz Boas, *Changes in the Bodily Form of Descendants of Immigrants*, 14 AM. ANTHROPOLOGIST 530 (1912).

Many aspects of the majority opinion seem to rely upon reasoning in clear opposition to *Ozawa*. First, the Court in *Ozawa* expressly relied upon certain district court cases to deny Mr. Ozawa citizenship that would indicate an opposite result for Mr. Thind. For example, in *In re Mohan Singh*, the court granted citizenship to a high-caste Hindu, finding that:

> [I]n the absence of any more definite expression by Congress, which is the body possessing the power to determine who may lawfully apply for naturalization, any members of the white or Caucasian race, possessing the proper qualifications in every other respect, are entitled to admission under the general wording of the statute respecting 'all free white persons.'

257 F. 209, 212 (S.D. Cal. 1919). Similarly, in *In re Mozumdar*, the court granted citizenship to a native of India on the basis that "it is now settled, by the great weight of authority, at least, that it was the intention of Congress to confer the privilege of naturalization upon members of the Caucasian race only," further noting that "[i]t is likewise true that certain of the natives of India belong to that race." 207 F. 115, 117 (E.D. Wash. 1913). In fact, in *Ozawa*, Justice Sutherland compliments these courts on their well-reasoned opinions on the matter: "[W]e should not at this late day feel at liberty to disturb it, in the absence of reasons far more cogent than any that have been suggested." 260 U.S. at 197.

Second, Justice Sutherland continues to twist the category of Caucasian to fit his purposes. Sutherland previously conjured up the category as a sword to exclude Mr. Ozawa and then, in this case, where the same definition should have shielded Mr. Thind from exclusion, it was again redefined to reject Mr. Thind as well. In *Ozawa*, he indicates that Caucasian is synonymous with white. *Id*. at 198. Notably, he relies on science when he indicates that the federal and state courts have decided naturalization issues correctly: "These decisions are sustained by numerous scientific authorities, which we do not deem it necessary to review. We think these decisions are right and so hold." *Id*.

This Court used their definition of Caucasian – as defined by previous cases and scientific authority – to deny entry to Mr. Ozawa, who by all other accounts the Court finds to be "well qualified by character and education for citizenship," *id*. at 189, because he falls outside of the current ethnographic, linguistic, and social scientific understanding of Caucasian. Yet when it comes to Mr. Thind, who would be understood to be Caucasian (as well as Aryan) by these standards, the Court throws out this category in favor of what a common person would understand the phrase "free white persons" to mean. *Thind*, 261 U.S. at 214. With this decision, therefore, the Court creates a new category of legal person today – the non-white Caucasian – who is closed out of the naturalization process in the United States.

Nor does the majority's discussion about legislative intent help to clarify these inconsistencies. It claims that the reinsertion of "free white persons" in the 1875 version of the Naturalization Act indicates that the category was meant to be exclusive rather than inclusive. *Id.* at 214. The majority argues that if Congress meant to include others who were neither white nor of African ancestry, it would have specified so in its language. But simply understanding that Congress meant to keep this category intact does nothing to clarify who is in the category itself. It is impossible to square all these different definitions of the category, including who the framers considered white in 1790; who was included as white in 1870 from among the groups that were immigrating at that time; who is included according to scientific ethnographic categories in *Ozawa*; and now, according to the majority, who the "common man" would include in this category.

If this Court means to have favored the common understanding standard, why speak of the Caucasian category at all in the *Ozawa* decision? While the Court may today choose to distance itself from cases that it approved of just three months ago, nothing in today's majority decision indicates that they are doing so. The reason may be that the science suited the aims of keeping Mr. Ozawa from naturalizing in the former case, but would not be entirely effective in keeping out Mr. Thind. To achieve the end it seeks, the Court therefore refutes the science and relies upon the common person. *Thind*, 261 U.S. at 209. As I will explore next, this resulting inconsistency makes more sense if the reasoning is understood as a way to simply reinforce exclusion.

V

Whiteness as Exclusion

In today's majority decision, the Court says: "What we now hold is that the words 'free white persons' are words of common speech, to be interpreted in accordance with the understanding of the common man, synonymous with the word 'Caucasian' only as that word is popularly understood." *Thind*, 261 U.S. at 214–15. The Court clearly chooses a populist alternative to the science it formerly relied upon in the *Ozawa* decision, and at the same time reinforces the idea that ethnology cannot trump the observation of the common man as to who qualifies as Caucasian or white: "[W]hatever may be the speculations of the ethnologist, it does not include the body of people to whom the appellee belongs." *Id.* at 215. Unlike the children of "English, French, German, Italian, Scandinavian, and other European parentage" who "quickly merge into the mass of our population and lose the distinctive hallmarks of their European origin," the Court states that those of "Hindu parents would retain indefinitely the clear evidence of their ancestry" and that "the great body of our people instinctively recognize it and reject the thought of assimilation." *Id.* Despite the majority's claim that "it is very far from our thought to suggest the slightest question of racial superiority or inferiority," *id.*, the Court does not acknowledge the hierarchy it creates by choosing such a test.

Here, now, is the crux of the matter. Who is assimilable in our society and who is not? In other words, who gets excluded? This seems to be the real test, which we

today have created by placing Mr. Thind on the other side of the border in a borderline case. Do the courts need to continue to police a line that is indefinite in the
first place? From a forward-looking perspective, what about the fact that such a line
leaves no room for immigrants who have otherwise met every standard for being an
American, as Mr. Thind has?

Judge Wolverton of the District Court of Oregon emphasized Mr. Thind's ability
to "westernize" himself and assimilate into American society, commenting that his
"character [has been] designated as excellent" by his commanding officer in the U.S.
Army and that he "professes a genuine affection for the Constitution, laws, customs,
and privileges of this country." *In re Thind*, 268 F. at 684. Like Mr. Ozawa before him,
he also possessed a high degree of education and knowledge of American culture.

Yet the Court finds that Mr. Thind is not assimilable today. The United States,
despite acknowledging that Mr. Thind is Caucasian as the word is currently understood, argued that the caste system made the people of India unassimilable. Part of
Mr. Thind's argument is that he had a claim to the Aryan heritage because of the
ways in which the caste system, as practiced in India, has for generations preserved
itself and its assigned statuses in society by preventing marriage and social mobility between the groups. The United States, however, uses the caste system in India
to argue that "at the time the first naturalization law was passed the Hindus were
regarded as a people wholly alien to Western civilization and utterly incapable of
assimilation to Western habits and customs, mode of life, political and social institutions." Br. for U.S. 14.

Further, Mr. Thind's relationship with the United States as a subject of the
British Empire may have played a role in determining his assimilability. The
U.S. Bureau of Investigation official, for example, informed the District Court of
Mr. Thind's political activities and of the United States and British intelligence
interest in the Ghadr party. Letter from Acting Chief, Bureau of Investigation, U.S.
Dep't of Justice to W.R. Byron, Esq. (June 24, 1919). Based on communications
provided by British intelligence officers, the Bureau identified Mr. Thind as within
a cohort of Hindus "prepared to help the radical element in this country at any
time," a belief they brought to the District Court's attention during his naturalization process. *See id.* The United States in its brief argues:

> The people of India were a subject-race, and, while the ideals of liberty, equality
> and fraternity were being preached in Europe and America, there is no reason to
> believe that any one seriously extended their applications to the people of India,
> or believed that those people were of the kind to be assimilated in citizenship in
> Western civilization.

Br. for U.S. 10. It cannot be that one's status as a colonial subject of a Western power
makes a person categorically unable to assimilate into the United States. Indeed,
there is something ironic about making such a distinction in a country that was
formerly comprised of colonies.

VI

The Potential Consequences of Today's Decision

Today, the Court rules on a question of the highest order. This decision may impact the life and liberty of those who have already been naturalized and all those people who are impacted by that individual's naturalization. Simply put, what happens if this decision is applied retroactively?

The impact will be devastating to those naturalized persons who own property, who are otherwise barred from ownership unless a citizen. *See, e.g.*, Alien Land Law, Initiative Measure No. 1 (1920). Greater still will be the impact on those, like Mr. Thind, who are subjects of the British crown but have already been naturalized as Americans. If they are stripped of their citizenship and have already renounced their British citizenship, they will be left stateless, between two worlds yet protected by none. This is also true of women who married naturalized citizens, only to find that those persons are no longer American citizens. It is still the law of this land that a woman's citizenship can be revoked if she marries a noncitizen man who is ineligible to naturalize. Those women will likewise be rendered among the stateless.

I harken back to Charles Sumner's solution nearly fifty years ago – remove the racial prerequisite language from the Revised Statutes. It no longer makes sense for our federal courts to police a term that cannot be defined. Our mighty Court demonstrated not once, but twice over the last three months how we are unable to reasonably determine what the meaning of white is, first in *Ozawa* and now in the present case. I dissent today on the matter of Bhagat Singh Thind's naturalization because our Court has failed to provide a reasonable and consistent interpretation of this statute and further ask that Congress recognize that all involved would be better served by striking the racial prerequisite language of a "free white" person in our naturalization laws.

6

Commentary on *Landon v. Plasencia*, 459 U.S. 21 (1982)

Sabrina Balgamwalla

In *Landon v. Plasencia* (1982), the Supreme Court considered whether a lawful permanent resident's attempt to return to the United States after a weekend trip to Mexico was an "entry" under § 101(a)(13) of the Immigration and Nationality Act (INA). The answer determined what kind of a hearing she would receive. The Court, in an 8-1 decision, determined that Maria Plasencia[1] was accorded sufficient due process in an exclusion hearing – in which she was found inadmissible due to her engagement in human smuggling – and that she was not entitled to the more robust process (and due process protections) of a deportation hearing. Professor Erin Corcoran, writing here as Justice Corcoran, has drafted a dissenting opinion that centers the discussion of due process on Maria Plasencia's interests in her immigration status and the principle of family unity, while laying bare the assumptions and anxieties about Central American migration at the heart of Justice Sandra Day O'Connor's original opinion.

BACKGROUND

On Friday, June 27, 1975, Maria and Joseph Plasencia made the two-hour drive from their home in Los Angeles, just over the border to Tijuana. Maria Plasencia, a citizen of El Salvador, was a lawful permanent resident (LPR) of the United States and a mother of four children. Her husband, Joseph Plasencia, was a U.S. citizen. Cross-border trips were not uncommon for denizens of southern California. Joseph was going to inquire about the cost of getting some dental work done, and the couple planned to do some shopping. However, this trip did not end like a routine weekend

---

[1] Many judicial opinions refer to parties by last name only, or as "respondent." Katharine T. Bartlett has noted the significance of including first names to "humanize and particularize," especially women, for whom "[f]irst names have been one dignified way in which women could distinguish themselves from their fathers and husbands." *See* Katharine T. Bartlett, *Feminist Legal Methods*, 103 HARV. L. REV. 829, fn. 1 (1990). Both the opinion and the commentary use the full name of Maria Plasencia and other noncitizen parties in other Supreme Court cases as a way of honoring the individuals whose lives were altered by these legal proceedings.

visit. As they sought to re-enter the United States on Sunday night, Maria Plasencia was taken into Immigration and Naturalization Service (INS) custody and scheduled to appear in court for an exclusion hearing the next morning.

While in Mexico, the Plasencias had met a number of Salvadoran nationals staying at their hotel. According to Maria Plasencia's testimony at her exclusion hearing, her husband had wanted to help some of them, and the couple agreed to drive six Salvadorans across the border to the United States. Some of the children in the car carried travel documents that belonged to the Plasencias' children. Based on these facts, Maria Plasencia was charged with inadmissibility under Section 212(a) (31) of the INA, which at the time denied a noncitizen admission when they "knowingly and for gain, encouraged, induced, assisted, abetted, or aided any alien to enter or to try to enter the United States in violation of the law." In her brief exclusion proceeding, Maria Plasencia was found to have engaged in human smuggling. Unable to appeal, she filed a writ of habeas corpus and was paroled into the United States, where she has apparently remained for the rest of her life.[2]

Law of Entry, Grounds of Inadmissibility, and the Privileges of Permanent Residence

The INA lays out two alternative processes for determining whether a noncitizen can enter or remain in the United States: exclusion proceedings and deportation proceedings. The Supreme Court's majority opinion in *Landon v. Plasencia* focuses on what level of due process is required for a noncitizen seeking entry to the United States, and whether LPR Maria Plasencia was in fact "entering" the United States as a matter of law upon her return from Tijuana.

Plasencia is grounded in the idea of borders as an expression of sovereignty, relying on *United States ex rel. Knauff v. Shaughnessy* as precedent.[3] In 1941, Congress authorized the Attorney General to deny entry to a noncitizen "if it were found that such entry would be prejudicial to the interest of the United States."[4] The regulations promulgated under the Act allowed the Attorney General to find a noncitizen excludable on that basis without a hearing, based on the premise that disclosure of the relevant information would harm the public interest.[5] In 1948, while attempting to immigrate to the United States as a war bride, Ellen Knauff was detained at Ellis Island for three years on allegations of espionage. Immigration officials claimed that

---

[2]   In addition to the transcripts and other documentation from the Immigration Court proceeding, Kevin R. Johnson's compassionate account of the case and accompanying investigation influenced this opinion and commentary. *See* Kevin R. Johnson, "*Maria and Joseph Plasencia's Lost Weekend: The Case of* Landon v. Plasencia," in David A. Martin and Peter H. Schuck eds., IMMIGRATION STORIES (2005).

[3]   338 U. S. 537, 338 U. S. 542 (1950).

[4]   Act of June 21, 1941, amending § 1 of the Act of May 22, 1918, 55 Stat. 252, 22 U.S.C. § 223, 22 U.S.C.A. § 223.

[5]   18 C.F.R. § 175.53(b) (1941).

her presence in the United States was a threat to national security, but they did not reveal their evidence and did not provide Ellen Knauff with an explanation as to why she was not allowed to enter the country. Justice Frankfurter's scathing dissent laments the lack of due process in her case, in which "the deepest tie that an American soldier could form may be secretly severed on the mere say-so of an official."[6] The majority in *Knauff*, however, maintained that "[w]hatever the procedure authorized by Congress is, it is due process as far as an alien denied entry is concerned."[7]

Three years later, in *Shaughnessy v. U.S. ex rel. Mezei*, the Supreme Court reiterated that for a noncitizen "on the threshold of initial entry" there is no right to a hearing, but that noncitizens "who have once passed through our gates, even illegally" require a hearing that conforms to due process standards.[8] The *Plasencia* majority noted that a deportation hearing – "the usual means of proceeding against an alien already physically in the United States" – generally takes place in an immigration court near the noncitizen's residence, and decisions made in those hearings can be appealed in federal court.[9] By contrast, an exclusion hearing takes place at the border and carries far fewer due process protections. An exclusion hearing cannot be appealed; a writ of habeas corpus is the only form of recourse. In a deportation hearing, the government bears the burden of establishing removability. In an exclusion hearing, by contrast, the noncitizen must establish eligibility for entry.

This is where the *Plasencia* case encounters another question – whether an LPR who has temporarily left the country is seeking "entry" at the border as a matter of law. A critical right associated with LPR status is the freedom to leave and return to the United States without relinquishing claims to privileged immigration status. Given that LPRs had at some point passed through the metaphorical "gates," it was unclear whether these noncitizens were entitled to deportation proceedings or a mere exclusion hearing.

In 1963, the Supreme Court decided *Rosenberg v. Fleuti*, addressing this very issue.[10] George Fleuti, a Swiss national and LPR of the United States, had traveled to Ensenada, Mexico (about 70 miles south of the border) in 1956. His time in Mexico lasted only a matter of hours. Years later, he was placed in deportation proceedings on the basis that he had left the United States and was inadmissible due to his affliction with "psychopathic personality" – that is to say, homosexuality. The Court observed that Congress intended to ameliorate the harsh consequences of such a departure, particularly where there existed a vested interest in residence tied to one's immigration status. Given his establishment of permanent residence, the Court reasoned, George Fleuti could not have intended to depart the United States.

---

[6] *Knauff* at 23.
[7] *Id.* at 11.
[8] 345 U.S. 206, 212 (1953).
[9] Landon v. Plasencia, 459 U.S. 21, 25 (1982).
[10] Rosenberg v. Fleuti, 374 U.S. 449 (1963).

Doing so would have triggered grounds for his exclusion, even where the underlying offense would be insufficient to deport him. This entirely nonintuitive approach – now referred to as "entry fiction" – reflects the immigration benefits conferred to LPRs in immigration law.

THE ORIGINAL OPINION

Maria Plasencia's situation was comparable to that of George Fleuti. She was an LPR who had resided in the country for years and traveled outside the country for only a weekend. However, in *Plasencia*, the Supreme Court departed from the entry doctrine liberalized in *Fleuti* and regarded Plasencia "on the threshold of initial entry," rather than as a returning LPR with continuous residence in the United States. The Court characterized Plasencia as an "initial entrant," thereby affirming the decision to deprive her of due process to a full deportation hearing on her claim to LPR status. The Court reasoned that if "the purpose of leaving the country is to accomplish some object which is itself contrary to some policy reflected in our immigration laws, … the interruption of residence thereby occurring would properly be regarded as meaningful." The Court concluded that, because Maria Plasencia engaged in human smuggling, her trip was not "innocent," and she therefore would be subjected to the summary process of an exclusion hearing.

Plasencia as Departure from the Law of Procedural Due Process

At first blush, *Plasencia* reads like a victory. The Supreme Court indicates that due process is warranted for an LPR seeking entry to the United States. However, the language rings hollow as the opinion glosses over the serious deficiencies in Maria Plasencia's exclusion proceeding. She found herself in court less than twenty-four hours after being arrested, pursuant to a notice issued only in English. She was not advised of her right to a continuance or legal representation. By contrast, had she been arrested by INS in the interior of the United States, Maria Plasencia would have been placed in deportation proceedings and had the opportunity to seek other relief. She would have had additional time to prepare her case, perhaps with the assistance of counsel. The hearing could have taken place near her home, in Los Angeles, where family and friends in her community could testify on her behalf.

In a deportation hearing, the government would have borne the burden of proving that Maria Plasencia was removable. This significant burden shifting may very well have changed the outcome. There was limited evidence that Maria Plasencia had left the United States with an intent to smuggle, much less with the intent to do so for personal gain. At the hearing, the government presented the testimony of only three of its six witnesses, and only one of them testified that she had an advance agreement to pay the Plasencias. Had Maria Plasencia been criminally charged with smuggling, where the government's burden of proof is "beyond a reasonable doubt," the evidence surely would have been insufficient to establish her guilt. Moreover, in a criminal proceeding, Maria Plasencia would have received constitutional due process protections, including the right to appointed and effective assistance of counsel, and protections from unlawful search and seizure and cruel and unusual punishment. As Justice Marshall pointed out in the dissenting portion of his opinion, "[v]igorous cross-examination by a competent attorney might well have led the Immigration Judge to resolve the disputed issue of fact in [Maria] Plasencia's favor."[11]

Plasencia is a notable divergence from the procedural due process analysis of the time. Cases from the 1960s and 1970s, such as *In Re Gault, Goldberg v. Kelly,* and *Mathews v. Eldridge,* reinforced the need for basic due process protections for individuals subjected to government proceedings against them, such as the provision of adequate written notice of a hearing[12] that includes notice of charges, as well as the right to counsel.[13] *Goldberg* expressly addressed due process protections in an administrative proceeding, including the right to notice as well as confrontation and cross-examination.[14] These due process cases were conscious of social vulnerability, considering age and income in the analysis of the need for due process. *Mathews* established a test in administrative proceedings that weighs the respective interests of parties and the government, balancing the rights at stake against the cost to the state.[15] *Plasencia* was an opportunity for the Supreme Court to similarly elaborate on due process rights associated with the interests of permanent resident status. Instead, the Court stated that it was positioned to decide the issue of Maria Plasencia's entitlement to due process, but not "precisely what procedures are due."

The Salvadoran Civil Conflict and the Political Anxieties of Immigration

The result in *Plasencia* is especially striking when one applies the balancing test in *Mathews* and considers the individual and government interests at stake. In the earlier cases of *Knauff* and *Mezei,* the Supreme Court focused not only on the acts of Congress authorizing denial of a hearing, but also the underlying national security rationales, grounded in fears of wartime espionage and communism. Although the smuggling allegations in Maria Plasencia's case prevented her from being lawfully admitted to the United States, they did not rise to the level of a security threat that would bar her from being paroled into the United States, or ultimately result in her removal. Nonetheless, the majority opinion sided with the government and

---

[11] *Plasencia* at 41 (opinion of J. Marshall, concurring in part and dissenting in part).
[12] *In Re Gault,* 387 U.S. 1 (1967);
[13] *Id.; see also* Lassiter v. Department of Social Services, 452 U.S. 18 (1981).
[14] Goldberg v. Kelley, 397 U.S. 254 (1970).
[15] Mathews v. Eldridge, 424 U.S. 319 (1976).

criticized Justice Marshall's dissenting opinion as "fail[ing] to discuss the interests that the Government may have in employing the procedures that it did."

Maria Plasencia's exclusion coincided with a new anxiety: an influx of refugees fleeing civil wars in Central America. Mere hours after Maria Plasencia's exclusion hearing, students at the National Autonomous University of El Salvador marched in protest of the military occupation of the Santa Ana campus. General Arturo Armando Molina ordered the Salvadoran National Guard to suppress the protest with machine guns and tanks. The massacre was one of four that took place in El Salvador that year. The protests in Santa Ana had the backing of Archbishop Oscar Romero, who made several appeals to the Salvadoran government to end its campaigns of repression and killing before he was eventually assassinated. Other civil conflicts – in which the United States played an undeniable role, arming and training government soldiers to wage war against civilians – were already underway in Guatemala and Honduras.

As a Salvadoran national who had recently returned from the country, Maria Plasencia was likely aware of the brewing political violence and the reasons why some of her compatriots wanted to escape to the United States. By the time the *Plasencia* case made its way to the Supreme Court, a military coup established the Revolutionary Government Junta of El Salvador and thousands of Salvadorans had fled to the United States seeking asylum. The Reagan administration, however, supported the right-wing Salvadoran government and labeled these refugees "economic migrants." The highly influential opinion letters issued from the Department of State, which were at that time mandatory for asylum claims, denied the existence of human rights violations in El Salvador. The effect on Central American asylum claims was devastating. In 1984, at the height of the civil conflict in El Salvador, INS statistics show a less than three percent approval rate for Salvadoran asylum claims.[16]

Justice O'Connor's opinion in *Plasencia* was consistent with the political messaging of the president who appointed her: Maria Plasencia's case was one of immigration for financial gain, not humanitarian necessity. However, U.S. asylum policies were already under scrutiny. Less than a month after *Plasencia* was argued, the District Court for the Central District of California ruled, in *Orantes-Hernandez v. Smith*, that INS agents had coerced Salvadorans to sign agreements for voluntary departure without advising them of their rights, strategically detained and isolated them to limit their ability to contact support networks and secure legal representation, and subjected them to serious mistreatment while detained.[17] Citing the clear and consistent reports of persecution in El Salvador, the court ordered a number of mechanisms be put in place to stop the coercive practices used by INS and facilitate

---

[16] *See* U.S. General Accounting Office, Factsheet Prepared for Arlen Specter, United State Senate, "Asylum: Approval Rates for Selected Applicants," June 1987.

[17] 541 F. Supp. 351 (C.D. Cal. 1982).

the ability of Salvadorans to apply for asylum as permitted under the 1980 Refugee Act. In 1985, a group of religious organizations, refugee legal assistance organizations, and human rights organizations filed suit against INS, the immigration court system and the Department of State, alleging discrimination against Salvadoran and Guatemalan asylum-seekers. The settlement in *American Baptist Churches v. Thornburgh* would allow reconsideration of asylum claims previously filed by Salvadorans and permitting new claims to be filed for Salvadorans who arrived in the United States prior to 1990. The Plasencias' six passengers could have easily been among them.

THE FEMINIST JUDGMENT

In her dissenting feminist judgment, Professor Erin Corcoran draws on feminist legal methodology to expand on Justice Marshall's minority opinion. In particular, Corcoran engages in an extensive due process analysis of *Gault*, *Goldberg*, and *Mathews* and extends their logic to immigration hearings for noncitizens with ties to the United States. Employing feminist practical reasoning – a methodology that "make[s] legal decisionmaking more sensitive to the features of a case not already reflected in legal doctrine"[18] – Corcoran argues that the Court ought to give substantial weight to the individual rights of noncitizens subject to exclusion, rather than automatically deferring to the state sovereignty interests traditionally privileged in immigration law. Corcoran also employs the feminist method of "widening the lens," questioning legal conventions in immigration law and encouraging a break from "the way things have always been done."[19] She argues that the majority's misinterpretation of the "innocence" requirement in *Fleuti* entrenches the moral authority historically given to immigration officials to assess the worthiness of prospective citizens. Corcoran also widens the lens on citizenship by calling out the historical convergence of immigration and respectability politics – social pressure to conform with "respectable" cultural and moral practices, generally those associated with white, middle-class heteronormativity.[20]

---

[18] Feminist practical reasoning is among the feminist legal methods outlined in Katharine T. Bartlett's seminal article *Feminist Legal Methods*, 103 HARV. L. REV. 829, 850 (1990).

[19] *See* Linda L. Berger, Introduction, FEMINIST JUDGMENTS: REWRITTEN OPINIONS OF THE UNITED STATES SUPREME COURT (2016) at 5, 17. The pluralistic lens and its relationship to feminism are famously discussed in bell hook's FEMINIST THEORY: FROM MARGIN TO CENTER (1984) and Audre Lorde's SISTER OUTSIDER (1984), and features prominently in Kimberlé Crenshaw's work on intersectionality, including the seminal articles *Demarginalizing the Intersection of Race and Sex: A Black Feminist Critique of Antidiscrimination Doctrine, Feminist Theory and Antiracist Politics*, 1 U. CHI. LEGAL F. 139 (1989) and *Mapping the Margins: Intersectionality, Identity Politics, and Violence against Women of Color*, 43 STAN. L. REV. 1241 (1991).

[20] Evelyn Brooks Higginbotham, professor of Afro-American Studies, African American Religion and the Victor S. Thomas Professor of History and African American Studies at Harvard University, introduced the term in her book *Righteous Discontent: The Women's Movement in the Black Baptist*

By situating Maria Plasencia alongside Ellen Knauff and George Fleuti, Corcoran establishes that due process would produce the same result for all three of these "Americans in waiting."[21]

In her feminist judgment, Professor Corcoran emphasizes Maria Plasencia's substantial ties to the United States – including her role as breadwinner, a wife to a U.S. citizen, and a mother of three minor children who were LPRs – as interests that require the robust protections of due process. Corcoran argues that due process analysis must give weight to rights of near-citizens, including the principles of family unity and realization of citizenship, rather than automatically tipping the balance in favor of the state's general sovereignty interests. Corcoran contrasts Maria Plasencia's case to that of Ellen Knauff, who was eventually granted a full hearing after an extensive public campaign and congressional action and mounted a successful defense. Corcoran points out that due process is critical to protect all noncitizens with ties to the United States, not just those with privilege and political know-how.

Professor Corcoran's dissent is concerned not just with the deficiencies in Maria Plasencia's exclusion hearing, but also the implications of the Court's preoccupation with Maria Plasencia's innocence when applying the *Fleuti* entry doctrine. Corcoran argues that such findings of wrongdoing should take place exclusively in criminal proceedings, where additional due process protections apply. She further points out that the majority's emphasis on "innocence" in *Plasencia* is particularly problematic given the historical use of immigration law to exclude people based on "undesirable" characteristics, including those pertaining to nationality, gender, and sexual orientation. Broadening the lens on citizenship, Corcoran unpacks the assumptions and interests inherent in the Court's decision to evaluate the morality of Maria Plasencia's conduct and her worthiness as a permanent resident, arguing that due process should intentionally break from the historic practices that authorized immigration officials to determine immigrants' deservingness of citizenship.

Professor Corcoran goes further, arguing that the standards traditionally used to evaluate the worthiness of prospective citizens are tied to white, heteropatriarchal norms. Corcoran draws a connection to the case of George Fleuti, who was apprehended not upon his return from Mexico, but rather after an INS investigation

---

Church, 1880–1920 (1993). Feminist immigration legal scholars have noted the role that gendered essentialization and respectability politics play in immigration law. *See, e.g.*, Kerry Abrams, *Polygamy, Prostitution, and the Federalization of Immigration Law*, 105 COL. L. REV. 641 (2005); Elizabeth Keyes, *Beyond Saints and Sinners: Discretion and the Need for New Narratives in the U.S. Immigration System*, 26 GEO. IMMIGR. L.J. 207 (2012); Jamie Abrams, *Enforcing Masculinities at the Border*, 13 NEV. L.J. 564 (2013).

[21] Corcoran intentionally uses this term, introduced by Hiroshi Motomura to describe individuals on a path to citizenship who manifest intent to make the United States their permanent home. *See* Hiroshi Motomura, AMERICANS IN WAITING (2006).

following his arrest by the vice squad for engaging in sex with another man in a park restroom.[22] George Fleuti's sexual orientation was discussed extensively by the lower court, with considerable emphasis placed on his "reform." Even so, his case went on for years after he was targeted for removal based on his sexual orientation. Corcoran identifies similar stereotypes and anxieties about Mexican and Latin American migration animating the arguments in *Plasencia*. The reversal of the liberalized entry doctrine in *Fleuti*, as well as increasingly harsh immigration consequences for human smuggling, similarly reflect these anxieties about immigration and the politicization of border enforcement.[23] Ultimately, both George Fleuti and Ellen Knauff – European immigrants with some means and privilege – were able to secure their futures in the United States as citizens. That Maria Plasencia was unable to do the same – according to Corcoran – highlights the necessity of due process protections applied to noncitizens equally, to prevent the recasting of citizenship as a single, narrow image.

Policy developments further eschewed due process in favor of deference to security-minded objectives in border enforcement. Following the passage of the Anti-Terrorism and Effective Death Penalty Act (AEDPA) in 1996, individuals can be summarily removed at the discretion of immigration enforcement officers, with no administrative hearing at all. A narrow exception to the summary expedited removal exists for individuals who request asylum. However, even these due process rights have been undermined. In *Department of Homeland Security v. Thuraissigiam*, for example, the Supreme Court restricted the ability of a Sri Lankan asylum-seeker to appeal his claim, because he was apprehended 25 yards from the U.S.-Mexico border. The Court determined that the petitioner's proximity to the border limited judicial review of his case to his writ of habeas corpus. Thuraissigiam's asylum claim was denied because he presented no evidence in his case, though it is well-established that both credible fear determinations and asylum claims can be based on testimony alone. In response to Thuraissigiam's argument that his due process rights were violated, the Supreme Court cited *Plasencia* in support of the premise that a noncitizen seeking admission "has no constitutional rights regarding his application, for the power to admit or exclude aliens is a sovereign prerogative."[24] Had Professor Corcoran's opinion been authored on behalf of the majority in *Plasencia*, or had the dissent gained traction in subsequent decisions, her reasoning would

---

[22] Rachel Rosenblum's work provides key context for the *Fleuti* case, specifically INS practices of collaborating with police to expose and deport gay noncitizen men through the early 1960s. See *Policing Sex, Policing Immigrants*, 104 CAL. L. REV. 149, 160 (2015).
[23] Regulations issued in 1990 expanded the inadmissibility grounds for human smuggling, providing a narrow waiver only for individuals who smuggled family members, and denying such waivers even in the presence of sympathetic reasons for assistance. INA § 212(d)(11). In 1996, Congress passed the Illegal Immigration Reform and Individual Immigrant Responsibility Act, amending INA § 101(a)(13). Subsequently, in *Matter of Collado-Munoz*, the Board of Immigration Appeals interpreted this amendment as eliminating the *Fleuti* doctrine entirely. 21 I&N Dec. 1061 (BIA 1998).
[24] Department of Homeland Security v. Thuraissigiam, 140 U.S. 1959, 1968 (2020) (citing *Plasencia* at 32).

have been a powerful safeguard against the erosion of due process protections for noncitizens at the border, particularly those seeking relief based on family connections or humanitarian necessity.

LANDON v. PLASENCIA, 459 U.S. 21 (1982)

Justice Erin Corcoran, dissenting.

On its face this case is about what type of hearing a lawful permanent resident (LPR) who returns to the United States after a brief departure is due when the government seeks to bar the LPR from returning to the United States. Specifically, when an LPR returning to the United States from a brief trip abroad is stopped at a border, is the LPR attempting an *entry* within the meaning of INA § 101(a)(13); 8 U.S.C. § 1101 (a)(13) and hence subject to exclusion proceedings? Or, is such return an exception to entry as interpreted by this Court and lower courts and codified by Congress in the INA, and, as a result, the LPR is entitled to deportation hearings and their greater procedural protections and different burden of proof?

Yet, this case is about more than statutory interpretation. Our decision determines whether a Salvadoran mother of four young children and wife of a U.S. citizen, lawfully residing in the country for years, will be afforded a full hearing and the opportunity to obtain discretionary relief and remain in this country with her family, or whether she will be deported to El Salvador, a country currently embroiled in violent civil war. This decision hinges on whether this country's long-standing commitment to family as a central organizing unit and value remains intact.

Family unity is a cornerstone of the current American immigration system and has been an animating value throughout. It first appeared explicitly as an immigration goal in the Emergency Quota Act of 1921. Emergency Quota Act of 1921, Pub. L. No. 67-5, § 2(d), 42 Stat. 5 (1921) (giving immigration preference to wives, parents, brothers, sisters, children under eighteen, and fiancees of U.S. citizens and LPRs present in the United States). Congress expanded family preferences in the McCarran–Walter Act of 1952. McCarran–Walter Act, Pub. L. No. 82-414, § 205, 66 Stat. 163 (1952) (providing for nonquota status for spouses and children of U.S. citizens and giving preference under the quota system for parents of U.S. citizens, spouses and children of LPRs, and brothers, sisters, sons and daughters of U.S. citizens). The 1965 Hart-Celler Act replaced the racially based national origins quotas program, but retained the emphasis on family unity as the centerpiece of U.S. immigration policy. Pub. L. No. 89-236, §§ 201(b), 203, 79 Stat. 911 (1965). The Hart–Celler Act provided that *immediate relatives* (defined as the children, spouses and parents of U.S. citizens) were not subject to annual numerical limitations. *Id.* at § 201(b). If a noncitizen proved the close family relationship, a visa was immediately available. Further, the Act gave preference to those with the following family relationships: unmarried sons and daughters of U.S. citizens, spouses, unmarried sons or daughters, and parents of LPRs, married sons or daughters of U.S. citizens, and brothers or sisters of U.S. citizens. *Id.* at § 204 (a).

Avoiding family separation has been a key concern behind the prioritization of family-based immigration. Immigration and Nationality Act: Hearing on S. 500 before the Subcomm. on Immigration and Naturalization of the S. Comm. On Judiciary, 89th Cong. 8 (1965) ("Under present law, we are forcing families to be separated – indeed, in some cases, forcing mothers to choose between America and their children."). Because of these family preferences, sixty-five percent of all LPR visas last year were family-based visas. U.S. Dep't Justice, Statistical Yearbook of Immigration and Nationality Service (1981).

Naturalization law likewise privileges family. Spouses of U.S. citizens need only three years of residence as an LPR to naturalize, as opposed to the five years of residency required for other LPR's. 8 U.S.C. §1430(a); INA § 319(a).

Moreover, embedded in our immigration system is a hierarchy of immigration statuses. At the bottom are short term visa holders like tourists. Next up the ladder are temporary visitors who are allowed longer, but time-limited, stays, like students and seasonal workers. At the top are LPRs. As the term suggests, they are permitted to remain in the United States indefinitely and work without any additional authorization required. Moreover, different from many temporary visa holders, LPRs are not restricted in the number of entries into the United States. They can, provided they are admissible, and their trips are not too long, freely come and go. To receive such a valued status, a noncitizen must show significant ties and pass through strict vetting.

The greater the connections a noncitizen forms with the American community, including family connections, the closer a noncitizen gets to U.S. citizenship. And the closer a noncitizen gets to U.S. citizenship, the more rights and legal protections she acquires. *Mathews v. Diaz*, 426 U.S. 67, 79 (1976) ("Congress may decide that as an alien's tie grows stronger, so does the strength of his claim to an equal share of [the country's] munificence.").

In this particular case, Respondent Maria Plasencia is a near citizen whose LPR status was conferred on her so that she, her U.S. citizen children, and her U.S. citizen husband could live together as a family in the United States. See *Landon v. Plasencia*, 1982 U.S. S. Ct. Briefs, LEXIS 1225, Joint Appendix, Transcript of Exclusion Hearing, June 30, 1975 at *11. Any attempts to revoke her status are not to be done lightly or arbitrarily. Revocation should only occur after an extensive process that provides her with an opportunity to fully present her case and requires the U.S. government to demonstrate that separating her from her family and cutting her cord to citizenship was necessary under the law.

Yet, Maria Plasencia was excluded from the United States after a brief trip to Mexico and an exclusion hearing that lasted less than an hour, when an immigration judge ruled that Maria Plasencia should not be allowed to return to the United States and should be deported back to El Salvador. And the majority today holds that the process provided to Maria Plasencia in that cursory exclusion hearing was sufficient. The majority contends that "[n]othing in the statutory language or the legislative history suggests that the respondent's status as a permanent resident entitles her to a suspension of the exclusion hearing or requires the INS to proceed only through a [more robust] deportation hearing." *Landon v. Plasencia*, 459 U.S. 21, at 28.

This conclusion ignores amendments made by Congress and decisions by this Court specifically designed to ameliorate the unfair harsh effects of the INA on LPRs with significant family ties like Maria Plasencia who briefly travel abroad. *Kwang Hi Chew v. Colding*, 344 U.S. 590 (1953) (holding that the Attorney General lacked the authority to order the exclusion and deportation of an LPR "without notice of the charges against him and without opportunity to be heard in opposition to them"); *Rosenberg v. Fleuti*, 374 U.S. 449, 462 (1963) (holding held that an LPR's return to the United States can only be deemed an entry if the departure was made with "an intent to depart in a manner which can be regarded as meaningfully interruptive of the alien's permanent residence."). The purpose of these holdings was to ensure that LPRs like Maria Plasencia would not summarily lose their status upon briefly departing from the United States.

Because I believe that an LPR like Maria Plasencia who takes a brief visit abroad cannot be subject to exclusion proceedings, I respectfully dissent. If the government attempts to remove Maria Plasencia and LPRs like her from the United States, it must do so via deportation hearings where the procedural and substantive protections for the noncitizen are greater and the burden is on the government to demonstrate through "clear and convincing" evidence that the individual is deportable from the country.

FACTS

Respondent, Maria Antonieta Plasencia, is married to a native-born United States citizen, Joseph Plasencia. She has resided in Los Angeles, California with their four children since she entered the United States as an LPR on March 6, 1970. She and her children are originally from El Salvador. Her children have been adopted by her U.S. citizen husband. Maria continuously resided in the Los Angeles area since her arrival to the United States. In that time, she and her husband had visited Mexico once before she was apprehended and detained. In addition, Maria had left the United States to return to El Salvador in order to bring one of her sons to the United States. In both cases, she fully complied with the law.

On Friday, June 27, 1975, Maria and her husband Joseph drove two hours from Los Angeles to Tijuana for a weekend trip. The purpose of the trip, Maria testified, was because "her husband wanted to see how much they would charge … for some dental work." 1982 U.S. S. Ct. Briefs, LEXIS 1225, Joint Appendix, Transcript of Exclusion Hearing, June 30, 1975 at *14. In addition, her husband wanted to get his car repaired. *Id.*

Two days later, at around 9:30 pm on Sunday evening, Maria was arrested by INS agents as she and her husband attempted to re-enter the United States by car at a border crossing. In the car with Maria and Joseph were six undocumented immigrants from El Salvador. *Id.* 14–16. Two of them were children who had family members living in the United States. Maria had provided several of them with minor alien registration cards and the social security cards of her own children. She testified that a woman in her community in Los Angeles had asked Maria to help bring the woman's young granddaughter fleeing El Salvador into the United States, and another man had asked her help in bringing a young boy who was a natural-born U.S. citizen back to the United States. *Id.*

The INS served Maria the next morning with a notice charging her with being inadmissible under Section 212 (a)(31) of the INA, which states a noncitizen seeking admission to the United States is excludable if "at any time [the individual] shall have knowingly and for gain, encouraged, induced, assisted, abetted, or aided any other alien to enter or to try to enter the United States in violation of the law."

In the notice, provided only in English, Maria Plasencia was also ordered to appear before an immigration judge for an exclusion hearing that same morning at 11:00 am. At this hearing, she appeared without counsel and the only evidence she presented was her testimony and that of her husband. The immigration judge accepted Maria Plasencia's waiver of the right to counsel at no expense to the government and did not inform her that the hearing could have been continued to a later date to afford her the opportunity to retain counsel and gather evidence in support of her case. 1982 U.S. S. Ct. Briefs, LEXIS 1225, Joint Appendix, Transcript of Exclusion Hearing, June 30, 1975 at *9–10. Instead, after an exclusion hearing that took less than an hour, the immigration judge found "clear, convincing and unequivocal" evidence that Maria Plasencia did "knowingly and for gain encourage, induce, assist, abet, or aid nonresident aliens" to enter or try to enter in violation of the law and ordered Maria to be excluded from admission. Oral Decision of Immigration Judge, 1982 U.S. S. Ct. Briefs, LEXIS 1225, Joint Appendix, Transcript of Exclusion Hearing, June 30, 1975 at *54–86. Maria had no right to appeal the decision. Her only path to relief was via a writ of habeas corpus.

I

*Procedural Due Process Requires that the Government Proceed
against Lawful Permanent Residents Who Take Brief Trips
Abroad in Deportation Hearings, Not Exclusion Hearings*

The majority in this case contends that the brief exclusion hearing provided to Maria Plasencia only hours after she had been arrested and detained satisfies due process requirements. While the majority concedes that *Kwong Hai Chew v. Colding*, 344. U.S. 590 (1953), stands for the principle that an LPR returning from a brief trip has a right to the same procedural due process as the resident would have if she never left the country, the majority holds that Maria Plasencia is not so entitled. This misconstrues the due process entitlements of LPRs like Maria Plasencia.

The Due Process Clauses of the Fifth and Fourteenth Amendments protect all persons within the boundaries of the United States, including persons whose presence in this country is unlawful. *Shaughnessy v. Mezei*, 345 U.S. 206, 212 (1953); *Wong Wing v. United States*, 163 U.S. 228, 238 (1896); *Yick Wo v. Hopkins*, 118 U.S. 356, 369 (1886). Moreover, LPRs are entitled to procedural due process, *Kwang Hi Chew v. Colding*, 344 U.S. 590 (1953), and a permanent resident does not lose such protections simply by making a brief trip abroad. *Rosenburg v. Fleuti*, 374 U.S. 449, 462 (1963); see also *Bridges v. Wixon*, 326 U.S. 135, 154 (1945) (recognizing that permanent residents attach great value in being able to reside in the United States and as such "meticulous care must be exercised lest the procedure by which [a resident alien is] deprived of that liberty not meet the essential standards of fairness.").

They key question here is how much process an LPR like Maria Plasencia who briefly traveled abroad should receive when the government seeks to revoke her LPR status upon return to the United States. *Goldberg v. Kelly*, 397 U.S. 254, 261–63 (1970) (discussing how benefits are statutory entitlements for the persons qualified to receive them and the termination of such benefits "involve state actions that adjudicates important rights"). "[T]his court has never held … that administrative officers, when executing the provisions of a statute involving liberty of persons, may disregard the fundamental principles that inhere in 'due process of law' as understood at the time of the adoption of the Constitution." *Yamataya v Fisher*, 189 U.S. 86 (1903). This Court has held that even unlawfully present immigrants are entitled to procedural due process when they are faced with expulsion from the United States. *Bridges v. Wixon*, 326 U.S. 135 (1945). Moreover, because of deportation's harsh consequences, "at times the equivalent of banishment or exile" *Fong Haw Tan v. Phelan*, 333 U.S. 6, 10 (1948), this Court has held that we must read deportation statutes and regulations in the light that is most favorable to the immigrant. *Id.* at 7.

Congress intentionally established two different types of administrative hearings for noncitizens to determine their eligibility to legally be present and remain in the United States: exclusion and deportation proceedings. Which hearing is used has significant consequences, both substantively and procedurally. *Leng May Ma v. Barber*, 357 U.S. 185 (1957).

Exclusion, in essence, is a government determination of who should be allowed to come into the United States to visit, live, or work. In an exclusion hearing, an individual seeking permission to enter the United States has the burden of proving that she is "clearly and beyond a doubt entitled to be admitted." INA § 291, 8 U.S.C. § 1361. There is no advance notice requirement to inform the noncitizen of the charges in an exclusion hearing "as long as the applicant is informed of the issues confronting him at some point in the hearing and he is given a reasonable opportunity to meet them." *In re Salazar*, 17 I. & N. Dec. 167, 169 (1979). Certain discretionary forms of relief like voluntary deportation, suspension of deportation, and adjustment of status, are not available in exclusion hearings. Finally, a noncitizen may not appeal an exclusion order to the Board of Immigration Appeals, but can only challenge it through a petition for a writ habeas corpus. 8 U.S.C. § 1105a(b).

Once a person has been vetted and granted leave to live, work or visit in the United States, the decision to remove (i.e., deport) them from the United States is different than the decision to originally allow them into the country. As such, Congress created a separate procedure for deporting an individual who has gained entry into the United States. The procedural protections in these deportation hearings are significantly greater than those in exclusion hearings, to protect against arbitrary decisions by government officials. *Yamataya v. Fisher*, 189 U.S. 86, 100–01 (1903) (holding actions of deportation officers must be measured by the Due Process Clause). In a deportation hearing, the government is required to provide notice of the charges levied against the noncitizen seven days prior to the hearing itself. 8 U.S.C. § 1252 (b); 8 C.F.R. 242.1(b). At a deportation hearing, the government has the burden to establish through "clear and convincing" evidence that the individual is deportable from the country. 8 U.S.C. § 1252.

Unlike in exclusion hearings, individuals in deportation proceedings can raise affirmative defenses to their removal and request that the immigration judge exercise discretion and allow them to remain in the United States even if they are deportable. *See, e.g.*, 8 U.S.C. § 1254. One of the primary defenses a noncitizen can assert is that her deportation would result in hardship to her family remaining in the United States. The immigration judge weighs these hardships to the family members against the government's interest in deporting the individual. If the judge finds that the family will suffer hardship, even if the individual has an immigration violation, the judge is permitted to allow the noncitizen to remain in the United States and keep her LPR status. Congress' decision to provide broad discretion to immigration judges in this context reflects its commitment to family unification. If the government prevails at a deportation hearing, the noncitizen may appeal directly to the court of appeals. 8 U.S.C. § 1105a(a) (1976 ed., and supp V).

The legal definition of entry has evolved over time. Early on this Court applied a rigid definition of the term and simply held "the word 'entry' .... includes any coming of an alien from a foreign country into the United States whether such coming be the first or any subsequent one." *United States ex rel. Volpe v. Smith*, 289 U.S. 422, 425 (1933). Over time courts, recognizing the harsh and even unfair consequences for certain noncitizens, softened their rigid understanding of entry to a more flexible one that did not consider any coming to the United States to be an entry. Instead, courts looked at whether such departures were voluntary and/or intentional. *See, e.g., Di Pasquale v. Karnuth*, 158 F.2d 878 (2nd Cir. 1947) (holding an that an LPR was not subject to reentry requirements when his train trip from Buffalo, NY to Detroit, MI unbeknownst to him was routed through Canada);

Delgadillo v. Carmichael, 332 U.S. 388 (1947) (holding that a merchant seaman's return from Cuba after his ship had been torpedoed was not an entry which could serve as a basis for deportation).

Subsequent to these judicial interpretations, Congress through statutory revision created explicit exemptions for LPRs leaving the United States for a variety of reasons, including voluntary and temporary departures. In addition to the plain language of the statute, the legislative history also reflects Congress' recognition that application of the term entry had been applied in ways that resulted in unfair and often harsh results. H.R. Rep. No. 1365, 82nd Cong., 2d Sess. 32 (1952); S. Rep. No. 1137, 82nd Cong., 2d Sess. 4 (1952) (articulating that the purpose of the bill was to provide a concrete definition of entry that also reflected evolving judicial precedents departing from the rigidity of the term entry).

In sum, LPRs who take brief trips abroad are not treated as seeking entry and therefore should not be subject to exclusion hearings. This would be consistent with the principle that increased connections to the country confer enhanced protections on noncitizens who reside here. And it does not undermine government interests in removing noncitizens who violate the conditions of their stay. If the government believes that a noncitizen's conduct before or during a trip abroad triggers a ground of deportation, the government can bring deportation charges and satisfy its burden of proof in a deportation hearing.

II

Procedural Due Process Protects Families from Separation

This Court has upheld the Attorney Generals' broad authority to exclude without a hearing those who seek entry but have claims to permanent status through the marriage to a U.S. citizen, *c.f. Knauff v. Shaughnessy,* 338 U.S. 537 (1950). However, history has demonstrated the importance of providing a hearing to protecting individual's claims to remain in the United States and preserve marriage and family unity.

Ellen Knauff, a German national, fled Germany during World War II and was granted refugee status in England in 1939. After the war she returned to Germany where she worked as a civilian employee for the U.S. War Department. It was there she met and subsequently married Kurt Shaughnessy, a U.S. citizen and World War II veteran. She attempted to enter the United States for the first time and naturalize pursuant to the War Brides Act, Act of Dec. 28, 1945, ch. 591, 59 Stat. 659, but was detained at Ellis Island and barred from entry. The Attorney General, claiming general concerns about public security, summarily excluded Ms. Knauff without providing specific reasons for denying her entry. Further, the government argued that Ms. Knauff was not entitled to an administrative hearing where the government would be required to provide the evidence used against her or an opportunity to rebut the government's decision to exclude her from entry.

This Court, in a 4-3 decision, affirmed that the Attorney General was authorized to exclude Ellen Knauff for security reasons without a hearing. It reasoned that the Attorney General had absolute power to exclude any noncitizen for security reasons even when the War Brides Act would have otherwise permitted Ellen Knauff entry. *Knauff*, U.S. 388 at 546. Specifically this Court held "[w]hatever the procedure authorized by Congress is, it is due process as far as an alien denied entry is concerned." *Id.*, at 544.

In dissent, Justice Frankfurter argued that national security concerns could be, and should be, protected by an *in camera* hearing. *Id.*, at 549 (Frankfurter, J. dissenting). Also dissenting, Justice Jackson was concerned that this absolute power to exclude was being used to break up a family and argued that Congress would have had to use more specific language before taking so drastic a step as denying entry without any hearing or evidence. *Id.*, at 551–52. This echoes the dissents in *Fong Yue Ting v. United States*, which argued that lawful residents have ties to the United States that justify greater legal protections. 149 U.S. 698, 734–37 (1893) (Brewer, J. dissenting); *id.* at 746 (Field, J. dissenting); *id.* at 762 (Fuller, J. dissenting).

After the Court's ruling, the Attorney General attempted to deport Ellen Knauff immediately. Such attempts were delayed through several stays of deportation, including one issued by Justice Jackson. Through public pressure and congressional action, Ellen Knauff was given a full hearing in which the government presented three witnesses to support its case. The government argued that Ellen Knauff was engaged in espionage while she was employed by the Army's Civil Censorship Division in Frankfurt, Germany. Because Ellen Knauff was able to see the evidence being used by the government, she was able to mount a defense. She successfully rebutted the testimony of each of the witnesses and produced evidence to prove that she had no access to any confidential or secret information. The Board of Immigration Appeals held that there was no substantial evidence that Knauff gave secret evidence to the Czechoslovakian authorities, nor was there any evidence to support any inference that Knauff would engage in any subversive activities if admitted to the United States. *In re Ellen Raphael Knauff*, No. A-6937471, at 18 (B.IA. Aug. 29, 1951).

Ellen Knauff's case shows the value of providing a full hearing. The information the government used to deny Ellen Knauff entry was faulty and inaccurate. Only because she was afforded a hearing, Ellen Knauff was able to rebut the inaccurate evidence against her and was able to remain in the United States with her U.S. citizen husband. Without a full hearing that includes sufficient notice and the opportunity for the immigrant to rebut the evidence being used to deny entry or deport, immigrants like Ellen Knauff and Maria Plasencia are banned from entering the country. This separates families and prevents them from pursuing naturalization based on their family connections.

Ellen Knauff was fortunate because, after being denied a full hearing by this Court, she was able to marshal media attention, congressional sympathies, and even convince the U.S. Department of Justice she should not be barred from entry. Most noncitizens, those like Maria Plasencia, are not so privileged or savvy. They are excluded summarily, and no one learns of their story. The law should demand full and fair process for deporting LPRs, so that the outcome is not left to the happenstance of media attention or the ability to captivate members of Congress or the executive branch. The role of the judicial branch is to protect those who don't have political representation or access to the political process.[25] Thus, it falls on this Court to, at the very least, provide procedural due process protections guaranteed under the U.S. Constitution to those who garner no affection among the political branches of government.

III

Fleuti Supports a Deportation Hearing for LPRs Returning from Brief Trips Abroad

While the text of the INA makes a distinction between those immigrants present within the United States and those "on the threshold of an initial entry," this Court has recognized that permanent residents returning from short trips abroad are not ordinarily subject to exclusion proceedings. *Rosenberg v. Fleuti*, 374 U.S. 449 (1963). A permanent resident is only subject to exclusionary proceedings upon returning to the United States if such a trip was "meaningfully interruptive" of resident status. *Id.* at 456–60.

A

Fleuti Bars the U.S. Government from Using Exclusion against LPRs Who Had Brief Trips Abroad

In *Rosenberg v. Fleuti*, we held that an LPR's return to the United States can only be deemed an entry by an LPR if the departure was made with "an intent to depart in a manner which can be regarded as meaningfully interruptive of the alien's permanent residence." 374 U.S., at 462. We noted that the "enlightened concept of what constitutes a meaningful interruption of the continuous residence which must support a petition for naturalization, reflecting as it does a congressional judgment that an alien's status is not necessarily to be endangered by his absence from the country, strengthens the foundation underlying a belief that the exceptions to section 101(a)(13) should be read to protect resident aliens who are only briefly absent from the country." *Id.*, at 459–60.

In March 1956, George Fleuti was arrested and convicted for having oral sex with another man in a park in Los Angeles. After this arrest and subsequent conviction,

---

[25] United States v. Carolene Products Co., 304 U.S. 144, 152 n. 4 (arguing that the role of heightened judiciary scrutiny is not just to protect economic and property rights but also to protect individual rights, particularly when those individuals are discrete and insular minorities).

INS issued an order to show cause and began deportation proceedings against Fleuti. However, the criminal conviction occurred prior to his brief visit to Mexico in August 1956 and was too minor to render him deportable for "moral turpitude" (a $200 fine). Therefore, the INS argued that when he returned from his brief trip to Mexico, the grounds of exclusion applied to him because he was "entering" the United States.

George Fleuti's contact with immigration authorities did not occur at a port of entry. Rather, he was placed into deportation proceedings three years after he had returned from a brief trip to Mexico when he was arrested by local police as part of a crackdown on "cruising areas" for engaging in a sexual act with another man. The government argued that Fleuti was excludable when he "entered" in August of 1956 because in December 1952 (after Fleuti had been admitted to the United States as an LPR) a new ground for exclusion was added to the INA for "persons afflicted with psychopathic personality." *Fleuti* at 451 (citing INA § 212 (a)(4)). This new exclusion ground was intended to keep "homosexuals and sex perverts" from entering the United States. *Fleuti v. Rosenberg*, 302 F.2d 652 (9th Cir. 1962), *vacated*, 374 U.S. 449 (1963). Congress viewed individuals who were involved in nonmonogamous or non-heterosexual relationships as socially deviant with reprehensible morals. *Boutilier v. INS*, 387, 134 n. 6 (1967) (noting that the original bill introduced in the Senate also barred "individuals who are homosexuals or sex perverts." *Id.*).

Such an exclusion ground is not new to our immigration statutory scheme. Many of the early exclusion grounds were designed to keep out those who were seen as dangerous or undesirable. Many targeted women and minorities, most notably Chinese immigrants. The first restrictive federal legislation to establish grounds for exclusion, the Act of March 3, 1875, known as the "Page Law" prohibited the entry of women who had entered into contracts for "lewd and immoral purposes," and made it a felony to bring women into the country for the purpose of prostitution. Act of Mar. 3, 1875 (Page Law), ch. 141, 18 Stat. 477 (repealed 1974). It included enforcement mechanisms specifically targeting Chinese women. *Id.* Congress was particularly concerned about Chinese practices of polygamy and prostitution gaining purchase in the United States. This bright line rule barring entry for prostitutes reflected Congress' judgment about women engaged in this activity and their unworthiness to be permitted into the United States. While our immigration framework has placed family at the center, the definition of family is heteronormative and narrow. Such exclusion grounds are designed to preserve traditional American conceptions about marriage and family in the federal immigration system.

Rather than ruling on a constitutional challenge to the "psychopathic personality" exclusion ground as impermissibly vague, the Court instead based its decision on a statutory interpretation of "entry." The Court was not willing to sanction INS' attempt to revoke Fleuti's LPR status because of his sexual orientation and held that Fleuti's return from his brief trip to Mexico did not constitute entry and thereby the grounds for exclusion were inapplicable to Fleuti.

The basis of the holding in *Fleuti* was INA section 101(a)(13). It defines entry as "any coming of an alien into the United States from a foreign port or place or from an outlying possession, whether voluntarily or otherwise." The statute, however, contains an exception for LPRs. They "shall not be regarded as making an entry into the United States for the purposes of immigration laws if the alien proves to the satisfaction of the Attorney General that his departure to a foreign port or place or to an outlying possession was not intended or reasonably to be expected by him or his presence in a foreign port or place or in an outlying possession was not voluntary." 66 Stat. 167, 8 U.S.C. §1101 (a)(13). Congress had amended the text to make it clear that an LPR who left for a short time and did not mean to abandon her status should not be treated as an applicant for entry. S. Rep. No. 1137, 82d. Cong., 2d Sess., 4 (1952); H.R. Rep. No. 1365, 82d Cong., 2d Sess., 32 (1952). Thus, this court concluded in *Fleuti* that "[c]ertainly if the trip is innocent, casual, and brief, it is consistent with all the discernable signs of congressional purpose to hold that the 'departure … was not intended' within the meaning and ameliorative intent of the exception to §101(a)(13)." *Fleuti* at 461–62.

B

Reliance on the *Fleuti* Innocence Factor Is Misguided Because It Distorts the Actual Facts of the Case

The majority concludes that Plasencia is ineligible to avail herself of the entry exception articulated in *Fleuti* because her brief trip to Mexico was not innocent because she engaged in activities contrary to the purpose of the immigration law, that is, she attempted to smuggle six noncitizens into the United States. *But see Maldonado-Sandoval v. INS*, 518 F.2d. 278, 280 (9th Cir. 1975) (holding that a brief journey by a permanent resident does not result in a loss of the procedural protections afforded by deportation proceedings even when allegations of fraud are involved). The majority makes too much of – and, indeed, profoundly misunderstands – the innocence factor in the *Fleuti* case. The majority's attempt to contrast the "innocent" actions of Fleuti with Maria Plasencia's alleged smuggling ignores the real politik of this Court's decision in *Fleuti*. Indeed, the INS in collusion with the local police was actively trying to deport Fleuti precisely because he was considered immoral and not innocent. The very reason the government sought to place him in exclusion proceedings was because they viewed him as a sexual deviant, unable to assimilate and unworthy of status in the United States. The central focus of the Court in *Fleuti* was the temporary duration of his time away from the United States and his intent to return. While one of the factors articulated by this Court in assessing the nature of Fleuti's time away from the United States was whether the trip was innocent; it was not dispositive. Instead the Court was being attentive to the legislative history and text of the amendments to the INA and the desire to ameliorate the harsh and often unfair consequences for noncitizens with a rigid interpretation of term entry.

Concluding that Maria Plasencia was engaged in the crime of smuggling as defined by the INA, 212 (a)(31), 8 U.S.C. §1182 (a)(31), when she returned to the United States with her husband and six noncitizens, the majority holds that her brief trip abroad was not innocent. As a result, she does not benefit from the holding in *Fleuti*, making the exclusion hearing the proper procedure. 459 U.S. 21, 30 (1982); (citing 8 U.S.C. § 1182(a)(31) (providing for the exclusion of any noncitizen seeking admission "who at the time shall have knowingly and for gain, encouraged, induced, assisted, abetted, or aided any other alien to enter or to try to enter the United States in violation of law")).

The majority has misappropriated the innocence language of the *Fleuti* test by asserting that motive for leaving the country is somehow central to determining whether or not an LPR meant to abandon their lawful permanent status. However, a careful and critical reading of *Fleuti* shows it does not support the majority's holding. *Fleuti* was a case in which this Court prevented the government from evading full process and stripping someone of LPR status via an exclusion hearing. The government is trying to do the same thing here to Maria Plasencia, and similarly should not be allowed.

Rather than focusing on the innocence discussed in *Fleuti*, the inquiry should focus on the core concern in *Fleuti*: whether the noncitizen intended to depart in a "manner which can be regarded as meaningfully interruptive of the alien's permanent residence." 374 U.S. at 462. The amount of time away from the United States and the circumstances an LPR faced if her return to the United States was delayed should determine whether an exclusion or deportation hearing is required. When determining meaningful interruption of residence, intended and continuous presence should be generously construed. "More specifically, both sections are intended to relieve aliens of the harsh results, and the unsuspected risks and unintended consequences, that would flow from a literal and rigid application of the provisions of the Act relating to expulsion and exclusion." (*Kamheangpatiyooh*, at 1256 (9th Cir. 1979) (*citing Fleuti* at 457–58, 462). Not only is the majority's application of the innocence factor a distortion of the *Fleuti* facts, in my view, the innocence of a departure is simply irrelevant to determining meaningful interruption of residence.

This Court did note in *Fleuti* that if "the purpose of leaving the country is to accomplish some object which is itself is contrary to some policy reflected in our immigration laws, it would appear that the interruption of residence thereby occurring would properly be regarded as meaningful." Id., at 462. However, it is not clear that Maria Plasencia's purpose of leaving the country was contrary to some policy reflected in the INA. Instead, her brief testimony indicates that she and her husband left the country for a dentist visit and to look for a car repair shop. While they did attempt to return with unauthorized noncitizens, it is not clear that their purpose in bringing them was to smuggle these individuals across the border for profit. The record instead suggests that the purpose in helping these individuals, while unauthorized, was for family unification, a policy central to our existing immigration laws. The majority has further narrowed a statutory provision designed by Congress to protect LPRs from having their status arbitrarily revoked by the INS. If the majority wanted to consider motive then they should have provided Maria with more notice and the opportunity to explain her circumstances and the political context motivating her decision to help individuals cross the border, as it was clearly not for personal gain. Before Maria and Joseph's trip, Maria met a woman named Margarita, whose son was separated from her. Margarita told Maria that her son Manuel was in Tijuana and had a birth certificate. She asked Maria to bring Manuel back from Tijuana to Los Angeles. Along with her own travel documents, Maria packed her children's minor alien registration cards (MICAs), and used one of them to try and bring Manuel back to Los Angeles. *Landon v. Plasencia*, 1982 U.S. S. Ct. Briefs, LEXIS 1225, Joint Appendix, Transcript of Exclusion Hearing, June 30, 1975 at *14–16. When the Plasencias arrived in Tijuana, there was not one boy but rather several children. According to Maria's testimony, her husband Joseph felt sorry for the children and took pity on them, deciding to bring them all back. "They cried to him and asked that they be brought across." *Landon v. Plasencia*, 1982 U.S. S. Ct. Briefs, LEXIS 1225, Joint Appendix, Transcript of Exclusion Hearing, June 30, 1975 at *14–16. When asked if she had anything to gain from bringing the passengers across the border, Maria said "Nothing before God, nothing." Maria testified that there was no payment discussed; indeed, the only financial exchange was a $25 contribution to the cost of gasoline, given to Joseph. *Landon v. Plasencia*, 1982 U.S. S. Ct. Briefs, LEXIS 1225, Joint Appendix, Transcript of Exclusion Hearing, June 30, 1975 at *14–16.

Motive matters. In a homicide case it can mean the difference between self-defense and murder. In asylum cases the reason a person flees their home country determines whether or not asylum is merited. The immigration definition of smuggling specifically requires a showing of personal gain as motive. In other words a smuggler profits from illegally transporting human persons across borders. A smuggler takes advantage of vulnerable individuals needing clandestine transport and literally makes money at the risk of these individuals' lives. If she is charged with smuggling, due process would require that Maria Plasencia be afforded an opportunity to provide evidence as the reasons she decided to bring these individuals across the border.

C

An Adjudication of the "Innocence" Factor Should Not Be Performed by Immigration Hearing Officers

I dissent also because the innocence factor as applied by the majority is not a proper issue for immigration officers in the context of brief exclusionary hearings. In fact as this Court noted in *Wong Yang Sung v. McGrath*, one of the fundamental purposes of the Administrative Procedure Act (5 U.S.C. §§ 1001 et seq.) as remedial legislation was "to curtail and change the duties of embodying in one person or agency the duties of prosecutor and judge." 339 U.S. 33, 41 (1950). Immigration proceedings must comply with the procedural requirements and separation of function mandates of the APA.

If an LPR is suspected of committing a crime, immigration court is not the venue to adjudicate criminal conduct. Criminal proceedings require additional constitutional protections, including the right to appointed counsel if a defendant is unable to afford counsel, the right to know the nature of charges and the evidence being used by the government, and right to confront witnesses. Immigration Court should not be used to effectively convict noncitizens of criminal actions without a criminal trial. A hearing officer's determination of guilt without requisite procedural protections falls short of due process. This is not to say that noncitizens cannot be held accountable for criminal acts. In fact, noncitizens who have been convicted through a criminal trial can be deported from the United States. *See, e.g., Palatian v. INS*, 502 F.2d 1091 (9th Cir. 1974) (upholding the deportation of an LPR after his federal drug conviction). Rather, a civil administrative proceeding where the government's burden of proof is minimal and the consequences are severe, that is, deportation and banishment from the United States and family, does not comport with Due Process, particularly when important procedural protections are lacking.

The exclusion hearing provided to Maria Plasencia, hours after she had been apprehended and detained overnight did not provide her the requisite time to gather corroborating evidence to explain her actions, to call her own witnesses or to demonstrate her community ties in Los Angeles. The INS provided Maria Plasencia with her notice to appear in English the same morning of her exclusion hearing. Without counsel Maria Plasencia's attempts to explain the reasons for her actions went unheard. Exclusion hearings by design do not provide enough procedural protections for a noncitizen to establish that her reasons for travel.

The majority's attempt to attribute a particular motive – personal gain – as the reason Maria decided to bring six noncitizens across the border also ignores the political realities in El Salvador at the time and how Maria understood herself a mother. She testified that her actions were animated by her desire to reunite Salvadoran children with family members living in the United States, not for personal or compensatory gain. *Landon v. Plasencia*, 1982 U.S. S. Ct. Briefs, LEXIS 1225, Joint Appendix, Transcript of Exclusion Hearing, June 30, 1975 at *14–16. Indeed, her actions to reunite family members echo U.S. immigration policy's commitment to family reunification. In describing the reasons Maria decided to bring six individuals including two children, she stated that she and her husband brought the children across "because my husband wanted to help them." *Landon v. Plasencia*, 1982 U.S. S. Ct. Briefs, LEXIS 1225, Joint Appendix, Transcript of Exclusion Hearing, June 30, 1975 at *16. El Salvador is currently in the midst of a civil war where death squads are targeting civilians and members of the clergy. Thousands of individuals have been "disappeared" and the death toll continues to rise. In all likelihood, the Salvadorans Maria and Joseph were attempting to help cross the border were fleeing such violence in an attempt to reunite with family members in the United States and find safe haven.

If the INS wants to proceed against Maria Plasencia, they may only do so in deportation proceedings.

CONCLUSION

By permitting the government to use exclusion proceedings to determine an LPR's right to remain in the United States, the majority opinion denies Maria Plasencia, an LPR and a spouse and mother of U.S. citizens, meaningful opportunities to explain her individual circumstances or ties to the United States. It ignores the primacy of family in our immigration architecture and discounts the proximity LPRs have to citizenship. And it runs afoul of rulings by this Court regarding the process constitutionally due to LPRs.

The majority has shown no regard for Maria as a mother, a wife, and a contributing member to the community. Blind to the political realities in El Salvador, the majority is content to have her excluded. I take no position on whether Maria should be allowed to remain in the United States. Such a decision, however, with grave consequences that will result in family separation for a near citizen, should be done with the aid and protections of the more robust procedures of a deportation hearing.

7

Commentary on *Plyler v. Doe*, 457 U.S. 202 (1982)

Michael A. Olivas

Plyler v. Doe is a kaleidoscope. The child's toy refracts different light rays by turning the instrument. Of course, *Plyler* is an immigration case, widely considered
the apex of immigrant rights, especially empowering undocumented immigrants
by allowing undocumented children to enroll in free public schools. It is a family
law case, affecting family choices by parents and their children. The education law
dimensions are also foundational, including traditional concepts of conflicts of law,
especially interpretations of residency, domiciliary, and durational requirements.
Although the case does not explicitly differentiate between immigrant men and
women, it can be usefully examined through feminist legal theory.

Plyler has not substantially influenced subsequent Supreme Court immigration
jurisprudence in the forty years since it was decided. In its aftermath, however, a
broad range of postsecondary *Plyler* issues have arisen, where most of the states with
larger numbers of undocumented schoolchildren, and even some with fewer such
students, have facilitated their enrollment in the public colleges and universities.
Even as states have ratcheted up their efforts to apprehend undocumented parents
and unauthorized workers, many other states carved out and maintained safe havens
for undocumented college children. The lasting influence of *Plyler* is in the wide
and deep accommodation that has been made for these children who have transformed into the success story of the well over million undocumented college students and the high visible political cohort of DREAMers.

The concurrence of Professor Shoba Sivaprasad Wadhia, in the voice of Justice
Wadhia, critiques the ways in which *Plyler* could have reached even further,
enshrining it even more obviously as the apex of immigrant rights. She takes issue
with the various ways in which the majority opinion characterizes the immigrant
children and their parents both in terms of nomenclature and subtle and nuanced
demonizing of parents in comparison to their innocent and victimized children.
Finding undocumented children to be a "suspect class," she details the ways in which
such a classification can be invidious, including the record of the prejudice against
Mexican children. Drawing from her own scholarship on prosecutorial discretion,
she firmly rejects the notion that undocumented children in the United States

are likely to deported. Throughout her opinion, she crucially highlights facts about who these immigrant families are and why they are in the United States. Her work of reconstituting narratives about such families is a core feminist legal tool, as featured in the chapters of this book.

THE ORIGINAL OPINION

In a 5-4 decision, the Supreme Court upheld the lower courts' findings for the children, striking down the Texas statute that denied state funds to school districts enrolling undocumented children.

In the first term of President Ronald Reagan, his Attorney General William French Smith testified to Congress and estimated the number of undocumented immigrants to be between three and six million, noting several proposals by the Administration to reform the immigration laws, including one to "legalize" many undocumented entrants who were then-currently residing in the United States. He noted that the subclass in our society was "largely composed of persons with a permanent attachment to the Nation, and that they are unlikely to be displaced from our territory."[1] He further testified that "'[w]e have neither the resources, the capability nor the motivation to uproot and deport millions of illegal aliens, many of whom have become, in effect, members of the community.'"[2] The majority opinion in *Plyler* relied in part on this inchoate federal permission to remain in holding that the State of Texas could not deny public education to undocumented children, either by banning them from schools or by charging tuition for the "free education" that attendance laws required. The Court termed the argument by Texas as "nothing more than an assertion that illegal entry, without more, prevents a person from becoming a resident for purposes of enrolling his children in the public schools."[3]

The Court used an equal protection analysis to conclude that a state could not make such a discriminatory classification of undocumented children "merely by defining a disfavored group as non-resident." It stressed the importance of residency and domicile in the country and in school districts, where elected school boards determined attendance zones for the public schools, conforming to geographic and political criteria. The Court considered and dismissed arguments proffered by the state in support of the challenged statute. First, the state had argued the classification or subclass of undocumented Mexican children was necessary to preserve the state's "limited resources for the education of its lawful residents."[4]

---

[1] Plyler v. Doe, 457 U.S. 202, 218 n.17 (1982).
[2] *Id.* These figures are subject to much dispute. Carefully conducted studies at the time of the case suggest the numbers are smaller than those proposed by Attorney General Smith. *See, e.g.,* Jeffrey A. Passel & Karen A. Woodrow, *Geographic Distribution of Undocumented Immigrants: Estimates of Undocumented Aliens Counted in the 1980 Census by State,* 18 INT'L MIGRATION REV. 656 (1984).
[3] Plyler, 457 U.S. at 227 n.22.
[4] *Id.*

A similar argument had been rejected in *Graham v. Richardson*, where the Court had held that the concern for preservation of resources could not justify an alienage classification used to allocate those resources and benefits.[5] Furthermore, the findings of fact revealed that the exclusion of all undocumented children would eventually result in some small savings to the state, but inasmuch as both state and federal governments based their school finance determinations primarily on the number of children enrolled and attending classes, any genuine savings would be uncertain and that barring those children would "not necessarily improve the quality of education."[6] "In terms of educational cost and need ... undocumented children are 'basically indistinguishable' from legally resident alien children."[7]

In addition, Texas had also enacted its statute to protect itself from a putative influx of undocumented parents and school-aged children. The Court acknowledged the state's concerns but found that the statute was not tailored to meet the stated objective, noting sharply, "[c]harging tuition to undocumented children constitutes a ludicrously ineffectual attempt to stem the tide of illegal immigration."[8] After all, parents make and undertake mobility decisions for minor children, who may or may not accompany or follow to join their families. Immigration and naturalization policy has always been within the exclusive powers of the federal government.[9] States may act to create legislation affecting immigrants if the law mirrors federal policy and furthers a legitimate state goal, but the Court determined no perceivable educational policy nor any state interests that would justify denying undocumented children an education.[10]

Finally, Texas maintained that undocumented children were singled out because their unlawful presence and that of their parents rendered them less likely to remain in the country and therefore less able to use the free public education they received in order to contribute to the social and political goals of the U.S. community. In response, the Court distinguished the subclass of undocumented immigrants who resided in the United States permanently as family units from the subclass of noncitizens who enter the country alone and whose intent is to earn money and stay temporarily. For those who remain, intent on making the United States their home, "[i]t is difficult to understand precisely what the State hopes to achieve by promoting the

---

[5] Graham v. Richardson, 403 U.S. 365, 374–75 (1971).

[6] Plyler, 457 U.S. at 207 (citation omitted).

[7] *Id.* at 229 (citing 628 F.2d 448, 461 (5th Cir. 1980)).

[8] *Id.* at 228 (citation omitted); *see, e.g.*, Toll v. Moreno, 458 U.S. 1 (1982) (allowing Treaty Organization visa-holders to establish residence for college fee purposes).

[9] Because Justice Brennan struck down the statute on Fourteenth Amendment grounds, he did not reach the issue of preemption. Plyler, 457 U.S. at 210. *See, e.g.*, DeCanas v. Bica, 424 U.S. 351 (1976) (analyzing whether state regulation was preempted by federal immigration law).

[10] "It is thus clear that whatever savings might be achieved by denying these children an education, they are wholly insubstantial in light of the costs involved to these children, the State, and the Nation." Plyler, 457 U.S. at 230.

creation and perpetuation of a subclass of illiterates within our boundaries, surely adding to the problems and costs of unemployment, welfare, and crime."[11]

As in many Equal Protection cases, the major issue in *Plyler* was the level of scrutiny to be accorded the Texas statute. Undocumented persons, without lawful status, prior to *Plyler*, had won constitutional protection in Fourth, Fifth, and Sixth Amendment cases, as well as in a range of civil litigation.[12] However, the Supreme Court had never been faced with the question of whether undocumented persons could seek equal protection under the Fourteenth Amendment. The Supreme Court had earlier held that undocumented persons are protected by the due process provisions of the Fourteenth Amendment.[13]

However, the State of Texas argued that because undocumented children were not "within its jurisdiction,"[14] they were not entitled to equal protection. Justice Brennan rejected this line of reasoning, drawing upon the legislative history of the Fourteenth Amendment and concluding that there "is simply no support for [the] suggestion that 'due process' is somehow of greater stature than 'equal protection' and therefore available to a larger class of persons."[15] Once he had determined that undocumented persons were entitled to equal protection, he determined the extent of scrutiny to be applied in the case. He discarded strict scrutiny, noting that undocumented persons were neither a "suspect class" nor was education a "fundamental right."[16] He also rejected the minimal scrutiny inherent in a two-tiered standard. Rather, he chose the "intermediate scrutiny" standard of *Craig v. Boren,* and found that the statute did not advance "some substantial state inter-est."[17] Therefore, he affirmed the judgments of the United States District Court and Court of Appeals invalidating the statute. While he reaffirmed the Court's decision in *San Antonio Independent School Dist. v. Rodriguez* that held public education not to be a fundamental right, he recited a litany of cases holding edu-cation to have "a fundamental role in maintaining the fabric of our society."[18]

---

[11] *Id.*

[12] Wong Wing v. United States, 163 U.S. 228, 238 (1896) (finding that all aliens are "persons" subject to due process guarantees of the Fifth and Sixth Amendments); Mathews v. Diaz, 426 U.S. 67, 77 (1976) (finding that undocumented immigrants are protected by the Fifth Amendment from invidious discrimination by the federal government); Torres v. Sierra, 553 P.2d 721, 724 (N.M. 1976) (affirming that an undocumented immigrant is a "person" within meaning of Wrongful Death Act); Arteaga v. Literski, 265 N.W.2d 148, 149 (Wis. 1978) (holding that undocumented immigrants may bring suit in personal injury actions).

[13] Yick Wo v. Hopkins, 118 U.S. 356, 369 (1886) (finding that the Fourteenth Amendment provisions "are universal in their application, to all persons").

[14] Plyler, 457 U.S. at 211.

[15] *Id.* at 213.

[16] *Id.* at 223. In dissent, Chief Justice Burger concurred that the Equal Protection Clause applies to undocumented immigrants. *Id.* at 243 (Burger, J., dissenting).

[17] *Id.* at 218, 218 n.16 (citing Craig v. Boren, 429 U.S. 190 (1976)). He continues "[o]nly when concerns sufficiently absolute and enduring can be clearly ascertained from the Constitution and our cases do we employ this standard to aid us in determining the rationality of the legislative choice." *Id.*

[18] *Id.* at 230.

Moreover, he determined that "illiteracy is an enduring disability,"[19] one that would plague the individual and society.

THE LEGAL INFLUENCE AND IMPACT OF *PLYLER*

Indeed, *Plyler* stands as settled law forty years later, and has never been seriously challenged in federal or state courts over the intervening years. Scholars who have looked carefully and thoughtfully at the case have determined it to be *sui generis*, not so much limited to its facts but as possessing weak doctrinal force and little constitutional significance. Its gravitational pull has not affected many subsequent cases, as none has come before the Court since then on all fours. Much of the considerable scholarly response to the Court's reasoning in the case has evinced surprise that the majority went as far as it did in rejecting the state's sovereignty. Professor Peter Schuck, for example, characterized the decision as a "conceptual watershed in immigration law, the most powerful rejection to date of classical immigration law's notion of plenary national sovereignty over our borders."[20] He reflects that "Courts are expositors of a constitutional tradition that increasingly emphasizes ... the universal, transcendent values of equality and fairness imminent in the due process and equal protection principles."[21] Notwithstanding, Dennis Hutchinson is among the most caustic doubter of *Plyler's* efficacy and significance: "Perhaps it is simply not appropriate to subject *Plyler v. Doe* to close analysis. Two of the concurring opinions warn against doing so."[22] Concerning *Plyler* and other similar cases, Professor Linda Bosniak has noted the ongoing tension between "alienage discrimination" and the "government's power to regulate the border and control the composition of membership in the national community."[23] She states that the questions concerning this tension "shape the law's conflicted understandings of the difference that alienage makes."[24]

All these views are likely correct, in that *Plyler's* incontestably bold reasoning has not substantially influenced subsequent Supreme Court immigration jurisprudence in the forty years since it was decided. The educational significance of the case, however, is still clear, even if it is limited to this subset of immigrants in the United States. Given the poor overall educational achievement evident in this population, this success story has significance in that it led to well over a million undocumented college students. Through the many pathways available in the immigration systems,

---

[19] *Id.* at 222.
[20] Peter H. Schuck, *The Transformation of Immigration Law*, 84 COLUM. L. REV. 1, 58 (1984).
[21] *Id.*
[22] Dennis J. Hutchinson, *More Substantive Equal Protection? A Note on* Plyler v. Doe, 1982 SUP. CT. REV. 167, 194 (1982).
[23] Linda Bosniak, *Membership, Equality, and the Difference That Alienage Makes*, 69 N.Y.U. L. REV. 1047, 1057 (1994).
[24] *Id.*

these students later surfaced as DREAMers, a highly visible political cohort, forming the ongoing progress and influence of *Plyler*.[25]

PLYLER AND THE POLITY

The political events since 1982 have not led to serious challenges on legislative
fronts, even as *Plyler* has always been vulnerable to federal legislating on the issue
of the education of undocumented children.[26] The Gallegly proposal was the one
serious attempt to preempt *Plyler's* holding at the federal level. Representative
Elton Gallegly (R-CA) led an unsuccessful effort in 1996 to ban undocumented
children from public schools, but his proposal was so polarizing it did not take
root or result in legislation. Even the two conservative Texas Republican Senators
did not support the proposed legislation because Texas educators and business
leaders had begun to make their peace with *Plyler's* result, growing the school-
aged population and providing labor.[27] Such federal efforts have not surfaced in a
serious vein since then.

Similarly, no serious state actions have threatened undocumented elementary and
secondary students' educational access in the four decades since *Plyler* was decided.[28]
The League of United Latin American Citizens (LULAC), for example, successfully
enjoined California's restrictionist Proposition 187 in *LULAC v. Wilson*. During a
deep economic recession, California voters had overwhelmingly passed a nativist
ballot initiative in 1994, Proposition 187, which restricted undocumented immigrants
from state public services, including access to public education, and required school
officials to report anyone suspected of being undocumented.[29] Notwithstanding
Plyler's continued validity, and subsequent cases like *LULAC* that rejected attempts
to limit undocumented students' access to schools, scholars have since chronicled a
number of secondary direct and diagonal threats targeting undocumented students.
Yet these cases in Albuquerque, New Mexico, Elmwood Park, Illinois, and El Paso,
Texas, all resolved anti-immigrant student policies in favor of the affected families,
whose children were singled out for school policies aimed at undocumented students.

Rather, the record shows a wide and deep accommodation of these children at the
individual school, district, and state levels – even as federal and state efforts to enact

---

[25] *See generally* MICHAEL A. OLIVAS, PERCHANCE TO DREAM: A LEGAL AND POLITICAL HISTORY
OF THE DREAM ACT & DACA (2020).

[26] MICHAEL A. OLIVAS, *The Story of* Plyler v. Doe, *The Education of Undocumented Children, and the
Polity, in* IMMIGRATION LAW STORIES 197, 212–13 (David A. Martin & Peter H. Schuck, eds., 2005).

[27] PHILIP G. SCHRAG, A WELL-FOUNDED FEAR: THE CONGRESSIONAL BATTLE TO SAVE
POLITICAL ASYLUM IN AMERICA 178 n. 33 (2000).

[28] Michael A. Olivas, *The Political Efficacy of* Plyler v. Doe: *The Danger and the Discourse*, 45 U.C.
DAVIS L. REV. 1, 11–12 (2011).

[29] MICHAEL A. OLIVAS, *Immigrant Children: Hiding in Plain Sight in the Margins of the Urban
Infrastructure, in* RESEARCH ON SCHOOLS, NEIGHBORHOODS, AND COMMUNITIES: TOWARD
CIVIC RESPONSIBILITY 327, 336–39 (William F. Tate IV ed., 2012).

stricter employment and immigrant legislation increased against adult workers without legal status, such as the Personal Responsibility and Work Opportunity Reconciliation Act of 1996 and Illegal Immigration Reform and Immigrant Responsibility Act of 1996. As but one example, Utah – not thought of as a particularly hospitable climate to immigrants – retained its postsecondary residency tuition status for undocumented college students as it moved to enact significant restrictionist employment and benefit legislation. Almost two dozen states have passed favorable college residency requirement laws that allow undocumented youth to attend college as in-state residents.[30] California, Texas, and other states have also made undocumented students eligible for state financial aid.[31] These are surely markers of how deeply the roots of *Plyler* have reached into the country's soil. The truth is that the United States needs this talent pool. In many highly technical fields, international scholars enroll in high numbers and, after consuming the benefits of our educational system, return to their countries. This is as it should be, as learning respects no borders, and recruiting internationally surely enriches U.S. institutions. However, the undocumented have every incentive to remain in the United States, to adjust their status through formal or discretionary means, and to contribute to the U.S. economy and community.[32]

THE FEMINIST JUDGMENT

Professor Wadhia, in her concurrence, begins with the ways in which *Plyler* sets forth a concerning narrative for immigrant parents and their children. She notes that even though the Plaintiff children and parents prevailed in the case, a subtle and nuanced blame-casting ("demonizing") occurred through Justice Brennan's nomenclature and innuendo by means of pejorative (and inaccurate) characterizations, particularly that of "illegal" and especially "illegal alien." Wadhia itemizes why this terminology is imprecise and ascribes criminality in a civil law domain. Her language is measured, but she gives short shrift to the casual use of such loaded language, even as the Plaintiffs prevailed in their claims. One can imagine the negative and prejudicial language that might have been employed had Texas and the school districts won the case. Furthermore, she highlights how the majority opinion regards the children to be innocents, while characterizing their parents as lawbreaking criminals. The perception of undocumented parents as inherently criminal has fueled anti-immigrant rhetoric that has influenced their exclusion from paths to legalization in comprehensive immigration reform policy proposals.

---

[30] Olivas, Perchance, *supra* note 25, at 145–48 (containing in Appendix 1 a detailed list of "State Laws Allowing Undocumented College Students to Establish Residency," as of 2019).

[31] *Id.* The Appendix also includes eligibility for state financial aid. *See generally* Michael A. Olivas, *Within You without You: Undocumented Lawyers, DACA, and Occupational Licensing*, 52 VALPARAISO L. REV. 1 (2018) (reviewing immigration status requirements for state occupational licensing laws).

[32] *See* Michael A. Olivas, *The Growing Role of Immigration Law in Universal Higher Education: Case Studies of the United States and the EU*, 37 HOUSTON J. INT'L L. 353, 386 (2015).

Professor Wadhia's next concern is the most fulsome part of her concurrence, and in several ways, the most critical in her determination that the majority employed the wrong level of scrutiny. Her concurrence critiques how the Court could have, on its own terms, found undocumented alienage of children to be suspect or, more satisfactorily, provided detailed criteria for measuring "enduring disability," so that legislatures could fashion more acceptable ends-means formulations in such instances.

Wadhia finds that the Supreme Court could have applied strict scrutiny to undocumented children as a "suspect class." She looks to the past holdings of the court with respect to alienage, such as in *Graham v. Richardson*. The Court's previous national-origin and alienage cases, read together, provide a considerable record of the "deep-seated prejudice" so manifestly evident in the state's treatment of undocumented persons. The majority held, however, that undocumented entry is "the product of voluntary action." Wadhia pushes back on this assumption by offering the many reasons that immigrant parents enter the United States with their children. She explains that some of these reasons like unsafe home country conditions and reunification with U.S.-based family members, remove the voluntariness of migration given the absence of safe and legal pathways to the United States.[33]

Professor Wadhia disagrees with *San Antonio Independent School District v. Rodriguez*, which held that education was not a fundamental right, and that the resource-poor school districts, while unequal, did not violate the rights of predominantly Mexican American school children. Wadhia would have applied "strict judicial scrutiny" because a fundamental right was implicated. She does not, however, seek to distinguish *Plyler's* "absolute deprivation [of education]" from *Rodriguez's* minimum education for all Texas school children, which did not ultimately constitute "an absolute deprivation." Rather, she focuses on a broader concept captured by Justice Marshall's dissent in *Rodriguez*: the fundamental importance of education, the unique status of public education in our society, and how it reflects our basic constitutional values. Wadhia might have added the far-reaching problematic impact of *Rodriguez* – the ability of states to allocate resources disparately across its school districts, resulting in unequal and discriminatory wealth differences in winner and loser subdivisions.

Finally, Wadhia's concurrence makes the significant point that undocumented children may very well be shielded from deportation because "the government simply lacks the resources to deport every person who is legally eligible to be deported." The Court itself recognized:

> In light of the discretionary federal power to grant relief from deportation, a State cannot realistically determine that any particular undocumented child will in fact

---

[33] *See* Katharine T. Bartlett, *Feminist Legal Methods*, 103 HARV. L. REV. 829, 851 (1990) (describing feminist practical reasoning as an approach to problems that pays attention to particular context).

be deported until after deportation proceedings have been completed. It would, of course, be most difficult for the State to justify a denial of education to a child enjoying an inchoate federal permission to remain.[34]

It is this "inchoate permission to remain" that suffuses *Plyler*, and likely paved the way to the 1986 Immigration Reform and Control Act (IRCA) that implemented *Plyler* and offered legalization to undocumented adults and parents. It eventually led even to President Obama's administrative actions, in his act of prosecutorial discretion embodied by the Deferred Action for Childhood Arrivals (DACA) program and his short-lived attempt to extend such discretion to undocumented parents of U.S. citizen and lawful permanent resident children with Deferred Action for Parents of Americans and Lawful Permanent Residents (DAPA). These are the very populations singled out for advantage in *Plyler*. Although the courts struck down DAPA as the legal equivalent of a bridge too far, these developments demonstrate the ways in which the government has enacted programs to shield individuals without legal status from deportation.[35]

One additional feature Wadhia might have addressed is the contradictory way in which the Court viewed "unlawful presence." The Court distinguished the subclass of undocumented persons who live in the United States as a family from the subclass of adult immigrants who enter the country alone and whose intent is to earn money and stay temporarily. It did so by recognizing that some reside in the United States with the intent of making it their home. Ultimately the states cannot have it both ways, disqualifying or precluding immigrants who have the genuine (if unarticulated) purpose to stay for the long haul, yet enacting laws or policies that do not allow such immigrants to establish deep roots, such as singling out their children for punitive purposes.

CONCLUSION

In sum, Wadhia's concurrence in *Plyler* could have had more traction, had it been the majority opinion. Given *Plyler*'s holding, it is hard to imagine more influence or reach. Writing as a first-generation Asian American, and the daughter of immigrants, however, Wadhia was able to draw on her own experience to admonish against demonizing parents and acknowledge the sacrifices that parents make for their children "to ensure they had the opportunities of achieving the American Dream." The issues that have arisen since the decision, such as those concerning school attendance zones, domicile and its effect on college residency requirements, and the extent to which undocumented parents have fewer corresponding rights than do their children would have been clarified. Her scholarship as a law professor has, in many respects, addressed these unresolved *Plyler* K-12 issues and the extension

---

[34] *Plyler*, 457 U.S. at 226.
[35] *Texas v. United States*, 809 F.3d 134 (5th Cir. 2015), *affirmed*, 579 U.S. 547 (2016).

to "Postsecondary *Plyler*" and DACA issues.[36] At the time of this writing, DACA is the can kicked down the road, and is in play with President Biden's agenda, with another Supreme Court case likely to determine its constitutionality. When that day arrives, Wadhia's writing will be essential.[37]

It has been forty-five years since IRCA, and persistent immigration quotas, country limitations, delays, and the four-year assault on immigration by the Trump Administration have taken a toll on undocumented immigration and delayed naturalizations, as well as over a million DACAmented students (800,000 in the program, and a similar number left at the gates when it was unlawfully suspended).[38] Wadhia has written a scathing analysis of the first eighteen months of the Trump Administration's disastrous immigration policies, including the "Muslim Ban," family separation, and the 2018 program called the "Migrant Protection Protocols" (MPP) – referred to as the "Remain in Mexico" program.[39]

Although the Biden Administration has swung into action to appeal and rescue DACA, DACA's future is uncertain. A district court in Texas has suspended new applications for the discretionary relief, which had allowed the 800,000 DACAmented students to hold employment authorization (EAD), be entitled to a Social Security Number (SSN), and be accorded lawful presence, much like the exact legal characteristics of the undocumented plaintiff children in *Plyler*.[40] There are attempts to get the DREAM Act, a law providing for a pathway to citizenship for undocumented youth, enacted into law.[41] However, as of Spring, 2022, it is unclear what will happen. In this climate, any attempt to enact more comprehensive immigration reform is unlikely to prevail.[42]

---

[36] *See generally* SHOBA SIVAPRASAD WADHIA, BEYOND DEPORTATION: THE ROLE OF PROSECUTORIAL DISCRETION IN IMMIGRATION CASES (2015).

[37] Professor Wadhia has also coauthored a comprehensive immigration casebook, showing her commitment to instruction and scholarship: LENNI B. BENSON, STEPHEN W. YALE-LOEHR & SHOBA SIVAPRASAD WADHIA, IMMIGRATION AND NATIONALITY LAW: PROBLEMS AND STRATEGIES (2020). *See also* SHOBA SIVAPRASAD WADHIA, BANNED: IMMIGRATION ENFORCEMENT IN THE TIME OF TRUMP (2019); Shoba Sivaprasad Wadhia, *National Security, Immigration and the Muslim Bans*, 75 WASH. & LEE L. REV. 1475 (2018); Shoba Sivaprasad Wadhia, *Darkside Discretion in Immigration Cases*, 72 ADMIN. L. REV. 367 (2020).

[38] OLIVAS, PERCHANCE, *supra* note 25, at 108–31 ("The 2016 Election of Donald Trump, the Recission of DACA, and Its Aftermath").

[39] *See* Shoba Sivaprasad Wadhia, *Immigration Litigation in the Time of Trump*, 53 U.C. DAVIS ONLINE 121 (2019).

[40] Texas v. United States, No. 1:18-CV-00068, 2021 WL 3025857, at *42 (S.D. Tex. July 16, 2021); OLIVAS, PERCHANCE, *supra* note 25, at 108–31; *see generally* Nicole Prchal Svajlenka & Trinh Q. Truong, *The Demographic and Economic Impacts of DACA Recipients: Fall 2021 Edition*, CTR. FOR AM. PROGRESS (Nov. 24, 2021), www.americanprogress.org/article/the-demographic-and-economic-impacts-of-daca-recipients-fall-2021-edition/.

[41] DONALD KERWIN, JOSÉ PACAS & ROBERT WARREN, READY TO STAY: A COMPREHENSIVE ANALYSIS OF THE US FOREIGN-BORN POPULATIONS ELIGIBLE FOR SPECIAL LEGAL STATUS PROGRAMS AND FOR LEGALIZATION UNDER PENDING BILLS 3 (2021).

[42] *See, e.g.*, David Axelrod, *It's Not Over for Joe Biden*, N.Y. TIMES, Dec. 28, 2021 (analyzing several complex strategies for enacting bills tied up in Senate).

No matter the legislative or litigation options, it will take time to sort out these issues. Meanwhile, *Plyler* itself, which gave birth to DACA, remains in place, undisturbed and widely accepted.[43] In many respects, had Professor Wadhia's concurrence been adopted as the majority opinion, much more light and nuance would have been possible. Following the tradition of feminist anti-subordination theory,[44] her recognition of the hierarchy created by the alienage classification, which also operated as a proxy for race, could have further illuminated the social oppression of undocumented immigrants.[45] Had hers been the majority view, *Plyler's* considerable light would have reached even further, enshrining it even more obviously as the apex of immigrant rights.

PLYLER v. DOE, 457 U.S. 202 (1982)

Justice Shoba Sivaprasad Wadhia, concurring.

This case centers on Texas statute § 21.031, which on its face permits the local school districts to exclude, or charge admission for, noncitizen children who entered the United States without immigration status. The questions before the Court are whether a noncitizen under the statute who is present in the state without legal status is a "person" and therefore in the jurisdiction of the state within the meaning of the Equal Protection Clause of the Fourteenth Amendment; and if yes, whether the statute violates the Equal Protection Clause. The plaintiffs in this case are school age children of Mexican origin residing in Smith County, Texas, who could not establish that they were legally admitted into the United States.

I join the opinion and judgment of the Court, holding that "A Texas statute which withholds from local school districts any state funds for the education of children who were not 'legally admitted' into the United States, and which authorizes local school districts to deny enrollment to such children, violates the Equal Protection Clause of the Fourteenth Amendment." I join the Court's conclusion about the important role of public education, the absence of a national policy to allow for a denial of public education, and the inclusion of undocumented children as "person[s] within its jurisdiction" under the Equal Protection Clause.

Like Justice Blackmun, in his concurring opinion, I believe that the Texas law denying public education to noncitizens without legal status "strike[s] at the

---

[43] For an overall assessment of Plyler's decades' long history, *see* MICHAEL A. OLIVAS, NO UNDOCUMENTED CHILD LEFT BEHIND: PLYLER V. DOE AND THE EDUCATION OF UNDOCUMENTED CHILDREN (2012); Olivas, *The Growing Role of Immigration Law*, *supra* note 32 (reviewing the international effect of *Plyler* and immigration issues in K-12 and colleges).

[44] Ruth Colker, *Anti-Subordination Above All: Sex, Race, and Equal Protection*, 61 N.Y.U. L. REV. 1003, 1007–10 (1986).

[45] *See, e.g.*, Erica O. Turner & Ariana Mangual Figueroa, *Immigration Policy and Education in Lived Reality: A Framework for Researchers and Educators*, 48 EDUC. RESEARCHER 549 (2019) (examining the lives and educational experiences of undocumented students using critical sociocultural approaches and critical race theories).

heart of the equal protection values by involving the State in the creation of permanent class distinctions."

I write separately however, for three reasons. First, in my view, the Court sets up a problematic differentiation between immigrant parents and their children. By casting the plaintiffs, who are undocumented children, as "illegal aliens," the Court creates a presumptively criminal class, which is inaccurate as a legal matter, and dehumanizing as a moral one. Remarkably, the term "illegal alien" appears more than ten times in the Court's opinion, normalizing the troublesome phrase for the reader and leaving an impression that the term is also accurate.

Second, I disagree with the conclusion by the Court that plaintiffs are not a suspect class. I believe they are a discrete class for which the strict scrutiny standard should apply. There are many forces that make the conditions of undocumented children worthy of a heightened analysis, including the fallacy that entry into the United States without legal status by parents with their children is a free choice and the ways that alienage is operating as a proxy for national origin discrimination. Further, I believe the Texas statute should be subject to strict scrutiny analysis because education is a fundamental right. While the majority adopts a less rigorous test to conclude that the State of Texas has failed to show how denying public education furthers a legitimate public purpose or substantial interest of the state, I believe the burden on Texas should be to prove that denying public education is a compelling interest, a showing that clearly fails here.

Finally, I wish to elaborate upon the Court's accurate conclusion that most children will never be deported and thus must be treated as if they will remain in the United States permanently. This is true not only because of the potential relief or legal status they may qualify for in the future, but also because of the inevitability and use of prosecutorial discretion in immigration law to protect minors.

I

First, the Court engages in a problematic narrative for immigrant parents and their children. By repeatedly labeling plaintiffs as "illegal aliens," the Court normalizes the concept of a presumptively criminal class, which is both inaccurate and dehumanizing. The Immigration and Nationality Act does not use the term "illegal aliens" to define a group of persons subject to deportation, nor does "illegal alien" appear in the governing regulations. Immigration and Nationality Act, Pub. L. No. 82-414, § 241, 66 Stat. 163 (1952). Rather than bring clarity, the Court's repeated use of "illegal alien" clouds the narrative and undermines the Court's own discussion about whether the term "person" includes all persons, citizen, and noncitizen alike, within the Equal Protection Clause of the Fourteenth Amendment.

The term "illegal alien" is also inaccurate because it places a permanent label on an immigrant who might at some point in the future adjust to a legal status or attain U.S. citizenship. For example, an immigrant who enters the United States without inspection as a toddler might many years later acquire the years of residence and equities or exhibit the personal hardships to be eligible for a waiver. The term "illegal alien" is also dehumanizing and conjures an image of both a lawbreaker and an outsider. "Even the term 'alien' (and especially the term 'illegal alien') connotes such a degree of strangeness as to be dehumanizing and tends to reinforce the attitude that such people are residents in the United States at the pleasure of the government." David F. Aberson, *Deportation of Aliens for Criminal Convictions*, 2 Pepp. L. Rev. 52, 58 (1974). When the term "illegal alien" is employed, the whole person is diminished by just one act. Such branding does not exist in other domains. When a person drives on the highway over the speed limit, we do not call them "illegal" even though they have technically broken the law. The term "illegal alien" is also alienating, as the phrase would suggest, marking a person as excludable or as someone who does not belong. Having already acknowledged the benefits of a public education and the inclusion of all people within the Equal Protection framework, including those who are undocumented children, the Court would be more consistent and accurate by using terms that are more inclusive and welcoming.

Further, the Court also creates a paradigm where the parents are at fault and the children are victims. When applying the rational basis test, the Court claims, "we may appropriately take into account its costs to the Nation and to the innocent children who are victims." 457 U.S. at 224. In finding no national policy for allowing States to deny educational benefits to children (a conclusion I agree with on its merits), the Court again casts children as innocent and the parents as at fault: "We are reluctant to impute to Congress the intention to withhold from these children, for as long as they are present in this country through no fault of their own, access to basic education." *Id.* at 226.

This narrative is problematic because it labels every parent in the United States from Mexico as blameworthy, as having freely chosen to enter the United States unlawfully. While we do not know the exact causes of migration from Mexico, such migrants have fewer options to enter the United States. The 1965 Immigration and Nationality Act for the first time set a limit of 120,000 overall visas for nationals from the Western Hemisphere and a cap of 20,000 visas for each country, without regard to demand or size. While Congress was successful in ending the discriminatory national origin quotas that pervaded the immigration law for decades, the 1965 amendments had the effect of numerically limiting legal pathways for Mexican nationals. Another limitation placed on migration from Mexico was the end of the "Bracero" program. The Bracero program, from 1942 to 1964, allowed hundreds of thousands of Mexicans to enter the United States for the purpose of labor. Gilberto Cárdenas, *United States Immigration Policy toward Mexico: An Historical Perspective*, 2 Chicano L. Rev. 66, 75–79 (1975). Related to this history is what the majority calls a "shadow population" of migrants "encouraged by some to remain here as a source of cheap labor, but nevertheless denied the benefits that our society makes available

to citizens and lawful residents." 457 U.S. at 219. Consequently, rather than placing blame on parents, one must examine the existing statutory framework and the
limited opportunities available for this same population to enter the United States
through a legal channel.

After showcasing the various benefits of education, the Court should not easily
criticize parents who enter the United States to provide their children with greater
opportunities or the chance to access education. When discussing the values of
education, the majority concluded:

> Both the importance of education in maintaining our basic institutions, and the
> lasting impact of its deprivation on the life of the child, mark the distinction.
> The "American people have always regarded education and [the] acquisition of
> knowledge as matters of supreme importance." We have recognized "the public
> schools as a most vital civic institution for the preservation of a democratic system
> of government."

Id. at 221 (citations omitted). Children who access education in the United States
and contribute to society may themselves reject the narrative by this Court that the
parents are to blame or should be treated differently. In the future, when they are old
enough to understand, these same children will be grateful for the sacrifices made
by their parents to ensure they had the opportunities of achieving the American
Dream. Rather than pit the child against the parent as the Court does here, the
Court should promote family unity, which in turn would bear consistency with
Congress' own commitment to family relationships and family unity. Immigration
and Nationality Act of 1965, Pub. L. 89-236, §§ 201–03, 79 Stat. 911–14 (1965) (current
version at 8 U.S.C. §§ 1151–53).

II

Second, I disagree with the conclusion that undocumented children are not a suspect class or that education is somehow not a fundamental right. Concluding that
education is a fundamental right and undocumented children are a suspect class, I
believe the Texas statute violates the Equal Protection Clause and should be subject
to a strict scrutiny analysis.

We have previously held that alienage is a suspect class, and we should not depart
from that conclusion. Classifications based on race, nationality, or alienage are well
established. *See, e.g., Graham v. Richardson,* 403 U.S. 365, 372 (1971). In *Graham,*
Arizona and Pennsylvania sought to restrict eligibility of benefits for noncitizens
"solely on the basis of a State's 'special public interest' in favoring its own citizens
over aliens in the distribution of limited resources such as welfare benefits." *Id.*
There, the Court concluded that "[a]liens as a class are a prime example of a 'discrete
and insular minority,' for whom such heightened judicial solicitude is appropriate."
Id. It further held that "a State's desire to preserve limited welfare benefits for its own

citizens is inadequate to justify Pennsylvania's making noncitizens ineligible for public assistance, and Arizona's restricting benefits to citizens and longtime resident aliens." *Id.* at 374. The Court agreed with the conclusion of the three-judge court in Pennsylvania that "limiting expenses is particularly inappropriate and unreasonable when the discriminated class consists of aliens. Aliens, like citizens, pay taxes, and may be called into the armed forces …. [They] may live within a state for many years, work in the state and contribute to the economic growth of the state." *Id.* at 376 (citation omitted). In short, the Court concluded that "alienage" was a suspect classification when analyzing state legislation and therefore should be subject to a strict scrutiny test.

Yet the Court's opinion distinguishes the plaintiffs here from those who might be treated as a "presumptively invidious" or "suspect class," based on conclusions that undocumented status is somehow mutable because it reflects a "conscious, indeed unlawful, action." *Plyler*, 457 U.S. at 220. But alienage and undocumented status are not things that can be changed simply. In my view, there are many forces that make the conditions of undocumented children immutable or a "suspect class" worthy of a heightened analysis requiring more than a rational or legitimate government objective.

It is misguided to conclude that parents have the freedom of choice to enter the United States. There are several reasons parents may enter the United States with their children without legal status. Some of these reasons include conditions in their home countries, opportunities for their children in the United States, and the absence of legislative reform. Congress' own immigration law has created a landscape that makes it impossible for children and their parents to enter from Mexico to the United States lawfully. While the 1965 Immigration Act was instrumental in opening immigration channels for immigrants from Asia, it also had the effect of reducing legal immigration from Mexico. "Mexican immigration was cut by almost 50% when the 1976 amendments to the Immigration and Nationality Act imposed a per-country limitation of 20,000 upon Western Hemisphere countries." Amicus Br. for Asian Am. Legal Def. & Educ. Fund (AALDEF) 16 n.29 (citing Act of October 3, 1965, Pub. L. No. 94-571, 66 Stat. 163)).

Further, parents and children are driven to reunite or remain with family members who hold U.S. citizenship. Indeed, several families living in the United States are in "mixed status" families, which means a single family may have a variety of immigration statuses, one undocumented, one as a green card holder, and the other as a U.S. citizen. *See* Josh Reichert & Douglas S. Massey, *Patterns of U.S. Migration from a Mexican Sending Community: A Comparison of Legal and Illegal Migrants*, 13 Int'l Migration Rev. 599, 610 (1979). Finally, and connected to my first point, is the Court's own casting of parents and children in this case as "illegal aliens," which in my view only bolsters the "presumptively invidious" group and vulnerability of undocumented immigrants.

The disproportionate impact of § 21.031 on Mexican children is evident. As described by the amicus brief filed by (AALDEF): "It is undisputed that the primary victims of section 21.031 of the Texas Education Code are children of Mexican origin, since almost all undocumented aliens in Texas are Mexican. Because immigration status has historically been used to discriminate against racial and ethnic minorities, § 21.031 should be considered within the broader context of discrimination against Hispanics as a minority group in Texas." Amicus Br. for AALDEF 14. In these ways, alienage is operating as a proxy for national origin – in this case, being Mexican.

This Texas statute should be subject to strict scrutiny. "[R]ace, nationality, or alienage is 'in most circumstances irrelevant' to any constitutionally acceptable legislative purpose. Instead, lines drawn on such bases are frequently the reflection of historic prejudices rather than legislative rationality." *San Antonio Independent School Dist. v. Rodriguez*, 411 U.S. 1, 105 (1973) (citations omitted) (Marshall, J., dissenting). I hope that in the future, this Court will revisit how undocumented children are cast in Equal Protection analysis.

Further, I agree with Justice Marshall who also writes separately today to hold that public education must be recognized as a fundamental right. This Court touts the values of education but refuses to acknowledge education as a fundamental right. Like the majority in today's decision, this same Court made a similar conclusion in the case of *Rodriguez*. In that case, the Court found that the Texas system of financing public education, which disadvantages a suspect class of "poor" people who reside in low property tax-based school districts, does not interfere with a fundamental right: "[t]hough education is one of the most important services performed by the State, it is not within the limited category of rights recognized by this Court as guaranteed by the Constitution." *Id.* at 2. This Court's conclusion today extends the dangerous precedent set in *Rodriguez*.

In fact, Justice Marshall's dissent in *Rodriguez* provides a tour into the case law and the ways the Court has previously made determinations of whether specific interests are fundamental. "[T]he fundamental importance of education is amply indicated by the prior decisions of this Court, by the unique status accorded public education by our society, and by the close relationship between education and some of our most basic constitutional values." *Id.* at 111 (Marshall, J., dissenting). He then points to the mandate for public education in all 50 states, the importance of education to "prepare citizens to participate effectively and intelligently in our open political system," and the intimate relationship between education and the political process, as among the reasons education should be recognized as a fundamental right. *Id.*

Amici also frame education as a fundamental right. As discussed in the amicus brief of Texas IMPACT, an interreligious nonprofit:

ACCESS TO PRIMARY EDUCATION IS A FUNDAMENTAL RIGHT. It is undisputed that the children in this litigation are protected by the due process clause of the fourteenth amendment. Mathews v. Diaz, 426 U.S. 67(1976); Wong Wing v. United States, 163 U.S. 228 (1896) …. [A]ccess to primary education, which is universally recognized as essential to a child's acquisition of basic literacy skills, surely ranks among those fundamental rights deserving of this Court's continued solicitude.

Amicus Br. for Tex. Impact 9–12.

Further, the National Education Association and League of United Latin American Citizens (NEA-LULAC) in their amicus brief explain how the language of *Rodriguez* signaled education as fundamental:

> As the Court in Rodriguez recognized, the absolute denial of basic education may unconstitutionally impede the meaningful exercise of the First Amendment freedom to impart and receive information and the effective utilization of the right to vote. The relationship between education and the proper functioning of a republican form of government is one which was frequently expressed by the original framers of the Constitution.

Amicus Br. for NEA-LULAC 9.

The NEA-LULAC brief also quotes the words of our Founders to underscore this position on education. It states that "John Adams also believed that education was essential to a republican form of government." *Id.* at 13. Adams stated that "Education is more indispensable, and must be more general, under a free government than any other …. [I]n a free government knowledge must be general, and ought to be universal." *Id.* at 13–14. It also notes the writings of Thomas Jefferson, an ardent proponent of public education, who viewed education as a necessary corollary of the right to an equal vote and of the right freely to transmit and receive information. *Id.* at 14.

Thus, I further conclude that education, like with other interests not specifically written into the Constitution, should be treated as a fundamental right.

III

Third and finally, I want to elaborate on the majority's apt conclusion that if children were denied public education, it is unlikely they would be deported. *Plyler,* 457 U.S. at 226. The clearest evidence to support this conclusion is the fact that some children who are undocumented today could in the future acquire durable status. The District Court acknowledged this very point: "the illegal alien of today may well be the legal alien of tomorrow." *Doe v. Plyler,* 458 F. Supp. 569, 577 (E.D. Tex. 1978). Rolan Heston, District Director of the Houston District of the INS, testified before the District Court that "undocumented children can and do live in the United States for years, and adjust their status through marriage to a citizen or permanent resident." *Id.* The District Court also identifies the legislative proposals in Congress to "legalize" those who entered the United States without status. *Id.* at 578.

An equally important reason that undocumented children would not be deported is prosecutorial discretion. Prosecutorial discretion refers to a choice by the Immigration and Naturalization Service (INS) to deport or not deport a person because of equities and limited resources. *See, e.g.,* Memorandum from Sam Bernsen, Gen. Counsel, INS, to Comm'r, Legal Opinion Regarding Service Exercise of Prosecutorial Discretion (July 15, 1976). Historically, young children, those with tender age or those who are living in the United States and going to school, have been among those protected through prosecutorial discretion. Similarly, undocumented parents caring for children in the United States have also been among those protected. *See also* Leon Wildes, *The Nonpriority Program of the Immigration and Naturalization Service Goes Public: The Litigative Use of the Freedom of Information Act,* 14 San Diego L. Rev. 42, 53–54 (1976). In 1975, the INS published "Operations Instructions" that require INS to consider the following equities:

> (1) advanced or tender age; (2) many years' presence in the United States; (3) physical or mental condition requiring care or treatment in the United States; (4) family situation in the United States—effect of expulsion; (5) criminal, immoral or subversive activities or affiliations—recent conduct. If the district director's recommendation is approved by the regional commissioner the alien shall be notified that no action will be taken by the Service to disturb his immigration status, or that his departure from the United States has been deferred indefinitely, whichever is appropriate.

INS, Operating Instructions § 103.1(a)(1)(ii) (Dec. 31, 1975). These discretionary protections are inevitable because the government simply lacks the resources to deport every person who is legally eligible to be deported. Plaintiffs in this case represent precisely the qualities that have been traditionally used to shield individuals from deportation.

In their amicus brief, the American Immigration Lawyers Association (AILA) also discusses the role of discretion in the immigration system and the ways the children who are the subject of this case could be protected through discretion. The brief from AILA summarizes the regulatory provisions that permit for a stay of deportation. This same brief also discusses the form of prosecutorial discretion known as deferred action, discussed above, which is most likely to apply to children living in the United States without immigration status. Such mechanisms provide the Attorney General with enormous discretion to protect children temporarily. AILA's amicus brief then concludes:

> This review of immigration law is to demonstrate that there is not a clear-cut status of "illegality" or that of being "undocumented" under the Immigration Act and Regulations, nor is the effect of a lack of immigration status clear. Great discretion has been granted to the Attorney General who, in turn, has delegated this discretion to the Immigration and Naturalization Service. Therefore, an alien who is patently without a lawful status under the Immigration Act may be allowed to remain indefinitely within the United States.

Amicus Br. for AILA 24–25.

* * *

Public education plays a crucial role in any democratic society and should be treated as a fundamental right when analyzing the State's interest in creating and enforcing § 21.031, a statute that is unconstitutional and worthy of a strict scrutiny analysis. Further, parents and children residing in a jurisdiction of the United States deserve to be treated with dignity regardless of their status, and courts should avoid dehumanizing them through labels that are often inaccurate. Finally, courts must consider the scope and role of prosecutorial discretion when interrogating the reasons why undocumented children are here to stay.

For the foregoing reasons, I concur in the ultimate decision rendered by the Court.

8

Commentary on *Jean v. Nelson*, 472 U.S. 846 (1985)

Raymond Audain

By the time Thurgood Marshall ascended to the Supreme Court of the United States, he was arguably the most consequential lawyer of the twentieth century. The grandson of an enslaved person, longtime leader of the NAACP Legal Defense and Educational Fund, Inc., and one of the architects of *Brown v. Board of Education*, Marshall helped to usher in the modern era of equal protection jurisprudence and contributed to the greatest social transformation in America since Reconstruction.[1] It is fitting, therefore, that this volume revisits *Jean v. Nelson*,[2] a landmark Supreme Court case that considered the constitutional rights of asylum seekers from Haiti. *Jean* is remembered primarily for Justice Marshall's forceful dissent, which signaled a watershed moment in the struggle for racial justice for immigrants. The case addressed a simple but fundamental question – is the federal government at liberty to discriminate against thousands of Black women, men, and children just because they are immigrants? For the communities that mobilized to challenge these practices, for the attorneys who supported their efforts, and for Justice Marshall, the answer had to be, no. Sadly, the *Jean* majority, towed the line of conventional immigration jurisprudence, granting extreme deference to the actions of INS officials at the expense of Black asylum seekers from Haiti who were mandatorily detained and summarily deported without due process of the law.

BACKGROUND

The relationship of the United States to Haiti has been, for centuries, punctuated by anti-Black prejudice, in part because Haiti long embodied a counterpoint and, some thought, posed an existential threat to American racial hierarchies.[3] By the end of the eighteenth century, French Saint-Domingue – as Haiti was then

---

[1] GILBERT KING, DEVIL IN THE GROVE: THURGOOD MARSHALL, THE GROVELAND BOYS, AND THE DAWN OF A NEW AMERICA 2 (2012).

[2] 472 U.S. 846 (1985) (*Jean III*).

[3] LAURENT DUBOIS, HAITI: THE AFTERSHOCKS OF HISTORY (2012); *see also* Jill Lapore, THESE TRUTHS: A HISTORY OF THE UNITED STATES 142–43 (2018).

148

known – was the world's largest producer of sugar, grew half of the world's coffee, and became the most profitable colony on earth. It was also a brutal slave state where between five and ten percent of the enslaved population died annually from overwork and disease. Many of the enslaved people who arrived in Saint-Domingue in the late eighteenth century were African soldiers captured in battle. As Laurent Dubois writes, Saint-Domingue's slavers were bringing "literally thousands of soldiers to their shores." In August 1791, enslaved persons on a sugar plantation ignited the largest slave revolt in history, and, within two years, every enslaved person in the colony was free. Professor Dubois explains that "the Haitian Revolution was an act of profound – and irreversible – transformation," which deeply unsettled the United States. For W. E. B. Du Bois, it offered abolitionists "an irresistible argument."[4] The United States refused to recognize Haiti's independence until 1862, and America's hostility persisted for a long time after that. In 1893, two years after he resigned from his post as U.S. minister and consul general to Haiti,[5] Frederick Douglass remarked, "Haiti is black, and we have not yet forgiven Haiti for being black or forgiven the Almighty for making her black."[6]

The U.S. government would repeatedly discriminate against Haitian immigrants. Discriminatory practices arguably reached their apogee in the 1970s and the 1980s, when tens of thousands of refugees fled Haiti by boat and sought asylum in the United States.[7] The U.S. government responded by deploying the so-called Haitian Program, in 1978. The Program's goal was simple: expel Haitian asylum applicants as quickly as possible while deterring others from seeking refuge in America. That entailed mass, perfunctory exclusionary hearings that sometimes occurred in closed courtrooms that barred the few lawyers available to help asylum seekers. Steven Forester was one such lawyer. "They locked the doors," he remembers, and, in order to avoid him, the government led the asylum seekers through back stairwells. The court also scheduled simultaneous hearings involving the same attorney, which made it difficult for asylum seekers to be represented by counsel. Forester found himself "running around literally three courtrooms to try to get there before an order was issued in the case." Moreover, Creole translators were so inadequate that Haitians often could not understand the proceedings or be informed of their rights.[8] When the hearings concluded, the applicants often received presigned asylum-denial forms that had been prepared in advance. Forester discussed the situation

---

[4] W. E. Burghardt Du Bois, The Suppression of the African Slave Trade to the United States of America 1638–1870 70–71 (1904).

[5] David W. Blight, Frederick Douglass: Prophet of Freedom (2018).

[6] Frederick Douglass, Lecture on Haiti (1893), in Great Speeches by Frederick Douglass 105, 106 (James Daley ed., 2013).

[7] Carl Lindskoog, Detain and Punish: Haitian Refugees and the Rise of the World's Largest Immigration Detention System 14 (2018); see also Haitian Refugee Center v. Civiletti, 503 F. Supp. 442, 450 (S.D. Fl. 1980).

[8] Jean I, 711 F.2d 1455 (1983).

with Judge Scroope, who presided over some of the hearings. "I remember him saying something like, 'The orders for this are coming from the highest levels from the Justice Department.'"

For many, it was clear that race – and racism – were at the heart of the government's approach. Irwin Stotzky, a law professor, worked with Haitian community leaders and advocates at the Haitian Refugee Center, a hub of activism. "We had a long talk with them about this," he remembers, "and they were furious that they were being treated, not like human beings, but just as numbers and figures, and they were being discriminated against." "This was not just a question of arid legal logic," Stotzky emphasized, "it was a question of defining them as human beings."[9]

A series of lawsuits ensued, including *Haitian Refugee Center v. Civiletti*.[10] *Civiletti* framed the issue starkly: "This case involves thousands of black Haitian nationals, the brutality of their government, and the prejudice of ours." The court noted that the plaintiffs were part of the first substantial flight of Black refugees, and it contrasted their treatment with that of their Cuban counterparts, explaining that "no greater disparity can be imagined." The court also detailed the harrowing journey many of the asylum seekers undertook, which often involved traveling by old, small, leaky wooden sailboats that were dangerously overcrowded. "The vast number," the court noted, "spent weeks adrift without food or water," and many "died in the attempt." Those who survived were "confronted with an Immigration and Naturalization Service determined to deport them." The court deemed the evidence "both shocking and brutal, populated by the ghosts of individual Haitians – including those who have been returned from the United States – who have been beaten, tortured and left to die in Haitian prisons."[11]

In addition to subjecting asylum seekers to illegitimate mass expulsion hearings, the United States also changed its decade's long practice of paroling asylum seekers while their claims were reviewed. Prior to May 1981, Haitian refugees for whom INS initiated exclusion proceedings were usually only briefly detained for public health screenings before being paroled.[12] In fact, the government had not resorted to widespread detention of undocumented immigrants since 1954, when large detention centers like Ellis Island were closed. By late 1981, however, the government adopted a vague new plan that called for a more restrictive use of parole and increased use of detention. But the plan did not include implementing regulations or guidelines – immigration officers were expected to use their discretion about whom to detain and whom to parole. A court found that "no one knew exactly what the policy was, and no one in authority attempted to supervise the exercise of discretion under the new policy. Not surprisingly, the discretion was exercised with harsh results. It

---

[9] Podcast Transcript, The Other Side of the Water, Episode 2: The Story of *Jean v. Nelson*.
[10] 503 F. Supp. at 442.
[11] *Id.* at 452.
[12] Louis v. Nelson, 544 F. Supp. 973, 981 (S.D. Fl. 1982).

concluded that, "[l]eft without guidance as to how to implement the undefined policy, the immigration inspectors enforced the detention policy as if it was intended to apply solely, and uniformly, to Haitians."[13]

The government detained thousands of Haitian asylum seekers for months and, in some cases, over a year. In 1982, the *New York Times* reported on sixty-eight Haitian women and men who had been detained for seven months in a former Navy brig in Brooklyn, with scarce access to the outdoors.[14] Others were detained in places like Big Spring, Texas; Morgantown, West Virginia; Ray Brook, New York; Ponce, Puerto Rico; and the notorious Krome Avenue Detention Center in Miami. Forester believes the government intentionally detained asylum seekers far "from any Haitian community that could provide any kind of comfort, or solace, or assistance, and they had no sense of what was going on the outside to try to help them. All they knew was that they were being indefinitely detained."[15] Larry Mahoney, a State Department spokesman who resigned in protest over the government's treatment of asylum seekers at Krome, described seeing "women sleeping under blankets so soiled and threadbare I mistook them for the contents of vacuum cleaner bags; guards so indifferent to suffering that they snickered at the helpless; sanitary facilities so squalid that they turned your stomach."[16] The detention policy was described as a moral disgrace.[17]

THE ORIGINAL OPINION

In 1981, Ira Kurzban, a young attorney who worked closely with Stotzky and the Haitian Refugee Center, came to work with some of the Haitian asylum seekers who had been subjected to the draconian immigration enforcement practices described above. And in December of that year, they filed a case challenging the detention policy, which culminated into *Jean v. Nelson*.[18] Kurzban and his clients were committed to litigating in a manner that centered questions of equal protection while also pursuing procedural claims. In the district court, they prevailed on the procedural claims, leading to the release of about 1,700 people. But the district court dismissed the equal protection claim. While Kurzban and his clients welcomed the decision to release the class members, the equal protection implications of the detention policy were so important to the petitioners that they cross-appealed that claim to the Eleventh Circuit.[19] According to Kurzban, there was a strong sense of injustice done to Haitians who were fleeing the horrible conditions under Duvalier,

[13] Jean I, 711 F.2d. 1455 (1983).
[14] Laurie Johnston, *83 Haitians in Brooklyn Still Fight for Asylum*, N.Y. TIMES (Feb. 28, 1982).
[15] Podcast Transcript, The Other Side of the Water, Episode 2: The Story of *Jean v. Nelson*.
[16] Lindskoog, *supra* note 17, at 44.
[17] Nelson, 544 F. Supp. at 976.
[18] Jean III, 472 U.S. at 847.
[19] Jean I, 711 F.2d at 1464.

and they wanted to remedy that injustice. "There was a very, very, very strong feeling in the Haitian community at the time that we need to go to court, that the courts will vindicate our rights," he recalled.[20] They were successful, at least initially. The Eleventh Circuit panel held that excludable immigrants had a right to be considered for parole in a nondiscriminatory fashion, therefore they could raise an equal protection claim.[21] The panel also reversed the district court's finding of insufficient evidence to prove discrimination. It found that the statistical evidence showed a "severely disproportionate impact" that revealed a pattern of discrimination "as stark as that in *Gomillion [v. Lightfoot]* or *Yick Wo [v. Hopkins]*."[22] The panel also considered the numerous prior lawsuits that challenged the disparate treatment of Haitian immigrants, extensive testimonial evidence that Haitians were targeted and mistreated, and evidence of the government's departures from the normal exclusion procedure. "All told," the panel explained, "plaintiffs mustered an impressive array of witnesses and equally impressive number of documents to demonstrate circumstantially, and to an extent, directly, intentional government discrimination against Haitians."[23] Kurzban said at the time that this was the first decision in American legal history where excludable aliens were found to be protected by the equal protection guarantees of the Fifth Amendment.

The victory was thrilling but precarious because race discrimination claims against the federal government in the immigration context were – and continue to be – especially challenging. The equal protection guarantee against intentional race discrimination has been undermined by the plenary power doctrine. Some believe it gives Congress and the President almost total latitude to discriminate against excludable immigrants, even on the basis of suspect classifications including race and gender.[24] The doctrine is rooted in the notorious *Chinese Exclusion Case*,[25] which reflects the same bigotry as *Plessy v. Ferguson*.[26] Louis Henkin described the doctrine as a "constitutional fossil, a remnant of a prerights jurisprudence that we have proudly rejected in other respects."[27]

---

[20] Podcast Transcript, The Other Side of the Water, Episode 2: The Story of *Jean v. Nelson*, www.jean vnelson35.org/the-story-of-jean-v-nelson.

[21] Jean I, 711 F.2d at 1483–84.

[22] *Id.* at 1489.

[23] *Id.* at 1494.

[24] See Hiroshi Motomura, *Immigration Law after a Century of Plenary Power: Phantom Constitutional Norms and Statutory Interpretation*, 100 YALE L. J. 545, 547 (1990); Catherine Y. Kim, *Plenary Power in the Modern Administrative State*, 96 N. C. L. REV. 77, 79 (2017).

[25] Chae Chan Ping v. United States, 130 U.S. 581 (1889).

[26] See Gabriel J. Chin, *Segregation's Last Stronghold: Race Discrimination and the Constitutional Law of Immigration*, 46 UCLA L. REV. 1, 22 (1998) ("The legislative history of the statutes approved by the Court in the plenary power cases indicates that they were not primarily motivated by a desire to influence foreign policy or international affairs, or even to protect American labor, but instead to foster white supremacy by defending white civilization against an undesirable race.").

[27] Louis Henkin, *The Constitution and United States Sovereignty: A Century of Chinese Exclusion and Its Progeny*, 100 HARV. L. REV. 853, 862 (1987).

Yet, in *Jean*, the government, which disparaged the litigation as an attack on their effort to protect its borders from "invasion," unabashedly embraced the plenary power doctrine. It contended that the asylees' immigration status rendered them powerless to assert equal protection rights. At oral argument, the government invoked the *Chinese Exclusion Case* to argue that "[t]he constitutional power of Congress and the Attorney General over aliens who have entered is very large. Over those who have not, it is a power that simply knows no counterpart in any other corner of our constitutional jurisprudence." By contrast, Kurzban argued that "given the history of discrimination here, given that continuing pattern and practice of discrimination, that it is necessary for this Court to issue a declaration making it clear that under the Constitution no race and nationality discrimination is permissible." Justice Stevens asked the government what may have been the pivotal question:

> You are arguing that constitutionally you would not be inhibited from discriminating against these people on whatever ground seems appropriate. But as I understand your regulations, you are also maintaining that … your agents in the field are inhibited by your own regulations from doing what you say the Constitution would permit you to do.

"That's correct," the Solicitor General responded, and that seemed to have satisfied the majority.[28] Richard Revesz, then law clerk to Justice Marshall, remembers leaving the oral argument believing that several of the Justices were trying to make the constitutional issue go away.[29] What emerged was a majority opinion sanitized of any description of the discrimination that Haitian refugees suffered or the deadly consequences many would face if forced to return to Haiti. A six-justice majority applied the doctrine of constitutional avoidance to sidestep the equal protection issue.[30]

Justice Rehnquist delivered the majority opinion of the Court. He noted that the Attorney General's 1981 policy decision to detain the Haitian asylum seekers without parole was not based on a new statute or regulation. Such a policy therefore required compliance with the Administrative Procedures Act which included even-handed treatment and prohibitions on considerations of race and national origin in parole decisions. According to the majority, however, the 1981 change in parole policy toward the Haitian asylum seekers did not discriminate among them on the basis of race. The Court found that the parole policy did not violate the Administrative Procedures Act. Further, in the absence of race discrimination, the Court concluded that it need not determine if the parole policy raised constitutional concerns. The Court acknowledged that the asylum seekers were eager to have their Fifth Amendment claim adjudicated, but the Court sided with the government's

---

[28] *Jean v. Nelson* oral argument, www.oyez.org/cases/1984/84-5240.
[29] Podcast Transcript, The Other Side of the Water, Episode 2: The Story of *Jean v. Nelson*.
[30] Jean III, 472 U.S. at 853–54.

interest and it demurred: "Because the current statutes and regulations provide petitioners with nondiscriminatory parole consideration … there was no need to address
the constitutional issue."[31] It affirmed the Eleventh Circuit's decision to remand the
case to the district court to determine whether INS officials were violating the new
regulations by discriminating based on race.

Justice Marshall dissented with a reserve that belied the magnitude of the case,
which was clear even at the time. "Every Supreme Court case is important," Revesz
recalls, "but some, frankly, are more important than others, and this one was widely
seen as an extremely important case because of the nature of what was at stake, the
people who were affected, [and] the obnoxiousness of the government policy."[32]
Marshall faulted the majority for crediting the government's assurances that the
INS officials would not engage in discriminatory conduct, and for failing to reach
the constitutional question. Marshall would have found that the Fifth Amendment
applied to the asylum seekers.

Marshall carefully characterized the question before the Court as "narrow," but
he also appreciated the far-reaching implications of extending equal protection guarantees to the petitioners, who were not simply noncitizens, but Black persons in the
United States, subjected to racially discriminatory governmental actions. Marshall
was, after all, an expert at persuading unsuspecting reactionaries to welcome-in the
thin edge of what often turned out to be a transformational wedge. Marshall's measured approach to persuasion may have reflected his lived experiences as a Black
civil rights lawyer during the Jim Crow Era, who set out to leverage the organs of a
white supremacist society to subvert white supremacy. This was tricky and dangerous work. Litigation had long been one of the few ways that Black Americans could
engage in social protest with a measure of safety,[33] but, even then, there were no
guarantees. In 1946, because of his successful criminal defense work in Columbia,
Tennessee, a deputy sheriff nearly killed Marshall on a dark road. At one point,
J. Edgar Hoover insisted that FBI agents protect him around-the-clock.

The *Jean* majority was unconvinced by Justice Marshall's dissent. Its colorblind
review of *Jean* permitted its deference to the exclusive authority of the Executive
and the Congress to regulate immigration matters. The salience of the race of the
immigrant petitioners and its clear relationship with the unprecedented and abusive conditions they experienced at the hands of INS officials, went ignored by the
Rehnquist majority. Instead, the *Jean* majority evaluated the case in a manner that
categorized the petitioners simply as a monolithic group of noncitizens, which justified the legitimacy of immigration enforcement against them, regardless of how
distinctly cruel it was.

---

[31] *Id.* at 854–55.
[32] Podcast Transcript, The Other Side of the Water, Episode 2: The Story of Jean v. Nelson.
[33] MICHAEL J. KLARMAN, FROM JIM CROW TO CIVIL RIGHTS: THE SUPREME COURT AND THE STRUGGLE
      FOR RACIAL EQUALITY 58 (2004).

THE FEMINIST JUDGMENT

Professor Patricia Winograd rewrites the *Jean* majority opinion as Justice Winograd. Her reimagined decision fully and unapologetically embraces the equal protection rights of the Black Haitian petitioners. Winograd's opinion does so foremost by humanizing and honoring the petitioners – even taking the care to say some of their names. By grounding its analysis in the "founding principles of our country" to reject the proposition that courts should unconditionally tolerate the exercise of unfettered discretion even when discretion is used to discriminate on the basis of race, the revised opinion, unlike the original, rejects the government's appeals to benighted precedent rooted in a long and awful history of prejudice and xenophobia. That jurisprudence should have been repudiated long ago, and Winograd's feminist revision offers an opportunity to imagine how recent challenges to discriminatory immigration policies may have turned out differently if such precedent had been reversed. The revised opinion also unflinchingly describes the injustices visited on the petitioners, who sought refuge in our country; it centers the desperation and vulnerability of the asylum seekers while reckoning with the special challenges they faced as Black immigrants; and it takes the government to task for failing to afford basic constitutional protections against racial animus.[34]

At the same time, however, Professor Winograd's revised opinion is imbued with optimism about America's commitment to the rule of law and basic fairness. It is also imbued with optimism about the role immigrants will continue to play in shaping America's contours and the place America will continue to hold in the imaginations of people who seek asylum. "The United States is a land of immigrants," the reimagined decision cites at the outset, and it explains that the petitioners undertook their terrifying journey so that they too might have a chance to exercise the rights and freedoms known only in America.

Professor Winograd's reimagined opinion is doctrinally akin to Justice Marshall's dissent. Both accept that the law permits immigration officials to enjoy wide but *not* unlimited discretion in policies and practices related to immigration regulation. Yet importantly, both are premised on an understanding of constitutional equal protection that applies to citizens and noncitizens alike. Winograd's feminist revision highlights this latter point in two important ways. First, she scrutinizes the plenary power and other conventions of immigration law as troubling pretexts for exclusionary laws that discriminate against immigrants of color. Second, Winograd's embrace of the petitioners' equal protection claim prioritizes the reality that the mistreated petitioners comprised a suspect classification under equal protection law, which calls for heightened scrutiny. This move, recognizes the Black Haitian asylum seekers as Black persons on U.S. territory, entitled to constitutional due process. Recognizing

---

[34] Kathryn Abrams, *Hearing the Call of Stories*, 79 CALIF. L. REV. 971 (1991); Toni Massaro, *Empathy, Legal Storytelling, and the Rule of Law: New Words, Old Wounds?*, 87 MICH. L. REV. 2099 (1989).

the petitioners as Black persons, relinquishes the legitimacy of the government's reliance on the plenary power to abuse its discretion with respect to noncitizens. As a result, Winograd's feminist revision reflects the broader range of possibilities available to racial justice advocates pushing for the rights of immigrants of color today. It also reflects an emerging consensus that discrimination against Black immigrants implicates core civil rights concerns.[35]

CONCLUSION

Several national organizations now operate squarely at the intersection of immigrant rights and racial justice, including the UndocuBlack Network and the Black Alliance for Just Immigration (BAJI). Even legacy civil rights organizations now readily conceptualize immigration issues as racial justice issues. The Trump administration's racialized approach to immigrants accelerated this development. In 2017, the NAACP filed a lawsuit to defend against the Trump administration's efforts to terminate DACA.[36] NAACP President Derrick Johnson declared that "there is no democratic dream for anyone if we don't allow our DREAMers to fully participate."[37] Recently, the Leadership Conference on Civil and Human Rights – which was founded in 1950 to address civil rights issues – led a successful campaign to support Haitian immigrants in the United States. Similarly, in 2018, the NAACP Legal Defense and Educational Fund filed suit to challenge the Trump administration's efforts to rescind TPS for Haitians in the United States.[38] For almost eighty years, LDF has focused on vindicating the rights of Black Americans across the United States, so litigating on behalf of Haitian immigrants may appear to be a new operational context. But, as LDF's leader explained, it would be unacceptable for LDF to afford the government any leeway to make a decision based on racial discrimination in *any* context.[39] This approach reflects the potential of feminist reasoning to encourage inclusive immigration values.[40] Cultural diversity, understood as an inclusive concept, promotes equality and tolerance of the individual and the collective, ideals that could promote a humanitarian immigration system.[41] Welcoming cultural diversity in our immigration laws would be a transformational change from the exclusionary norms that informed the immigration enforcement regime at the time of *Jean* and today. The reimagined decision demonstrates what it might look like to adopt those values into jurisprudence.

---

[35] Kevin Johnson, *Bringing Racial Justice to Immigration Law*, 115 Nw. U. L. Rev. Colloquy (2021).
[36] NAACP v. Trump, 298 F. Supp. 3d 209 (D.D.C. 2018).
[37] The Crisis, "NAACP Applauds Supreme Court Victory in NAACP v. Trump" (June 18, 2020).
[38] NAACP v. United States Department of Homeland Security, 364 F. Supp. 3d 568 (D. Md. 2019).
[39] *Don't Tell Your Story Too Soon*, Crooked: Pod Save the People (Feb. 27, 2018).
[40] Katherine T. Bartlett, *Feminist Legal Methods*, 103 Harvard L. Rev. 829 (1990).
[41] Nitya Duclos, *Lessons of Difference: Feminist Theory on Cultural Diversity*, 38 Buffalo L. Rev. 325 (1990).

JEAN v. NELSON, 472 U.S. 846 (1985)

Justice Patricia Winograd delivering the opinion of the Court.

This country has long been a beacon of freedom and fairness. On whatever continent one stands and over whatever body of water one may glance, enviable individuals look longingly "lòt bò dlo" (Haitian for "on the other side of the waters") with the hope of possessing the rights and freedoms known only in America. Risking life and limb to traverse vast oceans and dangerous territories, countless seek our refuge with confidence that liberty is inviolate on our shores.

The U.S. Refugee Act of 1980 amended the Immigration and Nationality Act of 1965 to require nonrefoulement and establish a uniform standard for adjudicating refugee and asylum claims. As stated during the hearings on the Refugee Act, H.R. 3056 Before the Subcommittee on Immigration, Citizenship, and International Law of the House Committee on the Judiciary, 95th Cong., 1st Session. 16 (1977):

> The United States is a land of immigrants, and since the founding of the Republic we have had a special national heritage of concern for the uprooted and persecuted....[We have a] … national ethos of humanitarian concern. It is decidedly in our foreign policy interest to project in countries around the world the image of U.S. humanitarian assistance for refugees. Such humanitarian assistance is a glowing example of the purposes and processes of the free democracy which we are, and of the free society which makes assistance possible.

The Refugee Act continues the Attorney General's longtime parole authority to permit the admission of potential asylees and refugees into the United States when it promotes the national interest and is justified by grave humanitarian concerns. The matter before us asks us to consider the constitutionality of the Attorney General's sudden reversal of its parole policy for asylum seekers and its implementation of a mandatory Detention Policy in the case of a class of Petitioners comprised of Black Haitian asylum seekers. We hold that the Attorney General's policies with respect to the petitioners, a suspect class who experienced racial discrimination at the hands of INS officers, unconstitutional in violation of the Fifth Amendment due process clause.

I FACTS

Petitioners are approximately 2,000 Black mothers and fathers, sisters and brothers, sons, and daughters who crossed the waters from their homeland in Haiti to the United States in the spring of 1981. Like thousands of immigrants before them, Lucien Louis, Wilner Luberisse, Jean Louis Servebien, Pierre Silien, Serge Verdieu, Milfort Vilgard, Josel Casimir, Job Dessin, Prophete Talleyvand, and other class members sought refuge in this Country for the promise of a better life, free from the harsh conditions and arbitrary executions perpetrated by the repressive Duvalier regime in their native land.

The Haitian Petitioners, having shown a credible and "well-founded fear of persecution," like other asylum seekers, warranted admission to the United States through parole pending the adjudication of their asylum and other humanitarian claims for relief from removal. *Louis v. Nelson*, 544 F.Supp. 973, 981 (S.D. Fla. 1982).

However, Immigration and Naturalization Services (INS) abruptly revoked that three decades-long parole policy – absent statute, regulation or even written instruction. In stark contrast to thirty years of parole policy for asylum seekers, and in direct contravention of a treaty requiring the humane treatment of Haitians, INS subjected petitioners to a mandatory Detention Policy described further below.

INS' subsequent actions stripped the Black Haitian men and women of their basic needs and fundamental rights while they awaited decision of their fate. Even medication required for their survival was taken from them. INS officials thereafter not only ensured that Petitioners would remain unaware of their rights, but also willfully and systemically deprived them of access to any who could help inform them of those rights. Further guaranteeing that there would be no careful, individual assessment of their asylum claims, INS officials hurriedly handled the Petitioners' claims *en masse* in clandestine and cloistered hearings behind closed doors. Countless local attorneys and community members waited in hallways and rooms to help the asylum seekers assert their rights, while INS officials diverted the Haitian asylum seekers through back channels away from counsel eager to represent them. Inadequate language interpretation during their exclusion proceedings prevented Petitioners from understanding the proceedings against them.

Not surprisingly, some of these hearings adjudged the Haitian asylum seekers excludable and deportable. By the Government's own admission, this was faulty and not in compliance with the law. For the detained Haitians, INS shuffled them around in what was identified by the court below as a "human shell game." *Louis v. Meissner*, 530 F. Supp. 924, 926–28 (S.D.Fla. 1981). INS herded the Black Haitian men and women around the country, often to desolate areas without access to counsel or any with whom they could communicate, far away from anyone who could provide assistance or comfort, including their families. If not imprisoned, they were kept in squalid conditions resembling that of a prison. During the pendency of this litigation, the Attorney General and other INS officials requested congressional funding of more than $30 million to build additional detention facilities adjacent to and as an extension of already-existing prisons to incarcerate the Haitians.

Many would go on to suffer lengthy, in some cases, year-long detention during which INS officials further deprived the Black Haitian asylum seekers of basic needs. Petitioners were separated from their children, isolated, dehumanized, and even physically abused. The following scenario was an all-too-familiar account of the callous disregard with which INS officials treated the Petitioners:

BY MR. KURZBAN

Q   Can you state your full name for the record please?
A   Hendrick DeSulme.
Q   Mr. DeSulme, when did you come to the United States?
A   August 9, 1981.
Q   Did you come here alone or were you accompanied by anyone?
A   Accompanied by my cousin and my child.
Q   How old is your child?
A   Two.
Q   Boy or girl?
A   A boy.
Q   Your cousin was in the camp at the time?
A   Yes. She was on the female side.
Q   They did not release your son at that time?
A   Never.
Q   How long was your son at Krome?
A   A month and a half.
Q   When your son was released, did you ask to be released also?
A   They had transferred me to Otisville. They had kept my child and released
    him after I left.
Q   Did you tell immigration anything with respect to whether or not you wished
    to be transferred because your son was at Krome?
A   When I was being transferred, I called Mr. Garcia and I told Mr. Garcia,
    my child is my own child. He has lost his mother. I am his mother. I am his
    mother and father both. That means that whatever I go is where he should be.
    He told me "shut up."

                    Louis v. Nelson, 544 F. Supp. 973, 982 (S.D. Fl. 1982).

    While this Court has long held that the Congress and the Executive enjoy ple-
nary authority over immigration matters, the discriminatory treatment suffered by
Petitioners in this case calls for constitutional judicial scrutiny, particularly when
Petitioners, Black Haitian asylum seekers, posed no apparent threat to public nor
national security.
    The Court of Appeals concluded that the Petitioners lacked the power to bring
a constitutional challenge to INS's actions. In order to accept its ruling, this Court
would need to accept its determination that Petitioners are not "persons" enshrined
within the protection of our Constitution. This we decline to do. The Fourteenth
Amendment guarantees that all are *persons* have a right to equal protection of the
law, regardless of citizenship status. The Fifth Amendment's due process clause
incorporates the Fourteenth Amendment's equal protection mandate. We granted

certiorari to consider the Petitioners' right to invoke the Fifth Amendment equal protection guarantee against race and nation origin-based discrimination by the INS's
execution of a mandatory detention policy against them. We hold that the Petitioners
unquestionably have this right. The Petitioners, as persons protected by the U.S.
Constitution, suffered invidious discrimination by the INS because of their race and
national origin as Black Haitians. Accordingly, we reverse the decision below.

II PROCEDURAL HISTORY

The procedural history in this case is long and complex yet provides important
context for the equal protection concerns raised by this case and examined below.
Petitioners initiated suit on behalf of themselves and a class of asylum seekers
against the Commissioner of the Immigration and Naturalization Service ("INS" or
"Nelson") responsible for handling their claims for asylum. Petitioners alleged that
the abruptly enforced Detention Policy to which they were newly subjected violated
the notice-and-comment rule-making procedures of the Administrative Procedure
Act ("APA"), 5 U.S.C. § 553, which prohibits an administrative agency from
adopting a substantive rule unless it first publishes notice and provides interested
persons with an opportunity to comment. *Louis v. Nelson*, 544 F. Supp. 973, 984,
993 (S.D. Fla.1982). Having failed to comply with this provision, INS unlawfully violated the APA in enacting the Detention Policy. *Louis v. Nelson*, 544 F. Supp. 973,
984 (S.D. Fla.1982). Petitioners further alleged that the Detention Policy had been
enforced against the Black Haitian asylum seekers because of their race in violation
of their equal protection rights. *Id.* Specifically, the Black asylum seekers alleged that
the Detention Policy was discriminatory on its face and in its application because it
imposed upon the Black asylum seekers a "double standard" in violation of the due
process clause of the Fifth Amendment. *Id.* They sought a writ of habeas corpus,
challenging their unlawful detention under 28 U.S.C. 2241. They also requested
declaratory and injunctive relief.

The District Court first certified the class of "all Haitian aliens who have arrived
in the Southern District of Florida on or after May 20, 1981, who are applying for
entry into the United States and who are presently in detention pending exclusion
proceedings … for whom an order of exclusion has not yet been entered …." *Louis
v. Nelson*, 544 F. Supp. 973, 1004, 1005 (S.D. Fla. 1982).

Defendants challenged the court's jurisdiction to rule on the claims alleged in the
suit. Defendants argued that judicial intervention in the matter brought to the fore
by the Haitian asylum seekers was inappropriate because: (1) Petitioners had not yet
exhausted their administrative remedies; (2) the case presented political questions
exclusively entrusted to the other political branches of government; and (3) judicial
review of agency decision governing parole is prohibited. *Id.* at 984–90. Rejecting
each jurisdictional challenge, the court turned to Petitioners' claims. *Id.* The District
Court agreed with Petitioners that the Detention Policy violated the APA. *Id.*

The District Court admonished the Policy for its implementation without "ever seriously undertaking the difficult task of drafting a set of guidelines concerning which aliens would be placed in detention – thus ... [remaining susceptible] ... to the dangers of arbitrariness and irrationality in the formulation of rules." *Louis v. Nelson*, 544 F. Supp. 973, 997 & 1003 (1982). Highlighting that the Detention Policy lacked "operating instruction[s], internal memorandum or other document," the District Court noted the Detention Policy's "obvious" impact on the Black asylum seekers:

> The new release criteria radically depart[ed] ... from the existing practice of regularly releasing Haitian aliens. It makes detention the rule, not the exception; and prescribes very narrow circumstances where parole will be allowed. Upon implementation, the new policy had an immediate and substantial impact on the Plaintiffs. The Court cannot think of any administrative action that would have a greater impact on a regulated group of people than a change in policy which results in their indefinite incarceration where, under the previous policy, they would have been free. *Id.* at 997.

The District Court also found that, under the Detention Policy, more Black Haitians had been detained and kept in detention for longer periods than persons of other nationalities. However, the District Court declined to uphold Petitioners' equal protection claim, reasoning that "regardless of its ultimate impact," it had been applied irrespective of race or national origin. *Louis v. Nelson*, 544 F. Supp. at 1004.

Because the INS had not published notice and allowed comment before implementing the changed policy, the District Court further held the Policy was null and void. *Louis v. Nelson*, 544 F. Supp. at 1003–04. As a result, the District Court: (1) ordered the release of all incarcerated class members; (2) enjoined the deportation of, and further exclusion hearings for class members unrepresented by counsel, and the enforcement of its policy detaining the Haitians until the INS complied with the APA rule making process; and (3) imposed a 30-day stay of its order to permit the INS to promulgate a new policy in accordance with the APA. *Id.*

Jean I

A panel of the Eleventh Circuit concurred with the District Court that the Detention Policy was unlawful and sanctioned its decision to release the Haitian asylum seekers. *Jean v. Nelson* ("Jean I"), 711 F.2d 1455 (1983). Echoing the District Court's pronouncement that the Administration had not complied with the APA's notice and comment provisions, the Court of Appeals agreed that the Detention Policy was invalid. *Id.* at 1474–75. Specifically, the Court of Appeals disagreed with the government's arguments attempting to justify its Detention Policy, including that the Policy did not fit within the APA's ambit because it was not a "rule." *Id.* The Court of Appeals took exception to the government's argument that it was not promulgating a new "rule," but rather implementing the statute – pointing out that such an interpretation misconstrued the requirements of the APA. *Id.* at 1475.

"An announcement ... [such as the Detention Policy here] ... that the INS will uni-versally enforce a detention policy while limiting parole is 'an agency statement of general applicability and future effect designed to implement, interpret or prescribe law or policy'" is a rule. *Id.*

The Court of Appeals also found without merit the government's contention that the Detention Policy fit within one of the several exceptions to the APA's rulemak-ing requirements. *Id.* at 1477–83. According to the Court of Appeals, it did not fit within the narrow foreign policy exception, which reflected Congress's intent that sensitive foreign policy issues need not be governed by the APA. *Id.* at 1477–78. The court further rejected the applicability of the Interpretive Rules exception asserted by the government. Given that the Detention Policy set forth a new course of action, it could not reasonably be interpreted as a mere "clarification" of exist-ing laws of regulations so as to fit within the Interpretive Rules exception. *Id.* at 1478. Nor could, despite the government's argument to the contrary, a "broad rule of detention with undefined exceptions" qualify as simply a "general statement of policy" that excepted it from the notice and comment rules of the APA. *Id.* at 1482. Particularly given the "harsh results" that ensued following the adoption of the Detention Policy, there was no justification to shift the balance that Congress has sanctioned away from affording a prior opportunity to challenge a rule that governs an agency's decision of such import. *Id.* (See Summary in Jean II, p. 8.)

The Court of Appeals affirmed the District Court's conclusion that class mem-bers could seek protection under the Fifth Amendment from discriminatory exer-cises of parole power. *Id.* at 1483. The Court of Appeals distinguished between a constitutional challenge to the right to be considered for admission (or decision concerning admission) and a challenge to the right to be considered for parole in a nondiscriminatory fashion. *Id.* The Court of Appeals stated clearly: "A statute, otherwise neutral on its face, must not be *applied* so as [to] invidiously discriminate on the basis of race." Id. at 1485 citing *Louis III* at 998–99 (emphasis added). Having established the right of Petitioners to legitimately challenge the discriminatory exer-cise of discretion in parole decisions, the Court of Appeals determined that "ample, unrebutted evidence" demonstrated that the Detention Policy was administered in a discriminatory manner in violation of the Haitians' equal protection rights. *Id.* In a lengthy opinion, the Court of Appeals described the anti-Black discrimination suffered by the Black Petitioners at the hands of lower-level INS officials. *Id.* at 1487–1503. According to the Court of Appeals, a "strong case of discrimination" sup-ported by substantial, unrebutted testimony in the record established that the Black refugees received discriminatory treatment in their asylum claims as compared to their non-Black counterparts. *Id.* at 1501.

Delineating the factors set forth by this Court in *Village of Arlington Heights v. Metropolitan Housing Dev. Corp.*, 429 U.S. 252 (1977), which outlines the proof needed to establish invidious discrimination by an acting government official, the Court of Appeals highlighted the direct and circumstantial evidence of unequal treatment here. The court found that the Petitioners had, in fact, established a prima facie case of discrimination and that the government had failed to rebut plaintiff's evidence. *Id.* at 1487. The court first accepted expert statistical evidence finding that the chance of so many more Haitians than non-Haitians being detained was "on the order of less than two in ten billion times" or a "statistical joke." *Id.* at 1488. In addition to the overwhelming statistical record, the Court of Appeals held that the District Court had erroneously disregarded other evidence of *Arlington Heights* factors that substantiated a finding of discrimination. *Id.* at 1490–91.

The Court of Appeals was persuaded by overwhelming documentary and testimonial evidence illustrating a historical pattern of "persistent targeting and mistreatment of Haitian immigrants" even prior to the filing of the case – all of which the district court erroneously discredited. *Id.* The Court of Appeals also detailed evidence the district court erroneously disregarded of "numerous departures from normal exclusion procedure" that singled out Haitians for discriminatory treatment. Among other things, Haitians, but not their non-Black counterparts were subject to mass exclusion hearings behind closed doors before they could present asylum claims. They were deported in a faulty manner. By INS' own admission, a special code within INS established just for the treatment of Black Haitians and departures from ordinary procedures, were followed in processing the Haitians that were not followed with any other group of refugees. *Id.* at 1492–93. INS' internal documents revealed the existence of the special discriminatory "Haitian Program" (denoted by documents bearing a special code (CO 243.85) accompanied by an awareness, at least by some, that the policy was not to be applied universally, but were designed to target Haitians. Ultimately, if the government officials did not intend it, which the record certainly indicates that they did, government officials knew that their detention policy would have its greatest impact on Black Haitians who amounted to a tiny fraction of asylum seekers similarly situated.

The Court of Appeals ultimately concluded this was a "classic case of unguided and unfettered discretion," which invoked the grave risk of "selective and discriminatory enforcement –" that could have used, at a minimum, the guidance of an administrative decision passed in concert with the APA. 711 F.2d 1502.

The Revised Detention Policy

Both parties appealed, but the appeals were not heard until after the INS promptly issued a new policy ("New Policy" or "New Detention Policy") in direct response to the District Court's order. The Attorney General's new policy was published in 1982. The New Policy incorporated the statutory standard pursuant to which the Attorney General had previously granted liberal parole to refugees. 8 U.S.C. 1182 (d) (5)(A). That statute, Section 1182, permits the Attorney General "in his discretion" to parole individuals into the United States temporarily under such conditions as he may prescribe *"for emergent reasons* or for reasons deemed strictly *in the public interest* any alien applying for admission to the United States" (emphasis added). 8 C.F.R. 212.5(a)(1)(1985).

This time, the Detention Policy purported to identify at least four specific categories of individuals that would generally qualify as satisfying the "emergent reasons" test justifying parole, including: (1) those with serious medical conditions; (2) pregnant women; (3) minors; and (4) individuals who will be witnesses in proceedings being, or to be, conducted by judicial, administrative, or legislative bodies in the United States. 8 C.F.R. 212.5(a)(1)-(4). However, the new regulations maintained a broader fifth category that included within the scope of individuals who would qualify for parole, those individuals whose continued detention "is not in the public interest as determined by" certain authorized immigration officials. 8 C.F.R. 212.5(a) (5). In other words, the revised statute explicitly reserved discretionary authority for lower-level INS officials.

The appeals were not heard until after the promulgation of the New Policy.

Jean II

Following the Eleventh Circuit panel opinion, the *en banc* Eleventh Circuit reconsidered the issues presented on appeal. *Jean v. Nelson (Jean II)*, 727 F.2d 957, 961–62 (11th Cir. 1984). *Jean II* found the Petitioners' APA claim now moot since none of the detainees were still being held pursuant to the regulations that were first held violative of the APA, *id.* at 962,

Jean II thus described the remaining "central question" as whether Petitioners' equal protection claims were valid – finding that they were not. *Id.* at 970. The Court of Appeals drew what it called a "fundamental distinction" between unadmitted noncitizens, those for whom "the decisions of executive and administrative officers … are due process of law," *id.* at 968; and noncitizens who succeed in "gaining entry" to the country, even by unlawful means, who have greater (though limited) due process rights. *Id.* Based on the fiction of this "entry doctrine," *Jean II* held that the Black asylum seekers could not raise a constitutional challenge to their detention or parole. *Id.* at 970.

According to the court, there was no basis to distinguish between a challenge to a parole decision and an admission decision since parole was simply a device of convenience that permitted INS to process asylum determinations without granting formal admission. *Id.* at 962. Yet, the court also noted that parole, although shorter-term and temporary, carried the same implications as did actual admission into the country. *Id.* at 971–72. For example, the court referenced, but distinguished decisions that allowed constitutional challenges by noncitizens, such as noncitizens' constitutional rights in the criminal arena, which could not be constrained by the federal government's plenary power over immigration. *Id.* at 973.

The Court of Appeals determined that Petitioners were entitled to some review of INS actions. However, it stated that the judiciary had a limited role in reviewing the discretionary decisions of executive officials. As such, the court could consider only whether the INS acted within the scope of their authority, and, if so, whether the lower-level immigration officials exercised their discretion in a manner consistent with their statutory grant of discretion. *Id.* at 978. According to the Court of Appeals, the only question left for review was whether the lower-level INS officials abused their discretion by discriminating on the basis of national origin in violation of facially neutral instructions from their supervisors." *Id.* at 979. Rather, *Jean II* focused exclusively on Petitioner's constitutional claims and reversed the decision of the panel on Petitioners' equal protection claim, remanding the case back to the District Court for further findings. *Id.* at 961–62.

We granted certiorari to address the significant issue concerning Petitioners' right to invoke Fifth Amendment protections to challenge the INS' execution of parole policy pertaining to Petitioners' detention and asylum claims pending admission to this country. Today, we hold that the Petitioners, while noncitizens, are persons, protected by the U.S. Constitution against arbitrary and discriminatory deprivations of life and liberty in the parole process.

III. FIFTH AMENDMENT EQUAL PROTECTION CLAIM

The text of the Fifth Amendment of the United States Constitution unequivocally grants to every *person* the right to be afforded due process under the law. Under this Amendment, persons are protected from governmental deprivations of life, liberty, and property without due process of law. Due process requires procedural fairness – guaranteeing to every person the right to receive fair and just judicial proceedings preceding any governmental deprivation of life, liberty or property. *Bolling v. Sharpe*, 347 U.S. 497 (1954). Due process under the Amendment also dictates substantive fairness. *Id.*

Substantive due process protects other fundamental rights. Although the freedoms to which liberty might extend have not expressly been delineated by this Court, it is well established that "liberty under law extends to the full range of conduct which the individual is free to pursue, and it cannot be restricted except for a proper governmental objective." *Bolling*, 347 U.S. at 500–01. We have long recognized that the liberty protected by the Fifth Amendment's Due Process Clause includes within it, the prohibition against denying to any person the equal protection of the laws. See *Bolling*, 347 U.S., at 499–500, 693; *Buchanan v. Warley*, 245 U.S. 60 (1917) (statute limiting the right of a property owner to convey his property to a person of another race was a denial of due process of law because it constituted discrimination on the basis of race); *Hampton v. Wong*, 426 U.S. 88 (1976). Discrimination may be violative of due process. Indeed, as long ago as 1896, this Court declared the principle "that the constitution of the United States, in its present form, forbids, so far as civil and political rights are concerned, discrimination by the general government, or by the states, against any citizen because of his race." *Gibson v. Mississippi*, 162 U.S. 565, 567 (1896).

A

There is no sound rationale that supports declining to extend our fundamental values of life and liberty afforded by the Fifth Amendment to Petitioners here. The Fifth Amendment applies to persons. Petitioners are – plainly – persons. The Fifth Amendment protects the Haitian immigrants, as clearly as it does all persons on our territory and in our midst. No clearer syllogism can be articulated.

That the Fifth Amendment's applies to all *persons* is evident by its express terms. Both the due process and equal protection guarantees of the Constitution are "universal in their application, to all persons within the territorial jurisdiction, without regard to any differences of race, of color or of nationality." *Yick Wo. v. Hopkins,* 118 U.S. 356, 369 (1886). Were there any doubt, our jurisprudence makes clear that noncitizens are persons who enjoy Fifth Amendment protection. *Mathews v. Diaz,* 426 U.S. 67, 77 (1975) ("even [a noncitizen][42] whose presence in this country is unlawful, involuntary, or transitory is entitled to that constitutional protection.") *See also Wong Wing v. United States,* 163 U.S. 228, 238 (1896) ("all persons within the territory of the United States are entitled to the protection guaranteed by [the fifth amendment]"); *Ex parte Milligan,* 71 U.S. (4 Wall.) 2 (1866) ("The Constitution ... covers with the shield of its protection all classes of men, at all times, and under all circumstances."). Simply put, the Fifth Amendment cloaks *all* persons, regardless of the color of their skin or the country from which they hail, in its protection. *Plyler v. Doe,* 457 U.S. 202, 210 (1982). As we stated in *Plyler,*

> [w]hatever his status under the immigration laws, an alien surely is a 'person' in any ordinary sense of that term. Aliens, even aliens whose presence in this country is unlawful, have long been recognized as 'persons' guaranteed due process of law by the Fifth and Fourteenth amendments. *Id.* at 210.

This Court has afforded Fifth Amendment protection to noncitizens in a broad array of contexts. For example, in *Russian Volunteer Fleet v. United States,* 282 U.S. 481 (1931), we upheld the invocation of the Fifth Amendment by a foreign corporation – a noncitizen – challenging an unlawful taking by the Federal Government. *Russian Volunteer Fleet v. United States,* 282 U.S. 481 (1931). There, we unequivocally stated that "as alien friends are embraced within the terms of the Fifth Amendment, it cannot be said that their property is subject to confiscation here because the property of our citizens may be confiscated in the alien's country." *Id.* If the Fifth Amendment protection should extend to "property" owned by a foreign individual or corporate entity duly organized under the laws of another territory, should it not follow that the same constitutional guarantees apply with equal force to protect the "life" and "liberty" of actual persons, even if foreign?

---

[42] Despite our nomenclature referring to those who seek our refuge as "aliens," this Court declines to use the term here.

For at least a century, persons detained at the border who are criminally prosecuted have received the same protections at trial afforded to a criminal defendant. *Wong Wing. V. United States*, 163 U.S. 228, 16 S.Ct. 977 (1896). We have made clear, albeit in dictum that, just as citizens within our borders, noncitizens cannot be punished without a "judicial trial ... [establishing] ... the guilt of the accused." *Id.* Lower federal courts have also acknowledged a noncitizen's right to due process protections at trial. *See, e.g., United States v. Henry*, 604 F.2d 908, 912–13; *United States v. Casimiro-Benitez*, 533 F.2d 1121 (1976). It strains credulity that the Constitution protects the criminally accused and foreign property owners, but not the "life" or "liberty" of the Petitioners.

B

The en banc Court of Appeals nevertheless declined to acknowledge Petitioners' constitutional rights under the Fifth Amendment because of a legal fiction. According to the Court of Appeals, during the time asylum seekers await a decision regarding their admission into this Country, they are not admitted (despite their presence on U.S. territory or in the Petitioners' case, in U.S. detention facilities), and therefore lack any constitutional right to challenge government action and treatment. *Jean II*, 727 F.2d at 968, 970. As the so-called "entry" fiction – adopted hook, line, and sinker by the Court of Appeals – goes, because asylum seekers have not "affected an entry" into the country, they have no constitutional rights; conversely, those who have received government approval to enter into this country do have constitutional rights. *Id.* In other words, even though immigrants are *physically* in our midst and in our custody, they must "be content to accept" whatever the government does in handling their claims because their presence into the country is only temporary and "unofficial" and cannot be deemed an "entry." Asylum seekers, then, are entirely at the mercy of our Attorney General and INS officials who not only are the ultimate arbiters of their potential status, but also have reserved unto themselves the right to be the ultimate arbiters of what to do with them while their status is determined.

The logic of the "entry doctrine" fiction neither comports with the underpinnings of due process nor the express words of our Constitution. Our Constitution nowhere suggests that one's status as a citizen or noncitizen in this country is determinative of the right to enjoy due process when subject to processes carried out by our government. Indeed, the "entry doctrine" fiction was created before the time the power of the Executive to parole asylum seekers was codified when immigration authorities handled asylum proceedings aboard vessels on which refugees traveled. Although created to reflect the needs of the time, its continuity should not be taken for granted where, as is the case here, its purpose and the means with which it is carried out is no longer justified. Justice Jackson's prescient words in his dissent in *Shaughnessy v. United States ex. Rel. Mezei*, 345 U.S. 206 (1953) warned of just the danger facing the Haitian Petitioners here were the logic of the entry doctrine fiction carried to its extreme:

> Because the respondent has no right of entry, does it follow that he has no rights at all? Does the power to exclude mean that exclusion may be continued or effectuated by any means which happen to seem appropriate to the authorities? It would effectuate his exclusion to eject him bodily into the sea or to set him adrift in a rowboat. Would not such measures be condemned judicially as a deprivation of life without due process of law? Suppose the authorities decide to disable an alien from entry by confiscating his valuables and money. Would we not hold this a taking of property without due process of law? Here we have a case that lies between the taking of life and the taking of property; it is the taking of liberty. It seems to me that this, occurring within the United States or its territorial waters, may be done only by proceedings which meet the test of due process of law. 345 U.S. at 226–27.

For too long now, we have endeavored to ascribe labels to immigrants seeking asylum within our borders. We have engaged in a sort of semantic gamesmanship used to justify and legitimize the plenary power of the government when dispensing justice at the border. However, just as we rejected the use of a fiction through passage of the Fourteenth Amendment so that newly freed slaves could rightly claim constitutional rights, we hereby resoundingly reject the use of a fiction that would serve to deprive "persons" within our borders the protection clearly afforded by the Fifth Amendment. We hold that whether she is just arriving at the border, being detained, or in the midst of proceedings, as long as she is subject to decision-making of U.S. authorities, she is entitled to be treated fairly in those decisions to the extent that due process affords. *Yick Wo. V. Hopkins*, 118 U.S. 356, 369 (1886).

C

The plenary power is not absolute. To the extent that the en *banc* Court of Appeals concluded that noncitizens' due process rights exist *only* when the plenary authority of the political branches to admit or exclude noncitizens is not implicated, *Jean II* at 972, this conclusion is squarely at odds with our long-standing jurisprudence, which the Court of Appeals itself tacitly acknowledged. See 727 F.2d, at 974–75. *Yick Wo. V. Hopkins*, 118 U.S. 356, 369 (1886); *Plyler v. Doe*, 457 U.S. 202, 210 (1982); *Rodriguez-Fernandez v. Wilkinson*, 654 F.2d 1382 (1981). See also *Augustin v. Sava*, 735 F.2d 32, 37 (2d. Cir. 1984) ("it appears likely that some due process protection surrounds the determination of whether an alien has sufficiently shown that return to a particular country will jeopardize his life or freedom"); *Yiu Sing Chun v. Sava*, 708 F.2d 869, 877 (2d. Cir. 1983) (a refugee's "interest in not being returned may well enjoy some due process protection"). As we stated more than a century ago:

> When we consider the nature and the theory of our institutions of government, the principles upon which they are supposed to rest, and review the history of

their development, we are constrained to conclude that they do not mean to leave room for the play and action of purely personal and arbitrary power. Sovereignty itself is, of course, not subject to law, for it is the author and source of law; but in our system, while sovereign powers are delegated to the agencies of government, sovereignty itself remains with the people, by whom and for whom all government exists and acts. And the law is the definition and limitation of power. It is, indeed, quite true that there must always be lodged somewhere, and in some person or body, the authority of final decision; and in many cases of mere administration, the responsibility is purely political, no appeal lying except to the ultimate tribunal of the public judgment, exercised either in the pressure of opinion, or by means of the suffrage. But the fundamental rights to life, liberty, and the pursuit of happiness, considered as individual possessions, are secured by those maxims of constitutional law which are the monuments showing the victorious progress of the race in securing to men the blessings of civilization under the reign of just and equal laws, so that, in the famous language of the Massachusetts bill of rights, the government of the commonwealth 'may be a government of laws and not of men.' For the very idea that one man may be compelled to hold his life, or the means of living, or any material right essential to the enjoyment of life, at the mere will of another, seems to be intolerable in any country where freedom prevails, as being the essence of slavery itself. *Yick Wo v. Hopkins*, 118 U.S. 356, 370 (1886)

Contrary to the Court of Appeals' assertion, our holding in *Shaughnessy v. United States ex rel. Mezei*, 345 U.S. 206 (1953) does not require us to reject Petitioners' equal protection claim here. *Mezei* involved the due process claim of Ignatz Mezei, a United States citizen who was excluded from the country and indefinitely detained after visiting his sick mother in Hungary. Ultimately, he was permanently excluded on national security grounds. *Id.* Having been denied a hearing to challenge his permanent detention, he sought a writ of habeas corpus. *Mezei*, 345 U.S. at 212. The narrow question decided in *Mezei* was whether his continued exclusion without a hearing in a case in which the Government raised national security concerns violated due process. *Mezei*, 345 U.S. at 207. The Court settled the due process question in the negative. *Id.* at 214–16.

Neither *Mezei* nor *United States ex. rel. Knauff v. Shaughnessy*, 338 U.S. 537 (1950) – also cited by the Government and relied on by the *en banc* Court of Appeals – carry any precedential weight in the resolution of Petitioners' constitutional claims here. To begin, any statements relating to the rights of an "excludable alien" to avail herself of constitutional protections were dicta and, as such, are without precedential force here. "It is a maxim, not to be disregarded, that general expressions, in every option, are to be taken in connection with the case to which those expressions are used." *See, e.g., Cohens v. Virginia*, 6 Wheat, 264, 399, 5 L.Ed. 257 (1821) (Marshall, C.J.). In any event, each of those cases presents a factual circumstance that is nonexistent here: a national security issue substantiating a detention where parole was "not in the public interest." Although the Government did not at the time of the proceeding reveal the basis for his exclusion, it was later determined that *Mezei* was excluded because of evidence that he was or had been a member of the Communist party. Although the facts and circumstances of *Knauff* were slightly different, Knauff's exclusion – security reasons that existed during wartime and confidential information that she may have been involved in espionage – was also upheld by the District Court, the Court of Appeals and affirmed by the Supreme Court.

This case does not present a national security issue. The Government here presented no evidence supporting any contention that Petitioners' parole was not in the public interest.

IV. CONCLUSION

Having determined Petitioners' clear right to constitutional protection, we now turn to the question of whether the incarceration practices and policies applied to Haitians and not their non-Black or non-Haitian counterparts violated Petitioners' equal protection rights. We find that INS officials invidiously discriminated against the Black Haitian asylum seekers in its incarceration practices in violation of the equal protection guarantee of the Fifth Amendment.

We do not here question (nor do Petitioners) that the Executive enjoys wide discretion over immigration policy. When, however, that discretion results in policy that is effectuated in a manner that discriminates on the basis of national origin and/or race, it must undergo strict constitutional scrutiny. Indeed, this Court long ago declared that "discrimination may be so unjustifiable as to be violative of due process." *Bolling v. Sharpe*, 347 U.S. at 499 & n.2.

The initial haste with which the Attorney General implemented the detention policy – coincidentally contemporaneous with the Haitians' arrival – begs the question whether the change in policy, following thirty years of adherence to an opposite policy indicates a sinister motive or purpose on the part of the Attorney General. Of course, that unwritten, undocumented policy cannot even be facially tested given that it is but a distant memory for only those in the inner circle of the Attorney General and his delegates. But Petitioners here do not challenge the original detention policy. Nor do they contend that the later incarceration standards adopted pursuant to the District Court's order are, on their face, discriminatory. Petitioners only challenge the implementation or application of the revised policy as it pertained to the Black Haitian asylum seekers.

Even a scant review of the voluminous evidence found by the Eleventh Circuit panel to satisfy the requirements of showing a discriminatory purpose under *Arlington Heights* belies any contention that it was not itself nor intended to be used to invidiously discriminate against the Black Haitian refugees pending decisions on their admittance. To be sure, the governmental regulations were implemented in a way that discriminated against Petitioners because of their race and national origin – suspect classifications requiring intensified scrutiny. To the extent that the

Eleventh Circuit relied on the government's unsubstantiated representation that the new policy did not discriminate on the basis of national origin, the Eleventh Circuit Court of Appeals erred.

The New Detention Policy under which Petitioners were incarcerated essentially reaffirmed the right of the Attorney General and his cadre of designees to exercise broad discretion in rendering decisions related to the detention of refugees and asylum seekers. The catch-all provision is the ultimate sanction: it leaves parole decisions entirely in the hands of lower-level designees charged with authority to make immigration decisions it deems "in the public interest" and to parole aliens whose continued detention is "not in the public interest."

Notably, the record reveals no prohibition delimiting INS officials' discretion or providing clear criteria to guide lower-level INS officials and agents to determine what is "in the public interest." Although the record reveals public statements at the time issued by the Attorney General and the President that the statute was intended to be applied neutrally, our inquiry does not end there. Indeed, even non-facial classifications may illegitimately discriminate against racial minorities and noncitizens if the effect of the statute harms individuals of a certain race or nationality and if the government had a purpose to harm members of such groups. *See, e.g., Personnel Administrator v. Feeeney*, 442 U.S. 256 (1979); *Arlington Heights v. Metropolitan Housing Dev. Corp.*, 429 U.S. 252 (1977); *Washington v. Davis*, 426 U.S. 229 (1976); *Jefferson v. Hackney*, 406 U.S. 535 (1972).

In the absence of clear guidelines to reduce the risk of error and abuse of discretion, imperceptible and implicit biases may influence the decision-making of rank-and-file INS agents. Even the well-intentioned, when making snap judgments, are susceptible to discriminatory stereotyping. That "unconscious racism" may be at play in these decisions is undeniable. *See* D. Bell, *Race, Racism and American Law* (2d ed., 1980); L. Bennet, *Before the Mayflower* (5th ed. 1982); J. Franklin, *From Slavery to Freedom* (5th ed. 1980); V. Harding, *There is a River* (1981); A. Higginbotham, *In the Matter of Color* (1978); J. Kovel, *White Racism: A Psychohistory* (1970); R. Delgado, *Words That Wound: A Tort Action for Racial Insults, Epithets and Name-Calling*, 17 Harv. C.R.-C.L. L. Rev. 133, 135–43 (1982).

But we need not rely on supposition or speculation that a discriminatory purpose evidenced by a particular course of action taken by the decision-makers here, INS officials, was undertaken because of its adverse effects upon the Black asylum seekers. We know from the proverbial horse's mouth (in the form of the trial testimony of countless INS officials) that intentional efforts were undertaken to discriminate against the Black Haitians. Policies disfavoring Blacks and others based on race, like those here, violate the equal protection clause unless they are necessary to further a compelling government interest. *Palmore v. Sidoti*, 466 U.S. 429 (1984); *Loving v. Virginia*, 388 U.S. 1 (1967).

Perhaps the presence of war-like conditions or another credible threat to our national security could justify a sudden change in the government's border enforcement policies. But only the most tortured reasoning could sanction the arbitrary, capricious, and discriminatory enforcement practices exercised against the Petitioners, no matter the stated governmental interest. In fact, the Government has provided no justification for discriminating against Black Haitians at the border. By the government's own admission, the Haitians were not incarcerated because they presented a threat to national security or a flight risk – the statutorily proscribed reasons to enforce and erect detention protocols on the basis of race and nationality – where their White counterparts did not. They were incarcerated and treated differently because, they were Black.

The very notion that we would welcome others to our lofty "land of the free" by placing them under arbitrary, capricious, and discriminatory rule offends our Constitution. The founding principles of our country do not countenance the exercise of unfettered discretion when it means that one may be deprived of life, liberty, or property based on the color of their skin, the sound of their creed or the country from which they hail. Neither the plenary power that grants the Executive and Attorney General the authority to regulate immigration at the border nor any other governmental function may be exercised in a manner that subjects persons to unequal treatment, without, at a minimum, a legitimate purpose. Certainly, should there be any reason to prefer one group over another, it would be because of the exigency that arises when another seeks protection within our borders in the face of their own peril and death, which, to be sure, existed for Petitioners here. The cruelty wielded upon Petitioners, is even more suspect in light of the treaty that our nation recently entered into, the Haitian Refugee Act of 1980, in which we committed to bestow upon the Haitians more humane treatment.

Unlike many of their non-Black counterparts, the Black Haitians risked life, limb, health, and well-being to traverse the rough seas to escape terror in their homeland only to arrive to an even worse fate. What they experienced upon their arrival in America was far from their mere hope of safety and survival; rather, their experience was reminiscent of a nightmare so ominous and tortuous as to cause some of them to beg to return to their own country – where death was a near certainty. The tales of abuse and suffering that would be the subject of memoirs thereafter tell of INS officials who afforded the Black Haitians not even a modicum of humanity, let alone due process and the equal protection of our laws.

The judgment of the lower court is reversed, and the case is remanded with instructions to release the Petitioners from detention and adjudicate their asylum claims.

9

Commentary on *Reno v. Flores*, 507 U.S. 292 (1993)

Lindsay M. Harris

In 1993, the U.S. Supreme Court's landmark decision in *Reno v. Flores*, authored by Justice Scalia, shaped the framework under which we still operate today for the detention of unaccompanied immigrant children. This decision and the subsequent 1997 Settlement Agreement have held steadfast relevance over the last three decades, as various humanitarian crises, combined with U.S. immigration policies, have led to large numbers of unaccompanied minors seeking protection in the United States.

The original *Flores* decision determined that the class of children – represented by named class member Jenny Lisette Flores, a then fifteen-year-old unaccompanied minor from El Salvador – had not established that their detention by the government violated their constitutional rights.

This decision has facilitated the ability of the U.S. government to detain hundreds of thousands of unaccompanied immigrant children – sometimes for prolonged periods of time – in problematic and, at times, inhumane conditions. What if this decision had come out differently? What if the humanity of unaccompanied children had been taken into account along with a compassionate interpretation of their fundamental rights? Professor Julia Hernández, writing as Justice Hernández, sheds some light on these questions in her rewritten opinion, while incorporating anti-racist, feminist, and child-centered principles into the decision.[1]

THE ORIGINAL OPINION

Writing for the majority in *Flores*, Justice Scalia framed the right asserted by the child plaintiffs as the "right of a child who has no available parent, close relative, or legal guardian, and for whom the government is responsible, to be placed in the custody of a willing-and-able private custodian rather than of a government-operated or

---

[1] *See* Meredith Johnson Harbach, *Feminist Legal Theory and Children's Rights, in* THE OXFORD HANDBOOK OF CHILDREN'S RIGHTS LAW 170 (Jonathan Todres & Shani M. King, eds., 2020) (explaining the way in which children's rights and feminist legal theory converge).

government-selected child-care institution."[2] Characterizing the right at issue in this manner allowed Justice Scalia to dismiss it, instead of viewing it as a "fundamental right" or acknowledging the liberty interest at stake. In doing so, Justice Scalia equated the government detention of these child plaintiffs with caregiving by parents, asserting that "juveniles, unlike adults, are always in some form of custody."[3]

In *Flores*, the child plaintiffs challenged a regulation by the Immigration and Naturalization Service (INS) permitting the release of a child only to a family member (parent, legal guardian, or other adult relative, including brothers, sisters, aunts, uncle, and grandparents). The regulations permitted release to an unrelated adult only in "unusual and compelling circumstances." The INS explained that it could not release to a broader class of people because it lacked the funding and expertise to engage in home studies.

The Court laid out a high bar to their facial challenge to the regulation: no set of circumstances must exist where the regulation would be valid. Given that the Court found no fundamental right to be at issue, it held that the government's approach survived rational basis review because it was "rationally connected to a government interest in 'preserving and promoting the welfare of the child.'"[4]

The Court presupposed that government-operated or government-selected child-care institutions provided adequate conditions for unaccompanied children that failed to trigger constitutional concerns. Referencing prior litigation and challenges to these detention conditions, resulting in the Juvenile Care Agreement (JCA),[5] the Court assumed that any conditions concerns were addressed by the government's "compliance with the extensive requirements set forth in the [JCA]."[6]

Further, the Court dismissed the best interests of the child standard as a "policy judgment rather than a constitutional imperative."[7] Without having to consider the best interest of the child, *Flores* made clear that the majority of Justices believed that the U.S. government was not required to expend resources and develop expertise to conduct home visits and assess the fitness of another adult for release of the child because the conditions of detention are "good enough."[8] While the plaintiffs argued that the INS regulation violated the statute because it relied on a blanket presumption of unsuitability of unrelated adult custodians, the Court found that the regulation was an appropriate and reasonable exercise of discretion by the Attorney General.

[2] Reno v. Flores, 507 U.S. 292, 303 (1993).
[3] *Id.* at 302 (quoting Schall, 467 U.S. 253, 265 (1984)).
[4] *Id.* at 303 (quoting Santosky v. Kramer, 455 U.S. 745, 766 (1982)).
[5] Memorandum of Understanding Re Compromise of Class Action: Conditions of Detention, Flores v. Meese, No. 85-4544-RJK (Px) (C.D. Cal. Nov. 30, 1987).
[6] 507 U.S. at 301.
[7] *Id.* at 305; *see also* at 304 (rejecting the best interests of the child standard as "not an absolute and exclusive constitutional criterion for the government's exercise of the custodial responsibilities that it undertakes").
[8] *Id.*

Finally, the Court dismissed any procedural due process concerns about how the INS made its determination to detain children. Although noncitizens in deportation proceedings are entitled to due process under the Fifth Amendment, Scalia believed that giving "juveniles" the right to ask for a hearing before an immigration judge was enough because he saw no evidence that the children were too young to assert that right, claiming that most unaccompanied immigrant children held in custody were sixteen or seventeen years old.

Throughout the *Flores* decision, the Court made clear that noncitizen children can be treated differently. Ultimately, the Court held that INS could continue to detain such children who could not be released to an available relative or legal guardian. In deferring to the federal government's plenary power over immigration, *Flores* concluded that the INS policy regarding the release of unaccompanied immigrant children from detention, though not ideal nor in the best interests of the children, was still legal and therefore, good enough.

THE LEGACY OF *RENO v. FLORES*

The Supreme Court's *Flores* decision in 1993 was followed by a Settlement Agreement between the parties, signed in 1997.[9] This Agreement set minimum standards for the detention of immigrant children. The Agreement allowed for the release of immigrant children to "an adult individual or entity seeking custody" as a last resort "when it appears that there is no other likely alternative to long term detention and family reunification does not appear to be a reasonable possibility."[10] The Settlement Agreement, in prioritizing the release of children from custody, did what the *Flores* decision failed to do, and came closer to implementing the best interests of the child standard. Despite this commitment to release children, litigation has repeatedly been brought over the years to enforce the terms of the Settlement.[11] Such litigation over the conditions and length of confinement and the release of parents accompanying their children into the United States might not have been necessary if the Supreme Court's 1993 decision had been issued with anti-racist, feminist, child-centered principles in mind.

Today it is easy to see the ways in which *Flores* condoned the incarceration of immigrant children and families. The Biden Administration, for example, has shifted from detaining children within Customs and Border Protection (CBP) facilities – where inhumane conditions have long been documented[12] – to holding

---

[9] Stipulated Settlement Agreement, Flores v. Reno, No. 2:85-CV-04544 (C.D. Cal. Jan. 17, 1997).
[10] *Id.* at ¶ 14.
[11] *See, e.g.*, Bunikyte v. Chertoff, No. A-07-CA-164-ss, 2007 WL 1074070, at *2 (W.D. Tex. Apr. 9, 2007) (challenging conditions at Hutto as a violation of the Flores Settlement); Flores v. Lynch, 212 F. Supp. 3d 907, 908 (C.D. Cal. 2015), *aff'd in part, rev'd in part*, 828 F.3d 898 (9th Cir. 2016) (challenging family detention as a violation of the Flores settlement).
[12] *See, e.g.*, Complaint ¶ 1, Doe v. Johnson, No. 15-cv-00250-DCB, (D. Ariz. June 8, 2015).

children en masse in non-licensed emergency sites, where they suffer some of the same neglect and delays in being released.[13] At a newly designated facility in Fort Bliss, Texas, 10,000 unaccompanied children have been held in cramped and crowded conditions, and allegations of sexual and physical abuse were made within the facility's first months of operation.[14] Family detention centers, which the Obama Administration closed and then subsequently reopened, hold children along with their parents.[15]

The anti-immigrant sentiment behind *Flores* also paved the way for the rise in adult immigration detention. If child detention is acceptable, there are no limits to what we can do to noncitizen adults. The detention of immigrants in the United States has massively increased in recent decades. César Cuauhtémoc García Hernández documents the rise of mass immigration incarceration in his book, which ably traces the emergence of imprisonment in the 1980s.[16] *Flores* did not anticipate the power-ful lobbying interests at play with the detention of immigrant adults and children, including private prison contractors like GEO Group and Core Civic (formerly Corrections Corporation of America). Today, more than 400,000 individuals per year spend time in immigration detention.[17] Conditions for adults are concerning, with medical attention lacking.[18] The COVID-19 pandemic brought these medical concerns sharply into focus.[19]

Flores dismissed concerns about the indefinite detention of children, and yet sadly these concerns were prescient. Although the Settlement Agreement was construed to limit immigration detention to approximately three weeks,[20] one toddler was held with his mother for twenty-two months, learning to walk and talk in confinement.[21] Statistics on the detention of unaccompanied immigrant children are not always clear, but many children are held for several months in government custody.[22] The average length of custody for children held by the U.S. government in FY 2020 was

---

[13] Shaw Drake & Bernardo Rafael Cruz, *Unaccompanied Children's Well-Being Must Come First at Fort Bliss and Across Texas*, ACLU (June 24, 2021).

[14] *Id.*

[15] *See generally* Lindsay M. Harris, *Contemporary Family Detention and Legal Advocacy*, 21 HARV. LATINO L. REV. 135 (2018).

[16] *See generally* CÉSAR CUAUHTÉMOC GARCÍA HERNÁNDEZ, MIGRATING TO PRISON: AMERICA'S OBSESSION WITH LOCKING UP IMMIGRANTS (2019).

[17] SHARITA GRUBERG, CENTER FOR AMERICAN PROGRESS, HOW FOR-PROFIT COMPANIES ARE DRIVING IMMIGRATION DETENTION POLICIES 1, 3 (Dec. 2015).

[18] OFFICE OF INSPECTOR GENERAL, DEP'T OF HOMELAND SEC., CONCERNS ABOUT ICE DETAINEE TREATMENT AND CARE AT FOUR DETENTION FACILITIES 2–3 (June 9, 2019).

[19] DONALD KERWIN, CENTER FOR MIGRATION STUDIES, IMMIGRATION DETENTION AND COVID-19: HOW A PANDEMIC EXPLOITED AND SPREAD THROUGH THE U.S. IMMIGRANT DETENTION SYSTEM 2 (Aug. 2020).

[20] Lynch, 212 F. Supp. 3d at 914.

[21] Laura Benshoff, *Judge Frees Mom, Toddler from Berks Immigrant Detention Center after 22 Months*, WHYY (Aug. 8, 2017).

[22] *Latest UC Data – FY 21*, HHS.GOV (Nov. 15, 2021).

102 days – more than three months.[23] Under the Biden Administration, the FY 2021 average is down to thirty-seven days in custody, but this will fluctuate depending on an Administration's priorities.

Experts have consistently maintained that the effects of even a "short period" of detention – for children detained alone or with their parents – can be extremely harmful. The American Academy of Pediatrics stated that "expert consensus has concluded that even brief detention can cause psychological trauma and induce long-term mental health risks for children."[24] Further, to the extent that unaccompanied children arrive with mental health challenges, the Department of Health and Human Services' own Office of Inspector General has found that the government struggles to address the mental health needs of children in its custody.[25] In short, the U.S. government, through its mass detention of immigrant children, is perpetuating and creating generations of traumatized individuals. The last three decades have seen repeated problems for immigrant children and families held in detention. In 2018, the country was in an uproar in response to the Trump Administration's zero tolerance policy, which resulted in children being physically separated at the border from their parents. The public's eyes were opened to the concept of "kids in cages," which had been happening for years as children were held in CBP temporary holding facilities prior to transfer to more permanent facilities managed by the Office of Refugee Resettlement under the Department of Health and Human Services. Some of what we know about unacceptable detention conditions comes from litigation involving adult detention or where complaints about inadequate medical care are filed on behalf of children detained *with* their parents.[26] Much of the evidence about children held on the border is sealed, but some information is publicly available, such as the stories included in an online exhibit from parents and children.[27]

While advocates have been able to limit the holding of *Flores* and use the 1997 Settlement Agreement to push for release, we continue to battle inadequate and shameful conditions for children in custody today. Let us imagine a world in which the Supreme Court in 1993 had recognized the best interests of the child standard and the harm that immigration detention has on children and human beings. That brings us to an analysis of the rewritten feminist judgment.

---

[23] *Unaccompanied Children: Facts and Data*, OFFICE OF REFUGEE RESETTLEMENT (Dec. 20, 2021).
[24] Julie Linton et al., American Academy of Pediatrics, *Detention of Immigrant Children*, 139 PEDIATRICS 1, 6 (2017).
[25] U.S. DEP'T OF HEALTH & HUMAN SERVS., OFFICE OF INSPECTOR GENERAL, CARE PROVIDER FACILITIES DESCRIBED CHALLENGES ADDRESSING MENTAL HEALTH NEEDS OF CHILDREN IN HHS CUSTODY 9 (Sept. 2019).
[26] *See, e.g.*, Letter from Lindsay M. Harris et al., CARA Pro Bono Project, to Megan Mack, Officer for Civil Rts. & Civil Liberties, U.S. Dep't of Homeland Sec., and John Roth, Inspector Gen., U.S. Dep't of Homeland Sec. (Oct. 6, 2015).
[27] THE FLORES EXHIBITS, https://flores-exhibits.org (last visited Dec. 25, 2021).

THE FEMINIST JUDGMENT

Professor Hernández's rewritten feminist judgment of *Flores v. Reno* masterfully reframes the issues at play with new language and appropriately recognizes immigration detention as incarceration and a deprivation of liberty. At the same time, Hernández calls out the racism underlying the INS policy, which undermines reunification of immigrant children with extended family or community members. She also introduces the concept of cultural humility and, importantly, acknowledges the geopolitical reality of migration from El Salvador to the United States. In doing so, she uses essential feminist narrative methods to focus on the reality of the lives of the actual people involved rather than simply on "objective" legal principles.[28]

Her opinion begins with the following: "Fifteen-year-old Jenny Flores traveled to the United States alone seeking refuge from the civil war in El Salvador and with the hope of reuniting with her mother." In contrast, Justice Scalia opens with: "Over the past decade, the Immigration and Naturalization Service has arrested increasing numbers of alien juveniles who are not accompanied by their parents of other related adults." A striking and immediate difference is language – the words used to describe the plaintiffs in the case. While Scalia refers to the plaintiffs as "alien juveniles," Hernández opens the decision by introducing the reader to one particular noncitizen child, Jenny Flores.

While Scalia immediately alludes to the potential criminality of the unaccompanied children by focusing on "arrests," Hernández signals their humanity by highlighting that Jenny was fleeing from civil war in El Salvador by "seeking refuge" and hoping to be reunited with her mother. While Scalia hints at fears of the "floodgates" opening – "increasing numbers" of children arriving – Hernández humanizes the children by focusing on one child and what she endured within the U.S. immigration system, which included "daily strip searches while being denied visitors, education, and recreation." From the very first sentence of the opinion, Hernández's rewritten opinion would have been a sea change in the way we think and talk not only about the detention of immigrant children but also about immigration more broadly in the United States.

Treating Immigrant Children as Children

Throughout the rewritten decision, Hernández uses narrative and storytelling to refer to the plaintiffs as they are – "children" rather than "alien juveniles." This powerful shift helps to reframe the crucial concerns fundamentally at interest in this case. In addressing the due process concerns at stake, Hernández frames the due

---

[28] *See* Margaret E. Montoya, Mascaras, Trenzas, y Grenas: *Un/Masking the Self While Un/Braiding Latina Stories and Legal Discourse*, 15 CHICANO-LATINO L. REV. 1, 31–32 (1994).

process rights of immigrants and the fundamental rights of children more generally. Recognizing the fundamental rights of children and the best interest of the child could have been revolutionary during this time. The United States contributed to the drafting of the 1988 United Nation's Convention on the Rights of the Child and signed it in 1995. But this was a largely symbolic gesture as the United States has still failed to ratify the Convention.

Professor Hernández holds that children have a fundamental right to be free from custody, explicitly rejecting the Court's characterization that children are always in some form of custody. Even shelter care is inherently incarceration, which triggers a substantive due process violation. Restraining a child's liberty is rarely in their best interest.

After identifying a fundamental right at issue, Hernández invokes strict scrutiny, requiring that the government interest be compelling, and the means narrowly tailored to effectuate that interest. After discussing the multiple harms of detaining children, Hernández questions the compelling government interest in "protecting and promoting the best interests of children." Rather, she determines that the government's chosen means – limiting release of children to a restricted class of relatives – is not narrowly tailored to that compelling government interest and that the government's "asserted interests appear to be pretextual stand-ins for invidious discrimination."

Professor Hernández also highlights the differences between children and adults. She makes apparent the real and realized risk of indefinite detention of noncitizen children. Further, she notes that putting children on "equal footing with adults" is "unacceptable." Specifically, children cannot defend themselves against INS officials in court who are responsible for their arrest and prosecution. Nor can they be expected to have the wherewithal to request a hearing to review their detention in the first instance. By emphasizing these facts, Hernández concludes that the INS regulation violates procedural due process.

In 2016, for example, former Immigration Judge Jack Weil made some rather ridiculous statements on the ability of children to represent themselves in removal proceedings: "I've taught immigration law literally to 3-year-olds and 4-year-olds … It takes a lot of time. It takes a lot of patience. They get it. It's not the most efficient, but it can be done."[29] Had the Supreme Court recognized the best interest of the child standard in 1993, it may have prevented the development of a norm of children defending themselves against trained prosecutors in removal proceedings.

Finally, Hernández finds the INS regulation at issue to be ultra vires because the federal statute governing immigration detention does not refer to children or minors in the detention provisions. Hernández concludes, through a plain language reading of the statute and using classical canons of statutory construction, that

[29] Jerry Markon, *Can a 3-Year-Old Represent Himself in Immigration Proceedings? This Judge Thinks So*, WASH. POST (Mar. 5, 2016).

"if Congress had intended to apply the statute to children, it would have explicitly said so." Ultimately, Hernández concludes that the agency merits no deference regulating in the area of child welfare, outside of its area of expertise, and that the regulation is not reasonably related to the purpose of the underlying statute. Hernández recognizes children not only as the bearers of rights themselves, but also as a group that requires special protection.

Cultural Humility and the Geopolitical Reality

The rewritten judgment would have introduced the concept of cultural humility into Supreme Court jurisprudence, recognizing that the INS policy forbidding release beyond a small group of relatives "devalues extended family and other caregiving structures embraced by large segments of the United States and global population, elevating a hegemonic definition of family that is inconsistent with precedent." Cultural humility can be defined "not as a discrete endpoint but as a commitment and active engagement in lifelong process that individuals enter into on an ongoing basis with patients, communities, colleagues, and with [oneself]."[30]

Hernández critiques the INS' limited view of family, recognizing that while prior Supreme Court jurisprudence has recognized that parents and related adults are likely to act in the child's best interests, "so too are extended family and other adults similarly situated through social or cultural norms."

Further, Hernández's decision situates the issues at play within the geopolitical reality. Noting that the four named plaintiff children are all from El Salvador – "where conditions of civil war and political violence currently exist" – Hernández skillfully acknowledges the role of the United States, far from a neutral actor, in shaping the situation on the ground in 1993.[31]

Immigration Detention as Incarceration

As Hernández astutely notes, the 1980s saw a rise in the detention of both child and adult migrants as an "increasingly central feature of immigration policing." Had this decision been issued in its rewritten form, emphasizing detention as the last resort, rather than the norm, may have curtailed the meteoric rise in immigration detention.

The rewritten judgment is very clear that the INS "institutionalization" of noncitizen children "amounts to detention" and is contrary to the best interest of children.

---

[30] Tariq El-Gabalawy, *Cultural Humility: A Guiding Principle for Changing Approaches to Teaching Criminal Law*, 25 U.C. DAVIS SOC. JUST. L. REV. 60, 62 (2021) (citation omitted).

[31] *See, e.g.*, Karen Musalo, *El Salvador – A Peace Worse than War: Violence, Gender and a Failed Legal Response*, 30 YALE J. L. & FEMINISM 3, 5 (2018).

A jail is a jail – no matter how cheery, colorful, or outwardly friendly to children – and the deprivation of liberty is detention. Framing the incarceration of children in this way might have prevented the arguments made by former President Donald Trump, with his supporters describing detention centers for children at the border as "summer camps."[32] Of course, the conditions in these facilities are a far cry from any summer camp.[33]

The decision does much to recognize the harm wrought by detaining immigrant children. Detention is bad for children, as has been borne out time and again by the U.S. government's various modes of detaining children, with and without their parents. As Hernández makes clear, "[t]he isolation of detention, compounded by tightly regulated access, creates a physical and psychological separation from society that disappears children within sterile institutions." Hernández's rewritten opinion skillfully uses the record to highlight the concerns regarding even the short-term detention of children, citing a study on the mental health of undocumented children from Central America.

Conditions and Alternatives to Immigration Detention

The rewritten opinion would have charted a different course forward in terms of litigation over conditions of confinement. While the opinion would have potentially rewritten the course of history with very few to no immigrant children held in confinement, what we have witnessed instead after the original *Flores* decision has been ongoing litigation regarding the precise conditions under which children are held. The decision as it stands laid the foundation for the abusive conditions we have seen repeatedly in headlines and litigation.

The rewritten opinion specifically considers alternatives to detention for children, pointing to the amicus brief from nongovernmental organizations which observed that community-based case management programs are "less expensive and less harmful to children because they are designed in children's best interests." This would have planted the seed for robust alternatives to detention and case management programs. We would not be at the embarrassing point we are today with the mass incarceration of tens of thousands of immigrant children and families, with the existence of only very small pilot programs, including the major pilot case management contract being awarded to a subsidiary of a private prison contractor back in 2015.[34]

---

[32] Avery Anapol, *Laura Ingraham: Migrant Child Detention Centers 'Essentially Summer Camps,'* THE HILL (June 18, 2018).

[33] *See, e.g.,* Matt Smith & Aura Bogado, *Immigrant Children Forcibly Injected with Drugs at Texas Shelter, Lawsuit Claims,* TEX. TRIB. (June 20, 2018).

[34] Chris Mill Rodrigo, *Record Number of Immigrants Funneled into Alternative Detention Programs,* THE HILL (Nov. 12, 2021).

Discrimination

By underscoring that immigrant children are, above all, children, Hernández finds that providing noncitizen children with lesser rights would raise significant Equal Protection issues. The rewritten opinion builds toward the ultimate conclusion that deciding this case in a different way would be undeniably racist.

One of the most powerful passages of the rewritten judgment is where Professor Hernández examines a government official's comments to help "shed light on the actual justifications for the new policy." Hernández takes Western Region Commissioner Ezell to task for his "xenophobic, classist, and racist public comments," which are not even mentioned in the original *Reno v. Flores* opinion. Naming and shaming his use of derogatory terms of migrants, including "wets" for "wetbacks," the rewritten decision would have brought to light this ugly, racist language. Pushing back on such rhetoric from the mouths of government officials in 1993 might have helped to avoid the foundation of hate-fueled othering and dehumanizing language about immigrants that catapulted Donald Trump to the presidency in 2016.

CONCLUSION

If Professor Hernández had graced the Supreme Court in 1993 and written a decision with feminist principles in mind, the best interests of the child standard would have been carried through all interactions between noncitizen children and the immigration system. Subsequent policies and litigation would have operated by treating children as children, no matter their citizenship status. The immigration carceral complex would not have grown to the enormous infrastructure we see today, and the default would be release. Finally, individualized decision-making, considering each child's particular circumstances, rather than whitewashing cultural and familial dynamics and nuances, would have governed, and thereby encouraged the release of children to loved ones in their communities to provide care rather than confinement.

RENO v. FLORES, 507 U.S. 292 (1993)

Justice Julia Hernández delivered the opinion of the Court.

Fifteen-year-old Jenny Flores traveled to the United States alone seeking refuge from civil war in El Salvador and with the hope of reuniting with her mother. But rather than the safety of her mother's care or the protection she sought from the U.S. government, Jenny was arrested and confined for months in a Los Angeles motel converted to a jail. The Immigration and Naturalization Service (INS) drained the swimming pool, barred the windows, and installed barbed wire around the building. Jenny was subject to daily strip searches while being denied visitors, education, and recreation. Although Jenny's uncle sought to care for her, INS kept her detained pursuant to an ad-hoc policy prohibiting a child's release to anyone other than a narrow class of immediate relatives. Under the policy, Jenny and other children in similar circumstances would be detained indefinitely until their deportation cases were decided.

Sadly, Jenny's story is not unique. Writ large, this case is about the government's detention of noncitizen children arriving at our borders, many of whom are refugees seeking asylum. The facts are reprehensible and replete with examples of xenophobia, racism, and a depravity toward migrant children and their families that cannot be tolerated. As such, we begin by unequivocally affirming that children arriving to our modern-day borders are, at least as far as the law is concerned, society's children. We make no constitutionally relevant detention-related distinctions between noncitizen and citizen children. There can be no doubt that the way we treat vulnerable people, such as those arriving at our borders, shines a light on the soul of this nation.

We are compelled to find that the best interests of children must inform all decisions made about children the government takes into custody, even for brief periods of time. It is axiomatic that detention is inimical to children's best interests. We reject INS' assertion that it is in a child's best interest to be detained rather than released to a responsible adult or organization. The INS' remaining justifications carry little weight when compared to incarceration's potential harm to children. And finally, a clear-eyed look at the facts reveals that the stated rationale for the policy simply amounts to a post-hoc, pretextual justification for invidious discrimination.

Procedural due process militates that children detained on suspicion of deportability cannot carry the burden to trigger their due process rights or to show entitlement to release as the regulation requires. To require such affirmative steps by a child newly arrived to the United States turns the Constitution back on itself. The Bill of Rights, activated to its full effect, maps out the boundaries of what the government cannot do, not the responsibilities of a vulnerable class like unaccompanied children. The Attorney General too has exceeded her authority in creating a regulatory scheme where children are presumptively detained because it is contrary to congressional policy that favors the release of juveniles.

Therefore, today we hold that detaining children for alleged immigration violations is unconstitutional, unless the government can affirmatively show by clear and convincing evidence before an impartial adjudicator that detention is required for the safety of the child or the public, and that no proposed plan for release would be sufficient.

We note the importance of this case because of the rise in detention of both child and adult migrants throughout the 1980s as an increasingly central feature of immigration policing.[35] Yet, the geopolitical context in which this case

---

[35] During the 1980s, INS steadily increased the number of people detained, corresponding with, and largely in reaction to, a major influx of Cubans, Haitians, and Central Americans. Human Rights Watch, *Brutality Unchecked: Human Rights Abuses along the U.S. Border with Mexico* 51 (1992).

arises speaks to the roots of much of the migration INS seeks to curtail. All four named plaintiff children hail from El Salvador, where conditions of civil war and political violence currently exist. Pls.' Compl. ¶¶ 12–15, 62. Although the government claims that "[t]he problem has been thrust upon INS by the combination of socioeconomic conditions in Central America beyond its control," Br. for Pet'rs 31, this characterization is reductive and incomplete. We cannot ignore the political, economic, and military relations between the United States and Central American countries, including El Salvador, that have shaped geopolitical realities undergirding migration today. Historically – and in the current conflict – the United States has not been a neutral nation. Alan Riding, *The U.S. Role in El Salvador*, N.Y. Times, Mar. 13, 1980. Rather, we have intervened directly and indirectly and cannot now claim that increased migration from El Salvador and neighboring countries is entirely the problem of those nations only. In what appears to be an era of increasing immigration enforcement, U.S. immigration systems must be oriented toward the assumption that people should live in freedom while pursuing their immigration cases, with detention being the exception, not the norm.

We begin with the factual and procedural background of the case, which originated as a class action in 1985. We then turn to due process, finding that detaining children during the pendency of deportation proceedings is presumptively unconstitutional. Finally, we reach the statutory question of whether the Attorney General lacks authority to issue the regulation, and conclude that she does not.

I

Background and Procedural History

This case is a challenge to the government's policy of detaining noncitizen children during the pendency of their immigration cases except when an immediate relative seeks their release. Detention in this circumstance is civil rather than criminal. Prior to the complaint filed in this case, to release noncitizen children encountered at modern-day borders, the INS followed the release policy established in section 504 of the Juvenile Justice and Delinquency Protection Act (JJDPA) of 1974. 18 U.S.C. § 5034. The JJDPA prefers release of children charged with criminal offenses to parents, guardians, or other responsible adults, including directors of shelter care facilities, upon the promise to bring the child back to court. Detention is a last resort, only if needed to ensure a timely court appearance. Despite the informal adoption of the JJDPA release provisions, at the time this case was filed, INS had no national unified policy on the detention or release of children in deportation proceedings.

In 1984, the INS Western Regional Office adopted a policy of limiting release separate from the JJDPA. This policy was not published in the federal register as required by the Administrative Procedure Act. 5 U.S.C. § 552(a). It restricted release to parents or lawful guardians except in "unusual and extraordinary circumstances." See Flores v. Meese, 934 F.2d 991, 994 (9th Cir. 1990) (quoting policy), vacated, 942 F.2d 1352 (9th Cir. 1991) (en banc). INS' initial justification for the new policy was to ensure child welfare and protect the agency against legal liability, Br. for Resp'ts 3–4 (quoting INS' Memo (Sept. 6, 1984)), although the agency admits that no allegations of harm to children released pursuant to the JJDPA policy have occurred, nor have any lawsuits ever been filed against INS on these grounds. Oral Arg. Tr. 6. In fact, the agency proffered no evidence as to why the policy change was necessary and further conceded that it had not consulted any professional guidance or recommended standards when adopting the policy. Br. for Resp'ts 7.

The policy came into play in this case when fifteen-year-old Jenny Flores was arrested pursuant to 8 U.S.C. §§ 1357(a)(2) and 1252(a)(1), which permits INS agents to arrest and detain people suspected of deportability. INS set bond for Jenny at $2,000. Jenny sought review of the bond determination before an Immigration Judge, who subsequently reduced the bond to $1,500. Only then did INS inform Jenny that she had to be released to a parent or legal guardian who must personally appear before the INS,[36] rather than her U.S. citizen uncle and legal permanent resident aunt who sought to care for her. Jenny unsuccessfully challenged the bond condition in front of the Immigration Judge. In July 1985, Jenny and three other children filed a class action lawsuit in the Central District Court of California.

The complaint alleged seven claims. The first two challenged the detention policy. The latter five concerned the conditions of the children's detention: denial of education, recreation, visitation, detention with unrelated adults, and unlawful strip searches. Although the conditions claims were resolved by settlement in November 1987 (JCA), and are therefore not before this Court, they remain relevant today. App. to Pet. for Cert. 148a–151a, 168a–205a. First, there is dispute as to whether the government is complying with the settlement. Amici assert that the conditions in INS detention facilities remain "abhorrent." Br. for Sw. Refugee Rts. Project et al., as Amici Curiae 15. Second, the history of the conditions litigation is relevant to our constitutional analysis because it provides additional context for the government's stated justifications for the policy.

The District Court certified the case as a class action. It then subsequently granted summary judgment to the children in a series of decisions finding that: (1) strip searches violated their Fourth Amendment rights; (2) INS' imposition of bond conditions violated due process; and (3) INS violated the Equal Protection Clause because it lacked a rational basis for treating minors differently in deportation versus

---

[36] INS officials acknowledged that undocumented adults who appeared to claim their children or relatives' children were subject to arrest and deportation. Patrick McDonnell, Children of Poverty, War Stagnate in Camps; Resurgence of Central American Immigration Points Up Plights of Youths Held by the INS, L.A. Times, Apr. 17, 1988.

exclusion proceedings (e.g., in exclusion cases, children could be released to other adults, including community-based organizations). INS then initiated a notice and comment process to equalize its deportation and exclusion policies. 52 Fed. Reg. 38245 (Oct. 15, 1987). The District Court deferred consideration of the Due Process claims until the final regulation was promulgated.

The final rule was published May 17, 1988. 53 Fed. Reg. 17449, 17450 (May 17, 1988) (codified at 8 C.F.R. § 242.24). It somewhat expanded possibilities for release beyond the original policy. It provides that a child "shall be released in order of preference to: (i) a parent; (ii) legal guardian; or (iii) other adult relative (brother, sister, aunt, uncle, grandparent) who are not presently in INS detention," unless a determination is made that detention is required to secure appearance at future proceedings or to ensure the child or other's safety. Id. at 17451. It permits release to unrelated adults only in "unusual and compelling circumstances." Id. In publishing the regulation, INS explained that the ultimate decision whether to release turned on the likelihood of appearance at future proceedings. INS' reason for not otherwise releasing to a wider class of people was because it would require "home studies for which the Service is neither adequately funded nor qualified." Id. at 17449.

The District Court then granted summary judgment and invalidated the regulatory scheme in three respects. App. To Pet. For Cert. 146a. First, it ordered INS to release any minor otherwise eligible for release to the enumerated categories in the regulation and any other responsible adult party. Second, it modified the regulation's requirement that the unrelated person formally agree to care for the child in addition to ensuring attendance at future proceedings. Finally, it required an automatic immediate hearing for any detained juvenile before an Immigration Judge about their detention and release.

A divided panel of the Court of Appeals for the Ninth Circuit reversed and remanded. Flores, 934 F.2d at 1013. The Ninth Circuit voted to rehear the case en banc and vacated the panel opinion and affirmed the decision of the District Court "in all respects." Flores, 942 F.2d at 1365. We granted certiorari and now affirm the Ninth Circuit's en banc decision.

II

Due Process

Freedom from government detention and other forms of physical restraint is at the core of the liberty interest that the due process clause protects. *Foucha v. Louisiana*, 504 U.S. 71, 80 (1992) (citing *Youngberg v. Romeo*, 457 U.S. 307, 316 (1982)). This liberty interest is enshrined in substantive and procedural rights when the government abridges an individual's freedom. See *U.S. v. Salerno*, 481 U.S. 739, 746 (1987).

Children also possess fundamental rights that the state must respect. *Tinker v. Des Moines Indep. Comty. Sch. Dist.*, 393 U.S. 503, 511 (1969); *Bellotti v. Baird*, 443 U.S.

622, 634 (1979). Due process applies to children, protecting their rights when faced with any deprivation of liberty. *In re Gault*, 387 U.S. 1, 13 (1967) ("whatever may be their precise impact, neither the Fourteenth Amendment nor the Bill of Rights is for adults alone"); *Parham v. J.R.*, 442 U.S. 584, 600 (1979) ("It is not disputed that a child, in common with adults, has a substantial liberty interest in not being confined unnecessarily for medical treatment."). Noncitizen children are therefore protected under due process as persons present in the United States who must be afforded substantive and procedural protections in conjunction with any deprivation of liberty.

When confining a child to an institution, current doctrine only allows it as a last resort for legitimate purposes and when the restriction is no greater than necessary to achieve those purposes. *See Schall v. Martin*, 467 U.S. 253, 269 (1984). In *Schall*, we held that pre-trial detention in juvenile delinquency proceedings was appropriate only upon a determination that release is not safe for the child or community, when such a decision is made by an impartial and detached official, and when justifications for detention are not punitive and are clearly stated. 467 U.S. at 266, 269–70. Today we question whether these protections are enough. But to provide noncitizen children in this context with lesser rights would raise significant Equal Protection issues. *See, e.g., Plyler v. Doe*, 457 U.S. 202, 224 (1982) (undocumented Mexican children's exclusion from public schools violated Equal Protection Clause); *Graham v. Richardson*, 403 U.S. 365, 376 (1971) (provisions of state welfare laws conditioning benefits on citizenship and imposing durational residency requirements on noncitizens violates Equal Protection Clause). Additionally, because the detainees in this case are children, their interests should be considered with special attention to their unique vulnerability and special needs. *See Eddings v. Oklahoma*, 455 U.S. 104, 115–16 (1982); *May v. Anderson*, 345 U.S. 528, 536 (1953) (Frankfurter, J. concurring).

A

Substantive Due Process

Substantive due process "prevents the government from engaging in conduct that shocks the conscience, … or interferes with rights implicit in the concept of ordered liberty" unless the infringement is narrowly tailored to serve a compelling state interest. *Salerno*, 481 U.S. at 746, 748 (quotations omitted). In its most elemental form, liberty is freedom from detention and restraint. *Id.* at 749 ("Respondents [invoke] … the 'general rule' of substantive due process that the government may not detain a person prior to a judgment of guilt in a criminal trial. Such a 'general rule' may freely be conceded"); *DeShaney v. Winnebago Cty.*, 489 U.S. 189, 200 (1989) ("In the substantive due process analysis, it is the State's affirmative act of restraining the individual's freedom to act on his own behalf – through incarceration, institutionalization, or other similar restraint of personal liberty – which is the 'deprivation of liberty' triggering the protections of the Due Process Clause"). Accordingly, liberty is the norm; government detention is the exception, only permissible when the state makes a strong showing of necessity.

A child's right to be free from government detention is a fundamental right. We readily conclude that the right to be free from government detention is "'[s]o rooted in the traditions and conscience of our people as to be ranked fundamental.'" *Salerno*, 481 U.S. at 751 (quoting *Snyder v. Mass.*, 291 U.S. 97, 105 (1934)). Our decisions have long protected and held sacred childhood. *See, e.g., Bellotti*, 443 U.S. at 634; *Planned Parenthood v. Danforth*, 428 U.S. 52, 74–75 (1976); *Parham*, 442 U.S. at 628 (Brennan, J., concurring in part and dissenting in part) ("[C]hildhood is a particularly vulnerable time of life, and children erroneously institutionalized during their formative years may bear the scars for the rest of their lives."). To hold otherwise would be repugnant to the morals and ethics this nation professes it aspires to embody.

Under the facts of this case, INS institutionalization amounts to detention, even though the detention here is civil rather than criminal in nature. The American Bar Association's Juvenile Justice Standards' definition of the word "detention" notes that a placement still constitutes detention even if the facility is seemingly decent and humane. Inst. of Judicial Admin., Am. Bar Ass'n, *Juvenile Justice Standards: Standards Relating to Interim Status* 45 (1980). "Whether it gives the appearance of the worst sort of jail, or a comfortable and pleasant home, the facility is classified as 'detention' if it is not the juvenile's usual place of abode." *Id.* While newly arrived children may not yet have a "usual place of abode," the general principle remains: a child is detained even if a facility is less harsh than a typical jail.

The INS argues that children in INS custody are not detained because the Juvenile Care Agreement (JCA) that settled the conditions claims requires "an open type of setting without a need for extraordinary security measures." App. To Pet. For Cert. 148a–151a, 168a–205a. But the JCA is not dispositive on the question of whether children in INS custody are in detention. The JCA itself requires "programs and strategies to discourage runaways and prevent the unauthorized absence of minors in care." *Id.* 173a. It is clear from the facts in this case – presented by both the government and class counsel – that these children have had their personal liberty restrained.

To accept the government's argument that children are not – or are no longer – held in detention facilities because of the JCA would be to deliberately close our eyes to the information before the Court that provides the facts on the ground. Amici note that "[a]s organizations with particular knowledge of INS detention practices and conditions, [we] wish to inform the court that this description of current conditions is grossly inaccurate." Br. For Sw. Refugee Rts. Project et al., 24. Further, the record shows that children are placed in juvenile jails and that the INS has ignored court orders prohibiting the practice of strip-searching children. *Id.* 29–30; *Flores v. Meese*, 681 F. Supp. 665, 669 (C.D. Cal. 1988). Amici also call our attention to a recently filed lawsuit alleging beating and psychological abuse of minors in a California facility. Br. For Sw. Refugee Rts. Project et al., 31–32. Facilities like the ones at issue here are like jails in that they are shielded from public view, effectively obscuring much of what happens inside the jail's enclosures. As one INS jailer testified, children in his facility could only "play in the dirt," or go out in the desert summer "and let their tongue[s] hang out in the heat." *Id.* 18. Given these factors, we are unconvinced that the conditions are as the INS claims them to be.

A child in government custody, therefore, experiences restraints on their liberty, striking at the heart of substantive due process. Custody is detention – a restraint on liberty – regardless of whether a facility resembles more closely a jail or an institution with fewer restrictions. The isolation of detention, compounded by tightly regulated access, creates a physical and psychological separation from society that disappears children within sterile institutions. Reducing the children's interests to a right to release to non-related adults turns the Bill of Rights on its head. We therefore find that the right at stake here is the right to be free from government detention.

Because this governmental custody inescapably denies children their liberty – a fundamental right – we apply strict judicial scrutiny. In this rigorous analysis, the government interest must be compelling, and the means chosen must be narrowly tailored to achieve that interest. *Salerno,* 481 U.S. at 748, 750. Protecting and promoting the welfare of children should be a compelling government interest.[37] *See Osborne v. Ohio,* 495 U.S. 103, 110 (1990). In support of its policy, INS has invoked no fewer than four justifications. First, INS has always claimed that its policy is to ensure the welfare and safety of children. Second, when the ad-hoc rule was initially implemented, then-Western Region Commissioner Howard Ezell stated that it was to protect the INS from potential liability if it were to release children to a broader class of adults. Br. For Resp'ts 3–4 (quoting INS' Memo (Sept. 6, 1984)). Third, in its promulgation of the final rule, INS stated that its purpose was to address the increasing number of unaccompanied children crossing the southern border. Finally, since issuing the final rule, INS has repeatedly stated that it favors government custody because the INS cannot vet all potential caregivers because it lacks sufficient resources and is not qualified to conduct home studies. 53 Fed. Reg. 17449 (May 17, 1988); Br. For Pet'rs 10.

These justifications hold little water. While ensuring the welfare and safety of children is a compelling interest, the detention of children is never in their best interests. Institutional settings are particularly harmful to children. Government

---

[37] The United Nations (U.N.) Convention on the Rights of the Child (CRC), entered into force in September 1990, is instructive here. Although the United States has not yet ratified the treaty, the CRC states that the best interest of the child should be the primary consideration in all actions concerning children.

custody often carries great risks, all of which are heightened when the detainee is a child. It is undisputable that institutionalizing children damages their ability to form close personal relationships, their global development, and ability to function in noninstitutional settings. Mary Ford & Joe Kroll, N. Am. Council on Adoptable Children, *Challenges to Child Welfare: Countering the Call for a Return to Orphanages* 8–12 (Nov. 1990); Br. Of Amici Curiae Child Welfare League of America et al., 26. Confinement can inflict long-lasting psychological, developmental, and physical harm. Even for short periods of time, detention is harmful to children. A child's sense of time is different than that of an adult because children cannot accurately assess the passage of time, making units of time stretch longer than an adult would perceive. Br. Of Amici Curiae Youth Law Ctr. et al., 11–16, *Flores v. Meese*, 942 F.2d 1352 (1991).

It is mystifying that an agency that imprisoned children with non-related adults in detention centers with barbed wire and uniformed guards, while denying them education, recreation, and visitation and subjecting the children to handcuffs and arbitrary punishment, could conclude that it is acting in children's best interests. With respect to potential liability, as we have recently held in *Deshaney*, government custody likely creates more liability than release: "[W]hen the State takes a person into its custody and holds him there against his will, the Constitution imposes upon it a corresponding duty to assume some responsibility for his safety and general well-being." 489 U.S. at 200.

Nor are their means chosen for promoting the best interests of children – limiting release of children to a narrow class of immediate relatives – narrowly tailored to that interest. There are numerous recommended standards by official entities, such as the U.S. Department of Health, Education and Welfare, the U.S. Department of Justice, and the Institute of Judicial Administration, finding that children should always be released to a parent, guardian, or other responsible party rather than detained.[38] INS ignored or rejected these standards when it adopted its policy. Many states around the United States also have laws that are consistent with these standards.[39] As we stated in *Schall*, "[t]he fact that a practice is followed by a large number of states … is plainly worth considering" as being part of our traditions. 467 U.S. at 268. Ironically, the INS seems to agree; it claims that state law and state forums are the most appropriate basis for deciding custody. Oral Arg. Tr. 17.

---

[38] *See, e.g.*, U.S. Dep't of Health, Education, and Welfare, *Model Acts for Family Courts and State-Local Children's Programs* 24 (1975); U.S. Dep't of Justice, Nat'l Advisory Comm. for Juvenile Justice and Delinquency Prevention, *Standards for the Administration of Juvenile Justice* 299 (1980); Inst. of Judicial Admin., Am. Bar Ass'n, *Standards Relating to Noncriminal Misbehavior* 41, 42 (1982).

[39] *See, e.g.*, Ala. Code § 12-15-62(a)(1) (1991) (release to "a parent, guardian, custodian or any other person who the court deems proper"); Conn. Gen. Stat. § 46b-133(b) (1990) (release to "parent or parents, his guardian or some other suitable person or agency"); Utah Code Ann. § 78-3a-29(3)(a) (1992) (release to "parent or other responsible adult").

The INS policy is also troubling because it devalues extended family and other caregiving structures embraced by large segments of the United States and global population, elevating a hegemonic definition of family that is inconsistent with precedent. While parents and other closely related adults are particularly likely to act in a child's best interests, so too are extended family and other adults similarly situated through social or cultural norms. We recognized as much in *Moore v. City of East Cleveland*, writing that "the Constitution prevents East Cleveland from standardizing its children and its adults by forcing all to live in certain narrowly defined family patterns." 431 U.S. 494, 506 (1977).

When the INS steps into the shoes of the parent, it must act in the child's best interests. It is incredible and unacceptable that the federal government cannot develop and put into practice a system for vetting caregivers. INS put forward no evidence that the economic cost of detention is less than the cost of hiring social workers to vet the backgrounds of potential caregivers. In fact, amici argue that its community-based refugee resettlement programs are less expensive and less harmful to children because they are designed with children's best interests in mind. Br. Of Amici Curiae U.S. Catholic Conf. et al., 12–14. No institutional care, no matter how benevolent, can supplant the care of a committed adult. In Jenny's case, it is obvious that instead of prolonged detention, releasing her to her uncle would have been in her best interests.

Rather, Western Region Commissioner Ezell's xenophobic, classist, and racist public comments shed light on the potential real justifications for the new policy. Taken together with the reality of detention conditions at the time this case began and evidence that undocumented parents who came forward to claim their children were arrested and placed in deportation proceedings, we find INS' justifications likely to be post-hoc, pretextual justifications for invidious discrimination. Sen. Dennis DeConcini (D-Ariz.) wrote to INS Commissioner Alan C. Nelson complaining that Ezell said, during a border tour, "'Sorry, I don't have time so we can go out and chase some wets.'" Jay Matthews, *Tough-Talking INS Official Raises Profile, Ire in the West*, Wash. Post, Mar. 24, 1986. The term "wets" is an abbreviation of "wetbacks," a derogatory, racist reference to individuals fording the Rio Grande into the United States. Against this background, INS maintains its position that institutionalization is in a child's best interest. Such an intractable position, however, reveals that INS' priorities are not to ensure that children are with relatives or other caring adults, but to expend few administrative resources while risking severe psychological, emotional, and physical harm to children. Such priorities certainly lead us to conclude that INS' purported interest in the welfare and safety of children is pretextual.

We therefore find that INS' policy cannot survive substantive due process scrutiny. The children here in INS custody have a fundamental right to be free from government detention and the policy is not narrowly tailored to a compelling government interest that does not otherwise appear pretextual. We next analyze Flores' procedural due process arguments.

B

Procedural Due Process

Flores argues that INS is constitutionally required to provide prompt, mandatory, and impartial review to each child in its custody. This inquiry would include whether probable cause to arrest exists, whether release or bond conditions are necessary to ensure appearance, and whether any suitable adult is available to care for the child. We agree that such safeguards are necessary to protect children's procedural due process rights.

Prior cases make clear what adequate due process requires. *See generally Schall v. Martin*, 467 U.S. 253 (1984); *U.S. v. Salerno*, 481 U.S. 739 (1987); *Foucha v. Louisiana*, 504 U.S. 71 (1992); *Parham v. J.R.*, 442 U.S. 584 (1979). In *Schall*, we only authorized pretrial detention upon a specific finding of serious risk that the child would commit a criminal act before the return date. 467 U.S. at 263–64. To make that determination, children are granted an individualized, adversarial probable cause hearing. *Id.* at 270. And when a child is detained, an expedited fact-finding hearing limits the time they can be held in pre-trial detention. *Id.* Likewise, in *Salerno*, the Bail Reform Act of 1984 required the government to demonstrate by clear and convincing evidence, after an adversarial hearing before a neutral adjudicator, that no pre-trial release conditions would reasonably assure the safety of the community. 481 U.S. at 750. The possibility of indefinite detention was limited by the Speedy Trial Act, 18 U.S.C. 3121 *et seq.* 481 U.S. at 747. In *Foucha*, we found that detention of criminal defendants acquitted by reason of insanity in state psychiatric institutions was not narrowly tailored or carefully limited because of the failure to provide the detainee with an adversarial hearing at which the state must prove by clear and convincing evidence that they are demonstrably dangerous to the community. 504 U.S. at 81, 86. Finally, in *Parham*, we required that an inquiry be conducted by a neutral factfinder when determining whether a child's involuntary institutionalization for mental health care met the statutory requirements for admission. 442 U.S. at 606.

In this context, INS' regulation is wholly insufficient. First, it provides for judicial review of the decision to detain or release only if the child requests it. 8 C.F.R. § 242.2(d). This unacceptably puts children on equal footing with adults. INS' justification for the policy is to protect children; that they need to be cared for by an adult and cannot be released without proper vetting of the release plan. We cannot recognize children's specific developmental realities in one breath and then discard them in the next by requiring that they request a hearing. Children cannot be expected to trigger a legal right, especially under conditions of detention in a foreign country where they likely do not speak or understand the language. Judicial review of the decision to detain or release must occur automatically.

Second, the regulation fails to require a hearing within a specified timetable. 8 C.F.R. § 242.24. This scheme is unlike the statutes at issue in *Schall* and *Salerno* that survived due process challenges; in those cases, the detention was strictly limited in time. Currently, children are detained for up to two years. *Flores v. Meese*, 934 F.2d 991, 1014 (1990) (Fletcher, J., dissenting). Flores' concerns regarding indefinite detention are not unrealistic. Therefore, any scheme authorizing the detention of children must require an immediate hearing to comport with due process.

Third, the decision of whether to release on recognizance, bond, or other conditions is made by INS officials, the same people who arrest and prosecute the child. The fact that the regulations specify that the hearing should be conducted by a "disinterested officer," 8 C.F.R. § 242.2(c)(2), does not cure this defect as an officer employed by INS cannot be a disinterested adjudicator. This fails to meet the procedural protections set out in the relevant decisions, which require review by a neutral decision-maker. We see no reason why procedural due process would offer less protection in this context. Accordingly, the hearing reviewing INS' custody determination must be conducted by an impartial adjudicator.

Finally, the statute fails to provide for individualized review. A presumptive rule in favor of detention, without individualized determination, is not narrowly tailored to children's best interests. Congressional policy, through the JDDPA for youthful offenders, establishes a presumption in favor of release. *See* 18 U.S.C. § 5034; S. Rep. No. 93-1011, at 56 (1974). In the absence of congressional intent to the contrary, we interpret this policy to extend to the children detained by the INS.

Our decision in *Stanley v. Illinois*, 405 U.S. 645 (1972) also compels this result. The presumption in *Stanley* – that unmarried fathers are unfit to care for their children – foreclosed individualized determinations the state was required to make. We found that:

> Procedure by presumption is always cheaper and easier than individualized determination. But when, as here, the procedure forecloses the determinative issues of competence and care, when it explicitly disdains present realities in deference to past formalities, it needlessly risks running roughshod over the important interests of both parent and child. It therefore cannot stand.

Id. at 656–57. That the children impacted by the INS policy are undocumented makes no difference; in this context, they require the same liberty the Constitution guarantees similarly situated citizens.

The District Court's order appropriately requires an automatic hearing "forthwith" before an immigration judge. It requires an inquiry into whether any nonrelative or organization who steps forward to care for the child presents a danger to the child and only allows release to a responsible adult when the child would be eligible for release to a relative otherwise. This approach is one that is required for the INS policy to comport with due process.

III

Statutory Claims

Although we determine that INS' regulation is unconstitutional, we do not end there. We address the statutory questions because they are intertwined with the constitutional questions. Congress possesses broad power to regulate immigration. *See INS v. Delgado*, 466 U.S. 210, 235 (1984) (Brennan, J., concurring in part and dissenting in part); *Galvan v. Press*, 347 U.S. 522, 530 (1954). When enacting the 1952 Immigration and Nationality Act (INA), Congress authorized the Attorney General to "establish such regulations … as he deems necessary for carrying out his authority." In turn, the Attorney General has discretion to determine whether and on what terms a noncitizen arrested on allegations of deportability should be detained pending a deportation hearing. 8 U.S.C. § 1252(a)(1). Specifically, § 1252(a)(1) provides that "any … alien taken into custody may, in the discretion of the Attorney General, and pending … final determination of deportability, (A) be continued in custody; or (b) be released under bond in the amount of not less than $500 with security approved by the Attorney General, containing such conditions as the Attorney General may prescribe." However, this discretion is not absolute. It is limited not only by what Congress intended but also based on what is permissible by the Constitution.

Flores argues that the regulation is ultra vires because it reaches beyond the scope of the Attorney General's discretion under 8 U.S.C. § 1252(a)(1). In particular, Flores argues that the rule is without reasonable foundation in its underlying rationale and reliance on blanket presumptions of unsuitability of potential caregivers, while the potential for indefinite detention represents an abuse of discretion.[40] We agree on all counts.

The test of whether a regulation is authorized is whether it is "reasonably related to the purposes of the enabling legislation." *Mourning v. Family Publications Serv.*, 411 U.S. 356, 369 (1973) (quoting *Thorpe v. Housing Auth. of Durham*, 393 U.S. 268, 280–81 (1969)). More specifically, the Attorney General's exercise of discretion "can only be overridden where it is clearly shown that it "was without a reasonable foundation." *Carlson v. Landon*, 342 U.S. 524, 540–41 (1952). We take into consideration indications of congressional policy as well as the principle that "a restrictive meaning must be given if a broader meaning would generate constitutional doubts." *U.S. v. Witkovitch*, 353 U.S. 194, 199 (1957). Accordingly, we look to whether agency decisions are "consistent with Congress' intent." *INS v. Nat'l Ctr. for Immigrants' Rights, Inc. (NCIR)*, 502 U.S. 183, 194 (1991). "When the validity of an act of the congress is

---

[40] Flores' initial Administrative Procedure Act (APA) was not renewed before this Court. The facts here may support Flores' claim that the promulgation of the regulation was arbitrary and capricious pursuant to 5 U.S.C. § 706. *See* Motor Vehicle Mfrs. Ass'n of U.S. Inc. v. State Farm Mut. Automobile Ins. Co., 463 U.S. 29, 41 (1983).

drawn into question, and even if a serious doubt of constitutionality is raised, it is a cardinal principle that this Court will first ascertain whether a construction of the statute is fairly possible by which the question may be avoided." *Witkovitch,* 353 U.S. at 201–02 (citation omitted).

While Congress gave the INS broad authority to issue regulations to carry out its authority under the statute, there are serious questions about whether Congress intended the statute to apply to children and whether INS' interpretation of its authority squares with congressional policy. Section 1252 is the only statute that addresses release or detention of noncitizens during the pendency of deportation hearings, and it has not materially changed since its enactment in 1952. A review of the legislative history fails to show any indication that Congress intended the detention provisions of the statute to apply to children. Regulations promulgated under this statute in 1963 also contain no reference to children. 8 C.F.R. § 242.2(c)(2). The plain language of the statute does not reference children or minors in its detention provisions. 8 U.S.C. §§ 1251–53. Reading the detention provisions in the context of the entire statutory scheme supports the conclusion that if Congress had intended the statute to apply to children, it would have explicitly said so. Indeed, the statute defines children and many of its provisions relate specifically to children. *See, e.g.,* 8 U.S.C. § 1101(b)(1); § 1154(d) (adoption of foreign-born children only permissible when state agency has done a home study); 8 U.S.C. § 1522(d) (assistance for refugee children).

Yet to date, Congress has not created a comprehensive legislative scheme for children arriving to the United States without a parent or guardian, even though it has legislated distinctly with respect to the custody of children in the federal criminal legal system via the JJDPA. The JJDPA demonstrates Congress' clear preference for release, specifically determining that institutional detention of juveniles is disfavored. *See* 18 U.S.C. § 5034; S. Rep. No. 93-1011, at 56 (1974). We reject INS' seeming conclusion that their regulation can depart from Congress' imperative because the children here are not citizens. In our view, Congress has spoken on the detention of children, dictating a clear presumption contrary to INS policy. INS' presumption that detention is better for children rather than release to an unrelated responsible adult or organization does not square with current congressional policy. We therefore must assume that should Congress break from its stated policy to apply such a consequential statute equally to children and adults, it would be clear.

In interpreting § 1252, the Board of Immigration Appeals has generally held that noncitizens should be released pending trial and that detention or bond is only appropriate upon on a finding of threat to the community or risk of flight from immigration authorities. *Matter of Patel,* 15 I&N Dec. 666, 666 (B.I.A. 1976) ("An alien generally is not and should not be detained or required to post bond except on a finding that he is a threat to the national security or that he is a poor bail risk") (citations omitted); *INS v. National Center for Immigrants' Rights, Inc. (NCIR),* 502 U. S. 183, 193–94 (1991). It is undisputed that neither of these rationales underly the detention in this case. Rather, INS argues that it lacks the expertise and resources to conduct a home study for every child. 53 Fed. Reg. 17449 (May 17, 1988). Flores argues that this rationale is a stand-in for administrative convenience. We agree. Rather than conduct home studies or contract with social workers to do so, the agency undertakes what it asks us to believe is the actual care of children, while at the same time claiming that it has no expertise in matters of child welfare. This reality makes INS' rationale patently unreasonable.

The regulations also allow for the possibility of indefinite detention. Although Congress' intent was to make the Attorney General's exercise of discretion presumptively correct and unassailable except for abuse, *Carlson*, 342 U.S. at 540, this possibility represents such an abuse. INS argues that the period of detention is limited by a pending deportation hearing, which must be speedy to avoid habeas. Yet INS concedes that these hearings take many months, if not years, and if the increase in migration to the United States is a bellwether of migration patterns to come, this timeline will indeed stretch longer still.

INS argues that it should be afforded deference in interpreting its enabling statutes. However, deference to an agency's rulemaking is only appropriate when the agency acts within its area of expertise. *See U.S. v. Shimer*, 367 U.S. 374, 381–82 (1961). Courts owe deference to the INS when it regulates immigration, its area of expertise and authority. *See Carlson*, 342 U.S. at 540–41. Indeed, INS has argued that it is not a child welfare agency and lacks the resources to carry out child welfare tasks. We therefore do not afford the agency deference in regulating child welfare. *See Hampton v. Mow Sun Wong*, 426 U.S. 88, 114–15 (1976) (invalidating an agency's determination in an area outside of its expertise). We find that the regulation is not reasonably related to the purposes of the enabling statute.

IV

Conclusion

Children should hold a special place and role in a humane and just society. They should be cared for by family, friends, or extended relatives with their best interests in mind, given their unique situations within their family and communities. This requires individualized decision-making. It is anathema to our professed morals and sense of justice to treat noncitizen children with any lesser degree of humanity than we would treat children who happen to be citizens. Today we hold that detaining children is presumptively unconstitutional unless the Government can affirmatively show by clear and convincing evidence before an impartial adjudicator that detention is required. Detention is limited to those exceptional circumstances when it is necessary for the imminent and articulable safety of the child or the public and there is otherwise no proposed plan for release that would be sufficient.

The judgment of the en banc Ninth Circuit is affirmed.

10

Commentary on *Zadvydas v. Davis*, 533 U.S. 678 (2001)

Nicole Hallett

Zadvydas v. Davis involved the government's long-term detention of noncitizens who had already been ordered deported.[1] The two petitioners in *Zadvydas* could not be removed from the United States because no country would receive them. Pursuant to a federal statute, however, the government was able to detain them indefinitely. The Court held that a six-month limitation must be read into the statute, at which point the government must show that removal is reasonably foreseeable.

Zadvydas was heralded as a landmark decision that took steps to unwind a century's worth of anti-immigrant due process jurisprudence. It rejected the idea that the government could detain noncitizens indefinitely solely because they had no right to remain in the country. And it pushed back on the government's contention that the plenary power doctrine over immigration laws trumped the Constitution, at least with respect to noncitizens already in the United States.

Yet a curious thing has happened in the twenty years since the case was decided. Rather than ushering in a new due process revolution, the decision represents something of a high-water mark in the fight for immigrants' rights. With one exception, noncitizens have lost every major immigration detention challenge to come before the Court since *Zadvydas*. As the rewritten concurrence makes plain, the way that *Zadvydas* was decided has contributed to its limited influence and has made it vulnerable to being overturned or limited to its facts.

At the same time, the abolition movement has changed the terms of the broader debate. Fundamentally, *Zadvydas* limited indefinite detention while leaving the detention system – and the deportation machine more broadly – intact. As more critical attention is directed toward the immigration system as a whole, it has become clear that *Zadvydas* did not go far enough in reigning in the government's immigration powers.

The tension between this new era of immigrants' rights advocacy and the Supreme Court's ever-narrowing view of due process means that *Zadvydas*'s legacy remains uncertain. It could be that in the decades to come, *Zadvydas* will represent a lost

---

[1]   533 U.S. 678 (2001).

era of immigrants' rights. Or maybe it will come to be understood as an artifact of a system that should have been abandoned long ago.

A LANDMARK IMMIGRANTS' RIGHTS DECISION

It is critical not to minimize how important *Zadvydas* was in the fight for immigrants' rights as a conceptual matter. For all its flaws, the decision treated noncitizens like human beings, not outsiders or foreign invaders.

Writing the *Zadvydas* majority opinion, Justice Breyer grounded his analysis in the Constitution, though it was not actually a constitutional decision. Instead, Breyer decided the case on constitutional avoidance grounds, reading a limitation into an ambiguous statute rather than striking it down. Justice Breyer situated his reasoning not in the plenary power doctrine, but in the Court's precedents establishing due process protections for other categories of individuals subject to prolonged civil detention, such as those with mental illness and sex offenders. The decision to treat immigration detention the same as other forms of civil detention, and therefore award noncitizens the same due process rights, was quite radical at the time, and not at all a foregone conclusion. At the same time, the majority opinion in *Zadvydas* does not grapple with the more fundamental question of whether immigration detention should exist at all.

The previous leading case on indefinite immigration detention, *Shaughnessy v. United States ex rel. Mezei*,[2] suggested a different outcome. In *Mezei*, a long-term resident of the United States was detained on Ellis Island and eventually issued an exclusion order because his "entry would be prejudicial to the public interest for security reasons."[3] The problem was that no country would accept him due to his uncertain nationality. The Court concluded that although he was entitled to due process, he had no right to be released into the country. Citing the Chinese Exclusion cases from the late nineteenth and early twentieth centuries, the Court concluded that the government had plenary power to detain him indefinitely because he stood on the "threshold of initial entry," a fact not changed by his long residence in the United States or his detention on U.S. soil.[4] The Court described Mezei's detention on Ellis Island as an act of "legislative grace" to someone with nowhere else to go, not a deprivation of liberty in the normal sense.[5]

Mezei could have provided grounds for the Court in *Zadvydas* to find that indefinite immigration detention was not a due process violation, but Justice Breyer resisted applying *Mezei*. Instead, he looked to the domestic civil detention context,

---

[2] 345 U.S. 206 (1953).
[3] *Id.* at 208.
[4] *Id.* at 212.
[5] Justice Clark revealed the absurdity of the argument that Mezei was "free to take leave in any direction except west" by pointing out that "[t]hat would mean freedom if only he were an amphibian!" *Id.* at 220 (Clark, J., dissenting).

where dangerousness alone is not enough to subject an individual to incarceration without trial. He also rejected the government's suggestion that noncitizen status itself could justify indefinite detention. Once removal is not reasonably foreseeable, Justice Breyer reasoned, the government has no special interest in keeping noncitizens detained.

The *Zadvydas* majority not only called *Mezei* into question, but also served as a partial repudiation of the Chinese Exclusion cases, which remain a stain on the Court's legacy even as other racist decisions have been overturned.[6] *Mezei*, decided one year before *Brown v. Board of Education*,[7] overruled *Plessy v. Ferguson*[8] and relied in large part on decisions rife with racial animus and reasoning that upheld statutes passed with clear racist intent.[9] Justice Scalia's dissent relies heavily on these cases, but Justice Breyer cites them only to distinguish them.[10] The one Chinese Exclusion case he cites approvingly is *Wong Wing v. United States*,[11] and only then for the proposition that the Due Process Clause protects noncitizens in deportation proceedings. That *Wong Wing* is the case that first upheld immigration detention goes unmentioned. Although Justice Breyer did not go so far as to overturn the Chinese Exclusion cases, he minimized their importance.

Finally, *Zadvydas* succeeded where other due process decisions have failed by setting out a bright-line six-month rule after which detention becomes presumptively unreasonable. Given the fact that very few detainees have the means to hire an attorney or the wherewithal to challenge their detention pro se, this bright line is important. It has had the effect of minimizing – though not eliminating – protracted litigation and has led to more noncitizens being released from detention rather than being kept locked up because of a judge's conservative interpretations of a fuzzier test.

THE AFTERMATH

Unfortunately, *Zadvydas* has had little influence on the Court's subsequent due process jurisprudence. Noncitizens have not fared well in other immigration detention decisions issued since *Zadvydas*.[12] The Supreme Court upheld a facial challenge to

---

[6] The Chinese Exclusion Cases are a series of Supreme Court decisions from the late nineteenth and early twentieth centuries interpreting the Chinese Exclusion Act of 1882 and other immigration statutes, often relying on racist stereotypes to uphold the broad power of the federal government over immigration.

[7] 347 U.S. 483 (1954).

[8] 163 U.S. 537 (1896).

[9] Kevin R. Johnson, *From Chinese Exclusion to Contemporary Systemic Racism in the Immigration Laws*, 97 IND. L.J. 1455, 1469 (2022).

[10] *Compare* Zadvydas, 533 U.S. at 695 *with* 533 U.S. at 703 (Scalia, J., dissenting).

[11] 163 U.S. 228 (1896).

[12] The one immigration detention case in which a noncitizen prevailed since Zadvydas was Clark v. Martinez, 543 U.S. 371 (2005). Justice Scalia's opinion in *Clark* held that the Court's interpretation of the statute applied to all classes of noncitizens, not only the classes to which Zadvydas and Ma belonged.

a different immigration detention statute in the 2003 case, *Demore v. Kim*, finding no due process concerns when detaining noncitizens with pending removal proceedings.[13] Subsequent attempts to read a six-month limitation into the statute – as the Court had done in *Zadvydas* – were rejected by the Supreme Court in the 2018 case, *Rodriguez v. Jennings*.[14] In 2019, the Court rejected an attempt to narrow the category of noncitizens subject to mandatory detention in *Nielsen v. Preap*.[15]

In the most recent foray into the issue, *Department of Homeland Security v. Thuraissigiam*, the Court, relying on *Mezei*, not only held that noncitizens apprehended near the border have no due process rights, but also concluded that such noncitizens could not even challenge their detention in court on a petition for habeas corpus.[16] The plenary power doctrine is also alive and well. In *Trump v. Hawaii*, Chief Justice Roberts relied on the doctrine to uphold President Trump's Muslim Ban,[17] marking yet another shameful chapter in our nation's history of court-sanctioned racism in immigration law. These recent decisions suggest that the *Zadvydas* decision was an anomaly rather than a beacon charting a new path forward.

Indeed, it is not clear if *Zadvydas* will survive a Supreme Court with a conservative supermajority. Justice Alito's dicta in *Jennings* that *Zadvydas* "represents a notably generous application of the constitutional-avoidance canon," suggests that there might be some appetite on the Court to revisit the decision.[18] The way *Zadvydas* was decided will make overruling it easier than if it had announced a new constitutional rule. It is much more difficult to strip rights once granted than it is to decide a statute is not ambiguous after all.

Even if *Zadvydas* is not overruled, the decision contains dicta that could be used to create a loophole broad enough to drive a truck through. In rejecting the government's argument that noncitizens pose special risks and need to be detained, Justice Breyer suggests that Congress could pass a statute that applied only to "specially dangerous" noncitizens. Congress responded by enacting the USA PATRIOT Act in the weeks after the September 11 terrorist acts. Section 412 of the Act allows the government to detain certain noncitizens indefinitely.[19] Although it purports to only allow detention based on national security risk, the statute's language is actually much broader, applying to any individual who "will threaten the national security of the United States *or the safety of the community or any person.*"[20]

---

[13]   Demore v. Kim, 538 U.S. 510, 529–31 (2003).
[14]   Jennings v. Rodriguez, 138 S. Ct. 830, 850–51 (2018).
[15]   Nielsen v. Preap, 139 S. Ct. 954, 965 (2019).
[16]   140 S. Ct. 1959, 1982–83 (2020).
[17]   138 S. Ct. 2392, 2418–20 (2018).
[18]   138 S. Ct. at 843.
[19]   8 U.S.C. § 1226a.
[20]   8 U.S.C. § 1226a(a)(6) (emphasis added).

While the government did not invoke this extraordinary authority for years, it did so recently against a long-time resident of the United States, who was convicted under the terrorism material support laws, based on the unilateral assessment by the government that he posed a risk to national security.[21] If and when Section 412 is considered by the Supreme Court, it will be a test case for just how resilient *Zadvydas*'s holding is.[22]

THE FEMINIST CONCURRENCE

Zadvydas is rightly celebrated as an immigrants' right victory, but Professors Stacy Caplow and Maryellen Fullerton, writing as Justices Caplow and Fullerton, help to highlight the flaws that have become apparent in the years since it was decided. The feminist concurrence does not go as far as envisioning a world without immigration detention, but it undertakes several interventions that make that future much more likely. Many of these interventions can be described as "feminist" because they humanize immigrants and focus on the practical implications of the current immigration detention system.[23] Their decision would not only be more durable but would also be more effective in ensuring that immigrants' constitutional rights are vindicated in individual cases.

First, Caplow and Fullerton have done what Justice Breyer would not and have declared the detention statute unconstitutional. If *Zadvydas* had followed the concurrence and struck down the statute, Congress would have undoubtedly followed the court's instructions and passed a new statute, particularly after the September 11 terrorist attacks. That new statute would be much more durable (especially given the current stalemate in Congress on immigration issues) than the *Zadvydas* decision may turn out to be. Similarly, it would have been much harder for the Supreme Court to resurrect *Mezei* in *Thuraissigiam* if it had been officially overruled, as it is in the rewritten concurrence. It turns out that Justice Scalia's scathing criticism that Justice Breyer had overruled *Mezei* without acknowledging it turned out not to be true after all.

Moreover, Caplow and Fullerton see the immigration system for what it really is, rather than how the government portrays it to be. For example, the majority assumed that the deportation system functions like a well-oiled machine that can remove all but a small handful of individuals within the ninety-day removal period.[24] As Caplow and Fullerton point out, this is a fiction. They also shed light on the

---

[21] Hassoun v. Searls, 469 F. Supp. 3d 69, 75–76 (W.D.N.Y.), *order vacated, appeal dismissed*, 976 F.3d 121 (2d Cir. 2020).

[22] *See generally* Nicole Hallett, *The Use and Abuse of National Security Detention*, 45 SEATTLE U. L. REV. 525 (2022).

[23] Katherine T. Bartlett, *Feminist Legal Methods*, 103 HARV. L. REV. 829, 849 (1990).

[24] Zadvydas, 533 U.S. at 682 ("[T]he Government ordinarily secures the alien's removal during a subsequent 90-day statutory 'removal period'").

functionally stateless individuals who have a nationality but whose countries will not accept them. This list of countries without repatriation agreements with the United States fluctuates over time. As of January 2020, the U.S. government listed ten countries as "recalcitrant" and twenty-three countries "at risk of non-compliance."[25] For individuals from these countries, removal is *never* reasonably foreseeable, even at the beginning of the ninety-day period. Yet *Zadvydas* allows the government to hold them for six months before an assessment is even made as to whether there is a realistic chance that they will be removed.

In other words, the deportation machine depends on cooperation with other governments to operate. People who are deported have to go *somewhere*. We cannot just set them adrift at sea on a lifeboat or shoot them into outer space. And yet, this goes largely unacknowledged in all of the debates about immigration policy. Currently, with the exceptions noted above, the United States is able to depend on other countries to repatriate their nationals, but this is hardly a fixed state of affairs. One could easily imagine a near or distant future in which climate change, warfare, famine, or disease has broken down the international system that exists today. In such a world, deportation would become an impossibility. What role would immigration detention play in that world? *Zadvydas* cannot help us answer this question.

The concurrence also pushes back on the legal fiction that deportation and immigration detention are not punitive, a laughable idea in 1893 when the Supreme Court first declared it to be true and an even more preposterous one today. Caplow and Fullerton accurately describe immigration detention as a "scheme that be[gan] as part of a civil regulatory effort [which was transformed] – without any intervening judicial factfinding or oversight – into an essentially punitive long-term sentence." Today, noncitizens are held almost exclusively in prison-like facilities, despite the fact that they are civil detainees. Many either served no time in criminal custody or spend much longer in immigration detention than they ever spent in prison. All have served their sentences and would be free if not for their citizenship status. The concurrence does not shy away from these facts, describing in detail the deplorable conditions that await immigrants in detention, including the petitioners Zadvydas and Ma.

The concurrence foreshadows the Supreme Court's 2010 decision in *Padilla v. Kentucky*, which recognized that deportation is a unique and severe consequence which might constitute a greater punishment than anything meted out to a criminal defendant at sentencing.[26] Consistent with a century's worth of jurisprudence, the *Padilla* Court found that deportation is not punishment. If the Court ever concluded that deportation was punishment, it would prompt a sea change that would leave an unrecognizable immigration system in its wake. *Zadvydas* did not raise the

---

[25] Cong. Rsch. Serv., IF11025, Immigration: "Recalcitrant" Countries and the Use of Visa Sanctions to Encourage Cooperation with Alien Removals 1 (2020).

[26] 559 U.S. 356, 365–66 (2010).

constitutionality of deportation, but if the majority opinion had followed the con-currence's lead, it would have been another nail in the coffin (though not the last) for the doctrine that deportation is not punishment, which has insulated immigra-tion laws from scrutiny for over a century.

Caplow and Fullerton also highlight the paucity of procedural protections for immigrants subject to indefinite detention, and the ample evidence when *Zadvydas* was decided that the government routinely failed to comply with its own insuffi-cient procedures. The same is true today after *Zadvydas*. Detainees often must file habeas petitions simply to get a custody review at six months as *Zadvydas* requires. Without lawyers, filing a petition often proves to be an insurmountable burden. Had it commanded a majority of the Court, the feminist concurrence would have required Congress to create a new custody review procedure and sent a strong signal to Congress that the procedural protections of this new regime would need to be robust to comply with the Due Process Clause.

The concurrence's clear and succinct assertion that not every noncitizen with a criminal record is a danger to the community stands in stark contrast to Justice Breyer's opinion, which seems to assume the dangerousness of noncitizens with criminal records, while holding that dangerousness alone does not justify their indefinite detention. It would be a game-changer if the government were to adopt the position of the concurrence. The immigration system has long been afflicted by the same trends of over-criminalization and over-incarceration as the criminal jus-tice system, aided by an extra dose of xenophobia. Even so, the concurrence could have gone further by, for example, explicitly repudiating Justice Breyer's suggestion that the Due Process Clause allows for the indefinite detention without trial of "spe-cially dangerous individuals."

The concurrence succeeds in humanizing immigrants, in acknowledging the current issues in the deportation system, in making clear, unequivocal statements about the unconstitutionality of the current detention regime, and in setting the immigration system on an altogether different path than the one we are now on. It notes the increasing reliance on the immigration detention system and predicts its problematic expansion. The number of detained immigrants has increased dramati-cally in recent decades, rising from 7,000 immigrants per day in 1994 to more than 50,000 per day in 2019, the last year before the coronavirus pandemic temporarily decreased the number in detention.[27]

Despite their recognition of the overuse of detention, however, Caplow and Fullerton, like the majority in *Zadvydas*, do not challenge the underlying premise that deportation is a valid exercise of state power and that detention is a necessary component of the deportation machine. Bail reform has decreased the number of pretrial detainees in some places who must await their day in court from jail, but

---

[27] Katharina Buchholz, *Number of Immigrant Detainees Rises Quickly*, STATISTA (Jan. 3, 2020).

there has been no similar reckoning about the need to detain immigrants who are litigating their removal cases or awaiting deportation.

It is far past time to rethink whether immigration detention is necessary. Congress passed the first statute authorizing immigration detention in 1891.[28] The Supreme Court sanctioned immigration detention five years later in *Wong Wing* as a power incidental to the government's sovereign authority to exclude or expel noncitizens.[29] The justification in more recent cases such as *Demore* has focused on the risk of flight and concerns that noncitizens would fail to show up to their removal hearings or deportation flights.

The majority in *Zadvydas* accepted without explanation the idea that detention was a necessary part of the immigration system, but it is not at all clear that this is true. When the Obama Administration put an "alternatives to detention" program in place for some families seeking asylum at the United States-Mexico Border, appearance rates at future court hearings were ninety-seven percent.[30] The government's interest in ensuring that noncitizens appear for removal hearings is similar to the government's interest in preventing voter fraud. The solution is worse than the problem by many orders of magnitude.

It is easy to forget that deportation did not become a feature of the U.S. immigration system until over a hundred years after the country's founding, and only then because of a reactionary ethno-nationalist response to Asian immigration. It is easier still to believe that deportation will always stand at the center of our immigration policy. But a true radical rethinking of the system requires us to challenge not only individual deportations, but the idea of deportation writ large.

Immigrants themselves have been at the forefront of the fight to end deportation. In 2013, over 500 organizations called for President Obama to put a moratorium on deportations into place as part of the #Not1More campaign.[31] In recent years, "Abolish ICE" has entered the mainstream lexicon, becoming a rallying cry for those who want a radical rethinking of the immigration system.[32]

Scholars have begun moving the debate in this direction too. In *The End of Deportation*, Angélica Cházaro dismantles the justifications for deportation and concludes that deportation is not only unnecessary but is a type of violence that modern civilization should not permit.[33] According to Cházaro, deportation cannot be justified as post-entry social control because it is premised on the idea of immigrants

---

[28] César Cuauhtémoc García Hernández, Migrating to Prison: America's Obsession with Locking Up Immigrants 27 (2019).

[29] 163 U.S. at 235.

[30] American Immigr. Lawyers Ass'n et al., *The Real Alternatives to Detention*, Nat'l Immigrant Justice Ctr.

[31] *Organizational Letter to the President: Suspend Deportations*, #Not1More.

[32] Sean McElwee, *It's Time to Abolish ICE*, The Nation (Mar. 9, 2018); *Abolish ICE*, United We Dream.

[33] Angélica Cházaro, *The End of Deportation*, 68 UCLA L. Rev. 1040, 1071 (2021).

as other, exemplified by the racist history of deportation. While historically, deportation laws were designed to keep out Asian immigrants, today ninety percent of deportees come from one of four countries: Mexico, El Salvador, Guatemala, and Honduras.[34] Deportation creates a racial caste system, though the nationality of the immigrants at the bottom of the hierarchy may change over time.

Deportation also cannot be justified without accepting an anachronistic conception of the nation-state. E. Tendayi Achiume has written about migration as an act of decolonization that corrects for centuries of oppression and subordination.[35] The nation-state's primary purpose is to protect the ill-gotten gains of the colonizers from the colonized who arrive at its borders. As Cházaro points out, deportation can only be justified as extended border control if the border is considered sacrosanct.[36]

The *Zadvydas* court, unsurprisingly, did not raise these questions. Neither does the rewritten concurrence, which concedes that the government's "interest in removal is legitimate." This concession seems appropriate. It is highly implausible that even a forward-thinking justice writing in 2001 would have questioned the legitimacy of the deportation machine. But we need make no similar concession in critiquing the decision today.

ZADVYDAS v. DAVIS, 533 U.S. 678 (2001)

Justices Stacy Caplow and Maryellen Fullerton, concurring in the judgment.

We agree with Parts I, II, and IIIA of Justice Breyer's opinion and we concur in the judgment. We believe that the statute at issue here, 8 U.S.C. § 1231(a)(6), as written and as applied, is unconstitutional so long as it permits indefinite detention of noncitizens ordered removed from the United States when the Government lacks the ability to carry out the removals. The Due Process Clause prohibits civil proceedings that result in the equivalent of life imprisonment due to conditions beyond the ability of noncitizens to control. The lack of procedural safeguards in the statute itself magnifies the constitutional defect. The statute's constitutional flaws are not cured by reading procedural conditions into the statute. Accordingly, we would strike this statute as unconstitutional and order the release of those confined pursuant to it who cannot be removed.

This view does not command a majority of the Court, however. The need to give practical effect to the decision of the Court rejecting the Government's position, therefore, compels us to join with our colleagues to order remand on terms closest to those we would impose. *See Screws v. United States*, 325 U.S. 91, 134 (1945) (Rutledge, J., concurring in the result). Although we would overturn 8 U.S.C. § 1231(a)(6), Justice Breyer makes a strong case that implicit temporal limitations

---

[34] *Id.* at 34, 40–41.

[35] E. Tendayi Achiume, *Migration as Decolonization*, 71 STAN. L. REV. 1509, 1510 (2019).

[36] Cházaro, *supra* note 33, at 1097.

permitting continued detention only for a period reasonably necessary to carry out removal could save the statute from unconstitutionality. We also support Justice Breyer's view that detention after six months is presumptively unconstitutional, and we appreciate his effort to salvage the statute by requiring reviews at six-month intervals to determine whether the Government has sufficient evidence that removal can be accomplished within a reasonably foreseeable time period.

We nonetheless believe this practical solution does not adequately protect against indefinite detention, even though this approach is likely to prevent some instances of serious harm. We take this opportunity to explain why we believe the harm inflicted by a statute that allows noncitizens to remain imprisoned even when they cannot be removed from the United States far outweighs any legitimate government goal.

I

A Preliminary Observation about Language

Before beginning our analysis, we offer a preliminary observation about language. We note with regret the language used by the immigration statutes and repeated by our colleagues. The statute refers to immigrants as "aliens," 8 U.S.C. § 1101(a)(3) ("any person not a citizen or national of the United States"), a frequent synonym for outsider, stranger, barbarian, intruder, squatter, interloper, or invader. *See Alien, Webster's New Pocket Thesaurus* (2000). Frequently, adjectives like "illegal" or "criminal" intensify this pejorative term. We believe that this demeaning language fuels unjust policies, such as those proffered by the Government in this case. These labels erase the humanity of the individual who may be a neighbor, classmate, fellow parishioner, or co-worker. They imply that individuals who are not United States citizens are a wholly different species, rather than a human being living next door or on the next block. Further, this debasing language perpetuates the myth of the immigrant as "other" and as lawbreaker despite the absence of evidence that immigrants in the United States have higher rates of criminality than United States citizens. To avoid perpetuating these negative stereotypes, we employ different vocabulary.

II

The Stateless Cannot Be Removed

The cases today remind us that there are, residing within our borders, large numbers of people who lack the right to be members of any political community. The stateless have no homeland; no country assumes the responsibility to accept and protect them. Statelessness is not a rare status; the Office of the United Nations High Commissioner for Refugees (UNHCR) estimates that there are millions of stateless individuals around the globe today. UNHCR, *The State of the World's Refugees: A Humanitarian Agenda* ch. 6 (1997). A significant international problem, stateless-ness is the subject of several international treaties. Convention Relating to the Status of Stateless Persons, Sept. 28, 1954, 360 U.N.T.S. 117; Convention on the Reduction of Statelessness, Aug. 30, 1961, 989 U.N.T.S. 175. Nor is statelessness a new concern in the United States. Almost fifty years ago, our Court called statelessness "a condi-tion deplored in the international community of democracies." *Trop v. Dulles*, 356 U.S. 86, 102 (1958).

Its causes are manifold – the dissolution of nations, war, and ethnic strife, gen-der discrimination in citizenship laws, administrative barriers to registering births, nomadic lifestyles, and more. Its human impact is widespread. Since the 1980s, a major hallmark of the ongoing oppression of almost two million Rohingya people in Myanmar has been their statelessness. UNHCR, *supra*, ch. 6, at 6. In recent years, the dissolution of the Soviet Union in 1991 and Yugoslavia in 1992 left hundreds of thousands of people stateless. *Id.* at 7–10. Warfare in Kuwait during the early 1990s dispersed some 250,000 Bidoon, causing long-term statelessness. *Id.* at 6.

Many stateless individuals have created new lives in our country but find them-selves without any legal basis for remaining and no country to which they can return. *See, e.g., Chadha v. INS*, 634 F.2d 408, 411 (1980), *aff'd by INS v. Chadha*, 462 U.S. 919 (1983) (student in the United States born in British colony of Kenya to Indian parents lacked citizenship in India, the United Kingdom, or Kenya after Kenyan independence). Many, like Kestutis Zadvydas, are not even aware of their lack of nationality until they run afoul of our immigration laws and are ordered removed from the United States.

The individuals before this Court are living examples of the harsh impact of a statute that imprisons the stateless indefinitely in order to remove them from the United States, despite the fact that removal is impossible because no country will receive them. But they are hardly alone or unique. Congress failed to realize that large numbers of stateless and functionally stateless individuals, including long-time lawful residents, could be detained indefinitely under the terms of the statute. This is fundamentally unfair and amounts to punishment for their stateless status. Consequently, we are compelled to state clearly that this statute's authorization of indefinite detention, untethered from any consideration of the likelihood of even-tual removal, violates both substantive and procedural due process.

A

As a stateless person, Kestutis Zadvydas cannot be deported. Born in a displaced per-sons camp in the maelstrom of post-war Europe, he lacks citizenship in Germany, where he was born; in Lithuania, where his parents may have been citizens; or in the United States, where he has lived as a lawful permanent resident for three decades, married, and raised a family. He led a seemingly uneventful life, punctuated when he was a teenager and a young man in his early twenties by two run-ins with the law. Two decades later he was convicted of a cocaine charge, served two years in prison, and was released on parole. Immigration officials arrested him upon his release from prison and held him without bond as they began proceedings to remove him from the United States. Unrepresented by counsel, he did not challenge his deportation and was ordered removed from the United States. To his surprise and the consternation of immigration officials, neither Germany nor Lithuania viewed him as a citizen. Now a grandfather, after thirty-five years as a lawful permanent resident of the United States, he discovered that he is stateless.

Zadvydas did not contest the Government's efforts to remove him from the United States. Indeed, he cooperated at every turn. Despite speaking only English, he volunteered to return to Germany, the land of his birth. He applied to return to Lithuania, the country where his parents had lived half a century earlier. He even followed INS instructions and twice applied for citizenship in Lithuania, only to be rejected.

Immigration officials argue that Congress authorizes them to detain Zadvydas permanently under the guise of effectuating his removal, despite the absence of evidence that removal will ever be possible. Countries are generally unwilling to accept deportees who are not their citizens. For example, immigration officials unsuccessfully sought to deport Zadvydas to the Dominican Republic, the homeland of his wife. Pet'r Zadvydas's Br. 6. Thus, this post-removal-period detention statute impermissibly consigns Zadvydas, and many other stateless individuals, to indefinite detention.

B

Some members of the American community are functionally, though not technically, stateless. Kim Ho Ma is one of them. His parents fled Cambodia and its genocidal leaders in 1979. After years in refugee camps, the United States granted them refugee status. The family entered the United States when Ma was only six, and they became lawful permanent residents. As a teenager in a poor neighborhood, Ma joined a Cambodian gang. This misguided choice led him to a violent encounter at age seventeen and a subsequent gang-related manslaughter charge. He was convicted and sentenced to three years in prison. Prison officials released him after two years based on his good behavior. Two decades after Ma arrived as a refugee child, the United States ordered him returned to Cambodia. Cambodia, which hemorrhaged refugees in the Khmer Rouge years, has no repatriation agreement with the United States; it refuses to accept Ma or any other Cambodian national. *See Ma v. Reno*, 208 F.3d 815, 818 (9th Cir. 2000).

Both Zadvydas and Ma received an early release from their criminal sentence based on good behavior. Both Zadvydas and Ma remained imprisoned for the purpose of deportation far longer than for their criminal convictions. Both Zadvydas and Ma remain in the United States because they fall through the cracks of the nation-state system. Since no country will accept them, they face indefinite – maybe permanent – detention in the United States.

C

We emphasize that the harm caused by this statute is not limited to one or two rare cases. Immigration officials have relied on this removal detention statute to hold thousands of human beings in jail even though removal is impossible. *See, e.g., Supreme Court Hears Arguments in Indefinite Detention Cases,* 78 Interpreter Releases 397 (2001) (approximately 3,000 currently subject to indefinite detention).

Some of them are from countries such as Cuba that lack diplomatic relations with the United States. *See* William G. Mayer, *Trends: American Attitudes Toward Cuba,* 65 Pub. Op. Q. 585, 588–90 (2001). Some of them are from nations like Laos, Cambodia, and Vietnam that have not entered repatriation agreements with this country. *See Ma,* 208 F.3d at 821. Some of them are from countries, for example, Somalia, undergoing such chaos and conflict that government functions have ground to a halt. *See* U.S. Dep't of State, *Country Report on Human Rights Practices 2000 – Somalia* (2001) (United States has no diplomatic representation in Somalia, where there is no functioning central government). Some of them cannot be removed because they are likely to face torture if they return to their home countries, yet our laws authorize their detention. 8 C.F.R. § 208.17(c). We recognize that some of the varied circumstances that prevent removal may disappear someday, but the mere possibility of change in the future cannot justify long-term detention.

Stateless and functionally stateless individuals exist in carceral limbo in deplorable conditions for extended periods of time. In many instances, they are treated far worse in immigration detention than those serving criminal sentences in the same facility. Br. of Catholic Legal Immigration Network, Inc. (CLINIC), et al., as Amici Curiae Supporting Resp't Ma 11, *Ma v. Reno,* 208 F.3d 815 (9th Cir. 2000). They also endure worse conditions than they experienced at the prisons where they had earlier served their criminal sentences because they are isolated and inaccessible to family and counsel. *Id.* 8, 11.

Zadvydas endured his prolonged inhumane incarceration for more than three and one-half years, far longer than his incarceration for cocaine use. During that time, he was confined to his cell twenty hours each day and permitted only two hours of exercise each week. Pet'r Zadvydas's Br. 16. Ma spent almost two and one-half years in immigration detention after two years in prison. *Ma,* 208 F.3d at 819.

Many similar stories were provided by *amici curiae.* For example, Thanh Cao Nguyen, a permanent resident of the United States, was ordered removed to Vietnam, which lacks a repatriation agreement with the United States. Nguyen was detained for removal for more than three and one-half years before immigration officials reviewed his indefinite detention. Although his family resides in California, Nguyen was transferred to five separate facilities, including locations in southern California, northern California, Minnesota, and Florida. In Florida, far from his support network, he was one of a small number of immigration detainees held in Coleman state prison. There prison officials detained him for administrative – not disciplinary – reasons in isolation under 23-hour lockdown for one year. He had limited access to telephone, legal materials, and recreation facilities. His attorney, though she had received advance permission from prison officials to visit, was denied access after traveling four hours to the prison. Ultimately, the attorney was able to meet with Nguyen for only twenty minutes to prepare an application for release from detention. CLINIC Br., *supra*, 4–5.

Julio Martull-Garcia, a permanent resident of the United States, has been in immigration detention for more than five years because he is a citizen of Cuba, which refuses to accept individuals removed from the United States. After four years of detention, he requested release, but was rejected in a letter noting only that release was not "warranted at this time." One year later, he requested an interview relating to his continued custody. He submitted letters from jail staff reporting that he "displayed excellent behavior," had no disciplinary reports, volunteered to tutor ESL students, and completed an alcohol treatment program. He also verified that he has four children who are U.S. citizens and need his support. Immigration officials did not respond to this request for release. CLINIC Br., *supra*, 5–6.

Jose Fernandes, a permanent resident of the United States from Angola, came to the United States as a child and settled in Rhode Island with his extended family. He became addicted to drugs which led to a criminal conviction and prison sentence. In prison, he completed multiple training programs, was an active participant in the Relapse Prevention/Drug Education Group, and joined a workshop on Alternatives to Violence. When placed in immigration detention and ordered removed to Angola, Angola refused to issue him travel documents. Though he pleaded with Angola, Portugal, and the Cape Verde Islands to accept him so he could escape from lifelong immigration detention, they all refused. He remained in prison for the purposes of removal for three years. Br. of the American Association of Jews from the Former USSR et al., as Amici Curiae Supporting Resp't Ma 16–17, *Reno v. Ma*, 208 F.3d 815 (9th Cir. 2000).

These are only a few examples of how indefinite detention has torn apart immigrant families, particularly those of refugees from Cambodia, Vietnam, Laos, and Cuba. *See id.* 7. With little choice but to flee the countries where they were born, many did so after assisting the U.S. Government. Most of these refugee families have built successful new lives in the United States, but their families are not immune from the problems that face all American communities. *Id.* 10–11. Many of them or their sons and daughters are the human beings locked up indefinitely after they have been ordered removed.

III

Due Process Violations

The cases before us concern the statutory framework for detaining and deporting noncitizens from the United States. Briefly put, the immigration laws of the United States authorize the removal of noncitizens on a staggering 130 enumerated grounds. *See, e.g.*, 8 U.S.C. § 1182(a); 8 U.S.C. § 1227(a). Once a noncitizen is subject to a final order of removal, the Government generally detains the noncitizen during the ninety-day removal period prescribed by statute. 8 U.S.C. § 1231(a). Detention is mandatory for noncitizens ordered removed on criminal or security grounds; it is discretionary for all others. 8 U.S.C. § 1231(a)(2). We note that mandatory detention applies in the removal period even if the criminal sentence did not impose any form of incarceration. If the Government cannot carry out the removal within ninety days, Congress authorizes a longer period of detention ("post-removal-period detention") in alternative circumstances: (1) noncitizens ordered removed on criminal or security grounds and all noncitizens who are inadmissible, as well as those who violated their nonimmigrant status or conditions of admission (known as "the disfavored groups") and (2) noncitizens determined by the Attorney General to be a risk to the community or a flight risk. 8 U.S.C. § 1231(a)(6). Any noncitizen determined to be a flight or public safety risk can be detained longer than ninety days; noncitizens in the disfavored groups can be detained even longer whether or not they pose these additional risks. Despite the long-term incarceration that the statute permits, it is silent about how the need for continued detention should be decided.

To the extent that this statute authorizes indefinite post-removal-period detention when the Government lacks the ability to effectuate the removal, the statute violates established principles of substantive due process.[37] To the extent that this statute authorizes post-removal-period detention without fair procedures to challenge the basis of the detention, it also violates procedural due process. We discuss each of these constitutional defects in turn.

A

Justice Breyer states that "[a] statute permitting indefinite detention of an alien would raise a serious constitutional problem." 533 U.S. at 690. Even Justice Kennedy, in dissent, acknowledges that "a substantial constitutional question is presented by the prospect of lengthy, even unending, detention in some instances." *Id.* at 706. We wholeheartedly agree. When removal detention rests on the unsubstantiated hope that removal from the United States may someday be possible, the Government's

---

[37] We note also that prolonged arbitrary detention is contrary to international law norms as well as prohibited by the International Covenant on Civil and Political Rights, Dec. 19, 1966, 999 U.N.T.S. 171, ratified by the United States in 1992.

action runs afoul of the Due Process Clause on two grounds. First, it is fundamentally unfair to continue to detain a person when the justification for detention disappears. Second, ongoing detention, in those circumstances, becomes solely punitive.

1

The Due Process Clause protects the liberty interests of all persons, including noncitizens, in the United States. *Wong Wing v. United States*, 163 U.S. 228, 238 (1896). The right to be free from physical custody is the paramount liberty interest. *E.g.*, *Foucha v. Louisiana*, 504 U.S. 71, 80 (1992); *Youngberg v. Romeo*, 457 U.S. 307, 316 (1982). And the substantive component of the Due Process Clause bars "arbitrary, wrongful government actions 'regardless of the fairness of the procedures used to implement them.'" *Foucha*, 504 U.S. at 80 (quoting *Zinermon v. Burch*, 494 U.S. 113, 125 (1990)). Yet the statute in question allows detention in prison-like facilities of broad groups of noncitizens even when there is no realistic likelihood of removal from the United States.

It is fundamentally unfair for the Government to detain people for the purpose of removal and to continue to detain them when the Government knows removal is impossible. In authorizing the indefinite detention of individuals who cannot be removed, Congress has ignored their fundamental liberty interest and has violated their right to due process. The violence inflicted by the Government's interpretation of 8 U.S.C. § 1231(a)(6) is particularly egregious when it falls on individuals, like the ones here, who have spent the majority of their lives as lawful residents of the United States.

Although Justice Breyer acknowledges the apparent unconstitutionality of the statutory text, he concludes that Congress must not have meant what the statute's words say. Accordingly, he relies on the doctrine of constitutional avoidance to construe the statute to include an implicit "reasonable time" limit on detention. *See Gomez v. United States*, 490 U.S. 858, 864 (1989) (explaining that courts must "avoid an interpretation of a federal statute that engenders constitutional issues if a reasonable alternative interpretation poses no constitutional question"); *see also United States v. Witkovich*, 353 U.S. 194, 201–02 (1957) (quoting *Crowell v. Benson*, 285 U.S. 22, 62 (1932)). He reads the statute to include an implicit requirement of hearings at six-month intervals to determine whether removal is likely in the "reasonably foreseeable future." 533 U.S. at 699. We agree with the concerns addressed by Justice Breyer, but are not persuaded by his reliance on the constitutional avoidance doctrine in this case.

The doctrine of constitutional avoidance comes into play when a court faces two statutory interpretations of equal plausibility. In such a circumstance, the court should choose the statutory construction that avoids confronting a constitutional question. *Crowell*, 285 U.S. at 62. This doctrine does not, however, allow a court to interpret a statute in a manner that is contrary to congressional intent. *See United States v. X-Citement Video, Inc.*, 513 U.S. 64, 78 (1994). In our view, this doctrine is not applicable here. The text of 8 U.S.C. § 1231(a)(6) is clear: Congress unambiguously authorizes post-removal-period detention without a time limit. We see nothing in the language, structure, or purpose of the statute that either explicitly or implicitly forbids indefinite detention.

Accordingly, we must review the terms of the statute that Congress actually wrote. The Government relies on 8 U.S.C. §1231(a)(6) to detain noncitizens for removal even though the Government does not anticipate being able to carry out the removal. In the cases before us and in many others, this form of post-removal-period detention has extended for multiple years even when there is no removal date in sight. Continuing to detain individuals indefinitely for a removal that is not reasonably foreseeable violates substantive due process.

2

This statute, as interpreted and applied by the Government, accomplishes a significant – and unconstitutional – sleight of hand. A detention scheme that begins as part of a civil regulatory effort is allowed to transform itself – without any intervening judicial factfinding or oversight – into an essentially punitive long-term sentence. The immigration removal system designed by Congress envisions a relatively brief period of detention for the purpose of carrying out the removal of noncitizens from the United States. Punishing noncitizens for the Government's inability to achieve its objective is not part of the legislature's intention. Yet punishment is exactly what ensues. Moreover, this punishment takes place despite our jurisprudence holding that the Due Process Clause forbids punishment of noncitizens for civil immigration violations. *Wong Wing v. United States*, 168 U.S. 228, 237 (1896).

It is true that noncitizens, like citizens, can be punished for crimes in criminal proceedings. It is also true that noncitizens can be deported from the United States in civil removal hearings. But our case law has steadfastly held that deportation, though it can result in grievous loss for noncitizens and their families, is *not* punishment.[38] *See, e.g., Fong Yue Ting*, 149 U.S. 698, 730 (1893); *Harisiades v. Shaughnessy*, 342 U.S. 580, 594–95 (1952); *INS v. Lopez-Mendoza*, 468 U.S. 1032, 1038 (1984). Deportation has long been viewed as a civil matter, and any consequent incarceration is also deemed a civil or administrative issue, justified only for the purpose of removing noncitizens from the United States.

The record in the cases before us reveals, however, that their "civil" incarceration subjected Zadvydas and Ma to the same loss of autonomy and confinement as a criminal sentence. Ironically, their prolonged immigration detention had none of the accompanying opportunities for rehabilitation that can accompany incarceration for those convicted of crimes. Because the immigration detention system has been established to remove individuals from the United States promptly, it is not surprising that training and rehabilitation programs are lacking. Nonetheless, the

---

[38] Although this aspect of our jurisprudence has generated debate, the parties have not raised this issue, and we leave a careful evaluation of this characterization to another day.

absence of support services in immigration detention intensifies the negative experience of life behind bars.

Our cases are clear that detention to carry out a regulatory objective is necessarily
conditioned on time limitations or narrowly tailored specific circumstances. *Reno v.
Flores*, 507 U.S. 292, 314 (1993) ("The period of custody is inherently limited by the
pending deportation hearing"); *Kansas v. Hendricks*, 521 U.S. 346, 357 (1972) ("The
statute thus requires proof of more than a mere predisposition to violence; ... [w]e
have sustained civil commitment statutes ... with the proof of some additional factor"); *see also United States v. Salerno*, 481 U.S. 739, 747–48 (1987) ("The Bail Reform
Act carefully limits the circumstances under which detention may be sought .... [A]nd
the maximum length of pretrial detention is limited by [] stringent time limitations").

In the cases before us, the detention is initially justified by the Government's interest
in removing noncitizens who have committed conduct that Congress has categorized
as grounds of deportability. The ninety-day removal period allows the Government to
make arrangements with other countries to effectuate the removals. The post-removal-
period detention might be justified in instances when the Government foresees
removal but has encountered logistical obstacles. The statutory text, however, puts no
limit on the length of the post-removal-period detention, and the Government insists
that Congress has authorized indefinite detention of noncitizens ordered removed,
even if removal is not possible. This is the point at which the regulatory justification
for detention evaporates and continued detention becomes punitive.

Accordingly, this form of immigration detention must be acknowledged as punitive and, as we discuss below, cannot be imposed without the due process protections associated with criminal matters. *See Kennedy v. Mendoza-Martinez*, 372 U.S.
144, 168–69, 186 (1962). Indicia of punishment are present here: (1) an affirmative
disability or restraint that is (2) disproportionate to the regulatory purpose assigned.
Id. Moreover, the conditions of confinement experienced by post-removal-period
detainees confirm its punitive nature. Not only are the noncitizens in question
deprived of their fundamental liberty but they are also subjected to conditions of
confinement that are frequently substandard and even abusive. As detention here is
incidental to removal, the observation in *Kennedy v. Mendoza-Martinez*, that "for-
feiture of citizenship and the related devices of banishment and exile have throughout history been used as punishment," is particularly cogent. *Id.* at 168 n.23.

Many "INS lifers" have been held in jails or prisons for years, have been transferred multiple times, and frequently have been stranded in parts of the country at
great distances from supportive family. Others have been detained in facilities where
they have faced inhumane conditions. *See* Human Rights Watch, *Locked Away:
Immigration Detainees in Jails in The United States* (1998) (describing frequent
transfers; use of disciplinary sanctions; lack of clothing and supplies; poor medical,
dental, and psychological health; and physical mistreatment). These detainees, with
no power over the countries that refuse to admit them, are warehoused behind bars
and treated like prisoners for indefinite, potentially lifelong periods. There is no
legitimate government interest that justifies this treatment.

It is both excessive and even irrational to detain noncitizens beyond the ninety-day removal period when the Government cannot remove them. The indefinite detention authorized by Congress in 8 U.S.C. § 1231(a)(6) is disproportionate to its regulatory purpose when there is no prospect of removal in the reasonably foreseeable future. Thus, it amounts to punishment. Accordingly, the Due Process Clause prohibits the Government from continuing to detain Zadvydas and Ma and other similarly situated individuals.

B

Because we conclude that detention pursuant to the post-removal-period detention statute can become punitive, we must examine whether the detention determinations are made with the procedural safeguards appropriate for such weighty decisions. The statute that authorizes post-removal-period detention is devoid of any procedural safeguards. The Government argues that implementing regulatory and administrative policies, which grant immigration officials unreviewable discretion to decide whether a noncitizen falls within the terms of the statute, provide sufficient procedure. We disagree. When physical custody is at stake, an opaque process that vests unreviewable discretion regarding detention in the same officers charged with enforcing the law is suspect. There must be fair and transparent processes for deciding whether there is a realistic chance of removal and for deciding whether noncitizens in post-removal-period detention constitute flight risks or public safety risks, as outlined in 8 U.S.C. § 1231(a)(6). We will discuss each of these in turn.

1

For more than half a century, our precedents have been clear: the Due Process Clause does not allow government officials to deprive individuals of their liberty via processes that lack a meaningful opportunity to be heard by an independent decision-maker. See, e.g., Goldberg v. Kelly, 397 U.S. 254 (1970); Mathews v. Eldridge, 424 U.S. 319 (1976). The Government must provide fair hearings for the termination of welfare payments, Goldberg v. Kelly, 397 U.S. at 261, for the elimination of disability benefits, Mathews v Eldridge, 424 U.S. at 332–33, for school suspensions, Carey v. Piphus, 435 U.S. 247, 266–67 (1978), for employment decisions, Arnett v. Kennedy, 416 U.S. 134, 151 (1974), and indeed, for all decisions in which an individual's liberty or property is potentially at risk, Wolff v. McDonnell, 418 U.S. 539, 557–58 (1974). The process to decide whether imprisonment should be extended must provide – at minimum – adequate notice, a meaningful opportunity to be heard at a meaningful time, and an impartial decision-maker.

To implement 8 U.S.C. § 1231(a)(6), the Government initially created a cursory two-paragraph regulation stating that the INS District Director can continue detention beyond the removal period in his or her discretion unless noncitizens can show by clear and convincing evidence that there is no danger to the community or flight risk. Inspection and Expedited Removal of Aliens; Detention and Removal of Aliens; Conduct of Removal Proceedings; Asylum Procedures, 62 Fed. Reg. 10,312, 10,378 (Mar. 6, 1997) (codified at 8 C.F.R. § 241.4). The regulation provided no opportunity for the noncitizen to receive notice of the District Director's decision-making process and no opportunity for the noncitizen to present evidence and discover and challenge the Government's submissions. Apparently recognizing the inadequacy of this statutory and regulatory approach to potential long-term detention of individuals in U.S. custody, various internal INS documents set forth rudimentary procedures for determining continued detention under 8 U.S.C. § 1231(a)(6). See, e.g., Michael Pearson, Exec. Assoc. Comm'r, Off. of Field Operations, INS, Memorandum on Detention Procedures for Aliens Whose Immediate Repatriation is Not Possible or Practicable (Feb. 3, 1999); Doris Meissner, Comm'r, INS, New Mandatory Review Policy for INS Long-Term Detainees (Apr. 30, 1999); Michael Pearson, Exec. Assoc. Comm'r, Off. of Field Operations, INS, Memorandum on Interim Changes and Instructions for Conduct of Post-Order Custody Reviews (Aug. 6, 1999). Two months before we heard arguments in this case, the procedures outlined in the INS internal memoranda were published as an official rule. Detention of Aliens Ordered Removed, 65 Fed. Reg. 80,281 (Dec. 21, 2000) (codified at 8 C.F.R. § 241.4).

While these procedures do require notice to the noncitizen and allow the submission of written information, they are insufficient to protect noncitizens' interest to be free of detention. Imprisoned individuals do not have the right to appear in person and present evidence on their own behalf. See 8 C.F.R. § 241.4(h)(1) ("[T]he district director *may in his or her discretion* schedule a personal or telephonic interview with the [noncitizen] as part of this custody determination.") (emphasis added). They do not receive the evidence on which the Government relies, so they are unable to challenge it or cross-examine the official furnishing the information. See 8 C.F.R. § 241.4(h)(2) (allowing the noncitizen to "submit information in writing" in support of release but granting no right to review and comment on evidence supplied by immigration officials). They are in custody and rarely, if ever, represented by counsel. See 8 C.F.R. § 241.4(h)(2) (allowing assistance by a representative at no expense to the government); *see also* Human Rights Watch, *Locked Away, supra,* at note 244 and accompanying text ("[O]nly about 11 percent of all detained immigrants are represented by legal counsel in immigration court"). Even fewer noncitizens in post-removal detention review proceedings have lawyers, although the regulation permits assistance by a representative at no expense to the government. 8 C.F.R. § 241.4(h) (2). The decision on continued custody is made by a single immigration official, not a neutral party. See 8 C.F.R § 241.4(h)(3)–(5) (authorizing only the district director or a staff delegate to decide whether to extend custody). In light of the magnitude of the liberty interest involved and the likelihood of errors in situations that lack two-sided testing of evidence, the regulations do not cure the statute's unconstitutionality.

In addition to the facial deficiencies of these regulations, there is evidence in the record that government officials consistently fail to comply with their own agency's custody review procedures, make biased and superficial decisions, and cause delay at every stage. For example, although the removal-detention period lasts only ninety days, more than six months passed after Ma received his final order of removal before the Government contacted the Cambodian Government. *Ma v. Reno*, 208 F.3d 815, 819 (9th Cir. 2000). The Government also failed to provide a custody review within ninety days, as required by 8 C.F.R. § 241.4(h)(1). *Id.* at 819 n.5. When Ma applied to be released from detention, the Government sent him a form letter denying his request without stating any reasons, as required by 8 C.F.R. § 241.4(d). *Id.* at 820. Though it lacked explanation for the denial, the form letter specified that there was no ability to appeal the decision. *Id.* For additional instances, see CLINIC Br., *supra*, 6–10 (describing that the INS took more than three years to review the custody status of a Vietnamese citizen ordered removed from the United States and provided detained noncitizens less than fifteen day's notice of a review of continued detention). When a person's liberty is at stake, these errors are troubling. When they are systemic, they raise grave constitutional concerns.

The two cases before us today involve noncitizens whose removal from the United States is unlikely, if not impossible. The Constitution requires that these noncitizens and others similarly situated must have access to fair hearing procedures in which they can raise the implausibility of their removal and seek release until circumstances change, permitting the Government to carry out the removals. If they are correct that removal is unlikely, there is no need to consider additional factors; the entire justification for removal detention is eliminated for noncitizens who can never be removed.

Justice Breyer's statutory construction would lead to periodic six-month review by immigration officials of the need for continued detention. We appreciate the concerns that motivate Justice Breyer, but we do not agree that the text of the statute lends itself to the cure he proposes. Moreover, we must emphasize that the current regulations already require periodic review, yet thousands whose removal is unlikely or impossible remain incarcerated indefinitely. For these reasons, we conclude that Justice Breyer's reading of 8 U.S.C. § 1231(a)(6) unacceptably shelters Congress from its constitutional responsibility to revise the statute to ensure that the Government does not impose long-term civil incarceration on noncitizens. The Government has proven to be untrustworthy in the current detention regime; we have no confidence that there will be meaningful protection of the constitutional rights of noncitizens in post-removal detention without a comprehensive revision of the custody review process. As one report states:

> The legislation imposing mandatory detention has caused immense—and unnecessary—suffering. But even in those areas where the INS retains the discretion to release individuals, it has failed to do so in a consistent or generous manner. It has been particularly remiss in its failure to explore alternatives to detention for vulnerable detainees and others who, particularly with appropriate supervision, would

represent neither a flight risk or a danger to the community. It has also failed to explore cost-effective, alternative forms of detention for those subject to mandatory detention.

Donald Kerwin, Mark von Sternberg, Juan Osuna, Mary McClenahan, Alicia Triche, Helen Morris, and Tom Shea, *The Needless Detention of Immigrants in the United States: Why Are We Locking Up Asylum-Seekers, Children, Stateless Persons, Long-Term Permanent Residents, and Petty Offenders?* 32–33 (2000).

Accordingly, we believe that the ball is in Congress' court to devise an appropriate framework to prevent detention past the ninety-day removal period when there is no prospect of removal in the reasonably foreseeable future. Congress might choose to include a clear articulation of the standard and burden of proof demanded of the Government for detentions longer than the ninety-day removal period. Congress could establish meaningful intervals for review to assess the likelihood of removal in the foreseeable future. Congress might require written decisions explaining the reasons for extending detention and codify the right to federal court review of the extensions of detention. Congress could require supervised release at the end of the ninety-day removal or other specified period if removal does not occur. Or Congress might develop an altogether different statutory scheme to avoid the constitutional challenges that indefinite detention triggers. In our system of government, it is up to Congress to design the immigration removal system consistent with due process.

2

The statute in question, 8 U.S.C. § 1231(a)(6), expressly authorizes indefinite post-removal-period detention when the Attorney General determines there is a risk of flight or a risk to the community. The Constitution demands that the Government must assess these risk factors in a fair procedure.

It is useful to examine each risk factor separately and to further distinguish between immigration detainees whom the Government cannot remove and those it has the ability to remove. We agree with Justice Breyer that the risk of flight evaporates when removal is impossible. 533 U.S. at 690. In those circumstances we conclude that noncitizens should no longer be detained at all. Consigning Zadvydas and Ma to indefinite detention in these circumstances has no regulatory purpose, which makes continued detention simply and unacceptably punitive. The statute provides post-release conditions of supervision that permit the Government to locate individuals if removal becomes possible. 8 U.S.C. § 1231(a)(3).

In contrast, for noncitizens whose removability is reasonably foreseeable even though it may take longer than ninety days to accomplish, flight risk may be a relevant consideration. In these situations, there must be individualized assessments of pertinent evidence. Noncitizens must have notice of the basis for the Government's contention that the noncitizen is unlikely to comply with the terms of release from custody, a meaningful opportunity to present evidence and to challenge the

Government's evidence, an impartial decision-maker whose conclusion is based on the record, and a written explanation of the decision.

Even if flight risk were relevant to their continued detention, the facts in the record show that Zadvydas and Ma were unlikely to flee. Turning first to Zadvydas, we note that he was held in detention more than three years after the expiration of the ninety-day removal period. *Zadvydas v. Caplinger*, 986 F. Supp. 1011, 1015 n.2 (E.D. La. 1997). During the years of post-removal detention, Zadvydas assisted immigration officials in their removal efforts. When these efforts were unavailing, Zadvydas sought release to live with his wife in Houston, Texas. His brother-in-law agreed to sponsor him. Zadvydas agreed to post a cash bond, to obtain employment and health insurance, and to report to immigration officials every month.

Kim Ho Ma was also a compliant detainee. After interviewing him and gathering letters from family members and friends, an immigration officer concluded that Ma had a "very supportive" family. The report noted that Ma's older brother, who owned his own business, promised to employ Ma, and that Ma was in frequent communication with his younger brother in an effort to prevent him from making the mistakes that Ma had made. Further, Ma would live in his parents' home and assist his handicapped elderly father. *Ma*, 208 F.3d at 819–20.

Thus, both Zadvydas and Ma have strong community and family ties that would minimize a risk of flight. It is no surprise to learn that they have complied with the conditions of release imposed by the courts that granted their petitions for habeas corpus.

The other statutory factor that justifies post-removal-period detention is risk to the community. In dissent, Justice Kennedy states that the public safety rationale justified continued detention in the cases before us. Justice Kennedy does not identify any evidence of individualized determinations that Zadvydas and Ma would present future public safety risks. Rather his conclusion appears to be based solely on the fact that Zadvydas and Ma each had been convicted of a crime in prior state proceedings. Justice Kennedy's perspective would transform every criminal conviction, no matter the particularized circumstances, into a permanent barrier to release from immigration detention. It would fly in the face of the trained and informed prison officials who made individualized decisions to release Zadvydas and Ma based on their good behavior before they had served their full sentences. More generally, it would effectively make a nullity of the "community risk" portion of 8 U.S.C. § 1231(a) (6). If prior convictions are a conclusive barrier to release, there would be no need to assess their post-removal-period detention as the statute contemplates.

The great majority of individuals in post-removal-period detention have removal orders based on a criminal conviction. Zadvydas and Ma each faced INS incarceration after they completed their criminal sentences. It is important to note, however, that many individuals in extended post-removal-period detention have never spent any time in custody because their criminal sentences did not include imprisonment. Further, the post-removal-period detention system also includes noncitizens ordered removed solely for violating their nonimmigrant status conditions. The variety of circumstances, noncriminal as well as criminal, that can land a noncitizen in post-removal-period detention is evidence of the widespread punishment this extended incarceration imposes.

We reject Justice Kennedy's perspective that all individuals with criminal convictions constitute a risk to the community. As we analyze the community risk factor set forth in 8 U.S.C. § 1231(a)(6), we again distinguish between noncitizens the Government cannot deport and those it reasonably believes it can remove after some further weeks or months. With regard to the first category, we believe that the Government must release from custody noncitizens whom the Government cannot deport. The purpose of the statute, and the purpose of the post-removal-period detention – to carry out the deportation – has evaporated. Therefore, the Government no longer has a legitimate reason to continue the removal detention, even of people with criminal records. Central to our reasoning is our understanding that Congress authorized post-removal-period detention in order to carry out removals, not for other reasons, such as punishment, or protection against risks to the community.

Even if executive determinations of community risk were sufficient to justify continued civil custody of stateless or otherwise unremovable noncitizens, a view we condemn in the strongest terms, there is no evidence that the Government meaningfully examined the risk of danger actually posed by either Zadvydas or Ma. Zadvydas's most recent conviction was for a nonviolent controlled substance offense. Ma's single conviction was for a violent crime, but his youth and evidence of his subsequent behavior suggest his rehabilitation was underway. Accordingly, the procedural deficiencies in their cases undermine their continued incarceration.

According to the record, neither Zadvydas nor Ma had a hearing at which he could present evidence that he was not a risk to public safety or counter any evidence the Government proffered to the contrary. Moreover, it appears that the Government's evidence of risk to the community in both their cases was the mere fact that each of them had been convicted of a crime. The view that past conviction alone is sufficient to establish future dangerousness has no support in our jurisprudence. See *Salerno*, 481 U.S. at 745. Ongoing detention based solely on a government official's determination of future hypothetical danger without the additional safeguards of a contested proceeding before a neutral adjudicator is nothing more than constitutionally disfavored preventive detention.

The second category of individuals, noncitizens whom the Government reasonably believes it can remove, are in a different position. In their cases, the purpose of post-removal-period detention has not vanished, and the Government has a legitimate interest in effectuating their removal. Continued detention may still play a role related to removal. At the same time, however, their constitutionally protected individual liberty is constrained, and Congress has set forth in 8 U.S.C. § 1231(a)(6) some grounds for their release pending removal. With so much at stake, they are entitled to individualized assessments of their risk to the community in proceedings with adequate notice, a meaningful opportunity to be heard, and an impartial decision-maker.

For the foregoing reasons, we conclude that the Due Process Clause requires fair procedures for decisions concerning continued detention pursuant to 8 U.S.C. § 1231(a)(6). Decisions about flight risks or public safety risks involve individualized assessments that require attention to context and nuance. Assessments about the realistic possibility of removing noncitizens to another nation also demand scrutiny of sensitive information relevant to the specific individual and the specific country. As the two cases before us have demonstrated, the liberty interests of noncitizens to be free from physical constraint is jeopardized by inadequate decision-making. We call on Congress to devise fair procedures that guard against indefinite detention of stateless and other noncitizens whom the Government cannot remove.

IV

Overruling Shaughnessy v. United States ex rel. Mezei

In his dissent, Justice Scalia agrees with the Government's argument that once noncitizens, including lawful permanent residents, receive a final order of removal, they lose all constitutional rights. He equates them with noncitizens outside the United States seeking permission to enter. He therefore concludes that Zadvydas and Ma, though physically present in the United States, have no rights under the U.S. Constitution.

This cannot be. As long as Zadvydas and Ma are physically within the United States and under control of U.S. officials, they are protected by the U.S. Constitution. Our longstanding precedents have made it clear that constitutional protections extend to noncitizens as well as citizens. *Yick Wo v. Hopkins*, 118 U.S. 356, 369 (1886). The Constitutional protections extend to noncitizens with removal orders, who cannot be forced by executive officials to do hard labor while they await removal. *Wong Wing v. United States*, 168 U.S. 228, 237 (1896).

Surely the Constitution prevents government officials from torturing noncitizens while they await removal, *see* Scalia, J., dissenting, 533 U.S. at 704, from interfering with noncitizens' rights to practice their religion during post-removal detention, and from denying medical care to noncitizens in immigration detention. The entry of a removal order against a noncitizen inside the United States does not transport the noncitizen to a constitution-free zone.

The Government supports its far-reaching argument with the infamous opinion in *Shaughnessy v. United States ex rel. Mezei*, 345 U.S. 206 (1953). In dissent, Justices Scalia and Thomas agree with the Government's reliance on *Mezei*. 533 U.S. at 703–05. *Mezei*, however, is distinguishable because Ignatz Mezei was applying for admission into the United States while Zadvydas and Ma are currently residing within our country. Furthermore, the Government's argument has a more fundamental flaw. *Mezei* was wrong when it was decided and is outmoded and indefensible now.

In *Mezei*, the Court reviewed a challenge to the detention on Ellis Island of a returning lawful permanent resident of the United States. The Court acknowledged that noncitizens "who have once passed through our gates, even illegally, may be expelled only after proceedings conforming to traditional standards of fairness encompassed in due process of law." *Mezei*, 345 U.S. at 212. Nonetheless, although Mezei was detained by U.S. officials for close to two years on an island in New York Harbor, the Court ruled that he was not entitled to due process. Ignoring the reality of long-term incarceration at the hands of U.S. government employees on U.S. territory, the Court determined that Mezei should be viewed as if he were still on board a private vessel in international waters: "[H]arborage at Ellis Island is not an entry into the United States." *Id.* at 213.

This is the origin of the "entry fiction" doctrine, in which U.S. immigration officials acknowledge the physical presence of an individual within the territory of the United States but deny that the noncitizen has "entered" the United States and, thereby deny the noncitizen the protection of the Due Process Clause. If this tortured logic were not so pernicious, it would be risible. The United States does not hesitate to enforce its laws on Ellis Island, nestled in New York Harbor. The U.S. Constitution must apply there too.

The *Mezei* opinion, with its fiction that presence on Ellis Island is *not* actual presence on U.S. territory, is a relic of the Cold War obsession with national security and reflects inadequate appreciation of current due process requirements. The perspectives of *Goldberg v. Kelly*, 397 U.S. 254, 269 (1970), and *Mathews v. Eldridge*, 424 U.S. 319, 335 (1976), had not yet become part of the fabric of our law.

Furthermore, subsequent developments in U.S. immigration law undermine *Mezei*. For example, thirty years after *Mezei*, we ruled that the U.S. Constitution requires the Government to provide fair hearings to lawful permanent residents who have left the United States when they attempt to reenter. Even when stopped at the border, "continuously present permanent resident [noncitizens have] a right to due process." *Landon v. Plasencia*, 459 U.S. 21, 33–35 (1983) (applying *Mathews v. Eldridge* due process balancing). As the *Plasencia* opinion held, noncitizens who seek reentry to the United States have weighty interests at stake. They may not only "lose the right to 'stay and live and work in this land of freedom'" but also "lose the right to rejoin [their] immediate family, a right that ranks high among the interests of the individual." 459 U.S. at 34 (quoting *Bridges v. Wixon*, 326 U.S. 135, 154 (1945)). Accordingly, the *Plasencia* court concluded that the Due Process Clause protects lawful permanent residents as they reenter the United States and commands that the Government provide fair procedures, as delineated by the *Mathews v. Eldridge* framework. 459 U.S. at 32–35.

It is no longer true that "[w]hatever the procedure authorized by Congress is, it is due process as far as [a noncitizen] denied entry is concerned." *Mezei*, 345 U.S. at 212 (quoting *United States ex rel. Knauff v. Shaughnessy*, 338 U.S. 537, 544 (1950)). We would formally repudiate that line of reasoning and overrule *Shaughnessy v.*

United States ex rel. Mezei. It is time for the Court to put *Mezei* to rest in all removal cases, especially those involving lawful permanent residents. We look forward to the day when the majority of this Court joins us.

V

The Overuse of Immigration Detention

This case concerns the constitutionality of a statute that effectively punishes large numbers of people held in civil detention. It is part of a deeper, even more worrisome, growing development in our immigration system: the overuse of detention of noncitizens to effectuate immigration laws. *See, e.g.,* 8 U.S.C. § 1225(b) (requiring detention of applicants for admission who appear subject to removal); 8 U.S.C. § 1226(a) (authorizing detention of noncitizens pending removal proceedings); 8 U.S.C. § 1226(c) (requiring detention of noncitizens removable for specified criminal activity or terrorist-related grounds after release from criminal incarceration); *see also* Kerwin et al., *supra,* at 32–33. Recent immigration legislation mandates detention at multiple junctures, affecting not only lawful permanent residents awaiting removal hearings and noncitizens awaiting deportation from the United States, but also many thousands of asylum seekers seeking entry at the border. *See* 8 U.S.C. § 1225(b)(1)(B)(iii)(IV); Amnesty International, *Lost in the Labyrinth: Detention of Asylum-Seekers* 2–3 (1999).

We recognize that the Government's interest in removal is legitimate, but we do not think it is greater than its interest in bringing criminal defendants to trial. Yet in the criminal setting, mandatory pretrial detention is unusual, if not exceptional. When mandatory detention occurs in criminal proceedings, the accompanying procedures are demanding and highly individualized. *See, e.g.,* 18 U.S.C. § 3142. Moreover, in criminal prosecutions, there are speedy trial protections that impose effective temporal limits on incarceration of those not convicted of a crime.

We are gravely concerned that our immigration law increasingly incorporates features of criminal law. One instance is the expansion of immigration detention generally, and post-removal- detention, in particular. As today's cases powerfully reveal, immigration law has adopted attributes of the criminal legal system without the robust procedural protections that the Constitution guarantees. Our apprehension is heightened as we increasingly encounter stories of large numbers of noncitizens who have been detained for immigration violations. Their numbers are outgrowing the federal immigration facilities. One serious consequence is that many noncitizens held for civil immigration violations have been placed throughout the country in state, local, and private custody at considerable cost. Peter H. Schuck, *I.N.S. Detention and Removal: A "White Paper,"* 11 Geo. Immigr. L.J. 667, 672 (1996). These nonfederal facilities, located throughout the country, only recently became subject to federal detention standards, 2000 National Detention Standards for

Non-Dedicated Facilities, but their conditions of confinement have sometimes been appalling. *See* Margaret H. Taylor, *Detained Aliens Challenging Conditions of Confinement and the Porous Border of the Plenary Power Doctrine,* 22 Hastings Const. L.Q. 1087, 1111–25 (1995); *see also* Human Rights Watch, *Locked Away, supra,* at notes 130–81 and accompanying text.

While the increasing reliance on detention in many facets of our immigration system is not directly before us today, we take the opportunity to draw attention to this growing phenomenon that extends into the state, local, and private sectors with little clear regulation or oversight. We predict that the substantial expansion of immigration detention, accompanied by the lack of adequate oversight and safeguards regarding the conditions of these facilities and the treatment of detainees, will lead to serious inequity and abuse. Heavy dependence on detention will encourage the flourishing of a nontransparent administrative system. When noncitizens are warehoused far away from their families and communities, immigration detention facilities will lack the "disinfectant" of sunlight. *Cf.* Louis Brandeis, *Other Peoples' Money and How the Bankers Use It,* ch. 5 (1914) ("What Publicity Can Do"). This bodes ill for the future of the immigration system in the United States.

Justice Breyer's opinion takes an important, albeit limited, step toward imposing limits on immigration detention. But, in the name of constitutional avoidance, it misses the opportunity to redress the incapacitating and punitive effects of 8 U.S.C. § 1231(a)(6) on its face and as applied by the Government. The overreliance on post-removal-period detention revealed by the record in this case may be the canary in the coal mine warning us of the greater problems that the overuse of immigration detention may generate.

***

The Due Process Clause of the United States Constitution protects noncitizens while they are in the United States. Even if noncitizens have lost their right to lawful permanent residence, they retain their fundamental liberty interest in remaining free from custody. We conclude that it is unconstitutional for immigration officials to imprison indefinitely noncitizens ordered removed whom the Government is not able remove. Nor can the Government continue to detain other noncitizens in the post-removal detention period unless fair procedures safeguard the release determinations.

We join Justice Breyer's opinion to vacate both decisions below and remand both cases for further proceedings.

11

Commentary on *Hoffman Plastic Compounds, Inc. v. NLRB*, 535 U.S. 137 (2002)

Ruben J. Garcia

Power analysis pervades the feminist judgment in *Hoffman Plastic Compounds, Inc. v. NLRB* by Professor Kati L. Griffith, writing in this volume as Justice Griffith. Her approach is unique because the 2002 opinion is usually viewed strictly as an interpretation of the National Labor Relations Act of 1935 (NLRA) and the Immigration Reform and Control Act of 1986 (IRCA), as these statutes apply to undocumented workers in the United States. Griffith widens the lens, however, by centering the power dynamics embedded in both statutes. This attention to power contrasts with the original 2002 opinion of the United States Supreme Court, which failed to recognize the power imbalances that Congress sought to remedy by enacting the NLRA, and denied the remedy of backpay to undocumented workers.[1]

Griffith's opinion also directly raises deeper questions about the unequal treatment of immigrants under law. Griffith asks, "should labor law remedies for employer violations yield when the employees they aim to protect are not authorized to work lawfully in the United States?" Put another way, why does immigration status justify unequal protection between two groups of workers who both suffer retaliation for exercising fundamental statutory rights? Griffith's opinion answers the question both in statutory terms, and by demonstrating the fundamental unfairness of different remedies applying to workers both considered "employees." Griffith's opinion thus represents an equalization of remedies for unfair labor practices that has been needed for some time.

Griffith also grounds her feminist judgment in *Hoffman Plastic Compounds* in the power dynamics that are embedded both in labor law, and in IRCA, the immigration law Congress passed in 1986.[2] "IRCA's provisions," she writes, "illustrate that Congress' main target was employers' ability to employ undocumented workers." This is a nuanced and novel way of thinking about immigration law that has heretofore been missing from judicial opinions and most scholarship on IRCA. The

---

[1] Hoffman Plastic Compounds, Inc. v. NLRB, 535 U.S. 137 (2002).
[2] Immigration Reform and Control Act of 1986, Pub. L. No. 99-603, 100 Stat. 3359 (codified as amended in scattered sections of 8 U.S.C.).

Supreme Court's blindness to power dynamics is why *Hoffman Plastic Compounds*, as I have argued elsewhere, is a prime example of the failure of courts to interpret labor and immigration laws in ways that prevent workers from falling through statutory cracks.[3]

The immanent power dynamics in immigration law are unique and central to Griffith's feminist judgment. In this commentary, I endeavor to explain the judgment as a natural outgrowth of the "immployment" law theory that Griffith herself coined and developed along with other scholars. This, coupled with the feminist analysis as outlined by Griffith, is an approach that is a road map to better reasoned judicial opinions in both labor law and immigration law.[4]

The respectful tone that Griffith takes toward the immigrant workers themselves also stands in stark contrast to the original opinion in *Hoffman Plastic Compounds*. To the Supreme Court majority, Castro is treated as the only lawbreaker in the situation, even though the employer also broke the law by laying off Castro and other employees in violation of federal labor law. Even after twenty years, and with several changes to the membership of the Court including the first Latina justice on the Court, several of the justices continue to use the epithet "illegal alien" in oral arguments, as they did during the *Hoffman Plastics* oral argument in 2002. This use of language has a demeaning impact on parties before the Court and on the public at large. In this commentary, I argue that little has changed over twenty years in how the Supreme Court views immigrant workers.

Until American politics allow for legislative change, the courts will remain the last resort for many immigrant workers. Until the composition of the Supreme Court changes, though, we can only hope for more enlightened feminist judgments like Griffith's.

THE ORIGINAL OPINION: TERROR PANIC JURISPRUDENCE LEADS TO LAW IN A POWER VACUUM

In 2001 and 2002, the landscape of immigration law and politics was strikingly similar to how it is today. Opportunistic politicians scapegoated immigrants, while lawmakers seeking to reform the system were stymied by systemic roadblocks such as border state politics and the filibuster.[5] Since 2002, the legacy of the September 11 terrorist

---

[3] RUBEN J. GARCIA, MARGINAL WORKERS: HOW LEGAL FAULT LINES DIVIDE WORKERS AND LEAVE THEM WITHOUT PROTECTION (2012).

[4] *See, e.g.*, Angela P. Harris, *Race and Essentialism in Feminist Legal Theory*, 42 STAN. L. REV. 581 (1990); Katherine Bartlett, *Feminist Legal Methods*, 103 HARV. L. REV. 829 (1990).

[5] *See, e.g.*, Leticia M. Saucedo, *Mexicans, Immigrants, Cultural Narratives and National Origin*, 44 ARIZ. STATE L.J. 305 (2012).

attacks has affected how the courts view immigrants. In twenty years, reform is still at a stalemate in Congress, and the politics of immigration remain highly charged.[6] During the relative détente of 1980s immigration politics, José Castro was hired by Hoffman Plastic Compounds in 1987, just one year after Congress passed IRCA. At that time, there was a rare legislative compromise around immigration policy. Congress enacted a sweeping amnesty for undocumented immigrants who had been in the country a certain number of years.[7] In addition, it enacted employer sanctions for the first time, placing the burden of employment verification on employers, and threatening penalties for those who failed to verify that their employees were authorized to work.[8]

Having entered the United States after the amnesty, Castro carried a triad of liabilities into his job – being Mexican, a low-wage worker, and undocumented in the United States. The racial context that Castro occupied further exacerbates the power differences that Griffith's opinion highlights. Unions are vehicles to try to remedy these kinds of power deficits. It is not entirely surprising then that when the employees of Hoffman Plastic Compounds began organizing a union with the United Steelworkers in 1988, Castro joined the effort. Unfortunately, Castro was also among the employees who were selected for layoff some weeks after. The union filed a charge with the NLRB challenging the layoffs as unlawful retaliation for their union activities. The Board prosecuted through the agency to the D.C. Circuit Court of Appeals, and finally to the United States Supreme Court, which agreed to hear the case two weeks after the September 11 attacks.[9]

In some ways, Castro's story fits the stereotypical mold of the lone male immigrant. Although it is often assumed that most immigrants coming from Mexico are men, there have been a growing number of women making that journey. The Pew Hispanic Center estimated in 2005 that fifty-six percent of adult unauthorized migrants were male.[10] Recent data from the Migration Policy Institute shows that fifty-two percent of undocumented immigrants are female.[11] The power dynamics the Supreme Court ignored in *Hoffman Plastics* (perhaps because the claimant

---

[6] See, e.g., SHOBA SIVAPRASAD WADHIA, BEYOND ENFORCEMENT: IMMIGRATION IN THE TIME OF TRUMP (2019); Michael G. Kagan, THE BATTLE TO STAY IN AMERICA (2019).

[7] National Public Radio, *A Reagan Legacy: Amnesty for Illegal Immigrants*, NEVADA PUBLIC RADIO (July 4, 2010).

[8] Brad Plumer, *Congress tried to fix immigration back in 1986. Why did it fail?*, THE WASHINGTON POST (Jan. 30, 2013).

[9] CATHERINE L. FISK & MICHAEL J. WISHNIE, *The Story of Hoffman Plastic Compounds, Inc. v. NLRB: Labor Rights without Remedies for Undocumented Immigrants* in Laura M. Cooper & Catherine Fisk, LABOR LAW STORIES (2003) at 421 (Hoffman's attorney Ryan McCortney believed that 9/11 "made all the difference" in the Court's decision to take the case.).

[10] Jeffrey S. Passel, *Unauthorized Migrants: Numbers and Characteristics*, PEW RESEARCH CENTER (June 14, 2005).

[11] Cecilia Esterline & Jeanne Batalova, *Frequently Requested Statistics on Immigrants and Immigration in the United States*, MIGRATION POLICY INSTITUTE (Mar. 17, 2022).

was male) are likely to have an even greater impact on the lives of female immigrant workers. They are more likely to lead to other forms of exploitation, such as unequal pay or sexual harassment.[12]

After the September 11, 2001 terrorist attacks, the mood in the country became highly suspicious of Muslims and immigrants of color. There also were many claims that the U.S.-Mexican border was a front for terrorists. And at the time that *Hoffman Plastics* was being considered at the Supreme Court, anthrax-laced envelopes were being received at the Court and in Congress.[13] This is the environment in which the Court made its decision, though it will never be known exactly how much this environment contributed to the opinion.[14]

For signs of the justices' views of immigrants, however, we can look at the transcript of the oral argument in the case, which took place on January 15, 2002. The justices' statements and questions reveal a great deal about their views of immigration and immigrants. For example, the late Justice Antonin Scalia immediately began peppering government attorney Paul R.Q. Wolfson with questions. Before Wolfson could even get the standard opening line to oral argument in the Supreme Court out of his mouth – "thank you, Mr. Chief Justice, and may it please the Court" – Justice Scalia interrupted him with the following pointed question:

> Mr. Wolfson, I just want to know … you're … going to argue that courts should pay illegal aliens money that it was unlawful for them to earn. [W]hat did the INS say to that?[15]

Wolfson struggled to get his opening line out and to address the barrage of questions: "Justice Scalia, may it please the Court: the position in our brief has been developed in consultation with the Immigration and Naturalization Service (INS) …" After more back and forth, and Wolfson affirming that his argument in favor of a backpay remedy for undocumented workers was the position of the United States including the INS, Justice Scalia retorted, "Well … it explains why we have a massive problem with illegal immigration in this country, if that's the way the INS feels about it."[16]

Wolfson proceeded with his argument, but it did not get much easier for the government's side. Justice Scalia was particularly dogged about several issues in

---

[12] *See generally* Sarah Cleveland, Beth Lyon & Rebecca Smith, *Inter-American Court of Human Rights Amicus Curiae Brief: The United States Violates International Law When Labor Law Remedies Are Restricted Based on Workers' Migrant Status*, 1 SEATTLE J. SOC. JUST. 795 (2003); *See also* ROBERT L. NELSON & WILLIAM P. BRIDGES, LEGALIZING GENDER INEQUALITY: COURTS, MARKETS, AND UNEQUAL PAY FOR WOMEN IN AMERICA 53–100 (1999), for an explanation of the organizational theory of discrimination and its relationship to the broader economic sociology literature.

[13] *See* National Public Radio, *Timeline: How the Anthrax Terror Unfolded* (Feb. 5, 2011).

[14] Muneer I. Ahmad, *Homeland Insecurities: Racial Violence After September 11*, 20 SOCIAL TEXT 101 (2011).

[15] Transcript of Oral Argument, at 27, Hoffman Compounds, Inc. v. N.L.R.B., 2002 WL 77224 (U.S. 2002).

[16] *Id.*, at 28.

the NLRB's case – including the ability of Castro to mitigate his damages through earning wages in the interim between firing and judgment. The NLRB requires workers who are seeking backpay after being fired illegally to be "available for work," and to deduct anything earned in the interim from the backpay award. After asking Mr. Wolfson whether there was a duty to mitigate, or find another job, Justice Scalia said, "mitigation is quite impossible, isn't it?" Justice Scalia asked incredulously:

> "How [is] this unlawful alien, supposed to mitigate" … "If he's smart, he'd say how I can mitigate, it's unlawful for me to find another job.… I can just sit at home and eat chocolates and get my back pay."[17]

Here, the assumptions of the Justices were on full display. Indeed, Justice Scalia suggested that Castro held the power to inflict damage on Hoffman Plastics by intentionally failing to mitigate.

Other justices viewed Castro primarily as an illegal alien, and a problem, not as a worker aggrieved by a powerful employee who requires a remedy. Justice O'Connor opined that workers who were undocumented somehow were "better off" than documented ones because they could get backpay without any right to be in the country:

> [T]he result is that back pay awards to illegal workers are likely to be greater than to legal ones under this board's policy, and that's so odd, and it gives the illegal alien an incentive to try to phony up more documents and to extend for the longest possible time the charade that the worker is here lawfully, and that's … surely strongly against the policies of the immigration act at the very least.[18]

Justice Kennedy, too, used the illegal alien label to question why the undocumented should even be allowed to join a union, asking the government attorney Mr. Wolfson: "[D]id it [the Government] give any consideration to the fact that a union ought not as a matter of policy to use illegal aliens for organizing activity?"[19]

Less than three months later, a five-member majority (Chief Justice Rehnquist, Justices O'Connor, Scalia, Kennedy and Thomas), struck down the NLRB's backpay remedy as "trenching upon" federal immigration law. Writing for the Court, Chief Justice Rehnquist concluded that the NLRB's remedy "trenched upon" IRCA's statutory scheme because backpay would serve as a magnet for migrants to come to the United States. The Court's opinion of course elides the fact that immigration law was "trenching upon" the NLRB's authority to remedy unfair labor practices.[20]

---

[17] *Id.*, at 32–33.
[18] *Id.*, at 38.
[19] *Id.*, at 34.
[20] Ruben J. Garcia, *Ten Years After Hoffman Plastic Compounds, Inc. v. NLRB: The Power of a Labor Law Symbol*, 21 CORNELL J. L. PUB. POL. 659 (2012).

In a dissenting opinion joined by Justices Stevens, Ginsburg, and Souter, Justice Stephen Breyer identified the lack of backpay as an incentive for the employer to hire and exploit undocumented workers. This goes against the entire purpose of controlling immigration that the Court majority claims to be prioritizing. While the dissent effectively rebuts the arguments of the majority about the twin and mutually reinforcing goals of the two statutes, there is much left to say about the ways in which Castro and other workers like him will be deterred from future organizing. Professor Griffith's opinion aptly puts the focus on the worker rather than the employer.

The *Hoffman Plastic Compounds* decision demonstrates that to the justices in the majority, immigration enforcement was more important than the prevention and remedying of labor exploitation. The dehumanizing use of the term "illegal alien" displays the views of several justices about undocumented immigrants. The argument showed even more clearly the devaluing of immigrants as people that Justice Scalia exhibited in his questions. "Illegal immigration" to Justice Scalia was a "massive problem" that threatened the nation. He also assumed that most undocumented workers are freeloaders, who would "eat chocolates at home" rather than look for work.

THE FEMINIST JUDGMENT: IMMPLOYMENT LAW CENTERS POWER ANALYSIS TO REACH A DIFFERENT OUTCOME

Unlike the justices in the original opinion, Professor Griffith recognizes the humanity of the undocumented worker whose backpay award is at issue. Griffith's use of the term "undocumented immigrant" is unique among justices of the Supreme Court. In the recent case *Kansas v Garcia*, both the majority written by Justice Samuel Alito and the dissent written by Justice Stephen Breyer used the term "illegal alien." Justice Breyer even used the term "Mr. Alien" in a question in oral argument.[21]

Further, Griffith brings her cross-doctrinal expertise on the intersection of immigration and employment law to a case that the majority of the Court saw resolved primarily by immigration concerns. Indeed, Griffith has pioneered an important area of scholarship, the interaction between immigration and employment law, hence resulting in the term she coined, "immployment law." Griffith's work mines deeply into several other areas as well, including the history of the Fair Labor Standards Act and issues of federalism and immigration law.[22]

---

[21] Kansas v. Garcia, 589 U.S. __ (2020). During the oral argument in Kansas v. Garcia, Justice Stephen Breyer asked the petitioner, "I-9, and these other papers you referred to You, Mr. Alien, go and give it to an employer for the purpose of pretending that you're somebody you aren't so you'll get a job, would that be preempted?" Transcript of Oral Argument, Kansas v. Garcia, at 25.

[22] Kati L. Griffith, *The Fair Labor Standards Act at 80: Everything Old IS New Again*, 104 CORNELL L. REV. 557 (2019).

Immployment law recognizes the interdependence of immigration with other bodies of law, and the ways that values affect the outcomes of the law.[23] As far back as the legal realists, the importance of values in juridical decision-making has been studied by scholars. Immployment scholars bring this approach to decisions affecting immigrants in the workplace. As with the *Hoffman Plastics* majority, most judicial opinions privilege immigration control over labor rights.[24]

Professor Griffith's feminist judgment is also important in centering the worker. As above, we might chalk this up to feminist theory's attention to labor as one of several axes of power dynamics and Griffin's humanistic approach to the workers. This has been the approach of many feminist scholars.[25] The feminist judgment is also more attuned to the empirical realities of immigration in the United States both in 2002 and now. The facts, supported by years of data, show the true cause of immigration is the availability of work, rather than the availability of backpay.[26] This underscores Griffith's argument that a ruling in favor of a backpay remedy is more likely to deter unauthorized immigration by reducing employers' incentive to hire undocumented workers.

Inequalities of bargaining power are central to feminist theory.[27] Griffith clearly makes that part of her analysis. The racialized underpinnings of the immigration system also contribute to the unequal bargaining power that leads to Griffith's feminist judgment, as seen in a number of judicial decisions. United States district judge Miranda Du in Nevada recently found the criminal felony provision in federal law for unauthorized reentry was a violation of the Constitution's Equal Protection Clause. Judge Du examined the legislative history of the statute and the racist origins of the 1924 Act and the McCarran-Ferguson Act.[28] As shown above there was a significant nativist bent to much of immigration law, and Judge Du's opinion provides a template for the examination of many other possible challenges, including the way that *Hoffman Plastic Compounds* treats similar workers differently based on their immigration status.[29]

---

[23] Keith Cunningham-Parmenter, *Fear of Discovery: Immigrant Workers and the Fifth Amendment*, 41 Cornell Int'l L.J. 27 (2008).

[24] Kati L. Griffith, *The Power of a Presumption: California as a Laboratory for Unauthorized Immigrant Workers' Rights*, 50 U.C. Davis L. Rev. 1279 (2016).

[25] Kati L. Griffith, *Discovering "Immployment" Law: The Constitutionality of Subfederal Immigration Regulation at Work*, 29 Yale L. & Pol'y Rev. 389 (2010). *See also* Martha Chamallas, Introduction to Feminist Legal Theory 5 (3rd ed. 2013) ("As a methodology, validation of personal experience has much to offer marginalized groups who lack the power to have their understanding of the world accepted").

[26] *See, e.g.*, Nolan Rappoport, To Tackle Illegal Immigration, Go After Employers.

[27] Martha Fineman, *Feminism, and the Difference It Makes*, 2 Colum J. Gender L. 1 (2005).

[28] Michelle Rindels & Riley Synder, *Nevada Judge Says Immigration Law Making Reentry a Felony Is Unconstitutional, has Racist Origins*, The Nevada Independent (Aug. 18, 2021).

[29] The inequality of remedies between undocumented workers and other workers has been recognized by several scholars. *See, e.g.*, Ruben J. Garcia, *Ghost Workers in an Interconnected World: Going Behind the Dichotomies of Domestic Immigration and Labor Laws*, 36 U. Mich. J. L. Reform 737 (2003).

CONCLUSION: IF COURTS DON'T CHANGE, BRING CHANGE TO THE COURTS

It is sometimes possible to overstate the importance of any one judicial opinion. Even before Hoffman, employers used the threat of deportation to retaliate against workers. One can also look at the history after the *Hoffman Plastic Compounds* decision and see many ways in which the decision did not affect immigrant worker organizing. In the twenty years since *Hoffman Plastic Compounds*, immigrant workers have continued to organize through unions and worker centers and continue to advocate for immigration reforms and an end to wage theft. Some examples include the National Day Laborer Organizing Network and its affiliate in Las Vegas, the Arriba Worker Center. The misclassification of the workers as independent contractors rather than employees, rather than the unavailability of backpay, is usually the most pernicious factor in keeping these workers from receiving the full worth of their labors.

The narrative of disempowered immigrant workers continues because many of the structural inequalities that existed before the opinion continue today. Even if the law changed to allow for backpay for unfair labor practices committed against immigrants, that would not resolve the tenuous status of the many undocumented workers in the country today. Until there is a permanent legislative solution which gives residency to millions of undocumented immigrants in the country, there will continue to be a caste of labor with unequal rights.

In the absence of legislative reform, Kati L. Griffith's feminist judgment in *Hoffman Plastic Compounds v. NLRB* shows a way toward full citizenship and worker power for immigrant workers that is consistent with both the goals of labor law and immigration enforcement.[30] In twenty years, the politics of immigration and labor law have hardened even more so that even with one party controlling both the presidency and Congress, movement on either priority seems very unlikely. Reforms of immigration and labor laws are necessary conditions to the full social incorporation of undocumented workers. This was exacerbated during the COVID-19 pandemic as many immigrant workers were considered "essential workers," without essential pay and safety conditions.[31]

All these pressures have been occurring in an environment of increasing polarization in the courts. The Supreme Court has become even more dominated by appointees of Republican presidents than it was in 2001. No longer is there much doubt about how the Court will decide cases involving union rights, after a string of cases defeating legislation aimed at supporting labor rights – from *Janus v. AFSCME*

---

[30] Fran Ansley, *Worker Solidarity and the Prospect for Immigration Reform*, 41 CORNELL J. INT'L L. 101 (2008).
[31] Ruben J. Garcia, *The Human Right to Workplace Safety in a Pandemic*, 64 WASH. U. J. L. & POL'Y 113 (2021).

Council 36, to, most recently, *Cedar Point Nursery v. Hassid*.[32] With the Supreme Court becoming more dominated by business interests, unless the composition (or size) of the Court changes, *Hoffman* will not likely be overruled.

Since it is unlikely that the Court will change soon, it is more apparent that court decisions will have to be changed through clear Congressional direction. Immigration and labor law reforms would increase overall worker power vis-à-vis their employers. For example, in 2019, the Protecting the Right to Organize (PRO) Act passed the House of Representatives, only to languish in the Senate because the filibuster requires super majority rule for enacting the legislation. If passed and signed by the President, the Act would reverse the result in *Hoffman Plastic Compounds*.[33] There is much more in the legislation, but when that happens it will reverse one of the greatest wounds that the Court has inflicted on immigration law and labor law. Until then, we can imagine the difference that a feminist judgment like Professor Griffith's would have made over the last twenty years.

HOFFMAN PLASTIC COMPOUNDS, INC. v. NATIONAL LABOR RELATIONS BOARD, 535 U.S. 137 (2002)

Justice Kati L. Griffith delivered the opinion of the Court.

This case is about power and inequality. It asks us to consider how labor law responds to vast power differentials in the relationship between employers and their undocumented immigrant employees (employees who labor in U.S. workplaces without proper immigration documentation to do so). It invokes New Deal era insights, long embodied in law, that low-wage workers in the United States do not have actual liberty to contract with their employers due to inequality of bargaining power between employers and employees. Employers "lay down the rules and the laborers are practically constrained to obey them" even when these rules are detrimental to laborers' health and well-being. *West Coast Hotel v. Parrish*, 300 U.S. 379, 393–94 (1937) (quoting *Holden v. Hardy*, 169 U.S. 366, 397 (1898)). This inherent employer power is further increased by undocumented workers' existence in the United States as "a shadow population" that lacks the right to vote and serves as a source of cheap labor. This reality "presents most difficult problems for a Nation that prides itself on adherence to principles of equality under the law." *Plyler v. Doe*, 457 U.S. 202, 218–19 (1981).

---

[32] Janus v. AFSCME Council 31, 585 U.S. __ (2018) (holding that state-enacted "fair share" agreements requiring public employees to pay union dues for services received are unconstitutional compelled speech); Cedar Point Nursery v. Hassid, 594 U.S. __(2021) (California regulation which allowed limited access to farms for informational organizing by unions was an unconstitutional per se taking of the growers' property).

[33] House Education and Labor Committee, *Protecting the Right to Organize*, at 5.

The facts of this case require us to consider how power and inequality inform the interpretation of the proper relationship between federal labor law, the National Labor Relations Act of 1935 (NLRA) and federal immigration law, most notably the Immigration Reform and Control Act of 1986 (IRCA). Specifically, should labor law remedies for employer violations yield when the employees they aim to protect are not authorized to lawfully work in the United States? Or, are the policies underlying both federal labor law and federal immigration law furthered when employers suffer consequences for violating employees' rights.

It is undisputed that Hoffman Plastics Compounds violated Section 8(a)(3) of the NLRA, 29 U.S.C. 158(a)(3), when it fired José Castro and three of his co-workers because of their activity in support of a labor union. It is also undisputed that Castro procured fraudulent documents to gain employment (an IRCA violation) and that he, like more than five million other individuals in the United States, lives in the United States without proper authorization under our immigration law regime. See U.S. Department of Justice, Immigration and Naturalization Services, 2000 *Statistical Yearbook of the Immigration and Naturalization Service* 271 (2000).

In this case, therefore, two distinct statutory regimes are at play in our analysis. Castro is both an "employee" with rights under labor law and undocumented (without authorization to be present in the United States) under immigration law. We are asked to consider how (if at all) the provision of an NLRA backpay remedy, requiring Hoffman Plastics to pay Castro for the time he would have worked had he not been illegally fired for union organizing, interacts with IRCA's goal to deter unauthorized employment by making fewer jobs available to undocumented immigrant workers. That is, we must resolve whether José Castro's undisputed immigration law violation prevents him from obtaining a remedy for Hoffman Plastics' undisputed NLRA violation.

To remedy the NLRA violation, the National Labor Relations Board (NLRB) calculated a backpay remedy from the day Hoffman illegally fired Castro for protected collective activity until the NLRB hearing when it was revealed that Castro was undocumented under immigration law. The NLRB ordered the employer to pay $66,951 plus interest to Castro. Hoffman filed a petition for review of the NLRB order in the U.S. Court of Appeals for the District of Columbia, which denied the petition. The court again denied the petition for review, after rehearing the case *en banc*, and enforced the NLRB's order. We granted certiorari, 533 U.S. 976 (2001), and now affirm.

Two related questions are at the core of this case:

1. Does the NLRB have authority to grant backpay to an undocumented immigrant employee as a remedy for an employer's NLRA law violation?
2. Would the provision of NLRA backpay to an undocumented immigrant employee contravene IRCA's goal to discourage unauthorized immigration by making it more difficult for employers to hire unauthorized workers?

Neither the NLRA's statutory language nor the IRCA's statutory language directly addresses questions about the intended relationship between these two statutory regimes.

We conclude that the NLRB does have authority to grant backpay to Castro and that the provision of backpay would not be in contravention of IRCA in any way. Considerations of power relations between employers and employees, key to Congressional intent underlying both the NLRA and the IRCA, guide our conclusions. The provision of the NLRA remedy is key to the promotion of a fundamental purpose of the NLRA to address power imbalances. Without the ability to join in collective activity with coworkers, "there would be created a subclass of workers without a comparable stake in the collective goals of their legally resident co-workers, thereby eroding the unity of all the employees and impeding effective collective bargaining." *Sure-Tan, Inc. v. NLRB*, 467 U.S. 883, 892 (1984). The NLRB's remedy is also consistent with the IRCA's goal to reduce employer power to hire undocumented employees. The provision of NLRA backpay makes undocumented workers less attractive to U.S. employers. It supports IRCA's goal to restrict employers' power to hire the unauthorized, thereby discouraging unauthorized immigration that is motivated by employment opportunities.

The most effective way to dissuade employers from unlawfully retaliating against collective activity among employees (a labor law goal) and to dissuade employers from preferring compliant undocumented employees (an immigration law goal) is to allow the NLRB to require employers to pay backpay to undocumented employees as a remedy for labor law violations. The provision of this remedy furthers labor law goals by protecting collective activity among documented and undocumented employees who share mutual concerns as workers. It protects those workers who have stepped forward to try to act collectively to gain power vis-à-vis their employers. It furthers the goals of immigration law by reducing employer incentives to attract an undocumented workforce that has inferior legal protections in the workplace. Allowing the employer to skirt backpay when the worker is not fully compliant with immigration laws would give the employer even more power in the employment relationship. It would be detrimental to both statutory regimes.

We base our ruling on proper consideration of power imbalances between employers and employees. Inequalities of power between employers and employees are explicitly acknowledged in the NLRA (Part I), implicitly acknowledged in the IRCA (Part II) and explicitly acknowledged in IRCA's fifteen-year-long legislative history (Part III).

I

Considerations of Power in the NLRA

Allowing the NLRB to grant backpay remedies when employers violate the rights of undocumented employees allows the NLRB to enforce the NLRA and its underlying policy to offset inequality of bargaining power. The NLRA explicitly considers the relative power of employers and an individual employee and acknowledges the need to offset power imbalances by protecting certain forms of collective activity among employees. A collective force of workers, rather than an individual worker, is in a better position to effectively bargain with powerful employers. The policies of the NLRA demand that workers that satisfy the NLRA definition of "employees," even when undocumented under immigration law, need to be able to join in collective action to offset employer power without the risk of employer retaliation. 29 U.S.C. § 152(3).

NLRA Section 8(a)(3) promotes collective action, and thus collective power, by making it unlawful for an employer "by discrimination in regard to ... tenure of employment ... to discourage membership in any labor organization." When Hoffman Plastics fired Castro and three of his colleagues for labor organization activity, it violated this labor law protection. *NLRB v. Transportation Mgmt. Corp.*, 462 U.S. 393, 398 (1983) ("if the employer fires an employee for having engaged in union activities and has no other basis for the discharge, or if the reasons that he proffers are pretextual, the employer commits an unfair labor practice."). The backpay remedy is necessary to dissuade employers like Hoffman Plastics from violating the NLRA because it requires employers to pay the wages it would have paid employees like José Castro if the employee had not been illegally fired. It thereby promotes collective action that can offset vast inequalities of bargaining power between employers and employees.

We have often referred to considerations of inequality of bargaining power as fundamental to the NLRA. *NLRB v. J. Weingarten, Inc.*, 420 U.S. 251, 261–62 (1975) (declaring that the elimination of inequality of bargaining power between employers and employees is a fundamental purpose of the NLRA). Indeed the NLRA's statutory text explicitly invokes notions of power and inequality. In Section 1 of the NLRA Congress found that inequality of bargaining power between employers and unorganized workers must be addressed. It declares:

> The inequality of bargaining power between employees who do not possess full freedom of association or actual liberty of contract and employers who are organized in the corporate or other forms of ownership association substantially burdens and affects the flow of commerce, and tends to aggravate recurrent business depressions, by depressing wage rates and the purchasing power of wage earners in industry and by preventing the stabilization of competitive wage rates and working conditions within and between industries. 29 U.S.C. § 151; *see also Am. Hosp. Ass'n v. NLRB*, 499 U.S. 606, 609 (1991); *Metro. Life Ins. Co. v. Mass.*, 471 U.S. 724, 753–54 (1985).

Sections 7 and 8 of the NLRA implement this policy goal to offset the difficulties that flow from inequality of bargaining power between the parties by encouraging and protecting collective action and collective bargaining among employees. *Am.*

Comm. NLRB v. City Disposal Systems, Inc., 465 U.S. 822, 835 (1984) ("[I]t is evident that, in enacting § 7 of the NLRA, Congress sought generally to equalize the bargaining power of the employee with that of his employer"); *Am. Comm'n Ass'n v. Douds*, 339 U.S. 382, 387–89 (1950) (referring to NLRA protections as aimed at "strengthening employee groups, [] restraining certain employer practices, and [] encouraging the processes of collective bargaining.").

Inequality and power considerations are so central to the NLRA that we have considered these dynamics not just in deciding remedies, but when assessing whether an employer has violated the NLRA in the first instance. In *Gissel Packing Co.*, we found it consistent with the NLRA to factor in power imbalances when concluding that an employer's seemingly general statements about job loss in the area before a union election was an implied threat to retaliate. We stated:

> Any assessment of the precise scope of employer expression, of course, must be made in the context of its labor relations setting.... [It] must take into account the economic dependence of the employees on their employers, and the necessary tendency of the former, because of that relationship, to pick up intended implications of the latter that might be more readily dismissed by a more disinterested ear. Stating these obvious principles is but another way of recognizing that what is basically at stake is the establishment of a nonpermanent, limited relationship between the employer, his economically dependent employee and his union agent, not the election of legislators or the enactment of legislation whereby that relationship is ultimately defined and where the independent voter may be freer to listen more objectively and employers as a class freer to talk. *NLRB v. Gissel Packing Co.*, 395 U.S. 575, 617–18 (1969).

To determine whether employees "heard" an implied threat when the employer talked about job loss, we concluded it was reasonable to consider the employees' inferior bargaining power. In other words, the NLRB can consider how a dependent employee would interpret the statements, rather than how an objective observer would perceive the situation.

Power considerations permeate NLRA cases. For example, in *J. Weingarten Inc.* we similarly considered how power (and an individual employee's lack thereof) shapes analyses of the NLRA. When concluding that an employee represented by a union has the right to bring a representative to an investigatory interview that could result in discipline, we again referenced inequality of bargaining power. We affirmed that:

> [r]equiring a lone employee to attend an investigatory interview which he reasonably believes may result in the imposition of discipline perpetuates the inequality the Act was designed to eliminate, and bars recourse to the safeguards the Act provided "to redress the perceived imbalance of economic power between labor and management." *J. Weingarten*, 420 U.S. at 261–62 (1975) (quoting *Am. Ship Bldg. Co. v. NLRB.*, 380 U.S. 300, 316 (1965)).

Based on an inequality of bargaining power rationale, all vulnerable workers, not just industrial workers like Castro, should be included in the NLRA's protective reach. This would properly extend protections to domestic workers and agricultural laborers, two groups that were excluded from the protections provided in the final bill that passed Congress in 1935. *See* Peggie R. Smith, *Organizing the Unorganizable: Private Paid Household Workers and Approaches to Employee Representation*, 21 N.C. L. Rev. 45, 109 (2000) (domestic workers "perhaps more than many groups of workers" need to join forces with other domestic workers to offset inequalities in bargaining power); Michael H. LeRoy & Wallace Hendricks, *Should 'Agricultural Laborers' Continue to be Excluded from the National Labor Relations Act?*, 48 Emory L.J. 489, 503, 536 (1999) (agricultural laborers often live and work in isolated settings, have "small bargaining power," and receive "poor earnings."). The decision to exclude these workers, which contravenes the broader Congressional acknowledgment of power differentials, seems to have been driven by political realities, namely a Southern Democratic push to exclude industries dominated by Black workers. *See* William E. Forbath, *Caste, Class, and Equal Citizenship*, 98 Mich. L. Rev. 1, 76–77 (1999) ("By allying with northern Republicans, or by threatening to do so, [Southern Democrats] stripped all the main pieces of New Deal legislation of any design or provision that threatened the separate southern labor market and its distinctive melding of class and caste relations, its racial segmentation, and its low wages."). Given that the same power dynamics are even more pronounced in agriculture and domestic service because of the isolation of those contexts, it is notable how out of step these exclusions are with the central policy of the NLRA.

Nonetheless, as these exclusions and this case remind us, economic inequality is not the only inequality of power relevant to the analysis. Inferior immigration status is a dynamic that further weakens employee bargaining power, especially if workers with this status are treated differently under the laws intended to protect employees who labor in U.S. workplaces. In a case not dissimilar from the one before us, we relied on considerations of inequality of power to conclude that undocumented immigrants can be NLRA "employees" despite their status under immigration law. *Sure-Tan, Inc. v. NLRB*, 467 U.S. 883, 892 (1984). If undocumented workers did not have NLRA rights, we reasoned, "there would be created a subclass of workers." *Id.* Thus, immigration status, similar to race and gender, is a "master status," that can foster inequalities of power between parties and can further workplace injustices. *See* Godfried Engbersen, *The Undocumented Outsider Class: Illegal Immigrants in Dutch Society*, in *European Societies: Fusion or Fission?* 97 (1999).

Racial power and gender power imbalances also inhibit low-wage workers from actual liberty to contract with their employers and should inform analyses that involve inequalities of bargaining power under the NLRA. Racism is at the core of U.S immigration law. John Higham, *Strangers in the Land: Patterns of American Nativism, 1860–1925* (2002); Kevin R. Johnson, *Race, The Immigration Laws, and Domestic Race Relations: A "Magic Mirror" into the Heart of Darkness*, 73 Ind. L.

J., 1128–30 (1998). Because race and gender are systems of power, not mere bio-logical attributes, racialized and gendered perceptions often implicitly inform how employers and employees perceive and interact with each other. *See* Michael Omi & Howard Winant, *Racial Formation in the United States: From the 1960s to the 1990s* at 59 (1994); Catharine A. MacKinnon, *Feminism Unmodified* 8 (1987) (referring to gender as "an inequality of power" and "a social status based on who is permitted to do what to whom.").

To offset these inequities in power, the NLRB needs remedies that will alter employer behavior, remedies that will discourage employers from exploiting vul-nerable employee populations. The NLRB has long used the monetary backpay remedy to deter employers from taking advantage of their superior bargaining power by retaliating against collective action among employees. *See NLRB v. J.H. Rutter-Rex Mfg. Co.*, 396 U.S. 258, 262–63 (1969) (stating that backpay has long been a core part of remedial arsenal of the NLRB). Beyond backpay, none of the NLRB's traditional remedies provide a monetary disincentive for employers to fail to comply with the NLRA. Posting of notices and cease and desist orders are important remedies, but they are not robust enough to alter employer behav-ior in the first instance. It not only hurts the undocumented employee when the NLRB cannot grant backpay to compensate for a labor law violation, it hurts all workers.

While we primarily consider relations between employers and employees, rela-tions between employers are relevant too. The need for universal application of the law to all employers also supports our ruling that the NLRB can grant backpay to undocumented workers. To rule that the NLRB cannot require employers to pay backpay to an undocumented immigrant employee would give law-breaking employers a "competitive advantage" over law-abiding employers. *See generally Brooklyn Sav. Bank v. O'Neil*, 324 U.S. 697, 710 (1945) ("An employer is not to be allowed to gain a competitive advantage by reason of the fact that his employees are more willing to waive claims for liquidated damages than are those of his com-petitor. The same considerations calling for equality of treatment which we found so compelling in *Midstate Horticultural Co., supra*, exist here."). If we deny the NLRB the ability to order backpay, employers who employ undocumented work-ers would have a competitive advantage over employers who do not employ such workers because they would have reduced exposure to monetary remedies if they violate the NLRA.

In sum, considerations of power permeate the NLRA's text and this Court's interpretations of the statute. Power imbalances are not just economic, they are also fostered by inferior status under immigration law, race, and gender dynamics. Deferring to the NLRB's decision to grant backpay to an undocumented immigrant worker to remedy an NLRA violation honors the NLRA's fundamental purpose to support collective worker action as an offset to employer power to define all of the non-statutory terms of the relationship.

II

Considerations of Power in the IRCA

Allowing the NLRB to grant backpay remedies when employers violate the labor rights of undocumented employees is also consistent with considerations of employer power in the Immigration Reform and Control Act (IRCA) of 1986. The IRCA was the first time Congress systemically targeted the workplace as a main site of immigration enforcement. Implicitly acknowledging the power of employers to attract undocumented workers through labor market opportunities, Congress put the main thrust of IRCA's restrictions on employers, not undocumented employees.

IRCA's provisions illustrate that Congress' main target was employers' power to employ undocumented workers. Most notably, IRCA makes it unlawful for an employer to knowingly employ or recruit undocumented workers. 8 U. S. C. §§ 1324a(a)(1)(A), (a)(2). It requires that employers verify that individuals have proper authorization to work in the United States. See §§ 1324a(a)(1)(B), (b). Employers who violate these provisions face possible criminal and/or civil sanctions. 8 U. S. C. §§ 1324a(e)(4), (f). The number of cases against employers for IRCA violations varies year to year. In 2000, immigration authorities completed close to 2,000 cases against employers, down from 8,000 cases closed in 1998. See U.S. Department of Homeland Security, Yearbook of Immigration Statistics 2002, Table 42.

In contrast to its treatment of employers, IRCA does not criminally sanction employees who seek to work or who actually work without proper authorization. The thrust of the requirements focus on employers, not employees. This emphasis on employer sanctions, rather than employee sanctions, is an acknowledgment that Congress did not want to make criminals out of undocumented workers like Mr. Castro who already face exploitation at the workplace.

Thus, taking away a labor law remedy from an undocumented employee who suffers an NLRA violation would not be consistent with Congress' attention on employer power to attract undocumented workers. Because undocumented workers may be less willing to speak up for themselves due to immigration retaliation fears, employers already have an incentive to prefer this more compliant workforce. A ruling denying backpay to undocumented employees who experience labor law violations would further that incentive. If there was a subset of employees with fewer protections than others, employers would actually be *more* incentivized to seek out undocumented employees. This circumstance would be in direct contradiction to the IRCA's goal of reducing the "magnet" of employment opportunities in the United States by making it more difficult for employers to hire undocumented workers. H.R. Rep. No. 682, 99th Cong., 2nd Sess. Pt. 1, at 45–46 (1986).

III

Considerations of Power in the IRCA's Legislative History

A systematic review of IRCA's fifteen-year legislative history affirms that the NLRB's provision of backpay remedies to undocumented employees is not in tension with the IRCA. Indeed, the provision of this NLRA remedy would actually support IRCA's goals. The legislative history communicates widespread congressional concern about the power imbalance between employers and undocumented immigrant workers. A wide swath of Congress saw employment protections for undocumented workers as essential to policy goals to curb unauthorized employment opportunities. Thus, taking protections away from undocumented workers would run counter to this immigration policy.

All thirteen congressional reports, written over a fifteen-year period, invoked concerns about labor conditions as a main thrust of IRCA's purposes. See H.R. Rep. No. 99-682, pt. 1, at 49 (1986); H.R. Rep. No. 99-1000 (1986); S. Rep. No. 99-132, at 1 (1985); S. Rep. No. 98-62, at 1 (1983); H.R. Rep. No. 98-115, pt. 1, at 30 (1983); S. Rep. No. 97-485, at 1 (1982); H.R. Rep. No. 97-890, pt. 1, at 29 (1982); Staff of S. & H.R. Committees on the Judiciary, 97th Cong., 1st Sess. Sess., U.S. Immigration Policy & Nat'l Interest No. 8 (Joint Comm. Print 1981) (the final report and recommendations of the Select Commission on Immigration and Refugee Policy with supplemental views by commissioners); Staff of Select Commission of Immigration and Refugee Policy, 97th CONG., Semiannual Report to Congress (Joint Comm. Print 1981); Cong. Research Serv., Staff of Select Commission of Immigration and Refugee Policy, 96th Cong., 2D Sess., Temporary Worker Programs: Background and Issues (Comm. Print 1980); H.R. Rep. No. 96-1301, at 11, 23 (1980); H.R. Rep. No. 94-506, at 2 (1975); H.R. Rep. No. 93-108, at 3 (1973).

All but one of the congressional reports mentioned concerns about the inferior treatment of undocumented workers. *See, e.g.,* H.R. Rep. No. 94-506, at 10 (1975); H.R. Rep. No. 93-108, at 6 (1973); see also H.R. Rep. No. 99-1000, at 25 (1986); H.R. Rep. No. 99-682 pt. 1, at 49 (1986); S. Rep. No. 99-132, at 16 (1985); H.R. Rep. No.98-115, pt. 1, at 17, 37 (1983); S. Rep. No. 98-62, at 20 (1983); H.R. Rep. No. 97-890, pt. 1, at 193 (1982); S. Rep. No. 97-485, at 19 (1982); Staff of Select Commission of Immigration & Refugee Policy, 97th Cong., Semiannual Report Congress, at 14 (Joint Comm. Print 1981); Cong. Research Serv., Staff of Select Commission of Immigration & Refugee Policy, 96th Cong., 2d Sess., Temporary Worker Programs: Background and Issues, at 104 (Comm. Print 1980). As a 1981 report put it, undocumented workers are "at the mercy of unscrupulous employers and 'coyotes' who smuggle them across the border" and thus "cannot and will not avail themselves of the protection of U.S [worker protection] laws." Staff of S. & H.R. Committees on the Judiciary, 97th Cong., 1st Sess., U.S. Immigration Policy & Nat'l Interest No. 8, at 42 (Joint Comm. Print 1981).

All but two of the thirteen reports referred to employer treatment of undocumented workers as exploitation. H.R. Rep. No. 98-115, pt.1, at 37 (1983); H.R. Rep. No. 97-890, pt. 1, at 193 (1982); Staff of S. and H.R. Comms. on the Judiciary, 97th Cong., U.S. Immigration Pol'y and the Nat'l Interest 13 (J. Comm. Print 1981); Cong. Research Serv., Staff of Select Comm'n of Immigration and Refugee Pol'y, 96th Cong., Temporary Worker Programs: Background and Issues 109 (Comm. Print 1980); H.R. Rep. No. 94-506, at 7 (1975); H.R. Rep. No. 93-108, at 8 (1973). For example, a 1975 House Report concluded that the legislation would "go a long way in eliminating the exploitation of [the undocumented] and the other consequences that flow from their illegal status in the United States." H.R. Rep. No. 94-506, at 10 (1975).

All eight reports that talk about the law's promotion of incentives portray that workplace protections to undocumented workers disincentivizes employers from preferring the undocumented over the documented workforce. H.R. Rep. No. 99-1000, at 25 (1986); H.R. Rep. No. 99-682, at 106 (1986); H.R. Rep. No. 98-115, at 37 (1983); S. Rep. No. 98-62, at 22, 120 (1983); H.R. Rep. No. 97-890, at 195 (1982); S. Rep. No. 97-485, at 120 (1982); Staff of S. and H.R. Comms. on the Judiciary, 97th Cong., U.S. Immigration Policy and the Nat'l Interest 344 (J. Comm. Print 1981); Cong. Research Serv., Staff of Select Comm'n of Immigration and Refugee Policy, 96th Cong., Temporary Worker Programs: Background and Issues, at 134 (Comm. Print 1980). Along these lines, one report declared that if the legislation did not pass "employers will continue to hire [undocumented workers] since such persons by virtue of their precarious status must work harder, longer, and often for less pay." H.R. Rep. No. 93-108, at 6 (1973).

Acknowledgment of the power imbalances between employers and employees, and the need to alter employer behavior permeates the legislative history. As several reports put it, the "weak bargaining power" that comes along with undocumented immigration status "depress[es] U.S. wages and working conditions" and deepens undocumented workers status as "a fearful and clearly exploitable group." S. Rep. No. 99-132, at 16 (1985); S. Rep. No. 98-62, at 20 (1983); S. Rep. No. 97-485, at 19 (1982). In a similar vein another report noted that "[a]n unscrupulous employer can exploit this vulnerability" by threatening to notify immigration authorities if the worker "does not agree to the employer's conditions of employment" thereby reviving the "specter of forced slavery and pardon[ing] the employer for illegal conduct." H.R. Rep. No. 97-890, pt. 1, at 193 (1982); see also H.R. Rep. No. 99-682, at 49 (1986); H.R. Rep. No. 99-1000, at 25 (1986); S. Rep. No. 99-132, at 16 (1985); S. Rep. No.98-62, at 20 (1983); S. Rep. No. 97-485, at 19 (1982).

The most explicit statement about Congress' intent not to affect the NLRB's remedial authority with its passage of IRCA in 1986 comes from a House report on the legislation the year it was passed. It states:

> [T]he committee does not intend that any provision of this Act would limit the powers of State or Federal labor standards agencies such as. ... the National Labor

Relations Board, or Labor arbitrators, in conformity with existing law, to remedy unfair practices committed against undocumented employees for exercising their rights before such agencies or for engaging in activities protected by these agencies. To do otherwise would be counter-productive of our intent to limit the hiring of undocumented employees and the depressing effect on working conditions caused by their employment. H.R. Rep. No. 99-682, pt. 2, at 8–9 (1986).

Nothing in IRCA's legislative history suggests that Congress intended to restrict the NLRB's authority to order backpay to undocumented employees whose employers violate the NLRA. Provision of backpay does not fun afoul of federal immigration. Instead, it supports immigration policy goals to reduce employer incentives to hire a more compliant undocumented workforce.

CONCLUSION

For these reasons, the Court holds that the NLRB does have the authority to grant backpay to an undocumented immigrant employee as a remedy for an employer's NLRA law violation. Our holding supports IRCA's goal to discourage unauthorized immigration by making it more difficult for employers to hire unauthorized workers.

Economic disadvantage, racial and gender inequities, and inferior treatment under the law (such as undocumented immigration status) foster unequal relations between employers and employees. These inequities can lead to injustices that run afoul of the NLRA's fundamental policies. Some employers exploit these inequities more than others. A proper consideration of power inequities, as both the NLRA and IRCA demand, makes it clear that the NLRB has the authority to require an employer to pay backpay to an undocumented employee. To rule otherwise would allow employers who exploit these inequities and fire employees for acting collectively to get off scot-free.

The judgment of the court of appeals is affirmed.

It is so ordered.

12

Commentary, *Padilla v. Kentucky*, 559 U.S. 356 (2010)

Gabriel J. Chin

The concurring opinion of Professor Marissa Montes, writing here as Justice Montes, is nothing short of compelling. It makes an overwhelming case that courts should extend the duty of defense counsel to advise clients regarding the so-called collateral consequences of criminal convictions, recognized in *Padilla v. Kentucky*,[1] to legal issues affecting clients beyond deportation. Deportation is extremely serious, but lifetime sex offender registration, as one example, is not obviously less so. The collateral consequences of unemployment, loss of parental rights, and eviction, among many others, are also harsh. Defense lawyers should consider these, as a matter of the general responsibility of lawyers to try to help their clients.[2] Even if, as some have argued, defense counsel for the poor should offer a specially truncated, limited and inferior form of service,[3] consideration of collateral consequences remains important to get the best sentence for their clients in whatever ration of legal services the lawyer is allocated.[4] I also agree with Montes that the framing of the modern U.S. criminal justice system as one of "mass incarceration" has the potential to mislead because most people with criminal records are in free society, not in prison.[5]

---

[1] 559 U.S. 356 (2010).

[2] For example, ABA Model Role of Professional Conduct 2.1 provides:

> In representing a client, a lawyer shall exercise independent professional judgment and render candid advice. In rendering advice, a lawyer may refer not only to law but to other considerations such as moral, economic, social, and political factors, that may be relevant to the client's situation.

[3] RICHARD A. POSNER, THE PROBLEMATICS OF MORAL AND LEGAL THEORY 163–64 (1999) ("[a] bare-bones system for defense of indigent criminal defendants may be optimal"; otherwise, "either many guilty people would be acquitted or society would have to devote much greater resources to the prosecution of criminal cases").

[4] Gabriel J. Chin, *What Are Defense Lawyers for? Links between Collateral Consequences and the Criminal Process*, 45 TEX. TECH L. REV. 151 (2012).

[5] I have argued instead for calling our time the era of "mass conviction." Gabriel J. Chin, *The New Civil Death: Rethinking Punishment in the Era of Mass Conviction*, 160 U. PA. L. REV. 1789 (2012).

ORIGINAL OPINION

The caselaw prior to *Padilla* rejected imposing on lawyers a duty to advise clients about collateral consequences of guilty pleas. Movement outside the courts was a significant part of the background leading to *Padilla*.[6] An important leader was Margaret Colgate Love, the U.S. Pardon Attorney in the Justice Department under Presidents Bush and Clinton, and my close colleague for over twenty years. She persuaded the ABA Criminal Justice Standards Committee to establish a project to draft ABA Standards for Collateral Sanctions and Discretionary Disqualification of Convicted Persons, which were approved by the ABA House of Delegates in 2003.[7] I served as Reporter. Among other things, the standards required that people pleading guilty be notified of applicable collateral consequences.[8]

There is a trick in the Standards. They provide that failure to give notice of collateral consequences "shall not be a basis for withdrawing the plea of guilty, except where otherwise provided by law or rules of procedure, or where the failure renders the plea constitutionally invalid."[9] So the Standards created a duty in one breath and in the next hint that it is unenforceable. But the ABA Standards themselves, the Supreme Court has ruled, help shape the content of the duty of defense lawyers under the Sixth Amendment.[10] As evidence of the normal practice of lawyers, they help shape the Constitution itself.

A distinguished lawyer from Vermont, Richard Cassidy, persuaded the Uniform Law Commission to start a project which ultimately became the Uniform Collateral Consequences of Conviction Act. I served that project as reporter as well. Again a major law reform institution took the position that collateral consequences were part of the criminal justice system. Mr. Cassidy was also instrumental in persuading Senator Patrick Leahy to support an appropriation to create a national inventory of collateral consequences; collecting them, obviously, would make it much more feasible for lawyers to warn their clients about them.[11]

When the Supreme Court granted certiorari in *Padilla*, I, along with Ms. Love, Professor Peter Margulies, and experienced appellate practitioner Daniel Leffell, wrote an amicus brief for the ABA.[12] One of the brief's main points was that the vast majority of states had recently held CLEs or published articles about the immigration

---

[6] Margaret Colgate Love, *Paying Their Debt to Society: Forgiveness, Redemption, and the Uniform Collateral Consequences of Conviction Act*, 54 How. L. J. 753, 780–98 (2011).
[7] Collateral Sanctions and Discretionary Disqualification of Convicted Persons (americanbar.org).
[8] ABA Standards for Criminal Justice, Standard 19–2.3(a).
[9] *Id.*
[10] Strickland v. Washington, 466 U.S. 668, 688 (1984) ("Prevailing norms of practice as reflected in American Bar Association standards and the like, ... are guides to determining what is reasonable, but they are only guides.").
[11] https://niccc.nationalreentryresourcecenter.org/.
[12] www.abanet.org/publiced/preview/briefs/pdfs/07-08/08-651_PetitionerAmCuABA.pdf.

consequences of criminal convictions. The courts might say that defense lawyers should have nothing to do with collateral consequences, but defense lawyers did not agree. Put another way, the question in *Padilla* was not whether lawyers should advise their clients about immigration consequences of criminal prosecutions; no competent lawyer would fail to do so. The question was what would happen when a lawyer breached the duty to do what every reasonable lawyer did.

At the time he was charged with a drug offense, Jose Padilla had been a lawful permanent resident of the United States for over forty years. He was married to a U.S. citizen, with several U.S. citizen children. He had been honorably discharged from the U.S. Armed Forced after serving during the Vietnam War. After four decades in the United States, avoiding deportation was one of his main concerns. So, before taking a plea, he asked his lawyer if his plea could get him deported. His counsel told him that he did not have to worry about being deported because he had been in the country for so long. In fact, the offense he pleaded guilty to triggered automatic deportation. Mr. Padilla claimed that, had he known so, he would have rolled the dice at trial because deportation was the same as "putting a gun" to his head.[13]

Mr. Padilla challenged his conviction, arguing that his lawyer's affirmative mis-advice violated his Sixth Amendment right to effective assistance of counsel. In a 7-2 decision authored by Justice Stevens, the U.S. Supreme Court agreed, holding that the Sixth Amendment requires defense attorneys to provide a client with accurate information regarding the potential deportation consequences of a guilty plea. Justice Alito, joined by Chief Justice Roberts, concurred, agreeing that a lawyer was required not to give misadvice, but was obliged only to warn in general terms that convictions could have immigration consequences. Justices Scalia and Thomas dissented, on the ground that immigration was a distinct domain from criminal prosecution, and therefore defense counsel had to pay it no mind.

Padilla was significant for recognizing the importance of plea bargaining to the criminal justice system. Because over ninety percent of criminal convictions result from guilty pleas, perhaps the most important service criminal defense lawyers perform is advising their clients whether to plead guilty and on what terms. In *Padilla*, the Court rejected the longstanding idea that the deportation consequences of criminal convictions were outside the scope of defense counsel's obligations. To the contrary, the Court acknowledged that deportation had become "an integral part – indeed, sometimes the most important part – of the penalty that may be imposed on noncitizen defendants who plead guilty to specific crimes." As such, the Court held that where it was clear that a criminal conviction triggered deportation, a defense attorney was required to advise a client about it.

The Court's recognition that deportation and criminal law were inextricably intertwined was long overdue. In the preceding decades, Congress had signifi-cantly expanded the list of convictions that could trigger, or mandatorily required,

[13]   Padilla v. Com., 381 S.W.3d 322, 327 (Ky. Ct. App. 2012).

deportation. By "dramatically rais[ing] the stakes of a noncitizen's criminal conviction," the Court concluded that Congress had made deportation consequences a critical consideration for noncitizen defendants like Mr. Padilla. As a result, the Sixth Amendment demanded that criminal defense attorneys accurately advise regarding the deportation consequences of guilty pleas.

Padilla was also significant for its rejection of the direct-collateral distinction running through effective assistance of counsel claims. Before *Padilla*, federal and state courts had held that criminal defendants were entitled to know the direct consequences of a plea, such as a term of imprisonment or fine. Anything else that flowed from a conviction (including such things as deportation, disenfranchisement, or loss of public benefits) was considered a "collateral consequence" and irrelevant to defense counsel's constitutional obligations. After *Padilla*, at least for deportation, the direct-collateral distinction no longer held.

Padilla was a victory for noncitizens, extending them critical Constitutional protections and helping them to bargain effectively with prosecutors for satisfactory pleas. Implementing *Padilla*'s mandate has proven a challenge. In the fractured and overburdened world of the defense bar, made up of independent federal, state, and local systems, public defenders and private defense counsel, answers have come haphazardly. Some public defender organizations have hired "*Padilla* attorneys" to do the job. Others contract with immigration law experts on an *a la carte* basis. Still others, often in rural or smaller counties, have no mechanism in place to ensure compliance.[14]

THE FEMINIST JUDGMENT

Padilla emphasized the "unique nature of deportation" which was "uniquely difficult to classify as either a direct or collateral consequence." By this language, the Court presumably meant to limit the holding's reach. Deploying several different techniques of feminist legal theory, Professor Montes show not just how, but why, the majority's logic must extend beyond deportation to any severe penalty linked to a guilty plea. In an approach consistent with an embrace of radical transformation typical of many feminist legal theorists, Montes gives us a legal regime that delivers justice where it is broadly demanded.

Montes recognizes and centers multiple axes of discrimination, demanding that the analysis "take into account the racism, classism, sexism and overall discrimination that plague our criminal system." Situating the opinion within its era of over policing, overcriminalization, and mass incarceration, Montes explains how collateral consequences reach far beyond the deportation of noncitizens in ways that are as devastating and important to defendants. Moreover, Montes shows that they have

---

[14] Ingrid Eagly, et al., *Restructuring Public Defense After* Padilla, 74 STAN. L. REV. 1 (2022).

distinctly impacted women and people of color. Deploying intersectional analysis,[15] Montes provides a crucial context the majority opinion ignored.

Montes focuses on one consequence – family unity – noting how guilty pleas interact with federal and state law regarding parental rights and custody to result in the breakup of families. Just as Jose Padilla was concerned with whether a plea would trigger his deportation, Montes observes that any reasonable parent would want to know that termination of their parental rights was a likely consequence of a plea. By centering the law's impact on family relationships, Montes's analysis reflects relational or difference feminists, who argue that law focuses on individual autonomy and rights and disrespects more traditional female values like connection and care.[16] By bringing family to the fore, Montes uncovers harms that women and people of color distinctively suffer that deserve redress as much as noncitizens duped into pleading to their own deportation.

Montes's concurrence also insists that instead of assessing professional norms by quoting standards from establishment institutions like the ABA, the law should incorporate the principles of rebellious lawyering into its analysis. Rebellious lawyering empowers poor clients, anchoring the practice of law in the world it tries to change. As Montes observes, rebellious lawyering "rejects the continued subordination of clients in the attorney-client relationship by recognizing clients as collaborators." Today (and at the time *Padilla* was decided), rebellious lawyering practices are not fringe practices. Many lawyers, at nonprofit service providers and firms big and small, ground their advocacy in the perspective of their clients. Nevertheless, no decided cases reference Gerald Lopez and rebellious lawyering when discussing the professional norms at issue in *Padilla*.

Montes's demand that the law use an alternative, progressive view of lawyering to determine reasonable representation reflects the feminist rejection of traditional sources of rules and power. Power and knowledge, she insists, run not just from the attorney to the client, but "in both directions." This reflects the feminist emphasis on collaborative, as opposed to hierarchical, relationships.[17] *Padilla* situates the answer to counsel's obligations in the clarity of the governing law, which is ascertainable only by the attorney or judge, and is decided without input from the client. In contrast, Montes makes the significance of the potential consequence to the client the triggering mechanism for an obligation to advise. This is something ascertainable only by the client and attorney working together. By centering a collaborative relationship in the standard for effective assistance of counsel, Montes rejects the traditional hierarchical construct of the lawyer-client relationship.

---

[15]   Kimberle Crenshaw, *Demarginalizing the Intersection of Race and Sex: A Black Feminist Critique of Antidiscrimination Doctrine*, Feminist Theory and Antiracist Politics, 1989 Univ. Chi. Legal Forum 139 (1989).

[16]   See Robin West, Caring for Justice (1997).

[17]   As Carol Gilligan observed in her book In a Different Voice (1982), women see "a world comprised of relationships."

Finally, collateral consequences, which disproportionately impact historically vulnerable and subordinated communities, are undoubtedly a feminist issue.[18] Montes alluded to this in her opinion when she argued that defense lawyers should be obliged to discuss collateral consequences affecting family unity. Of course, in absolute numbers, many women face criminal charges in the United States, and there are certainly aspects of the system rooted in patriarchy. But when it comes to being charged with and convicted of crimes, the gender disparity is profound. As is captured in the title of Vivian Berger's classic study of the law of sexual assault, "Man's Trial, Woman's Tribulation,"[19] criminal prosecution is, proportionally, largely an affliction of men. In 2020, the overall incarceration rate of women was less than a seventh of that of men.[20] One pair could be found where the traditional disparity was reversed: native women were incarcerated at a higher rate than Asian men. Yet, white men, a relatively privileged group, were incarcerated at more than five times the rate of a relatively disadvantaged group, African American women. Because of the gender disparity, when evaluating the criminal justice entitlements of defendants, we are evaluating, for the most part, the criminal justice entitlements of men.

Yet, collateral consequences imposed on men profoundly affect the lives of women. The men caught up in the criminal justice system are the sons of women and men, and the actual or potential husbands, partners, and fathers of other women and men. Collateral consequences are particularly important for those who are out of prison; for an inmate, the ability to get a license or public housing is not yet important. These circumstances underscore the irony that collateral consequences tend to be more significant the less serious the crime – someone serving ninety years in prison does not have to worry about their ability to live in public housing. That is, the ability of non-incarcerated men to work, have licenses and permits, to vote, to receive public benefits or live in public housing, has direct impacts on their family, and this is particularly so in communities where disproportionate numbers of non-incarcerated men have criminal records.

When he was President of the National District Attorneys Association, Robert Johnson wrote that prosecuting a parent who had committed even a misdemeanor offense against a child might result in deportation of the parent, and impoverishment or de facto deportation of the family, including the victim: In order the save the family, the law destroyed it.[21] Many women as well as men would say "no thanks" and Montes's feminist judgment would ensure that their voices are heard.

[18] Gabriel J. Chin, *Race, the War on Drugs, and the Collateral Consequences of Criminal Conviction*, 6 J. GENDER RACE JUST. 253 (2002).
[19] Vivian Berger, *Man's Trial, Woman's Tribulation: Rape Cases in the Courtroom*, 77 COLUM. L. REV. 1, 3 (1977).
[20] E. Ann Carson, *Prisoners in 2020 – Statistical Tables*, Bureau of Justice Statistics (Dec. 2021, NCJ 302776).
[21] Robert M.A. Johnson, *Collateral Consequences*, 35 THE PROSECUTOR 5 (May/June 2001).

WHY WE NEED REBELLIOUS LAWYERING: A PERSONAL
NARRATIVE AND PRACTICAL ARGUMENT

In the feminist tradition of narrative, I want to share some personal experiences that have colored my view of Professor Montes' opinion.[22] Reform of collateral consequences has been a central project of my professional life, so I cannot and will not resist supporting Montes's analysis with my own experiences.

After graduating from law school, I worked at a large, well-known law firm in a big city. From my own experiences, and those of classmates and colleagues, I know that when a good law firm represents a client, they consider all aspects and implications of the case. They do not limit themselves to "direct consequences" of the legal action or regulatory proceeding, but also consider second or third order possibilities. They do not limit themselves to automatic consequences, but also consider discretionary or contingent events. This is because as lawyers, they want to help their clients. Put another way, good lawyers, including lawyers representing business and rich people in civil cases, are "holistic,"[23] thinking about the goals and welfare of the client, not necessarily the narrow, technical legal problem. Clients of big firms, clients of any good lawyer, get the "rebellious lawyering" Montes calls for. Clients are taken seriously, lawyers try to understand their needs and goals in all of their complexity, and lawyers seek outcomes that the client rather than the lawyer sees as desirable. There is, in the law, no equivalent to the idea that "the operation was a success, but the patient died." It would not be considered good or acceptable representation for the law firm of White & Shoe to negotiate a settlement of a criminal, civil or regulatory matter with minimal "direct" consequences – say a $50,000 fine – and then have the client fold because as a result they lost a license or registration necessary to do business.

Having learned that lawyers were supposed to look out for the legal interests of their clients, I had a rude awakening when I joined the Criminal Appeals Bureau of the Legal Aid Society of New York in 1992. Even before the harsh innovations in federal immigration law which were to come, we had many noncitizen clients who faced possible adverse immigration consequences based on criminal convictions. Shades of *Padilla*, I was assigned a client whose lawyer had not warned him about the possible immigration consequences of his plea. But the law was adverse, and the powers that be forbade me to raise the issue for the client. My case, for a variety of reasons, was unlikely to have become *Padilla* only much earlier.

Nevertheless, one way the law changes is that courts are presented with arguments about injustice, again and again. Normally the way to get a legal issue to the U.S. Supreme Court is to raise the issue below, ideally, again and again so the Court

---

[22] *See, e.g.,* Carrie Menkel-Meadow, *Forward: Telling Stories in School: Using Case Studies and Stories to Teach Legal Ethics,* 69 FORDHAM L. REV. 787, 816 n.3 (2000); Robin West, The Word on Trial, 35 WM. MARY L. REV. 1101, 1113 (1994).

[23] *See, e.g.,* Michael Pinard, *Broadening the Holistic Mindset: Incorporating Collateral Consequences and Reentry into Criminal Defense Lawyering,* 31 FORDHAM URB. L. J. 1067 (2004).

sees that it is important. The difference between working at a private firm and working for poor people was driven home quite clearly to me. At the firm, we tried to win every single case where we had legitimate and just arguments.

Of course, big firms typically have more resources for paying clients than do public defenders appointed for indigent clients. But the basis of the rule that collateral consequences were none of defense counsel's concern, the supposition that it is impossible or even impractical for public defenders to offer such advice, is problematic for several reasons. First, what a monumental indictment of our legal system to say that lawyers cannot determine the collateral consequences of a criminal conviction. Is our law really so expansive and baroque that the implications of a criminal judgment are simply mysterious? It should not be, and, of course, is not.

To be sure, the law of immigration, public benefits, regulated industries, and other areas from which collateral consequences arise may be complex. However, that complexity has not prevented the states and the federal government from creating crimes in these areas, and, when a person accused of violating one of them is indigent, appointing ordinary defender agencies and individual defense attorneys to represent them. When it comes to putting people in prison, the system apparently has no doubt that ordinary lawyers are capable of figuring things out. Only when the argument was that lawyers should help clients were defense lawyers imagined to be incompetent to take on the task.

In addition, if lawyers, even public interest lawyers, are obliged to come up with information, it will not be the case that, for example, every public defender in North Carolina will wake up each morning and start looking at Section 1 of Title 1 of the North Carolina Code to locate collateral consequences. Instead, just as most jurisdictions prepare pattern jury instructions so lawyers and judges at least have a start, groups will collect and share lists and charts of collateral consequences, summarizing what they are, how they are triggered, and avoided.[24] Thus, while Montes is right to observe in her opinion that the "task [of advising about consequences of convictions] is not unreasonable because it is difficult," I am not convinced that it would be a difficult task once it is recognized as a routine duty.

Montes rightly argues that a distinction between direct and collateral consequences of a conviction is illusory. It has long been clear that the fancied distinction between criminal and civil consequences was nonexistent, at least to this extent: There were many examples of plea bargains and sentences which were affected by collateral consequences.[25] That is, injecting collateral consequences into a negotiation could influence the charge or sentence a prosecutor was willing to agree to. Accordingly,

---

[24] Thus, defense attorney Kara Hartzler wrote *Surviving Padilla: A Defender's Guide to Advising Non-Citizens on the Immigration Consequences of Criminal Convictions* (2011). For a list of collected collateral consequence inventories, see Compilations & inventories | Collateral Consequences Resource Center (ccresourcecenter.org).

[25] For a discussion of how immigration status can affect the traditional criminal process, see Gabriel J. Chin, *Quasi-Crime and Quasi-Punishment: Criminal Process Effects of Immigration Status*, 58 UCLA L. Rev. 1417 (2011).

any lawyer silly enough to accept the view of courts that a criminal prosecution was one thing, collateral consequences another, would be unilaterally discarding tools which could help get a better plea. Moreover, since so much of criminal defense practice is plea bargaining, it's foolhardy to believe that competent criminal defense attorneys see civil consequences of convictions as outside of their purview.

For these and other reasons, I was certain that the law before *Padilla* was not only unjust, but wrong.[26] Again, just as lawyers in civil practice ordinarily consider all legal implications of their advice, there is simply nothing in the text of the Sixth Amendment or any other law which arbitrarily carves out legal areas relevant to an outcome for a client in which a defense attorney need not or should not go. The Supreme Court has never held that criminal defendants are to be offered a lesser simulacrum of representation, by lawyers who have been hobbled or restrained from the normal obligation of offering legal advice on the legal consequences of legal actions.

The movement described above that set the stage for *Padilla* continues with respect to collateral consequences beyond immigration. In her opinion for this volume, Montes necessarily wrote from the perspective of the judiciary. A decade after *Padilla*, her imagined opinion goes farther than courts have been willing to go. So far, the courts have not done a great deal to advance their conceptualization of collateral consequences; the Supreme Court, for example, has not returned to *Padilla* other than to hold that it was not retroactive.[27] But the Court is not the only actor in the legal domain; sometimes it is not even the most effective, even if it has a view as broad as that of Montes.

For lawyers on the ground who struggle with the complexities of collateral consequences, Margaret Colgate Love started a nonprofit, the Collateral Consequences Resource Center (CCRC), to collect and disseminate information about collateral consequences, their relief, and reform. I serve on the board. The CCRC highlights the nonjudicial ways that collateral consequences can be alleviated and shows that *Padilla* is in a sense anachronistic despite its recency. The CCRC's reports depict a legal landscape which, with little judicial leadership, is reevaluating the role of collateral consequences in the law.

A 2017 report described remarkable progress by legislatures in ameliorating collateral consequences in a range of ways.[28] The latest 2022 report shows that the trends continue.[29]

---

[26] Gabriel J. Chin & Richard W. Holmes, Jr., *Effective Assistance of Counsel and the Consequences of Guilty Pleas*, 87 CORNELL L. REV. 697 (2002).

[27] Chaidez v. United States, 568 U.S. 342 (2013).

[28] COLLATERAL CONSEQUENCES RESOURCE CENTER, FOUR YEARS OF SECOND CHANCE REFORMS, 2013–2016 2–3 (2017). For example, almost all states have enacted reforms that prohibit employers from inquiring into an applicant's criminal history during the initial stages of the application process, a third of the states have expanded expungement and sealing authorities, and the availability and effect of deferred adjudication and diversion mechanisms has increased.

[29] Margaret Love & David Schlussel, FROM REENTRY TO REINTEGRATION: CRIMINAL RECORD REFORMS IN 2021 2 (2022) ("Overall, the productivity of state legislatures in 2021 mirrors their performance in 2019, itself a year that broke every record.").

This is not to say that a Supreme Court opinion like Montes's would be irrelevant. To be sure, courts should accept the reality on the ground that it is essential that collateral consequences be recognized as part of the criminal justice structure, and that defense lawyers have an important role to play not only in helping their clients dispose of criminal charges but in moving on with their lives afterwards. But it may well be more important that reintegration be recognized as important operationally than as a matter of judicial doctrine. It is better for the system to have a strong norm that it has a responsibility for collateral consequences and reintegration, and weak law, rather than the opposite.

PADILLA vs. KENTUCKY, 559 U.S. 356 (2010)

Justice H. Marissa Montes, concurring in the judgment.

I concur with the court's judgment that the Sixth Amendment requires defense counsel to advise a client whether a plea carries the risk of deportation. I write separately because, in my opinion, the court falls short by failing to recognize that its holding cannot be confined to immigration consequences of criminal convictions. Rather, the principle must extend to other consequences of conviction that significantly impact the livelihood of the accused irrespective of their immigration status.

The majority provides historical context for the intersectionality between immigration status and criminal prosecution. It goes into depth as to how Congress has expanded this country's immigration laws to purposefully "raise the stakes of a noncitizen's criminal conviction" to the point where, in some instances, the consequence of deportation is triggered the moment the noncitizen pleads guilty to a specified crime. *Padilla v. Kentucky*, 559 U.S. 356 (2010). The court depends on this ever-growing connection to justify its holding that defense counsel must inform their clients of potential adverse immigration consequences of a guilty plea.

But nothing about the Court's logic would limit the Sixth Amendment duty of counsel to advise to only our immigration laws. Rather, this same result must follow in other intersections where a criminal conviction can trigger drastic consequences. The list of such so-called "collateral consequences" is long,[30] and includes the ability to vote, access to public benefits, loss of employment opportunities and even access to higher education. *See* Elizabeth Hull & John Conyers, THE DISENFRANCHISEMENT OF EX-FELONS (2006). These collateral consequences affect citizens and noncitizens alike. And like deportation, which can separate families and prevent access to public benefits and employment opportunities, criminal convictions can carry those same results. This makes plain that a

---

[30] For the sake of simplicity, I use the familiar term "collateral consequence" throughout this opinion, even though I argue that many such consequences are actually direct consequences and should be analyzed as such.

much more comprehensive framework for dealing with collateral consequences as part of the criminal justice system is needed.

It is important that we recognize the historical context we currently live in: the era of over policing, abuse of prosecutorial discretion, and mass incarceration. It would be willfully ignorant to not acknowledge how each has influenced the growth in the number of U.S. residents affected by collateral consequences of criminal convictions. The United States currently has the largest incarcerated population in the world and an even larger number of individuals with convictions. *See* Jennifer Warren, *One in 100: Behind Bars in America 2008*, Pew Center on the United States 35 Table A-7 (2008) (comparing the inmate population of the United States with that of other countries by total inmate population, as well as by inmates per 100,000 residents). Our nation's focus on criminalization is not attributed to a rise in violent crime, but to changes in state and federal laws affecting sentencing, incentives for law enforcement agencies to make arrests, and incentives for prosecutors to overcharge crimes. *See* Marc Mauer, *The Causes and Consequences of Prison Growth in the United States*, 3 PUNISHMENT & SOCIETY 1, 9–20 (2001). This significantly increased the number of people charged and convicted of felonies. As a result of one such change – the War on Drugs, which concentrated police and prosecutorial resources on low-level drug offenders – from 1980 to 1998 alone, there were 1.6 million drug related convictions in the country. Many of those convicted faced mandatory sentencing penalties. *See id.* at 11.

The War on Drugs is only one example, part of a larger pattern of overcriminalization. Moreover, these shifts particularly impacted women and people of color. For instance, between 1986 and 1999, the number of women incarcerated in state facilities for drug-related offenses increased by 888 percent, far outpacing the rate of growth in the number of men imprisoned for similar conduct. By 2003, fifty-eight percent of all women in federal prison were convicted of drug offenses. Marc Mauer et al., *Gender and Justice: Women, Drugs and Sentencing Policy*, The Sentencing Project (1999). Women of color have disproportionately been impacted by this trend. Women of all races use drugs at approximately the same rate, but women of color are arrested and imprisoned at much higher rates. *See* National Institute on Drug Abuse, *Drug use Among Racial/Ethnic Minorities*, NIH Publication No. 03-3888 (1995) (revised 2003). Since 1986, African American women's incarceration rates for all crimes, largely driven by drug convictions, have increased by 800 percent, compared to an increase of 400 percent for women of all races. Many of these women were unwittingly, unknowingly, or only peripherally involved in drug related activities based on charges related to association and conspiracy. Lenora Lapidus, et al. *Caught in the Net: The Impact of Drug Policies on Women and Families*, ACLU Drug Law Reform Project (2005), www.aclu.org/caught-net-impact-drug-policies-women-and-families/. This widening net has had the effect of capturing more women, particularly women in relationships, some of which are abusive, with partners or family members who use or sell drugs. In addition, it has ensnared women who turn to the drug trade to supplement their family incomes in the absence of living wage jobs. *Id.*

I emphasize these numbers to show that when considering the duties of counsel under the Sixth Amendment, we must take into account the racism, classism, sexism, and overall discrimination that plague our criminal system. Collateral consequences affect a large number of US residents, most of whom hail from vulnerable communities that the United States has historically disenfranchised. The Court has classified noncitizens as a particularly vulnerable group due to dramatic changes in immigration law that have raised the stakes of a criminal conviction, and hence, rightfully interprets the Sixth Amendment to require advisal as to the collateral consequence of deportation. *Padilla*, 559 U.S. at 364. Yet, noncitizens are not the only vulnerable group targeted by our criminal system, nor are they the only ones who face severe collateral consequences. A proper analysis of *Strickland v. Washington*, 466 U.S. 668 (1984) demands that the Sixth Amendment duty to advise apply not just to deportation but to all significant collateral consequences.[31]

I

The Breadth of Collateral Consequences of Criminal Convictions

As prosecutions and incarceration have increased, so have the number, variety, and severity of collateral consequences suffered by defendants. These "invisible punishments" that accompany a sentence can result in the denial of a host of rights, privileges, and benefits. Dorothy E. Roberts, *The Social and Moral Cost of Mass Incarceration in African American Communities*, 56 STAN. L. REV. 1271, 1291 (2004). These consequences can touch upon every important area of a convicted person's life. Jenny Roberts, *Ignorance Is Effectively Bliss: Collateral Consequences, Silence, and Misinformation in the Guilty-Plea Process*, 95 IOWA L. REV. 119 (2009). Often unbeknownst to the offender, a conviction may make them ineligible for federally funded health and welfare benefits, food stamps, public housing and federal educational assistance. 21 U.S.C. § 862(a); 42 U.S.C. § 1437d(l)(6); 20 U.S.C. § 1091(r)(1). They also may trigger the automatic suspension of their driver's licenses. Cal. Veh. Code § 13200. They may make them ineligible for certain employment and professional licenses. N.Y. Unconsolidated Laws § 9821(e); N.Y. Real Prop. § 440-a; N.Y. Exec. Law § 435(2)(c)(l). In some instances, they may not be permitted to enlist in the military or possess a firearm. 10 U.S.C. § 504(a); 18 U.S.C. § 922. They may even lose their constitutional right to vote. *See, e.g.*, Ala. Const. Art. VIII, § 177(b).

---

[31] In *Strickland*, the Supreme Court held that the Sixth Amendment includes a defendant's right to effective assistance of counsel. The Court established that, to demonstrate a constitutional deficiency regarding effective assistance, (1) an attorney's representation must fall "below an objective standard of reasonableness" and (2) there must be a "reasonable probability that, but for counsel's unprofessional errors, the result of the proceeding would have been different." Strickland, 466 U.S. at 694.

Like the consequence of deportation, many of these collateral consequences flow automatically from conviction. Collateral consequences can be avoided through the plea-negation process. A criminal defense attorney aware of the collateral consequence landscape for an individual defendant can urge a prosecutor to agree to a plea that will not trigger a collateral consequence. Since these consequences may be more long-lasting and impactful than even a prison sentence, the duty of effective assistance of counsel must evolve to include a duty to affirmatively advise as to these consequences. A proper analysis of the first prong under *Strickland* would have yielded such a finding.

II

Strickland *Effective Assistance of Counsel Analysis*

Under *Strickland*, to demonstrate a constitutional deficiency regarding effective assistance of counsel (1) an attorney's representation must fall "below an objective standard of reasonableness" and (2) there must be "a reasonable probability that, but for counsel's unprofessional errors, the result of the proceeding would have been different." *Strickland*, 466 U.S. at 694. Like the majority opinion, I will my limit discussion here to the first factor.

A

Objectively Reasonable Defense Counsel

Strickland's first prong of constitutional deficiency is necessarily linked to the practice and expectations of the legal community. It asks whether counsel's conduct falls within the wide range of reasonable professional assistance. *Id.*, at 690. As such, "the proper measure of attorney performance remains simple reasonableness under prevailing norms." *Id.*, at 688. The Court has long relied on "prevailing norms of practice as those reflected in American Bar Association standards and the like ... as guides to determining what is reasonable ..." *Padilla*, 559 U.S. at 367. These are only to serve as guides and not inexorable commands. *Strickland*, 466 U.S. at 688; *see also Bobby v. Van Hook*, 558 U.S. 4 (2009) (per curiam).

The longstanding position of the federal courts has been that reasonable defense counsel generally needs to advise a client about only the direct consequences of a criminal conviction. *United States v. Gonzalez*, 202 F. 3rd 20 (1st Cir. 2000). As the majority here states, the Supreme Court has never distinguished between direct and collateral consequences in defining the scope of "reasonable professional assistance" required under *Strickland*. Instead, the majority states that such a distinction is not necessary to decide this case since deportation is neither direct nor collateral, but in its own "unique" category. *Padilla*, 559 U.S. at 357. The majority then uses the supposed special nature of deportation as partial grounds to require defense counsel to advise defendants about it as a potential consequence and to limit its rule to deportation. The majority's evasion of this issue places many defendants' Sixth Amendment right in jeopardy. The majority should have seized this opportunity to recognize that there is no meaningful Sixth Amendment distinction between direct consequences like prison and probation, and the many collateral consequences that flow directly from a criminal conviction. Put another way, nonsentence consequences, such as deportation, are in fact direct consequences of criminal convictions. As such, properly understood, the Sixth Amendment requires that defense counsel advise their clients as to both sentence and nonsentence consequences of significance that result from a conviction.

B

The Sixth Amendment Requires Counsel to Advise Their
Client of Any Collateral Consequence of Significance

Scholars have written extensively about the need for the Fifth and Sixth Amendments to catch up to the reality of the effects that criminal convictions have on the accused, their families, and greater communities. The work of one such scholar, Professor Jenny Roberts, inspired the rule I propose today of (1) eliminating the artificial divide between direct and collateral consequences and (2) requiring defense counsel to advise defendants as to any significant consequence resulting from a conviction. This rule can be practically implemented by defense counsel and will protect the constitutional values surrounding guilty pleas, including the right to an informed, voluntary process and the assistance of an effective lawyer. Jenny Roberts, *Ignorance Is Effectively Bliss, supra.* at 125.

There is no set definition of what is a "direct consequence" for purposes of the Sixth Amendment right to effective assistance of counsel. Lower courts have grappled with the concept and have essentially defined it as penal sanctions such as jail or prison time, and any probationary period or a fine which result from the conviction. *See id.*, at 119. This definition is insufficient as it omits drastic nonsentence collateral consequences triggered the moment a defendant enters a plea or is convicted. The majority here made this connection in regard to deportation by acknowledging how "recent changes in our immigration law have made removal nearly an automatic result for a broad class of noncitizen offenders," and thus, making it "most difficult to divorce the penalty from the conviction." *Padilla*, 559 U.S. at 357.

In that regard, though, there's nothing unique about deportation. The inability to divorce a collateral consequence from a conviction *is* what makes it a direct consequence. Thus, it should be incumbent on defense counsel to inform their client of *all* collateral consequences that may result from a criminal conviction. Doing so would protect the constitutional and ethical values that underlie a defendant's

right to decide whether to plead guilty based on full knowledge of a material consequence See Jenny Roberts, *Ignorance Is Effectively Bliss, supra*, at 121.

Though I remain firm in this position, I must acknowledge the constraints of
public defense counsel within our legal system. Nationwide, about eighty percent
of defendants cannot afford to hire an attorney and depend on state and federally
funded defense counsel. *Id.* at 147. Public defenders work tirelessly to provide adequate representation while managing crushing caseloads with limited resources.
Thus, imposing the additional requirement of advisement as to all collateral
consequences may be burdensome. Regardless, defense counsel must meet their
responsibility under the Sixth Amendment. Therefore, I would hold that they must
affirmatively warn their clients as to *significant consequences* of a conviction. This
rule coincides with the majority in recognizing that there may be instances where
a defendant would rather suffer a greater penal punishment than be handed a collateral consequence that could potentially affect an important area of her life for
perpetuity.

I propose a two-part test to determine when a consequence is significant. First,
counsel must advise as to any consequence that is significant or severe. If a reasonable person would consider a consequence as so severe to take into consideration
when deciding to enter a guilty plea, defense counsel must advise as to that consequence. Second, even where the consequence would not be severe under the
reasonable person standard, a consequence is significant if it is of particular importance to a client. This second factor must be determined on an individual basis. For
example, the loss of a driver's license may not be considered significant to someone
living in New York City who can readily access public transportation, but might be
very significant to someone living in a rural town in South Carolina who relies on
a vehicle for getting to work and accessing medical care. Though this factor may
seem daunting, it requires counsel to do no more than engage in a client interview
to determine collateral consequences of concern.

C

Deportation Is a Significant Consequence

Applied to deportation, the analysis is simple. As the majority recognizes, and this
Court has recognized for over 100 years, deportation is a severe consequence. *Fong
Yue Ting v. United States*, 149 U.S. 698, 740 (1893). A reasonable person would view
this consequence as severe enough that they must take it into consideration at the
time of deciding to enter a plea.

In addition, the facts in *Padilla* show how the second prong would lead to the
same conclusion. The petitioner, Jose Padilla, a Honduran national, has been a lawful permanent resident of the United States for more than forty years. *Padilla*, 559
U.S. at 356. He served in the Armed Forces during the Vietnam War, has established

a family, and is employed as a truck driver. *Id.* Given Padilla's life circumstance – a longtime resident with decades of established ties to the United States – counsel should have quickly recognized that the threat of deportation would be one of importance to him. In fact, Padilla affirmatively vocalized the importance of avoiding deportation to his counsel, and brought this claim forward on the basis that he would not have entered a guilty plea had he been properly advised.

D

The Possibility of Civil Confinement as a Collateral Consequence Can Be of Significance to a Defendant

Deportation is not the only immigration related consequence that can be classified as either severe or of particular importance. A reasonable person would consider the potential for civil confinement a significant collateral consequence. This consequence can impact defendants in a variety of ways, but is one that is often faced by noncitizens. Criminal convictions can cause noncitizen defendants to be subjected to mandatory immigration detention upon the completion of their criminal sentences. 8 U.S.C. § 1226. Mandatory detention is considered a form of civil confinement, but under conditions that are on par to criminal imprisonment. *See* Shirin Sinnar, *Patriotic or Unconstitutional? The Mandatory Detention of Aliens Under the USA Patriot Act,* 55 STAN. L. REV. 1419 (2003).

Immigrant detainees subjected to mandatory detention are usually disqualified from seeking bond and must remain in detention for the duration of their immigration proceedings, which often can take years. *Id.* When deciding to enter a plea, noncitizen defendants have a right to be informed of the possibility of their liberty being infringed upon after the completion of their criminal sentence.

E

The Sixth Amendment Requires Advisals Regarding Significant Consequences Outside the Scope of Immigration, Such as Those Impacting Family Unity

There are many other collateral consequences that, under my rule, would trigger a duty to advise. They include disenfranchisement, the denial of public housing, and the loss of employment opportunities. I write here in detail about one: the impact of convictions on family unity. I highlight this consequence specifically to draw a parallel to the consequence of deportation as an assault on a core American value: that of family unity. The majority notes that deportation threatens family unity, and uses that fact to stress why counsel must inform their client of the risk when considering a guilty plea. *Padilla,* 559 U.S. at 375 (noting the "concomitant impact of deportation on families living lawfully in this country"). Deportation is not the only consequence of a criminal conviction that causes harm to and separates families in the United States. Prolonged prison sentences and ever expanding collateral consequences have devastating impacts on American families. Given the disproportionate incarceration of parents of color and the rise of African American women in federal and state prison, this impact falls heavily on families of color. See Lenora Lapidus, et al., *Caught in the Net: The Impact of Drug Policies on Women and Families*, ACLU Drug Law Reform project (2005). Like those who have been deported, individuals who face imprisonment are forced to leave their homes, are separated from their families, and lose the ability to provide their families with economic and emotional support. In some instances, incarceration can lead to the permanent termination of parental rights. Under my two-factor test, the Sixth Amendment duty to advise would include family unity consequences of conviction.

In 1997, Congress passed and President Clinton signed into law the Adoption and Safe Families Act ("ASFA"). Pub. L. No. 105-89, 111 Stat. 2115 (1997) (codified in noncontiguous sections of 42 U.S.C.). ASFA was intended to reduce the length of time children spend in foster care, primarily by quickening the filing of termination of parental rights petitions to facilitate adoptions. As such, it presented a serious threat to family unity and parental rights. See Antoinette Greenaway, *When Neutral Policies Aren't So Neutral: Increasing Incarceration Rates and the Effect of the Adoption and Safe Families Act of 1997 on the Parental Rights of African-American Women*, 17 NAT'L BLACK. L.J. 247, 258 (2004). Once a child has been in foster care for fifteen of the most recent twenty-two months, ASFA requires the state to file a petition to terminate parental rights. 42 U.S.C § 629. The usual grounds for termination include abandonment, permanent neglect, mental illness, and severe or repeated abuse. ASFA has an unequal effect on children of incarcerated parents. See Greenaway, *supra*, at 258. The majority of United States prisoners are parents to minor children. Christopher Mumola, *Incarcerated Parents and Their Children* 1 (2000). Among federal prisoners fifty-five percent of fathers and eighty-four percent of mothers lived with their children prior to incarceration. *Id.* at 3 table 4. Out of this number, eighty percent of incarcerated mothers were single parents. *Id.* at 4 table 5. Many of these parents are serving lengthy prison sentences and will consequently face termination of rights based on abandonment or permanent neglect. See Greenaway, *supra* at 260–61. Once these rights are severed, children are placed for adoption and parents face an almost impossible battle to reunite with their children. In just five years following its enaction, ASFA caused a 250 percent increase in the number of parents who had their parental rights terminated while experiencing incarceration. Philip M. Genty, *Damage to Family Relationships As A Collateral Consequence of Parental Incarceration*, 30 FORDHAM URB. L.J. 1671, 1678 (2003).

The AFSA clock speeding up termination of parental rights petitions is not the only reason AFSA has increased the impact of convictions on family unity. Even where termination has not been completed during a period of incarceration, to reunify with their children, parents returning from prison must demonstrate that they can adequately care and provide for their children. But little help is available to parents in finding the suitable housing, employment and child care, that child welfare authorities require before permitting reunification. Jeremy Travis et al., *Families Left Behind: The Hidden Costs of Incarceration and Reentry*, Urban Institute 8 (2005), www.urban.org/research/publication/families-left-behind/. Indeed, ASFA sets out circumstances under which the government is relieved from its presumptive burden to make "reasonable efforts" to provide services and assistance that would help reunite parents with their removed children. One such instance when "reasonable efforts" are not required is where the parent has been convicted of certain criminal offenses. 42 U.S.C § 671(a)(15)(D). States have even broader provisions. For example, in Kentucky, parental incarceration whatever the underlying conviction can relieve the state of the duty to make reasonable efforts to reunify parent and child. Ky. Rev. Stat. Ann. § 600.020(2)(b), 610.127.

In my view, any reasonable parent would consider possible termination of parental rights as severe, and as a consequence they would weigh carefully when deciding to enter a guilty plea. The consequence of family separation affects the parent, family unit and the child. Immediate effects on children can include feelings of shame, social stigma, weakened ties to the parent, poor school performance, increased delinquency, and increased risk of abuse or neglect. *Travis, supra,* at 2. The family structure also changes financial relationships, income levels, emotional support systems, and living arrangements. *Id.* at 4. Hence, counsel must advise of *any* consequence that threatens family unity that may be applicable to their client within their respective jurisdiction.

F

Sixth Amendment Professional Norms Analysis Should Include Principles of Rebellious Lawyering

Finally, I write to clarify the "professional norm" component of *Strickland's* reasonableness standard. Under *Strickland,* the "proper measure of an attorney's performance remains simply reasonableness under prevailing professional norms." *Strickland,* 466 U.S. at 688. The American Bar Association's Model Rules of Professional Conduct state that counsel must pursue the interest of the client.[32] Given the proliferation of the consequences of criminal convictions, we can no longer conclude that a criminal sentence is all that is at stake in a criminal proceeding for a criminal defendant. For this reason, counsel needs to approach their

---

[32] "These principles include the lawyer's obligation zealously to protect and pursue a client's legitimate interests, within the bounds of the law, while maintaining a professional, courteous and civil attitude toward all persons involved in the legal system." Model Rules of Professional Conduct: Preamble § 9.

representation in a holistic matter that takes into account all collateral consequences that may be of importance to a client. As the majority here recognizes, sometimes the "most important part of the penalty that may be imposed" on defendants who plead guilty to specified crimes is not the sentence, but another consequence triggered by the conviction. *Padilla*, 559 U.S. at 365. In concluding that defense counsel must advise noncitizen defendants about the consequence of deportation, the majority gives weight to professional norms, including those set forth by American Bar Association ("ABA") and the National Legal Aid and Defender Association. *Id.* at 369. In addition to the norms set by the listed associations, I believe that the principles of rebellious lawyering should also be considered in determining professional norms and reasonableness.

The principles of rebellious lawyering, first developed by Professor Gerald Lopez, maintain that effective lawyers must *work with*, not just on the behalf of, their clients. *See* GERALD L. LOPEZ, REBELLIOUS LAWYERING: ONE CHICANO'S VISION OF PROGRESSIVE LAW PRACTICE 61 (1999). The idea stems from the fact that the client is in the best position to know the impact of a legal decision on their life. Involving a client in the stage of fact gathering and decision-making will improve a lawyer's advocacy by better assuring an identification of, and focus on, the client's preferred outcome. The practice of rebellious lawyering was created as a response to antiquated traditional lawyering models that failed to adapt to the growing crossover of our laws and recognize the importance of client empowerment. Traditional lawyering models center power and knowledge in attorneys and do little, if anything, to encourage lawyers to learn how formal changes in law penetrate the lives of the clients they serve. Rebellious lawyering rejects the continued subordination of clients in the attorney-client relationship by recognizing clients as collaborators. This requires lawyers to take into consideration their clients' experiences and informed judgments. This is particularly important for clients who are from historically marginalized backgrounds like those who have been disproportionately impacted by our criminal justice system.

The limitations of the traditional models are apparent in the facts of this case. Padilla's attorney assumed he knew what was best in striking a plea deal. He failed to adequately take into account Padilla's experience as a noncitizen and Padilla's concern about a conviction potentially triggering deportation and severely affecting his life. Counsel's willful ignorance went as far as causing him to misadvise Padilla as to the immigration consequences. Rebellious lawyering seeks to change this narrative by forcing lawyers to acknowledge that power and knowledge in an attorney client relationship runs in both directions. *Id.*, at 59. The reasonable lawyer does not limit herself to just knowledge of the law. Instead, she must be willing to learn from her clients, who are better able to assess the tolls that litigation and the impact a conviction may have on their finances, emotions, family, and community. *Id.*, at 50. Only after truly taking the time to understand their client's situation, may an attorney be effective in counseling and developing legal strategies that are best suited to protect that client's interest. Counsel must integrate their clients and empower them to engage in their own advocacy and this can only be done if they are fully aware as to how a conviction may impact their life. Though Padilla affirmatively informed his attorney of his concern about deportation, his attorney failed to take the extra rebellious lawyering step of respecting Padilla's situation and thus failed to investigate how a guilty plea could have dire consequences for him. Had he centered the interest of the client, he could have adequately protected or, at least, properly advised him.

The practice of rebellious lawyering is not limited to instances of deportation as a collateral consequence. It applies in any scenario where a client may face a consequence of importance. Employing this strategy also reaps benefits that extend beyond a client's personal life. The collateral consequences imposed on one individual often trickle down and out, impacting the livelihood of their families and communities. Hence, an attorney's action of identifying and advising of collateral consequences of importance can produce greater societal justice.

Rebellious lawyering also recognizes that the law and social structures are continually evolving, and hence, the act of lawyering must evolve to guarantee effective assistance of counsel. *Id.*, at 68. As Professor Lopez notes, nothing social stands still. Institutions, social arrangements, and the strategies deployed to control them inevitably evolve, even while appearing to remain constant. The majority recognizes this continued evolution in regard to our immigration and criminal laws. As public sentiment swings and enforcement priorities change, so too does the likelihood of deportation upon conviction. Recently, for example, many local law enforcement agencies have worked more closely and in coordination with federal immigration authorities to identify and facilitate the deportation of individuals caught up in the criminal justice system, increasing the likelihood of deportation for noncitizens with convictions. *See* U.S. Gov't Accountability Office, *Immigration Enforcement: Better Controls Needed over Program Authorizing State and Local Enforcement of Federal Immigration Laws* 4 (Jan. 2009) (finding that ICE was not properly controlling the program or supervising local actors). A lawyer attuned to the changing system is better equipped to identify and advise clients of collateral consequences that may impact their lives.

The ABA has echoed this same stance in its own standards in regard to the advising of collateral consequences. In its 1997 Standard for Pleas of Guilty, the ABA recognized that the evolving nature of criminal law has caused such an exponential growth in the number of significant potential collateral consequences that defense counsel must be obligated to inform clients about them. The ABA goes on to state that "to the extent possible defense counsel should determine and advise the defendant, sufficiently in advance of entry of any plea, as to the possible collateral consequences that might ensue from entry of the contemplated plea." The American Bar Association Standards on Pleas of Guilty, Standard 14-3.2(f) (1997). The fact that the ABA reflects rebellious lawyering principles confirms that rebellious lawyering is not a fringe expectation, but a professional norm.

In practice, it may be difficult for defense counsel to inform a client of a comprehensive list of potential collateral consequences given that they are vast, scattered and vary based on criminal conviction. But a task is not unreasonable because it is difficult. The law has created these significant consequences above and beyond incarceration. The law regarding effective assistance of counsel cannot ignore that. The ABA relies on a tenet of rebellious lawyering to overcome this issue by encouraging counsel to *learn* from their clients by taking the necessary step of interviewing their client "to determine what collateral consequences are likely to be important to the client given the client's particular personal circumstances and the charges the clients face." *Id.* The National Legal Aid and Defenders Association's (NALDA) Guidelines for Criminal Defense likewise task defense attorneys with inquiring at the interview stage as to a client's ties to the community and personal necessities, such as: family relationships, immigration status, employment, educational history and health related needs. *Performance Guidelines for Criminal Defense Representation*, National Legal Aid & Defender Association (2006), www.nlada.org/defender-standards/performance-guidelines/black-letter/. Through this line of questioning, defense counsel can easily identify collateral consequences that may affect the personal circumstances of their clients. Counsel then must only take the extra step of advising as to those potential consequences.

CONCLUSION

In all, I agree with the majority that Padilla's attorney's representation fell below an objective standard of reasonableness because of his failure to provide accurate advice regarding the likelihood of deportation resulting from Padilla's conviction. Unlike the majority, I would not limit the duty of counsel to advise to deportation consequences. Rather, I believe that in the interest of justice and in effort to protect the Sixth Amendment constitutional right it applies in all scenarios where a significant collateral consequence is at play. Both history and professional norms properly understood require us to make this finding.

13

Commentary on *Arizona v. United States*, 567 U.S. 387 (2012)

Kristina M. Campbell

Arizona enacted the Support Our Law Enforcement and Safe Neighborhoods Act (also known as S.B. 1070), in April 2010.[1] S.B. 1070 was the most comprehensive state attempt to restrict immigration at the time and gained notoriety for its infamous "Show Me Your Papers" provision.[2] The constitutionality of S.B. 1070 was quickly challenged, and four provisions of the law were enjoined.[3]

Arizona v. United States, decided by the Supreme Court in 2012, followed more than a decade of national litigation regarding the constitutionality of state regulation of immigration. The majority decision, written by Justice Anthony Kennedy, unequivocally held that regulation of immigration was wholly a matter of federal law that may not be usurped by the states.[4]

While the Court's decision in *Arizona* dealt a fatal blow to the controversial "mirror-image" theory of cooperative state enforcement of immigration law,[5] the majority declined to strike down Section 2(B) and ignored the racist context in which the law arose. Indeed, Chief Justice John Roberts began oral argument by getting the Solicitor General arguing the case against the Arizona law for the U.S. government to disclaim any argument based on racial discrimination. By contrast, Professor Annie Lai, writing here as Justice Lai, lays bare in her feminist judgment

---

[1] Ariz. Rev. Stat. Ann. § 11-1051.

[2] Section 2(B) provided that officers who conduct a stop, detention, or arrest must make efforts to verify the person's immigration status if they have "reasonable suspicion" to believe the person is undocumented. § 11-1051(B).

[3] *See* United States v. Arizona, 641 F.3d 339 (9th Cir. 2011).

[4] 567 U.S. 387 (2012) ("Arizona may have understandable frustrations with the problems caused by illegal immigration … but the State may not pursue policies that undermine federal law.").

[5] The "mirror-image" theory argues that states have an "inherent authority" to create and enforce state criminal immigration laws that are based on federal immigration statutes. *See* Kris W. Kobach, *The Quintessential Force Multiplier: The Inherent Authority of Local Police to Make Immigration Arrests*, 69 Alb. L. Rev. 179 (2006); ACLU, "OLC Memo on State and Local Law Enforcement of Immigration Laws," Sept. 7, 2005, available at www.aclu.org/press-releases/secret-immigration-enforcement-memo-exposed?redirect=immigrants-rights/secret-immigration-enforcement-memo-exposed.

the patently racist context of S.B. 1070 and brings to the fore the inevitable, and odious, human impact of the law on people of color. Using an antidiscrimination lens, Lai provides a powerful, alternative basis for finding all four challenged provisions of the Arizona law unconstitutional.

ORIGINAL OPINION

Justice Kennedy's majority opinion in *Arizona v. United States* squarely reaffirmed the supremacy of the federal government to legislate immigration matters. In his opinion, Justice Kennedy explained that S.B. 1070's "stated purpose is to 'discourage and deter the unlawful entry and presence of aliens and economic activity by persons unlawfully present in the United States' ... [and t]he law's provisions establish an official state policy of 'attrition through enforcement.'"[6]

The Court considered four provisions of S.B. 1070 that sought to regulate specific conduct of people present in Arizona without legal immigration status and included civil and criminal penalties for violation of these laws. While the most notorious provision of S.B. 1070 – Section 2(B)'s "show me your papers" provision – was upheld by the Court, the majority struck down the other three provisions as unconstitutional on the basis that federal immigration law preempts states from enacting their own immigration regulations.[7]

However, in finding much of the law preempted, the Court side-stepped the opportunity to address the motivation behind state immigration legislation like S.B. 1070. By declining to frame the preemption doctrine in a manner that took into account the discrimination driving state attempts to regulate immigration, the Court in *Arizona* ignored the reality of racial profiling that occurs when law enforcement polices immigrants and people of color. As a result, it also failed to consider the ways in which immigration federalism can be reimagined. Rather than simply affirming the status quo – that the federal government has "undoubted power over the subject of immigration and the status of aliens"– the Court missed the opportunity to honor the promise of our Constitution to fulfill "the perceptions and expectations of aliens in this country who seek the full protection of its laws" by emphasizing the antidiscrimination aspect of preemption doctrine.[8]

As Lai persuasively argues in her feminist judgment, preemption is not just about federal supremacy over the states in a given field. Drawing on the arguments of other legal scholars, she shows that "[t]he doctrine of preemption has long had an anti-discrimination component ... [and] the Court cannot ignore this dimension of

---

[6] 567 U.S. at 393.
[7] *Id.*
[8] *Id.* The argument in Lai's dissent about the myth of a comprehensive system for alien registration is discussed in further detail in Nancy Morawetz and Natasha Fernández-Silber, *Immigration Law and the Myth of Comprehensive Registration,"* 48 U.C. Davis L. Rev. 141, 187–90 (2014).

preemption in resolving the issues in this case." By critiquing the majority opinion's failure to put the racial tensions in Arizona surrounding S.B. 1070 into context, Lai highlights the importance of considering the intersectional experiences of immigrants when formulating immigration law and policy in the twenty-first century.

REIGN OF TERROR: SHERIFF JOE ARPAIO
AND THE TEMPLATE FOR S.B. 1070

Lai provides essential background information about the political climate in Arizona surrounding immigration prior to the passage of S.B. 1070 in 2010, when anti-immigrant sentiment combined with the white supremacist philosophies of prominent statewide leaders inflamed the populace and led to support for "attrition through enforcement" rhetoric. No discussion of S.B. 1070 would be complete without additional details about former Maricopa County Sheriff Joe Arpaio. Arpaio, long notorious for being the self-proclaimed "America's Toughest Sheriff," would reach an unprecedented level of global infamy as result of his cruel treatment of immigrants and people of color, in particular Latinx individuals, during his long reign.[9] As Lai demonstrates, the *Arizona* majority opinion's narrow approach to preemption represents a lost opportunity to address the antidiscrimination components of preemption theory that could have been used to condemn the tactics of Sheriff Arpaio.

Sheriff Arpaio's unlawful and racially discriminatory attempts to engage in local enforcement of immigration law in Arizona long pre-dated the passage of S.B. 1070 and served as a roadmap for the Arizona Legislature in crafting the law. Lai notes that certain Arizona state legislators, such as Russell Pearce, "appeared to be trying to codify Sheriff Arpaio's practices as a model for what law enforcement should be doing statewide." This is one of the reasons why, as destructive as S.B. 1070 was intended to be to the immigrant communities of Arizona, it was painfully reminiscent of previous instances in which communities of color were terrorized by both state and federal law enforcement about their immigration status.[10] By the end of 2005, Arpaio was making local enforcement of immigration law one of his signature issues.[11] Even before

---

[9] *See* Terry Greene Sterling and Jude Joffe-Block, Driving While Brown: Sheriff Joe Arpaio Versus the Latino Resistance (2021); *see also See* "Joe Arpaio: Life as 'America's Toughest Sheriff,'" BBC (Aug. 26, 2017).

[10] *See, e.g.,* David Holthouse, "Minutemen, Other Anti-Immigrant Militia Groups Stake Out Arizona Border," Southern Poverty Law Center Intelligence Report, 2005 Summer Issue (June 27, 2005) ("The night of April 3, armed vigilantes camped along Border Road in a series of watch posts set-up for the Minuteman Project, a month-long action in which revolving casts of 150 to 200 anti-immigration militants wearing cheap plastic 'Undocumented Border Patrol Agent' badges mobilized in southeastern Arizona ... At Station Two, Minuteman volunteers grilled bratwursts and fantasized about murder. 'It should be legal to kill illegals,' said Carl, a 69-year old retired Special Forces veteran who fought in Vietnam .... 'Just shoot 'em on sight. That's my immigration policy recommendation. You break into my country, you die.'").

[11] *See* Greene Sterling Joffe-Block, *supra* note 9, at 51.

gaining notoriety for his highly publicized "crime suppression sweeps," Arpaio was notorious for his "Tent City" jails. These Tent Cities, which were open-air facilities that Arpaio likened to concentration camps, were used to house thousands of individuals in Maricopa County custody.[12] The jails were known for the Sheriff's humiliating, demoralizing, and sadistic treatment of inmates.[13] Although the Tent City jails were not exclusively designed to incarcerate immigrants, in 2010 Arpaio announced his plans to open additional Tent City jails specifically to detain individuals arrested pursuant to the provisions of S.B. 1070, and offered to house individuals in Immigration and Customs Enforcement (ICE) custody in the Tent City jails if the government did not have adequate space to detain them in federal facilities.[14]

In 2007, Maricopa County entered into an agreement[15] with the federal government that allowed Sheriff Arpaio's deputies to assist ICE with the enforcement of immigration law in limited circumstances. Emboldened by his office's cooperation with the federal government, Arpaio created his own local immigration enforcement arm – the Illegal Immigration Interdiction ("Triple I") Unit within the Maricopa County Sheriff's Office – which engaged in vigilante-style enforcement of immigration law in Maricopa County.[16]

Although the agreement between Maricopa County and ICE was revoked in December 2011, Arpaio rapidly became notorious for racially profiling Latinx citizens on the suspicion that they lacked lawful immigration status.[17] A particularly persecuted group during the reign of Sheriff Arpaio was day laborers, who were routinely targeted by Arpaio's "Triple I" Unit on suspicion of being unlawfully present in the United States due to their race, color, and nationality.[18] But one of the men arrested by the "Triple I" Unit in 2007 – Manuel de Jesus Ortega Melendres – would

---

[12] *See* Stephen Lemons, "Joe Arpaio: Tent City a "Concentration Camp." THE PHOENIX NEW TIMES (Aug. 2, 2010) (In 2008 at the Arizona American Italian Club in Phoenix, responding to a comment from the audience wondering when he would start using concentration camps, Arpaio said "I already have a concentration camp.").

[13] *See* Greene Sterling Joffe-Block, *supra* note 9, at 28–29. ("By 1997, more than 560 male inmates lived in Tent City. They shared a total of eight showers, eleven sinks, eight permanent toilets, and twelve portable toilets … Arpaio banned jailhouse coffee, cigarettes, and salt and pepper. Journalists reported how Arpaio served inmates aged green bologna for lunch, cut daily inmate meals down to two, then served unseasoned vegetable proteins instead of meat. He initiated chain gangs as a disciplinary option … Arpaio's greatest stunt may have been requiring inmates to wear pink underwear.").

[14] www.motherjones.com/crime-justice/2010/07/arpaio-arizona-illegal-immigrants-tent-city/.

[15] *See* "Fact Sheet – The 287(g) Program: An Overview." AMERICAN IMMIGRATION COUNCIL (July 8, 2021) ("The 287(g) program is named for Section 287(g) of the Immigration and Nationality Act (INA) and became law as part of the Illegal Immigration Reform and Immigrant Responsibility Act of 1996 (IIRAIRA). Through the 287(g) program, state and local law enforcement officers collaborate with the federal government to enforce federal immigration laws.").

[16] www.globenewswire.com/fr/news-release/2007/10/17/1046633/0/en/Illegal-Immigration-Arrests-and-Crackdown-Follow-Judicial-Watch-Complaint.html.

[17] *See* "DOJ Report Slams Sherriff Joe Arpaio and DHS Restricts 287(g) and Secure Communities Programs," AMERICAN IMMIGRATION COUNCIL (Dec. 15, 2011).

[18] *See* Greene Sterling and Joffe-Block, *supra* note 9, at 97–108.

go on to be the lead plaintiff in the class action lawsuit that helped to end the tyranny of Joe Arpaio against the Latinx population.

ORTEGA MELENDRES, ET AL. v. ARPAIO: AN INTERSECTIONAL CHALLENGE TO WHITE SUPREMACIST LAW ENFORCEMENT

While the Supreme Court in *Arizona* clarified that immigration law is a federal domain, *Arizona's* pre-emption holding did not stop Sheriff Arpaio's attempts to enforce immigration law on the local level in Arizona. Rather, it was ultimately Arpaio's discriminatory pattern and practice of arresting and detaining individuals based on nothing more than the color of their skin that led to the successful class action civil rights suit, *Ortega Melendres, et al., v. Arpaio*,[19] in which the Maricopa County Sheriff's Office was found to have "engaged in racial profiling and unlawful traffic stops of Latinos" after a three-week federal trial in 2012.[20]

The plaintiffs demonstrated at trial that Sheriff Arpaio "acted on racially charged citizen complaints and requests for operations," and that he directed these complaints to his senior staff for law enforcement action.[21] Often, the citizen complaints that Arpaio relied on to direct his deputies to engage in law enforcement activities "criticized people based on little more than the color of their skin or the fact that they were speaking Spanish."[22] The evidence/citizen complaints used by the Sheriff's Office to justify traffic stops are shocking in their racial hostility toward immigrants and the Latinx community in general.[23]

The fact that private citizens felt emboldened to send nakedly racist communications to law enforcement, encouraging (and at times demanding) a law enforcement response based on the color of a person's skin demonstrates the climate of fear that Arpaio created in Maricopa County. Arpaio's "volunteer posse" of private citizens helped him identify and apprehend suspected undocumented immigrants within his jurisdiction and contributed to a rise in vigilantism by individuals who took matters concerning immigration enforcement into their own hands.[24]

In December 2011, U.S. District Judge G. Murray Snow certified the broad class of Latinx citizens impacted by Sheriff Arpaio's pattern and practice of racial profiling in law enforcement, and issued a preliminary injunction prohibiting Arpaio

---

[19] The author was co-counsel in the *Melendres* case in connection with her employment as a Staff Attorney at the Mexican American Legal Defense and Educational Fund (MALDEF) until July 2009.

[20] ACLU, www.aclu.org/cases/ortega-melendres-et-al-v-arpaio-et-al.

[21] *Id.*

[22] *Id.*

[23] *Id.* Examples of racist communications sent to the Sheriff's Office include the following correspondence: "If you have dark skin, then you have dark skin! Unfortunately, that is the look of the Mexican illegal who are here ILLEGALLY [...] They bring their unclean, disrespectful, integrity-less, law breaking selves here [...] I am begging you to come over to the 29thSt/Greenway Pkwy area and round them all up! ... They crawl around here all day and night.").

[24] *See* Greene Sterling and Joffee-Block *supra* note 9, at 53–54.

and his deputies from detaining immigrants who had not committed any crimes and turning them over to ICE. In October 2013, Judge Snow issued an Order that mandated specific changes to Maricopa County Sheriff's Office practices.[25] Among the ordered changes were "audio and video recording of all traffic stops, increased training for and monitoring of sheriff's office employees and the implementation of comprehensive record keeping."[26] Judge Snow also ordered a monitor to ensure that the Sheriff's Office complied with the changes mandated by the Court.[27]

Sheriff Arpaio and his office remained defiant. In May 2016, Judge Snow found Arpaio and his chief deputies in contempt of court for failing to comply with the Court's 2011 preliminary injunction. In his contempt ruling, Judge Snow found that:

> the Defendants have engaged in multiple acts of misconduct, dishonesty, and bad faith with respect to the Plaintiff class and the protection of its rights. They have demonstrated a persistent disregard for the orders of the Court, as well as an intention to violate and manipulate the laws and policies regulating their conduct.[28]

Judge Snow referred Arpaio to the United States Attorney for the District of Arizona for prosecution for criminal contempt of court.[29] The U.S. Attorney in Phoenix declined to prosecute due to an asserted conflict of interest, and referred Judge Snow's recommendation to the Department of Justice in Washington, D.C.[30] Finally, on October 11, 2016, an attorney with the Public Integrity Section in Washington announced that Arpaio would be prosecuted on one count of criminal contempt for violating Judge Snow's 2011 preliminary injunction.[31]

In the end, Joe Arpaio was convicted of criminal contempt of court for his conduct in the *Melendres* litigation, only to later be pardoned by then-President Donald J. Trump.[32] But the bigger lesson to be learned from the attempt to hold accountable Sheriff Arpaio and the Sheriff's Office, in my opinion, is that when the people lead, justice can become a reality.

THE FEMINIST JUDGMENT: PREEMPTION, REIMAGINED

Preemption is the favored litigation route of the government in attacking state regulation of immigration because it is straightforward – the supremacy of federal law over state law in immigration matters is incontrovertible in light of the death of the "mirror-image" theory. Professor Lai's opinion builds on preemption theory in a way that illustrates the importance of incorporating an intersectional approach to

[25] *Supra* note 20.
[26] *Id.*
[27] *Id.*
[28] *Id.*
[29] *See* Greene Sterling and Joffee-Block, *supra* note 9, at 240.
[30] *Id.* at 241–42.
[31] *Id.* at 246–47.
[32] *Id.*

immigration law and policy, explicitly noting the ways in which intersectionality is essential when analyzing the misogynist and white supremacist roots of immigration regulations such as S.B. 1070.

In her feminist judgment, Lai demonstrates how anti-immigrant measures and their discriminatory enforcement practices reflect the ways in which patriarchy and nativism reinforce and validate systems of oppression against historically vulnerable populations. She employs an intersectional analysis to critique how race, gender, and class have been used to both construct and reinforce harmful narratives about immigrant communities. As such, Lai's opinion deftly and convincingly illuminates the ways in which modern immigration law and policy disproportionately impacts women and people of color – and unjustly portrays immigrants as permanent "outsiders" in American society.[33]

In Lai's feminist judgment, we not only receive the historical context for the racial animus behind S.B. 1070, but the human stories of the individuals whose lives, and livelihoods, were harmed by Arizona's long history of anti-immigrant laws and policies. A critical part of the story of S.B. 1070, and a feminist re-imagining of the Court's decision in *Arizona v. United States*, is putting a human face on the persons who were the intended targets of the law. This includes not only recounting the ways in which the Latinx community in Arizona was profiled and victimized, but the ways in which they are heroes.

The story of *Arizona* requires reframing the narrative to include details about how the Latinx residents of the state of Arizona – and Maricopa County in particular – rose up and triumphed against the systems of white supremacy, patriarchy, and misogyny to claim victory in the Article III Courts. In using feminist legal theory and intersectionality to critique the Court's opinion in *Arizona*, Lai weaves the personal stories of women who were impacted by and decided to challenge S.B. 1070 and other anti-immigrant measures. Additionally, the inclusion of these women's stories in Lai's opinion demonstrates the power of using storytelling as a tool for crafting compelling legal arguments.[34] It humanizes the impact of a law that, due to

---

[33] As Kimberlé Crenshaw recently reflected, intersectionality is "a lens, a prism, for seeing the way in which various forms of inequality often operate together and exacerbate each other. We tend to talk about race inequality as separate from inequality based on hender, class, sexuality or immigrant status. What's often missing is how some people are subject to all of these, and the experience is not just the sum of its parts." *See* Katy Steinmetz, "She Coined the Term 'Intersectionality' Over 30 Years Ago. Here's What it Means to Her Today," TIME (Feb. 20, 2020).

[34] *See, e.g.*, MARTHA CHAMALLAS, INTRODUCTION TO FEMINIST LEGAL THEORY (3rd ed. 2013), at 5–6 ("The story of the recognition of sexual harassment is perhaps the best example of the grassroots development of a legal claim grounded in women's experiences … Starting with women's experiences, from women's perspectives, feminists were able to cast sexual behavior in a different light: to argue that what was pleasurable or inconsequential from the harasser's viewpoint was disturbing and serious when seen from the eyes of the target."); *see also* Katharine T. Bartlett, *Feminist Legal Methods*, 103 HARV. L. REV. 289 (1990) (setting forth legal methods that "reflect the status of women as 'outsiders,' who need new ways of challenging and undermining dominant legal conversations and of developing alternative conventions which take better account of women's experiences and needs.").

the complexity of the constitutional arguments in front of the Court, may otherwise get glossed over or lost entirely. Indeed, by infusing her opinion with the first-hand narratives of the brutality and trauma experienced by immigrant women and their families as a result of the unequal and biased enforcement of S.B. 1070, Lai has crafted a powerful feminist judgment that reminds us of the value of centering subjective experiences in order to provide a complete picture of the reasons why the law could not stand.

There are many heroes in the events leading up to *Arizona v. United States* that the Court's majority decision ignored completely. Unlike Lai's dissent, nowhere in the Court's majority opinion is there any recognition of the individuals whose lives were impacted by the passage of S.B. 1070. Aside from Justice Kennedy's brief attempt to wax poetic about the nobility of naturalized citizens' commitment to the responsibilities that come with choosing full membership in the United States, the same men and women whom he extolls as "shar[ing] a common destiny" because of their status as immigrants are erased entirely from his decision.[35] Justice Kennedy states that "[t]he history of the United States is in part made of the stories, talents, and lasting contributions of those who crossed oceans and deserts to come here."[36] However, by failing to include the struggles and the triumphs of the people who are the fabric of our nation's greatness, the *Arizona* Court's decision will be remembered not only for its reaffirmation of the preemption doctrine, but for its failure to take the opportunity to reflect on how the strength and courage of our nation's immigrants can be used to inform an antidiscrimination approach to preemption doctrine.

One of the powerful personal stories affirming Lai's appeal to expand the lens of our preemption analyses going forward is the one belonging to the lead plaintiff in the *Melendres* litigation, Manuel de Jesus Ortega Melendres. Throughout the entirety of the trial captioned with his name, Mr. Ortega Melendres remained silent.[37] It was not until December 2016, as the year came to a close, that Mr. Ortega Melendres finally spoke publicly about the racial profiling lawsuit, what it meant to him, and what he hopes it means for others going forward.[38] As recounted in his interview that month in the *Arizona Republic*:

> Ortega Melendres, now 63, entered the United States with a tourist visa through the Nogales Port of Entry in August of 2007. A month later, he was in the back of a patrol car in Cave Creek, handcuffed, in pain and tormented by the thought that he may never again see his family... "I was thinking a thousand things, that the worst was about to happen. I had heard that the authorities in the United States

---

[35] 567 U.S. at 416.
[36] *Id.*
[37] www.azcentral.com/story/news/local/phoenix/2016/12/26/phoenix-arrest-manuel-melendres-joe-arpaio-profiling-lawsuit/95041534/.
[38] *Id.*

were understanding, that they did not have a tendency to abuse their power. That day, they showed me the complete opposite of what I had heard. That's when the fear began," he said.[39]

Mr. Ortega Melendres is a husband, a father, a teacher, and a church leader.[40] All that was lost the day he was detained in Cave Creek happened not because of what he did or who he is, but because of what he looks like.

As Lai reminds us in her conclusion, "This case comes to us not as a challenge under the Equal Protection Clause but as a challenge under the Supremacy Clause. This is of course a consequence of how the federal government decided to frame its lawsuit." Lai shows how this decision by the Court is a lost opportunity to address the antidiscrimination dimension of the pre-emption doctrine in its majority decision. In the end, Lai demonstrates that we need not – and should not – sacrifice the antidiscrimination lens in our preemption analyses, lest we lose the stories of the real people affected by the law.

The reality of the discriminatory application of immigration law cannot continue to be lost by the erasure of the human experiences behind them. Reimagining pre-emption analysis through the antidiscrimination lens suggested by Lai allows us to buttress theory with reality. In the future, rather than simply reasserting the supremacy of federal law in immigration matters, applying Lai's call to heed the stories of the ways in which unconstitutional state immigration laws are enforced against oppressed communities will, I believe, allow us to move forward toward fulfilling her hope for utilizing "a fuller notion of preemption."

ARIZONA v. UNITED STATES, 567 U.S. 387 (2012)

Justice Annie Lai, concurring in part and dissenting in part.

Two years ago, Arizona captured the attention of the nation when it enacted the Support Our Law Enforcement and Safe Neighborhoods Act, or Senate Bill 1070, as amended by House Bill 2162 ("S.B. 1070"). Upon signing the bill into law, Governor Brewer declared, "[w]e cannot delay while the destruction happening south of our border – our international border – creeps its way north." Statement of Janice Brewer Upon Signing S.B. 1070 (Apr. 23, 2010). She noted, "[t]o my administration, and to me as your governor and as a citizen, there's no higher priority than protecting the citizens of Arizona." *Id.* Immediately, the law drew fury from groups across the country, leading to freedom marches, boycotts, and civil disobedience.[41]

I write separately today to examine more closely the motivations behind Arizona's attempt to enact its own state-level immigration policy and to consider the context

---

[39] *Id.*
[40] *Id.*
[41] *See, e.g.*, Evan Wyoge, *Thousands Take to Phoenix to Protest Arizona's New Immigration Law*, Ariz. Capitol Times (May 29, 2010).

for the public's opposition to the law. While I concur with the Court's decision as to Sections 3, 5(C), and 6 of S.B. 1070, I believe that majority's preemption analysis as to those sections is incomplete without this context and the narratives of those most likely to be impacted by the law. A more complete analysis reveals different rationales for striking down the three challenged provisions. Further, such analysis leads me to dissent from the majority's decision as to Section 2(B) of the law. I would find this provision to be unconstitutional as well.

I

The territory known today as Arizona was ceded by Mexico as part of the Treaty of Guadalupe Hidalgo in 1848 following the Mexican-American War, and subsequently, the Gadsden Purchase of 1854. Eileen M. Luna-Firebaugh, *The Border Crossed Us: Border Crossing Issues of the Indigenous Peoples of the Americas*, 17:1 Wíačzo Ša Rev. 159, 164, 166 (2002). When the new border was drawn, the population of the region was comprised almost entirely of indigenous peoples and people of Mexican descent. In fact, the international border divided what had previously been unified indigenous homelands, leaving a number of indigenous communities with no right of free passage. *Id.*

Although individuals of Mexican descent were given the choice to stay and become U.S. citizens, over the subsequent decades, they were eventually relegated to a type of second-class status by Anglo-Americans who came to the region intending to seize political and economic power. Eric V. Meeks, BORDER CITIZENS: THE MAKING OF INDIANS, MEXICANS, AND ANGLOS IN ARIZONA 11, 25–43 (2007). Repeated waves of nativism, particularly during periods of economic insecurity, led to a hardening of attitudes toward Mexicans and Mexican-Americans throughout the twentieth century, similar to what the country had seen with Asian immigrants starting at the end of the nineteenth century. *See* Mae Ngai, IMPOSSIBLE SUBJECTS: ILLEGAL ALIENS AND THE MAKING OF MODERN AMERICA, 7–9 (2004).[42]

Despite the many obstacles they faced, Mexican-Americans continued to forge robust communities in Arizona, sometimes even managing to hold political office.[43] But increasing militarization of the border in the 1990s contributed to a shift away from traditional migrant routes from Mexico in California and Texas and toward the Arizonan desert. Wayne A. Cornelius, *Death at the Border: Efficacy and Unintended Consequences of US Immigration Control Policy*, 27:4 Population & Dev. Rev. 661, 667 (2001). As more migrants crossed through the dangerous terrain on their way to other parts of the country, racialized tropes about foreign "hordes" overtaking

---

[42] For a detailed discussion of anti-Asian sentiment in the Arizona Territory, *see* Andrea Pugsley, "AS I KILL THIS CHICKEN SO MAY I BE PUNISHED IF I TELL AN UNTRUTH": Chinese Opposition to Legal Discrimination in Arizona Territory, 44:2 J. ARIZ. HISTORY 171 (2003).

[43] A notable example was the election of Mexican immigrant Raul Castro as governor of Arizona in 1974.

the state re-emerged. Vigilante groups began organizing patrols of the border. *See* Timothy Egan, *Wanted: Border Hoppers. And Some Excitement, Too*, N.Y. Times (Apr. 1, 2005). And enterprising lawmakers, seeing a chance to grow their popularity with constituents, began proposing measures aimed at making life so difficult for undocumented immigrants that they would decide to leave on their own accord.

No lawmaker was more renowned for espousing this strategy of attrition in Arizona than Russell Pearce, a former state senator and S.B. 1070's primary champion. After Pearce was first elected to the Arizona House in 2000, he introduced immigration-related legislation in a wide range of areas, from access to education and eligibility for state-funded benefits to employment verification, the availability of pretrial bail, and local enforcement of immigration laws, among other matters. *See* Kristina Campbell, *The Road to S.B. 1070: How Arizona Became Ground Zero for the Immigrants' Rights Movement and the Continuing Struggle for Civil Rights in America*, 14 Harv. Latino L. Rev. 1, 3–15 (2011). While Pearce's initial efforts were not successful, the tide began to change in 2004 with passage of Proposition 200, the Arizona Taxpayer and Citizenship Protection Act. Proposition 200 required Arizonans to provide proof of citizenship before they could vote and demanded that state benefits workers report suspected undocumented immigrants to federal immigration officials on pain of criminal prosecution. Ariz. Sec'y of State, 2004 Ballot Propositions: Proposition 200 (2004).

As Pearce gained power in the House, and then later the Senate, some law enforcement officials likewise made a name for themselves "cracking down" on immigrants. Maricopa County Sheriff Joe Arpaio, who previously believed that unlawful presence was not "a serious crime,"[44] realized he was on the wrong political cal side of the issue in 2005 when he took heat for publicly condemning vigilante Patrick Haab after Haab held up a carload of suspected migrants at gunpoint. Jana Bommersbach, *What Happened to Joe Arpaio?*, Phoenix Magazine, 26 (June 2008). By the end of that year, Arpaio emerged as an anti-immigrant crusader. He went on to establish an "illegal immigration hotline" for citizens to call in with tips about possibly undocumented neighbors, oversee workplace raids that resulted in the detention of hundreds of immigrant workers, and carry out regular "crime suppression patrols" or "sweeps" targeting day laborers and other Latinx community members through the use of pretextual traffic stops. A Justice Department expert examining the practices of Arpaio's agency later concluded that they involved "the most egregious racial profiling in the United States that he ha[d] ever ... seen." U.S. Dep't of Justice, United States' Investigation of the Maricopa County Sheriff's Department (hereinafter "DOJ Investigation Report"), 6 (Dec. 15, 2011).

* * *

---

[44] Indeed, as the majority explains, it is not a crime at all. *Arizona*, at 2505.

Likely responding to critics' prognostications that Arizona's S.B. 1070 will also lead
to widespread racial profiling, the Chief Justice's very first question for the United
States at the outset of the argument in this case sought to confirm that the government was not making any allegation about profiling.

> CHIEF JUSTICE ROBERTS: Before you get into what the case is about, I'd like to
> clear up at the outset what it's not about. No part of your argument has to do with
> racial or ethnic profiling, does it? I saw none of that in your brief.

The Solicitor General acquiesced:

> GENERAL VERRILLI: Where—that's correct, Mr. Chief Justice. ... We're not
> making any allegation about racial or ethnic profiling in the case.

Transcript of Oral Argument at 33–34, Arizona v. United States, 132 S. Ct. 2492 (2012)
(No. 11-182).

While it is true that the government's challenge to Arizona's law sounds in preemption, not equal protection, the Solicitor General did not have to answer in
the way he did. The doctrine of preemption has long had an antidiscrimination
component.

In Hines, for example, a case cited repeatedly by the majority, this Court struck
down Pennsylvania's registration law for noncitizens, finding that states could not
enter the field of "alien registration" "in any respect." Arizona, at 2502 (discussing
Hines v. Davidowitz, 312 U.S. 52 (1941)). In our reasoning, we referred to the comprehensive federal registration scheme as the product of a compromise reflecting a
distaste for laws that unnecessarily burdened the individual rights and liberties of
noncitizens and that "singl[ed] out aliens as particularly dangerous or undesirable
groups." 312 U.S. at 69–71. We noted that "the Constitution and our Civil Rights
Act have guaranteed to aliens 'the equal protection of the laws[.]'" Id. at 69 (citing
Yick Wo v. Hopkins, 118 U.S. 356, 369 (1886)). State regulation that compromised
the character and uniformity of the national scheme was therefore impermissible.

In Plyler v. Doe, a rare case where this Court decided to rule on equal protection
grounds instead of preemption, we recognized the close connection between these
two analytical frameworks. 457 U.S. 202, 225–26 (1982). In reaching the conclusion
that Texas's law permitting school districts to deny undocumented children access
to public education violated equal protection, we observed that no identifiable congressional policy supported imposing such a disability on this class of schoolchildren. Id. at 225. In fact, we noted that "the classification reflected in [the Texas
statute] [did] not operate harmoniously within the federal program." Id. at 226.

The relationship between antidiscrimination principles and preemption law has
been recognized and further theorized by legal scholars. See Lucas Guttentag,
Discrimination, Preemption, and Arizona's Immigration Law: A Broader View, 65
Stanford L. Rev. Online 1 (2012) (arguing that preemption doctrine should consider
the effect not only of federal immigration law but of civil rights laws enacted by the

Reconstruction Congress that banned discrimination against immigrants); Hiroshi Motomura, *The Rights of Others: Legal Claims and Immigration Outside the Law*, 59 Duke L. J. 1723, 1736–46 (2010) (describing the role preemption often plays as a proxy for equal protection-based individual rights challenges to subfederal laws that target undocumented immigrants due to the hurdles associated with succeeding on equal protection grounds). As Professor Kevin Johnson notes, numerous cases addressing the constitutionality of state and local laws dealing with immigration have undeniable civil rights implications. Kevin Johnson, *Immigration and Civil Rights: State and Local Efforts to Regulate Immigration*, 46 Ga. L. Rev. 609, 629–30 (2012).

In my opinion, the Court cannot ignore the antidiscrimination dimension of preemption in resolving the claims in this case. The backdrop against which Arizona's law was enacted makes clear that S.B. 1070 – like the Arizona measures and policies that came before it – gave expression to xenophobic sentiment, cloaking that sentiment with the power of law.

For example, during the legislative debate over S.B. 1070, lawmakers spoke of the need to "protect" Arizona against a "foreign invasion." Test. of Sen. Gould, Final Reading of S.B. 1070, S. Floor Sess. (Apr. 19, 2010). In similar remarks then-Representative Pearce made several years earlier, he had urged colleagues to not stand by "while we watch the destruction of our country" and "the destruction of neighborhoods" by undocumented immigrants. Test. of Rep. Pearce Regarding H.B. 2779, House Gov't Comm. Hearing (Feb. 20, 2007). Indeed, in proposing S.B. 1070, Pearce appeared to be trying to codify Sheriff Arpaio's practices as a model for what law enforcement should be doing statewide.[45] There was a moment when it seemed like Pearce might not get the votes he needed for the bill's passage, but then Arizona border rancher Robert Krentz was killed in late March 2010. Although authorities had no suspects and no information about the killer's identity at the time, S.B. 1070 supporters immediately capitalized on Krentz's death by publicly speculating it was the work of an undocumented Mexican immigrant. *See* Andrea Christina Nill, *Latinos and S.B. 1070: Demonization, Dehumanization, and Disenfranchisement*, 14 Harv. Latino L. Rev. 35, 41 (2011). S.B. 1070 passed the House shortly thereafter, and on April 23, 2010, was signed into law by the Governor.

An antidiscrimination lens for preemption analysis would give more authentic expression to the objection that many members of the American public actually have to S.B. 1070. That objection is grounded in the understanding that people of color will inevitably bear the brunt of any attempts to enforce the law. *See Arizona's*

---

[45] *See* Editorial, *Resist Stampede to State Mandates for Immigration Enforcement*, East Valley Trib. (Oct. 23, 2009). Pearce also seems to have intended for S.B. 1070 to return to Arpaio immigration enforcement powers that Arpaio had lost after the federal government had initiated a civil rights inquiry into his agency. Press Release, *Sen. Pearce Demands End to Sanctuary City, 'Catch and Release' Policies* (Oct. 21, 2009); Jeremy Duda, *Immigration and Customs Enforcement: If Sheriff Arpaio Continues Sweeps, It will be Under State, Not Federal, Law*, Ariz. CAPITOL TIMES (Oct. 16, 2009).

Immigration Crackdown: The Backlash Begins, The Economist, 71 (May 7, 2010). Further, if the experience with Arizona's laws and policies leading up to S.B. 1070 is any indication, vulnerability under the law will fall not only along lines of race and ethnicity, but gender.

Others have discussed the importance of applying an intersectional analysis to policies and practices that impact people of color – in other words, examining how "the imposition of one burden ... interacts with preexisting vulnerabilities to create yet another dimension of disempowerment"[46] – and immigration laws are no exception. Though less attention has been paid how Latinx women in particular will be affected by S.B. 1070, there is little doubt that, as with white supremacy, patriarchy affects how Arizona's immigration measures are understood, defended, and enforced. As sociologist Mary Romero explains, anti-immigrant discourse in Arizona has portrayed Mexican women as a threat to ideal nativist notions of family and patriotism. Mary Romero, *Constructing Mexican Immigrant Women as a Threat to American Families*, 37:1 *Int'l J. of Sociology of the Family* 49 (2011). Indeed, Proposition 200's provisions regarding reporting by benefits workers appears to have been targeted at immigrant women perceived as overusing public benefits to the detriment of "American" (white) children. These racialized gender stereotypes may also help explain the shocking actions of Maricopa County Sheriff's Office ("MCSO") deputies toward women like Lorena Escamilla of Laveen, Arizona, who was stopped by deputies in her driveway while five months pregnant and repeatedly slammed into the hood of her car, belly-first, after she refused to consent to a search of her vehicle,[47] or the actions of deputies toward Elaine Sanchez of Guadalupe, Arizona, who was followed home and pushed to the ground with a knee in her back, all because she allegedly had a license plate light out.[48] Even when women are not themselves directly targeted for investigation, arrest, or detention, they have felt the impact of the arrest of their husbands, brothers, fathers, and sons – and as caregivers, are left to pick up the pieces.

For Latinx people in Arizona, the immigration measures of the 2000s culminating in S.B. 1070 have brought back painful memories of the "Chandler Roundup," in which hundreds of citizens and noncitizens alike were profiled, harassed,

---

[46] Kimberlé Crenshaw, *Mapping the Margins: Intersectionality, Identity Politics, and Violence against Women of Color*, 43 STAN. L. REV. 1241, 1249 (1991). *See also* Mari J. Matsuda, *Beside My Sister, Facing the Enemy: Legal Theory Out of Coalition*, 43 STAN. L. REV. 1183, 1189 (1991) (encouraging us to always ask the "other question," as doing so forces us to probe "the obvious and non-obvious relationships of domination, helping us to realize that no form of subordination ever stands alone").

[47] Declaration of Lorena Escamilla in Support of Plaintiffs' Motion for Summary Judgment, Melendres v. Arpaio, No. CV 07-2513-PHX-GMS (D. Ariz. Apr. 29, 2011).

[48] Order on Summary Judgment, Sanchez v. Arpaio, No. CV-0901150-PHX-LOA (D. Ariz. Oct. 5, 2010). Ms. Sanchez and her family are Yaqui; though frequently mistaken for Mexican, their indigenous ancestors had settled in Arizona long before the arrival of many Anglo Americans. The Yaqui are an example of a people who were cut off from their homeland due to a hardening of the southern border. Luna-Firebaugh, *The Border Crossed Us*, at 167.

interrogated, and, for some, ultimately arrested by the Border Patrol over five days in 1997. *See* Mary Romero, *Racial Profiling and Immigration Law Enforcement: Rounding Up of Usual Suspects in the Latino Community*, 32 Critical Sociology 447, 453 (2006). Rather than being limited in duration and geographic scope, however, the attacks at the state and local level are now more widespread and relentless, a constant reminder of these communities' perceived "outsider" status.

* * *

Having set out the relevant context in which S.B. 1070 was enacted and the reality informing how S.B. 1070 will be enforced, I will now address each of the challenged provisions of S.B. 1070 in turn.

II

Section 3

The majority concludes that Section 3 of S.B. 1070, which creates a new state misdemeanor based on a violation of federal registration requirements for noncitizens, is preempted because Congress has "occupied the field of alien registration." *Arizona*, at 2501. In such a case, under our existing preemption precedents, any complementary regulation by the state is *per se* disallowed because it "detract[s] from the 'integrated scheme of regulation' created by Congress." *Id.* at 2502 (internal citations omitted).

As I noted at the outset, I agree with the majority's determination that Section 3 is preempted. In reaching its determination, though, the majority places significant weight on what it describes as a "comprehensive" system of registration at the federal level. *Id.* I do not agree that the federal registration system, as currently set up, is as comprehensive as the majority suggests. Indeed, as the Leadership Conference for Civil and Human Rights and other organizations explain in their amicus curiae brief, the notion that federal law requires all noncitizens to register their presence with the government and carry registration documents at all times is a myth. Brief for the Leadership Conference on Civil and Human Rights et al. (hereinafter "LCCHR Amicus Brief"), Arizona v. United States, No. 11-182, 13-23 (Mar. 26, 2012). While our country's history is punctuated with periods where the government attempted to impose a broader registration requirement, today's federal code only obligates those who are *issued* a registration document (and over 18 years of age) to carry one. 8 U.S.C. § 1304(e). And it only imposes penalties for failing to register on those who are specifically required to do so. 8 U.S.C. § 1306(a). Individuals who entered the country without inspection – which make up a significant number of undocumented immigrants – are not provided any registration document, and in fact, for decades have had no way to register. LCCHR Amicus Brief at 14–17.

Further, of the remainder of noncitizens, multiple classes are exempt, or are not issued a registration document despite having technically applied for registration. Id. at 17–21; *see also, e.g.*, 8 U.S.C. § 1303(b).

What the majority characterizes as an "integrated" scheme, *Arizona*, at 2502, is more a patchwork of rules that have become increasingly fragmented over time with the proliferation of different types of immigration status. *See* 8 C.F.R. § 264.1. The majority suggests that the federal government has strengthened the registration requirements since this Court examined the scheme in *Hines* (e.g., by adding a carry requirement), *Arizona*, at 2502, but, taken as a whole, just the opposite is true. Since *Hines*, the registration scheme has become more ad hoc and obsolete, applying to a comparatively smaller cross-section of the noncitizen population. Few cases of a violation of the registration statutes are prosecuted today.[49]

Ironically, the myth of a comprehensive federal registration system is what allows state officials to continue to insist that their laws simply complement federal law. While the majority may believe that presenting the federal system as exhaustive offers a quicker route to a finding of preemption, there are costs to this approach. First, it fails to directly rebuke Arizona's true intent with Section 3 – to criminalize undocumented immigrants' presence in the state. *See* LCCHR Amicus Brief at 15–16. This intent is made apparent by the fact that those noncitizens actually subject to federal registration and carry requirements, that is, noncitizens who have received permission to be in the United States, are *exempt* from application of the provision, Ariz. Rev. Stat. § 13-1509(F), while those who are not authorized to be in the United States – and who, as discussed above, often have no way to register – are not. Section 3, working in tandem with Section 2(B) of S.B. 1070, also ensures that Arizona law enforcement officials need nothing more than suspicion of unlawful presence to initiate a stop, detention, or arrest, since such presence is now a state crime. Rather than seeking to "assist" in the enforcement of the federal scheme, Arizona's aim was clearly to implement its own immigration scheme, one that targets individuals perceived to be undocumented for additional punishment. *See Arizona*, at 2503 (describing sanctions imposed by Section 3 not present in federal law).

Second, the majority's approach obscures the ugly history associated with more consummate federal registration schemes of the past. One such system was established as part of the Chinese exclusion laws. The Act of 1882 required Chinese workers to obtain and carry "certificates" showing they had been present in the United States prior to the institution of race-based bans on admission. Geary Act of 1892, ch. 60, § 6, 27 Stat. 25, 25 (1892); *see also Chae Chan Ping v. United States*, 130 U.S. 581, 609 (1889). The 1940 Registration Act in place during *Hines* was enacted in the lead up to World War II at a time when the government was actively trying to ferret out suspected Communists and other leftist "subversives." *See Harisiades v.*

---

[49] Data on prosecutions for violation of registration statutes can be found at https://tracfed.syr.edu/index/index.php?layer=cri.

Shaughnessy, 342 U.S. 580, 590 (1952). And more recently, in the wake of September 11th, the federal government instituted a controversial Special Registration program requiring male nonimmigrant visa holders from predominantly Arab and Muslim countries to show up at immigration offices to be photographed, fingerprinted, and interrogated. American-Arab Anti-Discrimination Committee and the Penn State Dickenson School of Law Center for Immigrants' Rights, *NSEERS: The Consequences of America's Efforts to Secure its Borders* (2009). S.B. 1070's Section 3 is reminiscent of these earlier efforts to track and target groups on the basis of race, religion, or political belief. By glossing over this history, the majority renders this connection of S.B. 1070 to our past less clear.

Arizona's scheme is offensive to the Supremacy Clause, not only because it is based on an inaccurate understanding of the federal scheme, but because it invites precisely the type of "distinct, unusual and extraordinary burdens" on less-favored groups that we warned of in *Hines.* 312 U.S. at 65–66. An antidiscrimination lens for preemption offers a more forthright, and I believe, ultimately less fragile, alternative path to the result reached by the majority.

III

Section 5(C)

With respect to Section 5(C) of S.B. 1070, I agree with the majority that Arizona may not enforce a "state criminal prohibition" on undocumented immigrants "know-ingly apply[ing] for work, solicit[ing] work in a public place or perform[ing] work as an employee or independent contractor" where "no federal counterpart exists." *Arizona,* at 2503 (quoting Ariz. Rev. Stat. § 13-2928(C)). The federal scheme at issue here is the one regulating the employment of unauthorized immigrants enacted by Congress as part of the Immigration Reform and Control Act of 1986 (IRCA).

Of course, Section 5(C) is not Arizona's first attempt to create a state-level scheme to address what lawmakers describe as the problem of immigrants "steal-ing" "American" jobs. In 2007, the state enacted a wide-ranging measure called the Legal Arizona Workers Act (LAWA). LAWA prohibited employers from know-ingly hiring unauthorized workers and required them to use the federal E-Verify system, a system that the federal government itself has acknowledged contains per-sistent errors. U.S. Government Accountability Office, *Employment Verification: Federal Agencies Have Taken Steps to Improve E-Verify, but Significant Challenges Remain,* GAO-11-146 (Dec. 17, 2010). Despite going beyond IRCA in notable ways and threatening to incite discrimination against workers on the basis of national origin by "radically skewing the relevant penalties" faced by employers, *Chamber of Commerce v. Whiting,* 563 U.S. 582, 616 (2011) (J. Breyer, dissenting), a plurality of this Court determined that LAWA tracked federal law closely enough to be constitutional. *Id.* at 600–01, 607.

Other provisions of LAWA not challenged in *Whiting* created new Arizona felony offenses for the use of personal information of another, whether real or fictitious, with the intent to obtain employment. H.B. 2779, § 1 (2007) (codified at Ariz. Rev. Stat. § 13-2009(A)(3)); *see also* H.B. 2745, § 1 (codified at Ariz. Rev. Stat. § 13-2008). These provisions were transparently targeted at undocumented workers. And, predictably, Maricopa County officials soon began using them to conduct large-scale raids at businesses with Latinx employees, arresting those who could not show lawful presence. DOJ Investigation Report at 7–8. During this time, lawmakers also considered proposals directed at day laborers who gather in public places to signal their availability to work to potential employers. Campbell, *The Road to S.B. 1070*, at 13–14. While those proposals did not become law, the Town of Cave Creek managed to pass an anti-solicitation ordinance that law enforcement officials used to arrest day laborers. Jacques Billeaud, *3 Day Laborers Sue Cave Creek Over Its Curbs on Soliciting Work*, Associated Press (Mar. 26, 2008). Meanwhile, Arpaio's earliest "crime suppression patrols" were aimed at day laborers. Ryan Gabrielson and Paul Giblin, *Reasonable Doubt Part III: Sweeps and Saturation Patrols Violate Federal Civil Rights Investigations*, East Valley Tribune (July 11, 2008).

Arizona's enforcement of laws against day laborers and other immigrant workers have followed a racialized course. Indeed, it is of little surprise that day laborers were among the first to be singled out in Arpaio's patrols (and that they are specifically called out in S.B. 1070). Primarily Latinx, day laborers in Arizona present the most visible manifestation of the "problem" in the eyes of white residents – that is, brown-skinned people encroaching on their neighborhoods. In a letter from Sheriff Arpaio's personal file, a constituent complained that on her way to Walmart one day, a "large amount of … Mexicans" had been standing outside the Home Depot "swarmed" her car and she was so scared that she had no choice but to "manually direct them away from [her] car." Statement of Facts in Support of Plaintiffs' Partial Motion for Summary Judgment ("Ortega Melendres SOF"), Ortega Melendres v. Arpaio, No. CV 07-2513-PHX-GMS, 23 (D. Ariz. Apr. 29, 2011). Although Arpaio acknowledged the letter did not describe any crime, he nevertheless shared it with his Chief Deputy. *Id.; see also id.* at 22-26 (describing a similar response by Arpaio to other complaints). Another letter from a constituent lamented that all the workers were speaking Spanish at the local McDonald's and suggested that Arpaio conduct an operation in her town. *Id.* at 23. Two weeks later, deputies came to the area to conduct a patrol. *Id.* To find and arrest day laborers while on patrol, deputies generally staked out corners and watched for vehicles that picked up those who appeared to be Mexican immigrants, then followed them until they could "establish probable cause for a traffic stop." Gabrielson and Giblin, *Reasonable Doubt Part III*. Similarly, during worksite raids, Arpaio's deputies rounded up Latinx workers for interrogation, leaving white workers free to go about their business. Statement of Facts in Support of Plaintiffs' Partial Motion for Summary Judgment, *Mora v. Arpaio*, No. 2:09-cv-01719-DGC, 3–5, 9, 16 (D. Ariz. Dec. 28, 2010).

Arizona's efforts to criminalize undocumented workers cannot be untangled from the racialized enforcement of its laws, as stigmatizing portrayals of the Latinx immigrants have transformed their attempts at subsistence into another reason they should be feared and despised. In the final reading of S.B. 1070 on the Senate floor, Senator Pearce warned of a "job-taking, wage-depressing tsunami" and urged his colleagues to "stand up for Americans." Test. of Sen. Pearce, Final Reading of S.B. 1070, S. Floor Sess. (Apr. 19, 2010). In a public address soon after S.B. 1070's passage, co-sponsor Representative John Kavanagh likewise denigrated day laborers, claiming "All these strange men walking around …. I think most people recognize that most of these people are illegal aliens. Legal residents don't have to solicit labor in the street like hookers." Ariz. Capitol Television, Capitol Forum: Rep. Kavanagh Talks About SB 1070 (June 21, 2010). The likening of immigrant day laborers to another scorned group, the latter largely women, allowed Kavanaugh to invoke race and gender to shame and further dehumanize both populations.

Not surprisingly, the dehumanizing rhetoric and constant threat of arrest has made for a highly exploitable workforce in Arizona. Local advocacy groups and worker centers have called attention to the issue, with some offering know your rights presentations and a safe place for workers and day laborers to gather. *See, e.g.*, Complaint, Friendly House v. Whiting ("Friendly House Complaint"), 2:10-cv-01061-SRB, 11–12, 15–16 (D. Ariz. May 17, 2010). But they face an uphill battle.

While I ultimately agree with the majority that Arizona's most recent bid to punish immigrant workers is preempted, it is not clear to me that the federal scheme has done a substantially better job at protecting workers from exploitation. *See, e.g.*, Michael J. Wishnie, *Prohibiting the Employment of Unauthorized Immigrants: The Experiment Fails*, 2007 U. Chi. Legal F. 193, 205–16 (2007) (observing that IRCA has led to substantial employment discrimination and contributed to the erosion of wages and working conditions across the labor market, including for U.S. born workers). It is certainly notable that Congress, in enacting IRCA, declined to impose criminal penalties on workers simply for engaging in unauthorized work. *Arizona*, at 2504. However, by delegating immigration enforcement powers to private employers, IRCA also gave employers a powerful new tool by which to keep immigrant workers in the shadows and suppress workers' rights. *Id.* at 195. Moreover, rather than serving as a basis to preempt anti-immigrant laws, courts have often pointed to IRCA as a reason why undocumented immigrants should be *denied* certain remedies for labor violations, since making those remedies available would supposedly contravene the federal goal of deterring unlawful employment. *Id.* at 211–13. Rather than extolling the federal scheme as "careful[ly] balance[d]," *Arizona*, at 2505, I would instead give greater consideration to the nativist impulses behind Section 5(C) described above to reach the same conclusion as the majority.

IV

Section 6

Section 6 of S.B. 1070 attempts to expand the arrest authority of Arizona law enforcement officers by permitting them to conduct a warrantless arrest of any person whom
officers have probable cause to believe has "committed a public offense that makes
the person removable from the United States." Ariz. Rev. Stat. § 13-3883(A)(5). It is
not entirely clear what is meant by the term "public offense." The Arizona criminal code defines the term as referring to any "conduct for which a sentence to a
term of imprisonment or of a fine is provided by any law of the state in which it
occurred … and, if the act occurred in a state other than this state, … would be so
punishable under the laws, regulations or ordinances of this state or of a political sub-
division of this state[.]" Ariz. Rev. Stat. § 13-105(27).⁵⁰ This would certainly include
criminal offenses that could render a person inadmissible or deportable under the
Immigration and Nationality Act (INA). The drafters could have also intended for
the term to include the new state immigration-related offenses created by S.B. 1070,
including Sections 3 and 5(C) discussed above, or even the federal offense of entry
without permission, *see* 8 U.S.C. § 1325(a). Whatever the meaning of the phrase, it is
evident that Arizona was attempting in Section 6 to endow its officers with the power
to conduct arrests for civil removability. Teresa A. Miller, *Citizenship & Severity:
Recent Immigration Reforms and the New Penology*, 17 Geo. Immigr. L.J. 611, 616–17
(2003) (explaining that despite being based on commission of prior criminal offenses,
removability under the INA is still treated as civil in nature).

    Section 6 is likely a response to the Ninth Circuit Court of Appeals decision in
Gonzales v. City of Peoria. There, the court determined that Peoria police officers
were only authorized to enforce the criminal provisions of the INA under then-
existing Arizona law. 722 F.2d 468, 476 (9th Cir. 1983), *overruled on other grounds*,
Hodgers-Durgin v. de la Vina, 199 F.3d 1037 (9th Cir. 1999) (en banc). Several of my
colleagues who dissent from the majority's decision with respect to Section 6 suggest that Arizona may amend its laws to assert "inherent authority" to enforce federal
immigration law, including its civil provisions. *See Arizona* at 2516–17 (J. Scalia,
concurring in part and dissenting in part); *id.* at 2523 (J. Thomas, concurring in part
and dissenting in part); *id* at 2528, 2532–35 (J. Alito) (concurring in part and dissenting in part) (believing that it is "well established that state and local officers generally have authority to make stops and arrests for violations of federal criminal laws"
and that federal law likewise does not preclude state and local officers from arresting
noncitizens who have committed removable offenses, so long as such arrests are permitted by state law). The majority does not address the question of inherent authority directly, though it does explain that federal law does not contemplate state and

⁵⁰ At the time S.B. 1070 was enacted, this definition appeared at Ariz. Rev. Stat. § 13-105(26).

local officers making arrests based solely on civil removability "absent any request, approval, or other instruction from the Federal Government." *Arizona*, at 2507; *see also Arizona*, at 2509 (implying that prolonging a stop or detention on this basis would impermissible).[51] For the reasons below, I would go further than the majority and expressly find state and local officers to be prohibited from enforcing the civil and criminal provisions of the INA.

As others have observed, the merger of immigration enforcement with criminal law enforcement involves bringing together two of the most powerful regulatory tools in the state's arsenal against an individual. *See, e.g.*, Juliet Stumpf, *The Crimmigration Crisis: Immigrants, Crime, and Sovereign Power*, 56 Am. U. L. Rev. 367 (2006); Douglas Husak, Overcriminalization: The Limits of the Criminal Law 95 (2008). Both areas of law harness the force of the state to "punish and [] express societal condemnation" – with the potential to do a great deal of damage in the process. Stumpf, *The Crimmigration Crisis*, at 379; *see also* Robert M. Cover, *Violence and the Word*, 95 Yale L. J. 1601 (1986). With any exercise of state power, we must be attentive to the potential for abuse. We should be particularly wary of efforts to combine one zenith of state power with another.

While my colleagues writing in dissent invoke historical examples of states enacting laws restricting immigration, *Arizona* at 2511–12 (J. Scalia, concurring in part and dissenting in part), the systematic involvement of local officers in federal immigration enforcement efforts is a more recent prospect, one espoused by Kris Kobach, who apparently helped Pearce craft S.B. 1070. In a 2005 law review article, Kobach proposed that state and local police could act as "force multipliers" in the fight against unauthorized immigration to cast a far wider "net" over the immigrant population through their everyday encounters with the public. Kris Kobach, *The Quintessential Force Multiplier: The Inherent Authority of Local Police to Make Immigration Arrests*, 69 Albany L. Rev. 179, 181 (2005). But that is precisely the problem with such efforts. Kobach seeks to bring the full, concentrated reign of the state to every sidewalk and street corner, dramatically increasing the stakes of each police-civilian encounter by making it a potential trigger for detention and deportation.

The majority focuses its analysis of Section 6 on ways that Arizona goes further than the immigration arrest authority Congress granted to federal officers. *Arizona*, at 2505–06. For example, federal officers may only conduct a warrantless arrest on the basis of possible removability when a noncitizen is likely to escape before a warrant can be obtained while Section 6 contains no such limitation. *Id.* at 2506–07 (citing 8 U.S.C. § 1357(a)(2)). But federal officials frequently don't abide by their own arrest limitations. *See, e.g.*, Complaint, Moreno v. Napolitano, No. 11-cv-05452 (N.D. Ill. Aug. 11, 2011) (alleging that U.S. Immigration and Customs Enforcement ("ICE") frequently issues immigration detainers without a warrant or any determination that

---

[51] The majority declines to address whether state and local officers have authority to detain a person for a violation of federal criminal immigration law. Arizona, at 2509–10.

individuals subject to detainers are likely to escape). And while the majority states that S. B. 1070 undermines the discretionary power entrusted to the federal government to decide who should be subject to enforcement action, ICE sometimes makes arrests of persons that the agency has elsewhere claimed are not enforcement priorities. *See* American Immigration Lawyers Association, *Immigration Enforcement Off Target: Minor Offense with Major Consequences*, AILA Doc. No. 11081609 (Aug. 16, 2011). While these realities do not give Arizona license to enter the fray, they do make it harder for the federal government to argue that Arizona's attempt do so will muddy otherwise clear waters.

In my view, the greater reason to keep Arizona out of the business of immigration enforcement is the augmented impact it will have on the individual rights of people of color. While determinations of removability, especially removability based on past criminal legal system involvement, are no doubt complex, this is not a question of training on the particulars of immigration law. Sheriff Arpaio lost his agency's 287(g) powers amid concerns that deputies were intentionally using their powers to violate civil rights.[52] Returning that authority to Arpaio through the back door of Section 6 will simply invite the Sheriff (and other law enforcement agencies in Arizona) to revive the discriminatory practices that led the DOJ to investigate MCSO in the first place. And as we have seen, once immigration and criminal law enforcement are conflated with each other, little can be done to quell the inflammatory generalizations that can follow.[53]

This Court must recognize that endowing state and local officials (who already have primary dominion over the enforcement of criminal laws) the blanket ability to enforce federal immigration laws is simply too treacherous a proposition for us to accept. For the same reasons why civil rights mandates could not give way to arguments about states' rights in the 1960s, here too we cannot permit Arizona to install its own immigration enforcement regime in the name of states' rights.

Because it grants state and local law enforcement officials a concentrated power greater than what Congress is likely to have countenanced, Section 6 is preempted.

V

Section 2(B)

While I agree with the majority that Sections 3, 5(C), and 6 of S.B. 1070 are preempted, I part ways with the majority's decision regarding Section 2(B). The thrust

---

[52] *See* Arizona, at 2506 (describing agreements under 8 U.S.C. § 1357(g)(1)).
[53] *See, e.g.*, Test. of Sen. Pearce Regarding S.B. 1070, H. Military Affairs and Pub. Safety Comm. Hearing (Mar. 31, 2010) (citing fabricated statistics that "Phoenix number two in the world in kidnappings ... the home invasion, carjacking, [and] identity theft capital of the nation" and that "60% of the homicides in Phoenix involve illegal aliens"); Robin Lubitz, Op-Ed, *Expert Questions Pearce's Numbers*, Ariz. Republic (June 26, 2009).

of the majority's reasoning for declining to find Section 2(B) preempted is that doing so would be premature. *Arizona*, at 2510. However, as I explain below, this Court has all of the information it needs to find Section 2(B) preempted at this stage, even though the law has not yet gone into effect.

A significant concern raised by the United States and various amici about Section 2(B) is that its mandate to Arizona officers to verify immigration status will lead to extended detentions or delays in a person's release following an arrest. The majority believes there's a chance Arizona can implement Section 2(B) in a way that will avoid this possibility. *Arizona*, at 2509. But as the court below recognized, the very structure of Section 2(B) ensures that individuals will be held for additional time pending status checks with ICE. *United States v. Arizona*, 641 F.3d 339, 347–48 (9th Cir. 2011).

The first sentence of Section 2(B) requires that officers make a reasonable attempt to ascertain the immigration status of a person stopped, detained, or arrested, when practicable, where the officer has reasonable suspicion that the person is undocumented. Ariz. Rev. Stat. § 11-1051(B). The third sentence sets forth how such status is to be determined, that is, through verification with federal authorities. The majority claims that the terms "reasonable" and "when practicable" should signal to officers they cannot prolong stops for this check. *Arizona*, at 2509. But that is a remarkably rose-colored assumption, particularly when neither term connotes on its face that a status check should be terminated when the state law basis for a detention has ceased to exist and when Arizona itself has stated that its guiding framework for S.B. 1070 is "attrition through enforcement." S.B. 1070 § 1. As additional evidence that prolonged detentions will be endemic, a recent analysis of traffic stops conducted by the MCSO during the period when it was engaged in immigration sweeps shows that deputies took twenty-one percent to twenty-five percent longer to complete a stop of a vehicle when at least one Latinx motorist or passenger's name or ID was checked. Ortega Melendres SOF at 53.

Section 2(B)'s mandate is even clearer with respect to cases where a person is arrested. The plain language of the second sentence requires officers to perform a status check not only for a subset of individuals but for *all* arrestees. Ariz. Rev. Stat. § 11-1051(B). Nothing in the text of that sentence suggests that a person's status need not be checked if the person is otherwise ready to be released from custody.

In short, while the majority believes "it is not clear at this stage … that the verification process would result in prolonged detention," *Arizona*, at 2509, there is simply no way prolonged detentions can be avoided, especially with the anticipated rise in the number of status check inquiries federal authorities will have to field from Arizona officers. *See* Brief for Appellee United States of America at 56–57 (explaining that verification process may involve checking multiple databases, and in thousands of cases, produces an indeterminate answer, thus requiring "search[ing] additional databases and even paper files in an effort to resolve the inquiry").

But extended detentions are not the only concern raised by Section 2(B). In the same way that the very structure of the provision guarantees extended detentions, the structure of the provision also virtually guarantees investigations based on race. In order for the verification mandate to be triggered out in the field, officers must first conduct a "lawful stop, detention, or arrest[.]" Ariz. Rev. Stat. § 11-1051(B). But this hardly acts as a limitation. Officers who want to pull a vehicle over are almost always able to do so by developing probable cause for a minor traffic or vehicle violation. An MCSO deputy recently testified that when he was out investigating potential violations of immigration law, it took him only about two minutes to establish probable cause to stop just about any vehicle he was tracking. Ortega Melendres SOF at 29. Indeed, in an email Kris Kobach sent to Senator Pearce when Arizona legislators were considering amendments to S.B. 1070, Kobach urged Pearce to make sure that Section 2(B) captured not only stops, detentions, and arrests in the enforcement of any state law, but municipal ordinances too. See Andrea Nill, *Email from Author of Arizona Law Reveals Intent to Cast Wide Net Against Latinos*, Think Progress (Apr. 30, 2010). Kobach's aim was to make the provision as broad as possible. Examples of municipal ordinance violations he gave were of "cars on blocks in the yard" and "too many occupants of a rental accommodation," violations often used as a pretense to target low-income communities of color. *Id.*; *see generally* Lindsay Nash, *Expression by Ordinance: Preemption and Proxy in Local Legislation*, 25 Geo. Immigr. L. J. 243, 251–58 (2011) (tracking the connection between nuisance-related regulation and local anti-immigrant sentiment).

In fact, Arpaio – who is facing trial in a case alleging racial profiling by his agency later this year – has publicly stated, in response to critics, "Where do you think 99 percent of the people come from?" Ortega Melendres SOF at 5. When asked what his deputies look for when they are investigating individuals who may be unlawfully present, he cited factors such as "what they look like [and] if they look like they came from another country." *Id.* The majority points to language in Section 2(B) that prohibits officers from relying on "race, color or national origin" in developing reasonable suspicion a person is undocumented, *Arizona*, at 2507–08 (citing Ariz. Rev. Stat. § 11-1051(B)), but that is hardly reassuring. The statement is qualified by the phrase "except to the extent permitted by the United States or Arizona Constitution." *Id.* And race and appearance have long been permissible factors in developing reasonable suspicion of an immigration violation under the precedents of this Court and Arizona courts.

In *United States v. Brignoni-Ponce*, for example, this Court stated that "apparent Mexican ancestry," while not enough to give rise to reasonable suspicion to believe someone is present in violation of immigration laws on its own, can nevertheless be a "relevant" factor. 422 U.S. 873, 886–87 (1975). The case was cited in training that ICE provided to MCSO officers in connection with their 287(g) agreement. 287(g) Officer Training Workbook, Hickey Decl. Ex. 57, *Ortega Melendres v. Arpaio*, No. CV 07-2513-PHX-GMS, 23 (D. Ariz. Apr. 29, 2011). This rule has also been echoed in decisions of the Arizona Supreme Court. *See, e.g., State v. Gonzalez-Gutierrez*,

927 P.2d 776, 780 (Ariz. 1996) (citing *Brignoni-Ponce*, 422 U.S. at 885–87). Under an earlier version of S.B. 1070, Arizona lawmakers' intent was even more apparent. That version stated that officers may not rely *"solely"* on "race, color or national origin." S.B. 1070, § 2(B) (2010) (emphasis added).

But even if Arizona had not qualified the prohibition on racial profiling in Section 2(B), it would have made little difference, since it is not difficult to mask such profiling by ostensibly relying on factors that essentially act as proxies for race and ethnicity. Soon after S.B. 1070 was enacted, the Arizona Peace Officer Standards and Training Board ("AZ POST") issued guidance identifying factors that could be considered in developing reasonable suspicion of unlawful presence, including "dress," difficulty communicating in English, and being "[i]n [the] company of other unlawfully present aliens." AZ POST, Implementation of the 2010 Arizona Immigration Laws Statutory Provisions for Peace Officers 3–4 (2010). The list is similar to lists that MCSO provided its deputies after the agency lost its 287(g) task force agreement, and those evidently did little to abate the pattern of racial profiling. *See* MCSO News Release, Hickey Decl. Ex. 59, *Ortega Melendres v. Arpaio*, No. CV 07-2513-PHX-GMS, 23 (D. Ariz. Apr. 29, 2011).

Finally, Arizona has provided a list of documents that give rise to a presumption that a person is lawfully present in the U.S. *See* Ariz. Rev. Stat. § 11-1051(B). Having one of these forms of identification will not insulate a person from investigation, but even this supposedly "neutral" list of documents will inevitably lead to discrimination, since women, the elderly, low-income people and people of color are less likely than others to have accurate identification documents.[54]

The outrage Arizona lawmakers have expressed in response to concerns that racial and ethnic profiling are inevitable is telling. It suggests they have had little experience with hostile police contact themselves. But despite the claims of lawmakers, the law can be seen as one designed to keep minorities under surveillance and control, with significant and far-reaching impacts.[55]

One need look no further than the experiences of those who've stepped forward to participate in legal challenges to S.B. 1070 to see the effects of Section 2(B). For example, C.M., a plaintiff in a challenge brought by civil rights groups, is a high school student in Gilbert, Arizona. Friendly House Complaint at 20. She lives in fear that she will be stopped and questioned about her immigration status due to her "dark skin and the fact that she speaks a foreign language." *Id.* Notably, C.M. is

---

[54] *See, e.g.*, Brennan Center for Justice, Citizens Without Proof, 2–3 (2006) (finding that sixteen percent of Latinx citizens and twenty-five percent of African-American citizens did not have government-issued photo IDs and that only sixty-six percent of voting-age women had any proof of citizenship with a current legal name).

[55] George A. Martinez, *Arizona, Immigration, and Latinos: The Epistemology of Whiteness, the Geography of Race, Interest Convergence, and the View from the Perspective of Critical Theory*, 44 Ariz. S. L. J., 175, 182–85, 186–88, 191 (2012) (describing consequences such as alienation, retreat from social institutions and civil life, and the exacerbation of structural inequality).

not Latinx but a Haitian immigrant who, despite having been granted Temporary Protected Status (TPS) by the federal government, does not have a registration document or any document enumerated in Section 2(B). *See* Ariz. Rev. Stat. § 11-1051(B). She faces discrimination not only as an immigrant who speaks Haitian Creole, but as a Black person living in a majority white state.

As another example, a Jane Doe in the same case, also from Haiti, is a survivor of domestic violence. Friendly House Complaint at 23. Although she was granted permission by an immigration judge to stay in the United States pursuant to the Violence Against Women Act (VAWA), she has no proof of this other than the order from the immigration judge. *Id.* As numerous advocacy groups have pointed out, Section 2(B) is particularly concerning to survivors of violence, who often face marginalization along multiple lines, including gender, race, and socioeconomic status. *See* Amicus Curiae Brief of Legal Momentum in Support of Plaintiffs' Motion for Preliminary Injunction, *Friendly House v.* Whiting, 2:10-cv-01061-SRB, 2 (D. Ariz. July 7, 2010).[56] These factors increase their distrust of police as well as their vulnerability to police contact, and although federal immigration laws do provide some remedies for this group, the remedies are imperfect and often leave survivors in a liminal immigration status. See Friendly House Complaint at 23; LCCHR Amicus Brief at 18–19. Defenders of S.B. 1070 might point to the exception in Section 2(B) for situations where an investigation of immigration status could "hinder or obstruct an investigation" of a crime, such as domestic violence, Ariz. Rev. Stat. § 11-1051(B), but interpretation of this provision is left to the discretion of officers. Any departmental rule exempting victims or witnesses from investigation would likely violate S.B. 1070's prohibition on policies "limit[ing] or restrict[ing] the enforcement of federal immigration laws to less than the full extent permitted by law." Ariz. Rev. Stat. § 11-1051(A). Moreover, as an increasingly intersectional survivors' advocacy movement has recognized, many who have experienced domestic violence are themselves criminalized and treated as *targets* of law enforcement, particularly when they don't fit the stereotype of an ideal "victim." *See, e.g.*, Mary Gilfus, WOMEN'S EXPERIENCES OF ABUSE AS A RISK FACTOR FOR INCARCERATION, VAWnet: THE NATIONAL ONLINE RESOURCE CENTER ON VIOLENCE AGAINST WOMEN (Dec. 2002). The exception in Section 2(B) therefore offers little protection to immigrant survivors of crime.

A broad cross-section of grassroots groups, legal organizations, criminal defense attorneys, faith, labor, business, law enforcement representatives, and even foreign governments have shared experiences illuminating the likely harms of Section 2(B).[57]

---

[56] *See also* Ashley Arcidiacono, *Silencing the Voices of Battered Women: How Arizona's Immigration Law 'SB 1070' Prevents Undocumented Women from Seeking Relief Under the Violence against Women Act*, 47 CAL. WESTERN L. REV. 173, 194–97 (2010); Giselle Aguilar Hass, Nawal Ammar, and Leslye Orloff, BATTERED IMMIGRANTS AND U.S. CITIZEN SPOUSES, LEGAL MOMENTUM (2006).

[57] *See, e.g.*, LCCHR Amicus Brief; Brief of the American Civil Liberties Union et al., Arizona v. United States, No. 11-182 (Mar. 23, 2012); Brief of the National Immigrant Justice Center et al., Arizona v.

This provision is fundamentally different than any of the forms of "cooperation" incorporated into federal law and cited by the majority, *Arizona*, at 2508, because of its sheer reach and its categorical command that Arizona officers act as de facto immigration agents. I would affirm the preliminary injunction with respect to Section 2(B).

* * *

While the United States advances only a single ground for its claim against Section 2(B) and the other challenged provisions, the ample evidence of inevitable racial and ethnic profiling suggests that S.B. 1070 may also be susceptible to challenge under the Equal Protection Clause of the Fourteenth Amendment. Such a challenge would no doubt face some hurdles under the precedents of this Court. *See, e.g., Washington v. Davis*, 426 U.S. 229 (1976). Nevertheless, it is worth at least a brief discussion.

Under *Village of Arlington Heights v. Metropolitan Housing Development Corporation*, a plaintiff may contest a facially neutral law on the theory that unlawful discrimination was a "motivating factor" in its enactment. 429 U.S. 252, 265–66 (1977). Factors that may serve as circumstantial evidence of discriminatory intent include: (1) the legislative history, especially contemporaneous statements by members of the legislature; (2) "the historical background" or "sequence of events leading up to the challenged decision"; (3) the disproportionate impact of the challenged decision on a protected group; and (4) substantive or procedural departures from usual decision-making norms. *Id.* at 266–68.

Here, as detailed above, the legislative history is replete with statements made by lawmakers conflating immigrants with crime and undocumented immigrants with Latinx people generally. Legislators also used racially coded language, referring to the need to protect against hostile foreign "inva[ders]." *See also* Nill, *Latinos and S.B. 1070*, at 54. Indeed, the other legislative acts leading up to S.B. 1070 reflect a multiyear effort to target the Latinx community. *See also* H.B. 2281, 48th Leg., 2d Reg. Sess. (Ariz. 2010) (Arizona bill, considered in the same legislative session as S.B. 1070, penalizing schools that offer ethnic studies courses). Moreover, the Arizona Legislature appears to have departed from its typical practice when it *removed* officer and police department discretion (through Section 2(B)'s mandatory status checks) rather than enhancing it. *See* Ariz. Rev. Stat. §§ 11-1051(A)-(B), (H). These and other

United States, No. 11-182 (Mar. 26, 2012); Brief of the American Bar Association as Amicus Curiae, Arizona v. United States, No. 11-182 (Mar. 26, 2012); Brief of Arizona Attorneys for Criminal Justice et al., Arizona v. United States, No. 11-182 (Mar. 26, 2012); Brief of the United States Conference of Catholic Bishops et al., Arizona v. United States, No. 11-182 (Mar. 26, 2012); Brief of Amici Curiae National Council of La Raza., Arizona v. United States, No. 11-182 (Mar. 26, 2012); Brief of State and Local Law Enforcement Officials, Arizona v. United States, No. 11-182 (Mar. 26, 2012); Brief of the United Mexican States, Arizona v. United States, No. 11-182 (Mar. 26, 2012).

facts could certainly form the scaffolding for an equal protection claim. I expect that courts will begin to see more such challenges to state-level immigration laws soon.[58]

VI

This case comes to us not as a challenge under the Equal Protection Clause but as a challenge under the Supremacy Clause. This is of course a consequence of how the federal government decided to frame its lawsuit. That the United States and the State of Arizona are the two parties in this case may render less visible the profound stake that civil society has in our decision today. But it does not relieve us from considering those interests.

Analyzing the federal government's claims through an antidiscrimination lens for preemption allows us to confront the broader set of issues at play with Arizona's latest experiment with "attrition through enforcement." It may also better guide courts called on to evaluate future state laws that may be less obviously targeted at immigration. Ultimately, I hope this might offer some measure of comfort to those who feel ardently that this case is about more than *who* gets to detain or arrest them, their loved ones and their neighbors, and restore their faith that the law will protect them, like all others who make up our national community.

Applying this fuller notion of preemption, I would find all of the challenged provisions unconstitutional.

---

[58] *See, e.g.,* Friendly House Complaint at 56.

14

Commentary on *Jennings v. Rodriguez*, 138 S. Ct. 830 (2018)

Ahilan Arulanantham

Jennings v. Rodriguez presented the Supreme Court with the opportunity to address a simple question of profound importance: can the government incarcerate noncitizens for prolonged periods – often for years – without hearings to determine whether their confinement is necessary? But the Court did not decide it. Instead, a fractured 3-2-3 Court held the immigration statutes authorize such incarceration for the groups of noncitizens at issue in the case, and remanded for lower courts to decide if those statutes are constitutional.

In contrast, Professors Sarah Sherman-Stokes and Sarah Schendel, writing here as Justices Sherman-Stokes and Schendel, address the constitutional questions that lie at the heart of *Rodriguez*. Their feminist judgment concludes the Due Process Clause does not permit the government to confine noncitizens for lengthy periods without bond hearings, and goes further, stating that immigration detention and deportation are a form of punishment, and therefore likely unconstitutional regardless of what civil process accompanies them.

I have litigated *Rodriguez* since its inception in 2006 and argued it (twice) in the Supreme Court. As such, it feels strange to comment on the case, particularly because it remains pending as of the time of this writing (May 2023), and the class-wide injunction the district court ordered in 2012 remains in place. Nonetheless, I am delighted to comment on the fascinating opinion authored by Professors Sherman-Stokes and Schendel, which speaks directly to some of the profound issues that the litigants in *Rodriguez* briefed at great length, but the Supreme Court ignored.

I focus my commentary on two of them. *First*, Sherman-Stokes and Schendel reconceive the "plenary power doctrine," a concept that has proven foundational in immigration law for more than one hundred years. Courts often invoke that somewhat vague concept to set aside normal modes of constitutional analysis in favor of approaches that provide greater deference to the "political branches" – Congress and the Executive – to set immigration policy. Sherman-Stokes and Schendel reject plenary power by extending *Padilla v. Kentucky*, 559 U.S. 356 (2010) – which held the Sixth Amendment requires counsel to provide noncitizen criminal defendants with accurate immigration advice – to hold that deportation is itself a punishment. *Second*, building on that conclusion, Sherman-Stokes and Schendel suggest immigration detention itself is likely unconstitutional because, as punishment, it cannot be imposed without procedures that comply with the Sixth Amendment.

Thus, Sherman-Stokes and Schendel do more than establish that the constitutional claim we raised in *Rodriguez* has merit. They also point the way to an argument for invalidating virtually all immigration detention.[1]

THE *RODRIGUEZ* LITIGATION

The conditions that gave rise to *Jennings v. Rodriguez* can be traced to changes in the immigration laws enacted in 1996, when the population of immigrants incarcerated by the federal government under the immigration laws exploded after Congress enacted the Illegal Immigration Reform and Immigrant Responsibility Act. That statute both dramatically restricted access to asylum and greatly expanded the set of convictions that render people deportable. It also overhauled corresponding provisions governing immigration detention. In particular, 8 U.S.C. 1225(b) expanded the government's authority to jail asylum seekers pending adjudication of their cases; and 8 U.S.C. 1226(c) required the government to jail people convicted of certain crimes while their removal cases remained pending. These changes gave the government vast new authority to jail immigrants.

Unsurprisingly, they also led to litigation by jailed immigrants seeking freedom. The first such case to reach the Supreme Court was *Zadvydas v. Davis*, 533 U.S. 678 (2001). That case involved lawful permanent residents born in countries that would not take them back after they were ordered removed based on criminal convictions, including many who had been brought here as children from Vietnam, Cambodia, and Laos. The applicable statute had no explicit time limit dictating how long someone could be detained while awaiting deportation. By 2001, there were thousands of such individuals facing potentially indefinite incarceration by immigration authorities. The government invoked "plenary power" authority to hold these individuals until they could be physically deported, regardless of how long that might take.

The Supreme Court rejected that view. It construed the post-removal order detention statute to contain an implicit "reasonable time" limitation – which it set at a "presumptive" six months – to avoid the serious constitutional problems associated with prolonged and potentially permanent immigration detention. In describing those constitutional problems, *Zadvydas* relied extensively on civil detention doctrine from outside the immigration context. *Zadvydas* also relied on *Wong Wing v. United States*, 163 U.S. 228 (1896), in which the Court first justified immigration detention by reference to the pretrial criminal context (where custody hearings for

---

[1]   I use the term "immigration detention" because the Court has done so consistently. Nonetheless, it is misleading. Most people entering an immigration detention center would believe they are in a prison.

individuals facing punishment have long been required).[2] And *Zadvydas* rejected the Government's request for deference based on plenary power doctrine because "that power is subject to important constitutional limitations," *id.* at 695.

Zadvydas appeared to signal the Court was well on its way to limiting plenary power authority in the immigration detention context. However, just two years later (during which the 9/11 attacks occurred), the Court appeared to reverse course. In *Demore v. Kim,* 538 U.S. 510 (2003), the Supreme Court upheld the constitutionality of "brief" periods of *mandatory* detention – that is, detention without the opportunity even to ask for release on bond – for noncitizens convicted of certain crimes who were litigating their immigration cases. The Court relied on statistics presented by the government purporting to show that it needed just a few weeks in most cases to complete removal proceedings before an Immigration Judge, and about four and a half months to resolve most cases involving appeals. It characterized the case of Mr. Kim himself as an outlier, as it had taken about six months (thus far).

Based on the assertion that detention under the statute would be brief, *Demore* upheld it. The Court reached that result without ever citing the civil detention doctrine on which *Zadvydas* had relied. Instead, *Demore* justified its holding in part by reference to a traditional tenet of plenary power doctrine: "that Congress may make rules as to aliens that would be unacceptable if applied to citizens."[3] As to the constitutional constraints on such rules, *Demore* stated "when the Government deals with deportable aliens, the Due Process Clause does not require it to employ the least burdensome means to accomplish its goal,"[4] thus suggesting that "deportable" noncitizens have lesser rights to liberty than other persons.

The *Rodriguez* litigation arose in the shadow of *Zadvydas* and *Demore.* In working with populations of jailed immigrants, my colleagues and I found the government routinely incarcerated people for *much* longer periods than those described in *Demore* – three and a half years in Mr. Rodriguez's case, to give just one example.[5] Yet the government refused to provide them with hearings to determine whether their confinement remained justified, citing *Demore. Rodriguez* challenged those claims. Relying on *Zadvydas, Demore,* and Ninth Circuit cases we had litigated post-*Demore*, we asserted that the immigration statutes must be read to permit hearings to assess the need for detention after six months, and that the Due Process Clause required such hearings.

---

[2]   Zadvydas, 533 U.S. at 694 (discussing Wong Wing); *see also* Wong Wing, 163 U.S. at 235 ("Detention is a usual feature of every case of arrest on a criminal charge, even when an innocent person is wrongfully accused; but it is not imprisonment in a legal sense").

[3]   538 U.S. at 522.

[4]   *Id.*, at 528.

[5]   The Government would eventually acknowledge both that the data it submitted was inaccurate and that the Court had erred in interpreting it. *See* Letter from Ian Heath Gershengorn, Acting Solicitor General, to Hon. Scott S. Harris, Clerk, Supreme Court 1–3 (Aug. 26, 2016), Demore v. Kim, 538 U.S. 510 (2003) ix (No. 01-1491).

Rodriguez would have been an easy case absent plenary power doctrine. The central constitutional question presented – whether the Due Process Clause permits prolonged confinement under the immigration laws *without a bond hearing* – is not close under normal civil detention doctrine. No other civil detention system permits incarceration of such length without the modest process afforded by a bond hearing. At least during peace-time, the cases governing every other confinement system make a hearing like the one we sought in *Rodriguez* available well before six months, and usually in a matter of days.[6] Because these rules establish the "process" due "persons" under the Fifth and Fourteenth Amendments, absent plenary power one would think they apply to *Rodriguez* by fairly straightforward analogy. After all, *Rodriguez* class members, like all people subject to immigration enforcement, are "persons." Put most starkly: if the government cannot incarcerate someone pending trial on a criminal charge for more than a few *days* without a hearing on whether their pretrial confinement is necessary, how could it incarcerate them for *months*, let alone *years*, pending adjudication of a deportation charge without providing any such hearing at all?

However, plenary power doctrine remains very much a part of the Supreme Court's immigration jurisprudence. Mr. Rodriguez and other members of the *Rodriguez* class shared some characteristics with the petitioner in *Demore* – most of them were held under statutes that arguably required their detention for the duration of their cases, and their cases were still pending. On the other hand, the petitioners in *Rodriguez* were jailed for *far* longer periods than *Demore* considered. The Court had found comparable detention lengths likely unconstitutional in *Zadvydas*. Thus, resolving the central constitutional question in *Rodriguez* by reference to existing doctrine requires reconciling *Demore* with *Zadvydas* and explaining the role of plenary power doctrine in this context.

For the last seventeen years of *Rodriguez* litigation, the Supreme Court has refrained from answering that question – despite holding two oral arguments, the second of which was ostensibly devoted only to the constitutional question. Instead, it rejected the immigrants' statutory arguments, and left the constitutional questions for resolution by lower courts.

THE FEMINIST JUDGMENT

Professors Sherman-Stokes and Schendel take a fundamentally different approach. They eschew detailed textual analysis of the statutes, focusing instead on the serious constitutional problems with the existing immigration detention

---

[6]   *See* United States v. Salerno, 481 U.S. 739, 747, 750 (1987) (upholding pretrial criminal detention only with bond hearings that must occur "prompt[ly]," usually within days); Schall v. Martin, 467 U.S. 253, 270–71 (1984) (upholding scheme permitting preventive detention of juveniles where judges hold hearing within four days); Foucha v. Louisiana, 504 U.S. 71, 81–83 (1992) (requiring individualized findings of mental illness and dangerousness for civil commitment beyond brief period).

regime that the Supreme Court's controlling opinion ignored. They also trace the modern history of immigration detention, revealing its strikingly recent origin. As Sherman-Stokes and Schendel explain, the federal government ended virtually all immigration detention in 1954, and detained only a small fraction of the number of people incarcerated today as late as 1994. Their feminist judgment also reaffirms the importance of class action litigation as a mechanism for providing voice to marginalized individuals who lack the ability to bring due process claims before the courts without the class device.

While these strands of their opinion all deserve sustained attention, I focus this commentary on two doctrinal moves of particular importance in Sherman-Stokes and Schendel's opinion: their rejection of the plenary power doctrine as applied in this context, and their strong suggestion that immigration detention itself is unconstitutional – not just when it lasts for months without bond hearings (as in *Rodriguez*), but in *all cases*.

Rethinking Plenary Power

In their Feminist Judgment, Sherman-Stokes and Schendel offer a strikingly original way to resolve the doctrinal puzzle at the heart of *Rodriguez*. They do not engage directly with the tension between *Zadvydas* and *Demore*, but instead reject application of plenary power doctrine primarily by reference to *Padilla v. Kentucky*, 559 U.S. 356 (2010). *Padilla* held the Sixth Amendment requires counsel to provide accurate advice as to the immigration consequences of a potential conviction to noncitizen criminal defendants facing trial. Sherman-Stokes and Schendel extend *Padilla* to hold that deportation is itself punishment. They first describe *Padilla* as providing "a more nuanced – and indeed more honest – appraisal of detention and deportation," quoting its statement that deportation is "sometimes the most important part of the penalty" noncitizens face when convicted of deportable offenses. They then "denounce the lie we have been telling since 1893," and declare unambiguously that "immigration detention and deportation are punitive."

Sherman-Stokes and Schendels' focus on *Padilla* echoes a classic feminist approach to critical legal analysis, insofar as *Padilla* eschews focus on the formal distinction between civil sanctions and criminal punishment in favor of a deeper, "more honest" analysis of what deportation actually does to the lives of those deported.[7]

Padilla also serves as a powerful doctrinal basis on which to build the fundamental shift Sherman-Stokes and Schendel envision. It is more recent than *Demore* and *Zadvydas*, and one of the few Supreme Court cases in the last four decades expanding the constitutional rights of immigrants in any context. Perhaps most importantly,

---

[7] *See generally* Katharine Bartlett, *Feminist Legal Methods*, 103 HARV. L. REV. 829, 850 (1990).

seven justices supported the judgment in *Padilla*, including Chief Justice Roberts and Justice Alito, and the Court has since extended it.[8]

Nonetheless, extending *Padilla* to hold that deportation and detention incident to it are punishment presents difficulties. First, *Padilla*'s rationale focuses on the immigration consequences of *criminal convictions*; it has no obvious application to cases that do *not* involve convictions. *Padilla* recognized that deportation "is not, in a strict sense, a criminal sanction," but held that "deportation is nevertheless intimately related to the criminal process." 559 U.S 336, 365 (2010). And while the spirit of *Padilla* suggests courts should focus on the practical realities of deportation rather than its formal classification as a civil "penalty," its rationale tells us very little about why deportation (and detention pending deportation) constitutes punishment for the many detained immigrants who do *not* face deportation on criminal grounds. For example, Sherman-Stokes and Schendel discuss class representatives Mr. Farah and Mr. Abdikadir, both of whom sought asylum when they presented themselves for entry. DHS officers jailed them under 8 U.S.C. 1225(b) even though they had no criminal history. If deporting them constitutes a punishment, it cannot be because deportation is "intimately related to the criminal process."

Second, if deportation is a punishment, then the government can *never* impose it without the protections afforded by the Sixth Amendment. Yet it is far from obvious that deportation should *always* be viewed as punishment. I agree that in many cases deportation should be understood as punishment; it seems obvious that deportation constitutes punishment for someone like Mr. Rodriguez – a lawful permanent resident brought to this country as an infant who resided here for decades and is now the father of three American children.

Sherman-Stokes and Schendel buttress their claim by narrating the stories of class representatives in *Rodriguez*, utilizing a paradigmatic method of feminist jurisprudence: "narrative to illuminate the effects of the law on individual plaintiffs."[9] The contrast with the actual *Rodriguez* opinion is sharp, as it contains no comparable acknowledgment of our clients' humanity.

Nonetheless, the claim that *all* deportations constitute punishment strikes me as implausible. For example, the deportation of tourists present for only short periods – whether because they were convicted of deportable crimes or because of other violations of the terms of their visas – surely should not be classified in all cases as punishment. Similarly, deporting at least some individuals who arrived very recently and assert no asylum claim cannot plausibly be described as punishment.[10]

---

[8] *See* Lee v. United States, 137 S.Ct. 1958 (2017) (permitting criminal defendant to withdraw guilty plea based on attorneys' failure to advise that plea would lead to mandatory deportation).

[9] FEMINIST JUDGMENTS: REWRITTEN OPINIONS OF THE UNITED STATES SUPREME COURT 15 (Kathryn M. Stanchi, Linda L. Berger, & Bridget J. Crawford eds., 2016).

[10] Unfortunately, the doctrinal tests for identifying punishment are so malleable as to be almost useless on this point. *See, e.g.*, Kennedy v. Mendoza Martinez, 372 U.S. 144, 168 (1963) (describing seven nonexclusive factors).

Although Sherman-Stokes and Schendel ground their rejection of plenary power primarily on *Padilla*, they offer a tantalizing hint of another basis in a line referencing the doctrine's racist origins. They assert "this Court is troubled by overreliance on case law from the 1800s and early 1900s, that gives credence to immigration detention being civil, given its disturbing and racist origins." They then cite the racist holding and language in *Fong Yue Ting v. United States*, 149 U.S. 698 (1893), which upheld the "one white witness" rule for Chinese people seeking to prove they had resided here prior to passage of an exclusion law.

Sherman-Stokes and Schendel say nothing more on this subject, but it could serve as a strong distinct basis for abandoning plenary power. Although the Supreme Court has not applied the Constitution's prohibition on intentional race discrimination to its own prior opinions, the logic of that doctrine would suggest it could. The Court's most recent formulation of the rule comes from *Village of Arlington Heights v. Metropolitan Housing Development Corp., et al.*, 429 U.S. 252 (1977). It requires courts to strike down state action motivated by racial animus, unless the state establishes "that the same decision would have resulted even had the impermissible purpose not been considered." *Id.* at 265, 271 n.21.

By analogy, applying *Arlington Heights* to prior *judicial* decisions would require a court applying precedent that rests on racial animus to determine anew whether the underlying rule is justified under modern (hopefully not racist) doctrine. While a full exploration of such an approach is beyond the scope of this commentary, it undoubtedly could be fruitful for a project aimed at rejecting plenary power doctrine. Sherman-Stokes and Schendel allude to this possibility when they note the racism underlying the nineteenth century cases from which plenary power doctrine purportedly originates. In doing so, they implicitly invoke strands of feminist legal theory that understand antidiscrimination doctrine as driven by principles of anti-subordination, and also that see a comprehensive critique of law's patriarchy as necessarily connected to a critique of racial subordination.[11]

The Constitutionality of Immigration Detention Itself

As I described above, the central constitutional question presented and unanswered in *Rodriguez* – whether the Constitution permits prolonged detention under the immigration laws without a bond hearing – is easy to resolve if we take Sherman-Stokes and Schendel's cue to disregard plenary power. Wartime aside, the Due Process Clause always requires hearings where the state has to explain why incarceration is necessary. Therefore, the feminist judgment's holdings that

---

[11] *See generally* Ruth Colker, *Anti-Subordination Above All: Sex, Race, and Equal Protection*, 61 N.Y.U. L. Rev. 1003 (1986); Kimberle Crenshaw, *Demarginalizing the Intersection of Race and Sex: A Black Feminist Critique of Antidiscrimination Doctrine, Feminist Theory and Antiracists Politics*, 1 Univ. Chi. Legal Forum 139 (1989).

"[t]he constitutional right to due process encompasses eligibility for bail," and that "[t]o prevent the prolonged, unreviewable detention of thousands of noncitizens within the United States, the statute must be read to require a bail hearing," are the only conclusions consistent with modern due process doctrine.

While *Rodriguez* would be an easy case absent plenary power, lurking beneath it is a harder question concerning the constitutionality of immigration detention itself. Although Sherman-Stokes and Schendel's opinion does not appear to *hold* that immigration detention itself is unconstitutional, it describes both deportation and detention as punitive. If true, that conclusion would render immigration detention unconstitutional in all cases unless it were imposed *as punishment*, utilizing procedures that comply with the Sixth Amendment.

A skeptical reader – even one who accepts that deportation is sometimes punishment – might disagree with that rationale. Even if deportation constitutes punishment, it does not necessarily follow that detention pending completion of deportation proceedings is also punishment. After all, under current due process doctrine, *jail* generally does not constitute punishment even though imprisonment after a conviction does.[12] So long as incarceration is necessary to ensure appearance at trial or to prevent danger to the community, and so long as it lasts no longer than reasonably needed to serve its underlying purpose, it satisfies Due Process.

Sherman-Stokes and Schendel's opinion responds to this potential objection with an eye to the lived experience of those subject to the law. It quotes a remarkable passage in which Justice Sotomayor interrogated the Associate Solicitor General during the *Rodriguez* argument, noting that jailed immigrants wear orange suits, are shackled, and "referred to by number, not by name," before asking "[i]n which ways is immigration detention different than criminal detention?"[13] Again invoking substance over form, they argue immigration detention must constitute punishment if the conditions of incarceration are indistinguishable from those used to punish.

While this approach to challenging the constitutionality of immigration detention is undoubtedly powerful, the rationale on which it rests is actually quite narrow, as it suggests that improved conditions of confinement would render immigration detention permissible. However convincing that rationale would be with respect to current conditions of immigration detention, it does not provide a strong foundation on which to rule all immigration detention necessarily unlawful.[14]

---

[12] *See generally* Bell v. Wolfish, 441 U.S. 520, 536–37 (1979).

[13] There is support for this approach in some civil detention doctrine. *See, e.g.,* King v. County of Los Angeles, 885 F.3d 548, 557 (9th Cir. 2018) (conditions "presumptively punitive" if sufficiently "similar to" prison).

[14] Conditions in immigration detention centers have not improved since we compiled the record describing them in *Rodriguez*. *See* Brief for Respondents Alejandro Rodriguez, et al., No. 15-1204, at 8–9, Jennings v. Rodriguez, 138 S. Ct. 830 (2018) (describing "prison-like conditions"). Indeed, conditions grew worse during the pandemic. *See generally* ACLU, *The Survivors: Stories of People Released from ICE Detention During the COVID-19 Pandemic* (2021) (available at: www.aclu.org/report/survivors).

I agree with Sherman-Stokes and Schendel that proper application of modern civil detention doctrine would render virtually all immigration detention unconstitutional, but for different reasons. Although the *Rodriguez* petitioners did not argue that all immigration detention is unconstitutional, the basis for such an argument is available in the record.

The two permissible rationales courts have recognized for immigration detention are flight risk and danger to the community. Neither supports immigration detention, at least in anything like its present form. As with all civil detention, immigration detention for the purpose of ensuring appearance at removal hearings (or for physical removal, if necessary) is not permissible if the government can ensure appearance through other methods. As a result, to defend this form of civil confinement, the government must show that other methods of supervision cannot accomplish its goal.

Whether or not the government could ever have made that showing – an issue hotly contested in *Demore* itself – it could not make it today. The record in *Rodriguez* includes the testimony of the government's own witness stating that Intensive Supervision programs ensure appearance at removal proceedings close to 100 percent of the time. Reports published by the government's contractors corroborate what its witness said, showing appearance rates consistently above ninety-five percent. More recent studies of programs focused on immigrant families have shown similar success. And such programs are now ubiquitous. Indeed, on any given day DHS now has far more people under supervision programs than it confines in detention centers.[15] While the government could perhaps show, in a very unusual case, that a particular individual's history proves they are among the one in a hundred people who will not appear, such cases would be vanishingly rare.

Immigration detention also cannot be justified to ameliorate the risk of danger to the community. Noncitizens who present a danger can already be held under laws that apply to citizens. If law enforcement officials in the criminal law system have chosen not to detain a given noncitizen, it makes no sense for the immigration laws to require their confinement based on danger. Unlike in the criminal context, people detained under the immigration laws have generally served their time for any underlying criminal offenses, and in all cases remain subject to criminal confinement if any outstanding criminal charges remain. In that sense they differ – and fundamentally so – from individuals held prior to criminal trial.

Put another way, if the law permits the release of a citizen with a given criminal history, it cannot require the incarceration of a noncitizen with that same criminal history *based on their dangerousness*, because "the alien's removable status itself … bears no relation to a detainee's dangerousness." *Zadvydas*, 533 U.S. at 692. While I believe this basic doctrinal infirmity sufficient to refute any argument for the

---

[15] *See* Transactional Records Access Clearinghouse, "Over 180,000 Immigrants Now Monitored by ICE's Alternatives to Detention Program" (available at: https://trac.syr.edu/immigration/reports/678/).

preventive detention of noncitizens under the immigration laws, it also bears mention that no evidence shows such detention works to protect the public. In fact, overwhelming evidence has established that immigration enforcement as a whole has no public safety benefit, even when purportedly targeted to focus on people who have committed serious crimes. Numerous studies have established this fact.[16]

Thus, whether analyzed under a "least restrictive means" test or some more permissive due process standard, it is very hard to defend immigration detention in any form – regardless of the conditions of confinement – as a constitutionally permissible measure for preventing flight or protecting the community.

CONCLUSION

We filed *Rodriguez* in September 2006. We won the injunction requiring bond hearings in 2012. For more than ten years since that time, the *Rodriguez* injunction has provided people incarcerated under the immigration laws with a modicum of due process – a bond hearing after six months of confinement, so long as their cases remain pending. But what is perhaps most striking about *Rodriguez* now, seventeen years after we filed it, is how modest it seems. Even as the Supreme Court has grown more hostile to immigrants' rights, legal scholars, advocates within the immigrants' rights movement, and social scientists studying immigration enforcement have shown that the legal justification for immigration detention is remarkably thin. It must be defended primarily by reference to cases that draw critical support from racist nineteenth century caselaw, and it lacks any policy justification given modern measures of its effectiveness.

Professors Sherman-Stokes and Schendel's Feminist Judgment imagines a Supreme Court that rejects the racist foundations of plenary power doctrine, declares current deportation and immigration detention schemes punitive, and affirms the modest relief provided by the *Rodriguez* injunction. In doing so, it also creates space for elaboration of a basic point we could never make in our *Rodriguez* briefing: that because noncitizens are "persons," the Fifth Amendment prohibits their incarceration without trial pursuant to the immigration laws, whether or not they receive a bond hearing after six months.

JENNINGS v. RODRIGUEZ, 138 S. CT. 830 (2018)

Justices Sarah Sherman-Stokes and Sarah Schendel, for the majority.

Every day, tens of thousands of noncitizens[17] endure prolonged detention in jails and prisons, for the purpose of seeking the right to remain in the United States. The

---

[16] *See generally* Anna Flagg, *Deportations Reduce Crime? That's Not What the Evidence Shows*, NEW YORK TIMES (Sept. 23, 2019) (collecting studies).

[17] This Court will refrain from using the derisive term, "alien." The term is legally and factually inaccurate, and serves only to dehumanize a class of persons.

question before this Court is simple: whether and for how long the United States government may separate noncitizen parents from their children, noncitizen caregivers from their dependents, and noncitizen breadwinners from their households without individualized review of their custody status, and detain them in prisons and jails in notoriously dangerous conditions. *See* 8 U.S.C. § 1225(b) (requiring the detention of inadmissible noncitizens arriving at or near U.S. borders until they are removed, or until there is a finding that they have a credible fear of returning to their home country and are thus eligible to apply for asylum); 8 U.S.C. § 1226(a) (permitting the detention of noncitizens in removal proceedings who are a danger to the community or flight risk); 8 U.S.C. § 1226(c) (requiring the detention of certain noncitizens convicted of certain crimes).

In this case, we specifically consider the rights of three distinct classes of noncitizens, (1) asylum seekers; (2) those noncitizens who have been convicted of a crime and have completed their sentence; and (3) noncitizens who are physically present within the United States but who, legally, are considered to be "seeking admission" to the United States.

But a bland description of the classes of noncitizens impacted tells us nothing about their lives, or the impact of prolonged detention on those lives. The wife of class member Abdirizak Adan Farah, for example, was left by the U.S. Government to raise their three-month-old U.S. Citizen baby alone while Abdirizak sat in immigration detention, unable to present evidence that he was neither a flight risk nor a threat to the community. Class member Abel Perez Ruelas' wife, a U.S. Citizen nurse at a senior-living facility, raised their children for more than 560 days without her co-parent. The four children of Yussuf Abdikadir were similarly without their father for more than 202 days. Although the court would prefer to refer to them by name, the plaintiffs have not disclosed the names of their family members, a decision which this court respects and understands in light of ICE's ongoing harassment of immigrants and their families. While the average length of detention is 365 days, some members of these classes have been apart from their families for 387 days, 438 days, 446 days, 561 days, 608 days, 831 days, and in one case, 1,095 days. They have missed birthdays – in some cases year after year – as well as celebrations, holidays, milestones and family rituals.

The fathers, husbands,[18] long term residents, workers, and community members in this case argue that the relevant statutory provisions – §§ 1225(b), 1226(a), and 1226(c) – do not authorize "prolonged" detention in the absence of an individualized bond

---

[18] This Court takes notice that all of the named class members in this case are men. The stories of women, gender nonconforming, gender nonbinary and trans immigrant detainees are significant. These groups of detainees face special challenges and dangers in immigration detention, including increased rates of abuse and sexual assault. *See* Lauren Zitsch, *Where the American Dream Becomes a Nightmare: LGBT Detainees in Immigration Detention Facilities*, 22 Wм. Mary J. Women L. 105 (2015); Our Moment for Reform: Immigration and Transgender People, National Center for Transgender Equality (2013).

hearing at which the Government proves by clear and convincing evidence that the class member's detention remains justified. Further, the Petitioners argue, the absence of such a hearing violates the Due Process Clause of the Fifth Amendment. On both points, we agree. Justice Alito believes that the relevant statutory provisions cannot be read to require bond hearings every six months "without doing violence to the statutory language[.]" *Jennings v. Rodriguez*, 138 S. Ct. 830, 848 (2018). But in fact, we do catastrophic violence to immigrant families and communities when we use "doing violence" to a legal statute as a justification for caging human beings for months, and years, at a time without meaningful review.

The Due Process Clause applies to all "persons" within the United States, including noncitizens, whether they are here lawfully or not. See *Yick Wo v. Hopkins*, 118 U.S. 356, 369 (1886); *Wong Wing v. United States*, 163 U.S. 228, 238 (1896). This Court will no longer engage in the legal fiction that noncitizens, held in detention facilities, jails and prisons within the United States are not "in the United States." They are on United States soil, within the jurisdiction of the United States, and they are protected by the laws of this country. See *Wong Wing*, 163 U.S. at 238.

We have recognized before that prolonged mandatory detention without meaningful review raises serious Constitutional concerns. And as this Court did previously in *Zadvydas*, we construe the statute to impose a six-month limit on detention because the Constitution requires periodic review of custody. *Zadvydas v. Davis*, 533 U.S. 678 (2001). And as was done following the Court's decision in *Zadvydas*, the immigration agency should also create an administrative review structure to provide for bond hearings after that time.

I

"Civil" Detention

While the use of immigration detention in the United States is longstanding, the number of those detained has ebbed and flowed over the years. The Immigration and Nationality Act (INA) was passed in 1952 and established the grounds upon which noncitizens could be denied entry into the United States and detained. INA, 8 U.S.C. §§ 1101–1407 (1952). The INA also granted immigration authorities discretion to release from detention on bond certain noncitizens, based on community ties and pending a final determination of removability.

Though there remained targeted detentions and deportations throughout the 1950s, 1960s, and 1970s, there was a decline in the systemic use of immigration detention during this time. Indeed, in 1954 the United States announced it would end detention except in extraordinary circumstances. See Att'y Gen. Herbert Brownell, Jr., Address at Naturalization Ceremonies (Nov. 11, 1954). Until 1988, release was the presumption for noncitizens arrested by immigration authorities and the burden was on the government to demonstrate that a noncitizen was a danger and/or a flight risk, thus justifying their detention under the INA. *See* 8 C.F.R. §§ 212.5(a)(2)(ii), 242.24 In 1994, an average of 6,785 persons were detained by immigration authorities on any given day. Will Matthews, *The Big Business of Inhumane Detention of Immigrants* (Nov. 1, 2011) (available at: www.aclu.org/blog/big-business-inhumane-detention-immigrants). In 2017, while the unnamed partners, parents and loved ones waited at home for people like Abel, Alejandro, Yusuf, Jose, and Abdirizak to return, over 323,000 people were booked into an ICE detention facility. Immigration and Customs Enforcement, *FY 2017 ICE Enforcement and Removal Operations Report*, Figure 11, at 11 (available at: www.ice.gov/sites/default/files/documents/Report/2017/iceEndOfYearFY2017.pdf).

In 1893, we held in *Fong Yue Ting* that the power to deport a noncitizen is as absolute and unqualified as the power to exclude. *Fong Yue Ting, v. United States*, 149 U.S. 698, 746–47 (1893). This holding, an extension of the principle announced in *Chae Chan Ping* four years prior, was an extraordinary leap – granting plenary power to the federal government insofar as the regulation of noncitizens was concerned, whether or not they were inside, or outside, the United States. *See Ping v. United States*, 130 U.S. 581 (1889). Together, *Chae Chan Ping* and *Fong Yue Ting* set the stage for how this Court, and by extension this country, would view immigration detention in the decades to come, including which procedural and substantive protections would attach, and which would not. The Court in *Fong Yue Ting* declared that an order of deportation is not punishment for a crime, but rather "a method of enforcing the return of [a noncitizen] who hasn't complied." *Fong Yue Ting*, 149 U.S. at 730. The ghost of this dicta – that detention and deportation are not criminal, but civil – has haunted more than a century of immigration jurisprudence, and destroyed the lives of millions of noncitizens and their families in the decades since. *See Reno v. American-Arab Anti-Discrimination Committee*, 525 U.S. 471, 491 (1999) (holding that removal is not punishment, irrespective of the acknowledged reality that removal may result in severe penalties including the loss of life, liberty and property); *INS v. Lopez-Mendoza*, 468 U.S. 1032, 1038 (1984) ("A deportation proceeding is a purely civil action … [and is not intended] to punish an unlawful entry …."); *Harisiades v. Shaughnessy*, 342 U.S. 580, 594 (1952) ("Deportation, however severe its consequences, has been consistently classified as a civil rather than a criminal procedure."). As recently as 2001, this Court noted that "[t]he proceedings at issue here are civil, not criminal, and we assume that they are nonpunitive in purpose and effect." *Zadvydas*, 533 U.S. at 690. It is doubtful that the more than 323,000 persons in immigration detention in 2017, to say nothing of those already deported, and the family members left behind, would feel similarly.

In 2010, this Court opened the door to a more nuanced – and indeed more honest – appraisal of immigration detention and the profound impact of deportation on individuals and their families. *See Padilla v. Kentucky*, 559 U.S. 356, 364 (2010). In *Padilla*, we acknowledged that, "[t]he importance of accurate legal advice for noncitizens accused of crimes has never been more important … *as a matter of federal law, deportation is an integral part – indeed, sometimes the most important part – of the penalty that may be imposed on noncitizen defendants who plead guilty to specified crimes." Id.* (emphasis added).

In this case, the Court has the opportunity and obligation to denounce the lie we have been telling since 1893: that immigration detention and deportation are not punitive. Plainly, immigration detention and deportation are, in fact, punishment. Justice Sotomayor's rhetorical questioning at oral argument is illustrative:

> In which ways is immigration detention different than criminal detention? I mean, I–I understand right now that when you detain aliens, you put them in orange suits, they are shackled during visitation and court visits, they are subject to surveillance and strip searches, they are referred to by number, not by name. So in which ways is immigration detention different than criminal detention?

Transcript of Oral Reargument at 8, *Jennings*, 138 S. Ct. 830 (No. 15-1204).

We must answer truthfully: there is no difference. Immigration detention is criminal rather than civil. If we are to maintain a system of detaining noncitizens, then from that recognition should flow concomitant procedural and substantive safeguards not currently available. *See, e.g.*, Anil Kalhan, *Rethinking Immigration Detention*, 110 COLUM. L. REV. SIDEBAR 42 (2010) (discussing the possibilities and limits of a "truly civil detention system" in recognizing that the immigration detention is criminal and the limited protections in light of this); Robert Pauw, *A New Look at Deportation As Punishment: Why At Least Some of the Constitution's Criminal Procedure Protections Must Apply*, 52 ADMIN. L. REV. 305 (2000) (arguing that deportees "are being punished not only as a matter of ordinary discourse, but also as a matter of law" and as such "at least some of the constitutional safeguards that traditionally apply in the context of criminal prosecutions must apply in cases like these"); César Cuauhtémoc García Hernández, *Immigration Detention as Punishment*, 35 IMMIGR. & NAT'Y L. REV. 385 (2014) (arguing that though immigration detention is criminal, the constitutional limitations imposed by criminal procedure are ill-equipped to address immigration detention); Gabriel J. Chin, *Illegal Entry as Crime, Deportation as Punishment: Immigration Statute and the Criminal Process*, 58 UCLA L. REV. 1417 (2010). Primary among these protections should be regular individualized custody determinations and a limit on the length of detention authorized under the statute.

In coming to this conclusion, we discount the precedential authority of case law from the 1800s and early 1900s, that gives credence to immigration detention being civil, and we note its disturbing and racist origins. *See, e.g., Ping*, 130 U.S. 581; *Fong Yue Ting*, 149 U.S. at 706–07, 732 (finding a statute constitutional which required "hearing the testimony of a credible white witness," because "persons of the Chinese race" were not credible witnesses); *id.* at 743 (Brewer, J., dissenting) ("It is true this statute is directed only against the obnoxious Chinese[.]"); *Harisiades v. Shaughnessy*, 342 U.S. 580 (1952); *Shaughnessy v. United States ex rel. Mezei*, 345 U.S. 206 (1953).

II

Due Process in Criminal and Civil Cases

Prior to the injunction issued by the District Court for the Central District of California, the detained class members in the instant case had no individualized hearing to determine whether they pose a safety or flight risk justifying their continued detention. And some of them have been detained for almost three years without such review.

Noncitizens within the United States, including asylum seekers and arriving noncitizens as in the instant case, are protected by the Constitution. Relevant to this case are the Constitution's protections against excessive bail spelled out in the Eighth Amendment and the right to due process in the Fifth Amendment. *See Carlson v. Landon,* 342 U.S. 524, 545 (1952). The Fifth Amendment's Due Process Clause forbids the Government to "depriv[e]" any "person ... of ... liberty ... without due process of law." Freedom from imprisonment – from government custody, detention, or other forms of physical restraint – lies at the heart of the liberty that Clause protects. See *Foucha v. Louisiana,* 504 U.S. 71, 80 (1992). That is, the Due Process Clause applies to all "persons" within the United States, including noncitizens, whether their presence here is authorized, unauthorized, temporary, or permanent. See *Plyler v. Doe,* 457 U.S. 202, 210 (1982); *Mathews v. Diaz,* 426 U.S. 67, 77 (1976); *Kwong Hai Chew v. Colding,* 344 U.S. 590, 596–598, and n. 5 (1953); *Yick Wo v. Hopkins,* 118 U.S. 356, 369 (1886); cf. *Mezei,* supra, at 212 (noncitizens "who have once passed through our gates, even illegally, may be expelled only after proceedings conforming to traditional standards of fairness encompassed in due process of law"). The Constitutional right to due process encompasses eligibility for bail. *See United States v. Salerno,* 481 U.S. 739, 748–51 (1987); *Schilb v. Kuebel,* 404 U.S. 357, 365 (1971).

The civil label was first applied to deportation proceedings in 1893. *See Fong Yue Ting,* 149 U.S. at 730. In more than a century of scholarship and case law since then, it has become plain that deportation is punishment or worse, violence. *See, e.g., id.* at 755–57 (Field, J., dissenting) (noting the historic distinctions between the power to exclude, which was civil, and the power to expel, which was criminal); Daniel Kanstroom, *Deportation, Social Control, and Punishment: Some Thoughts About Why Hard Laws Make Bad Cases,* 113 HARV. L. REV. 1890, 1893–94 (2000) (explaining that, "deportation of long-term lawful permanent residents for post-entry criminal conduct seems in most respects to be a form of punishment"); Stephen H. Legomsky, *The New Path of Immigration Law: Asymmetric Incorporation of Criminal Justice Norms,* 64 WASH. & LEE L. REV. 469, 471 (2007) ("The underlying theories of deportation increasingly resemble those of criminal punishment."); Pauw, *supra,* at 313 ("It is this refusal to give serious consideration to the family rights at stake that makes deportation look much more like punishment ...."). Indeed, deportation has

long been compared to a kind of sentence, and even a death sentence, for noncitizens; and an "exile, a dreadful punishment." *United States ex rel. Klonis v. Davis*, 13
F.2d 630, 630 (2nd Cir. 1926); *see also Harisiades*, 342 U.S. at 660 (Douglas, J., dissenting) (referring to deportation and stating bluntly, "banishment is punishment in
the practical sense"); Bryan Schatz, *Our Immigration Courts Aren't Ready to Handle
Millions of Deportations*, MOTHER JONES (Mar. 21, 2017), www.motherjones.com/
politics/2017/03/immigration-court-deportations-trump-asylum/ (Chief Immigration
Judge Marks explaining, "I often say that we do death penalty cases in a traffic court
setting. With the case of an asylum seeker – that's life or death"); Tom O'Connor,
Iraqi Christians Face 'Death Sentence' as Trump Prepares Mass Deportations,
NEWSWEEK (June 14, 2017), www.newsweek.com/iraq-christians-trump-death-
sentence-deportation-625722 (comparing deportation to a death sentence for Iraqi
Christians); Chloe Sang-Hun, *Deportation a 'Death Sentence' to Adoptees After a
Lifetime in the U.S.*, N.Y. TIMES (July 7, 2017), www.nytimes.com/2017/07/02/world/
asia/south-korea-adoptions-phillip-clay-adam-crapser.html (comparing deportation to a death sentence for Korean adoptees who did not become United States
citizens); Tom Hayden, *When Deportation is a Death Sentence*, LA TIMES (June
28, 2004), http://articles.latimes.com/2004/jun/28/opinion/oe-hayden28 (comparing
deportation to a death sentence for alleged gang members from Central America).
As we affirmed in *Padilla*, deportation is a "drastic measure." *Padilla*, 559 U.S. at
356. And as this court has held, "even where detention is permissible … due process
requires 'adequate procedural protections' to ensure that the government's asserted
justification for physical confinement 'outweighs the individual's constitutionally
protected interest in avoiding physical restraint.'" *Casas-Castrillon*, 535 F.3d at 950
(*quoting Zadvydas*, 522 U.S at 690).

So, while historically these proceedings have been treated as "civil," this Court
today announces that they are henceforth punitive proceedings. These are adversarial proceedings in which unrepresented noncitizens are out resourced by highly
trained government attorneys and in which noncitizens may be facing not only a
loss of liberty and "all that makes life worth living," but also stand to face permanent banishment from the United States. *See Bridges v. Wixon*, 326 U.S. 135, 147
(1945). Because the noncitizens in these classes are protected by the Constitution,
the punitive proceedings to which they are subject require the concomitant safeguards and procedural protections afforded to criminal defendants. Specifically,
they are entitled to periodic, and meaningful, hearings on the status of their custody. A "meaningful" hearing is one in which the detained noncitizen can fairly
present her case, including presenting evidence on her behalf and challenging any
evidence presented by the government.

There are few comparable civil proceedings where custody is at issue. This itself
is notable – it should be exceedingly rare that a civil matter results in detention, let
alone detention of this prolonged and indefinite kind. Where custody is a feature, an
individualized hearing or similar is provided. *See, e.g., Kansas v. Hendricks*, 521 U.S.

346 (1997) (finding that involuntary confinement does not violate the due process clause and is nonpunitive under the Kansas Sexually Violent Predator Act, though such persons get a hearing prior to confinement and the right to annual review); *United States v. Comstock*, 560 U.S. 126 (2010) (holding that a federal statute allowing a district court to order civil commitment, beyond the date an inmate would otherwise be released, of a 'sexually dangerous' federal prisoner was constitutional under the Necessary and Proper Clause). The Court finds no reason not to "treat like cases alike" and will do so here. See H.L.A. HART, THE CONCEPT OF LAW 160, 163–66 (Penelope A. Bulloch & Joseph Raz eds., 3d ed. 2012); CHAÏM PERELMAN, JUSTICE (1967); CHAÏM PERELMAN, DE LA JUSTICE (1945). Moreover, the Court has previously found periodic bail hearings to be required in a number of other immigration contexts. See, e.g., *In re Ah Moy*, 21 F. 808 (C.C.D. Cal. 1884); *Wong Wing*, 163 U.S. at 235 (finding detention Constitutional, but making analogy to criminal detention); *Tod v. Waldman*, 266 U.S. 113 (1924) (providing for release on bail); *Michel v. I.N.S.*, 119 F. Supp. 2d 485, 498 (M.D. Pa. 2000) (citing *Chi Thon Ngo v. I.N.S.*, 192 F.3d 390, (3d Cir. 1999)); *Zadvydas*, 533 U.S. at 690; *Wilks v. U.S. Dep't of Homeland Sec.*, No. CIV. 1:CV-07-2171, 2008 WL 4820654, *2 (M.D. Pa. Nov. 3, 2008) (citing *Prieto–Romero v. Clark*, 534 F.3d 1053, 1065–66 (9th Cir. 2008)). The Court will not depart from that trend in this case. To prevent the prolonged, unreviewable detention of thousands of noncitizens within the United States, the statute must be read to require a bail hearing.

III

The Plenary Power Doctrine and Constitutional Exceptionalism in Immigration Law

In 1889, this Court held that the United States' power to exclude is an "incident of sovereignty." *Ping*, 130 U.S. at 609. In upholding a ferociously racist statute excluding Chinese citizens from admission to the United States, this Court held that the power to exclude noncitizens is so basic to nationhood that the Constitution cannot limit it. *Id. Chae Chan Ping*, despite, or perhaps because of, its xenophobic origins, has come to stand for the proposition that the political branches enjoy extremely broad discretion over whom to admit to the United States and how to treat them while it decides, and that courts should not scrutinize those choices too closely. *Id.* at 626 ("Legislation for such regulation, limitation, or suspension was [e]ntrusted to the discretion of our government …."). *Chae Chan Ping* has never been overruled and in fact has been relied upon to support a stunning breadth of congressional power in immigration law. We are deeply concerned by the lack of Constitutional limits placed on the so-called "plenary power" and what has come to be known as a kind of "immigration exceptionalism." *See, e.g.,* GERALD L. NEUMAN, STRANGERS TO THE CONSTITUTION: IMMIGRANTS, BORDERS, AND FUNDAMENTAL LAW (Princeton University Press 1996);

Gabriel J. Chin, *Is There a Plenary Power Doctrine? A Tentative Apology and Prediction for Our Strange but Exceptional Constitutional Immigration Law*, 14 GEO. IMMIGR. L.J. 257 (2000). Though outside the scope of the instant case, this Court's historic reluctance to carefully examine immigration statutes for Constitutional problems, is troubling. As immigration legal scholars have suggested, this approach is misguided, outdated and overdue for reexamination. *See, e.g.*, Hiroshi Motomura, *Immigration Law After a Century of Plenary Power: Phantom Constitutional Norms and Statutory Interpretation*, 100 YALE L.J. 545 (1990).

IV

Absent Individualized Bond Hearings, §§ 1225(b), 1226(a), and 1226(c) Violate the Constitution

Ensuring due process rights are fulfilled in the form of a bond hearing not only corrects a historical wrong, it will also allow for greater access to lawyers, reunification with families, and fair access to resources denied to those detained.

For more than twenty years, this Court has recognized that freedom from prolonged immigration detention lies "at the heart" of the Due Process clause of the Constitution; that all persons, including immigrants, are protected from being deprived of their liberty without due process of law. *Zadvydas*, 533 U.S. at 679, 690. It is for these reasons, and applying the statutory canon of constitutional avoidance, that the lower court in this case has previously read a six-month limit into the statute for those in post-removal order detention; finding that unless the government could show that removal was reasonably foreseeable, noncitizens facing deportation are entitled to periodic reviews of their custody status. *Rodriguez v. Robbins*, 804 F.3d 1060, 1086, 1090 (9th Cir. 2015), rev'd sub nom. *Jennings*, 138 S. Ct. 830.

The Government would have this court believe that §§ 1225(b), 1226(a), and 1226(c) authorize detention without review until the conclusion of removal proceedings without jeopardizing due process. It points to *Demore v. Kim* as support. *Demore v. Kim*, 538 U.S. 510 (2003). In *Demore v. Kim* we held that Congress did not run afoul of Due Process rights under the Fifth Amendment in holding that noncitizens can be detained pursuant to the no-bail provisions of the INA. *Id.*, at 531. In that case, we considered the government's concern that released noncitizens would fail to appear at their removal hearings against the noncitizens' liberty interest. In dissenting from the majority opinion in *Demore*, we wrote, "[t]he issue is whether [the plenary power] may be exercised by detaining a still lawful permanent resident [noncitizen] when there is no reason for it and no way to challenge it." *Id.*, at 576.

We must interpret an immigration statute to require judicial review of a detention decision because "[a] statute permitting indefinite detention of a [noncitizen] would raise a serious constitutional problem." *Zadvydas* at 690. Put another way, "even where detention is permissible … due process requires 'adequate procedural protections' to ensure that the government's asserted justification for physical confinement 'outweighs the individual's constitutionally protected interest in avoiding physical restraint.'"] *Casas-Castrillon v. Dep't of Homeland Sec.*, 535 F.3d 942, 950 (9th Cir. 2008) (*quoting Zadvydas*, 522 U.S at 690).

The passage of time has revealed that our majority opinion in *Demore* was not only misguided, but based on clearly erroneous – and later disproven – data presented by the Government. The Court believed that the issue in *Demore* was distinct from that at issue in *Zadvydas* because detention under § 1226(c) has "a definite termination point": the conclusion of removal proceedings.[19] *Demore v. Kim*, at 512, 529. While such a distinction may allay concerns about prolonged detention that collides with due process, the truth is more harrowing in light of the Government's post-decision concession that the statistics presented in *Demore* were inaccurate. In briefing, the Government asserted that the average length of detention was four months, and five months in appealed cases. This, we know now, grossly understated the realities facing noncitizen detainees. In fact, the actual average length of detention was 382 days – or more than one year of being locked up, in jail, apart from their families and communities. Debra Cassens Weiss, *Justice Department Discloses "Several Significant Errors in Information Provided for SCOTUS Case*, A.B.A. J. (Aug. 31, 2016), www.abajournal.com/news/article/justice_department_discloses_several_significant_errors_in_information_prov. Were this Court aware of the true duration of detention without review at issue in *Demore v. Kim*, we would have held that due process demanded periodic review at regular intervals. Such review is necessary to consider the individual facts and concerns specific to each detained noncitizen and avoid unjustified years-long detention.

V

Class Actions: Embracing Power in Numbers While Valuing Individuality

This case reaches the Court as a class action, aggregating claims of many similarly situated noncitizens. While each claimant has a valuable, and individual, story to tell, much of their power in challenging their prolonged detention is in their numbers. Because we are concerned that the government wishes to disable future class action lawsuits, we pause here to consider the value of the class action and to affirm its role in this case, and in future cases.

---

[19] The Court also notes that during oral argument, Counsel for the Petitioners suggested that a noncitizen "always has the option of terminating the detention by accepting a final order of removal and returning home." Transcript of Oral Reargument at 25, *Jennings*, 138 S. Ct. 830 (No. 15-1204). This option, presented as neutral, is not. Many noncitizens are facing permanent separation from their family and community, or even danger or harm, if removed to their countries of origin. What's more, some noncitizens may no longer consider their country of removal "home" if they have made a life in the United States.

Following Rodriguez' habeas petition arguing that he was entitled to a bond hearing, Rodriguez subsequently moved for class certification on these claims in the Central District of California. The certification of the class and subclasses is not before this court. Our focus is on what process – having constituted a class – they are due.

We are particularly struck by one dynamic in this case's construction. The classes have been constituted for the reasons common to class actions – the power of commonality, of numbers, and the ability to represent a multitude of individuals impacted by the procedures and policies in question. In doing so, in joining together, it is perhaps inevitable that the individual circumstances of each class member become obscured, to the detriment of the Petitioners and this Court. This is particularly meaningful in this case, as what Petitioners ask for is not only the potential end to their prolonged detention, but for an individualized hearing, and the attention of a judge to the unique, fact-specific considerations in their case.

A significant challenge for this Court in cases such as this is holding in mind the position of each individual immigrant, whose experience is entirely her own, while making decisions about one of the many groups to which she may belong. We must be careful that the power of the class action – its number and scope – not overshadow its goal of making the less powerful, the too-often unseen, visible.

The modern class action is a result of movements for social change and equality among the too often marginalized. *See* Brooke D. Coleman & Elizabeth F. Porter, *Reinvigorating Commonality: Gender and Class Actions*, 92 N.Y.U. L. REV. 895 (2017) ("The modern class action, the modern feminist movement, and Title VII of the Civil Rights Act of 1964 were all products of the creativity and turmoil of the 1960s."); *see also id.* at 896 (arguing that "the theoretical concept of commonality – cohesion, unity – in the women's movement has had a significant impact on the ability of women to seek collective redress for work-place discrimination through class actions"). Class actions allow groups to overcome "classic barriers to judicial justice such as lack of resources, lack of access to lawyers, and retaliation" by defendants/respondents "against individuals who file suit." *Id.* at 898. At their most impactful, class action lawsuits have the potential to "force industry-wide change, even in the most entrenched, male-dominated industries." *Id.* (*quoting* Anita Hill, *Class Actions Could Fight Discrimination in Tech*, N.Y. TIMES (Aug. 8, 2017)). Whether this is viewed as a feature or a bug of the class action is open to interpretation, and is part of a broader "fight over ideas about litigation's proper role in a democracy." David Marcus, *The History of the Modern Class Action, Part I: Sturm Und Drang*, 1953–1980, 90 WASH. U. L. REV. 587, 590–92 (2013) (explaining that "[c]onsumer advocates, civil rights practitioners, and plaintiffs' lawyers" have argued for a "regulatory conception" of Rule 23, where class actions offer an "important substitute for, or addition to, public administration, and courts should deploy the device aggressively to maximize regulatory efficacy").

That this case is a class action is, by itself, an important indicator of the vast number of immigrants impacted by these laws. At the outset of the case, Rodriguez and his fellow petitioners were among over 350 detainees in the Central District of California alone who had endured at least six months of incarceration without an individualized hearing to determine the legitimacy of their ongoing detention. Amended Complaint, J.A. at 18–42, *Jennings*, 138 S. Ct. 830 (No. 15-1204). Specifically, Petitioners represent all people within the District who (1) are or will be detained for longer than six months pending completion of removal proceedings; (2) are not detained pursuant to one of the national security detention statutes; and (3) have not been afforded a hearing to determine whether their prolonged detention is justified. The subclasses are defined and represented as follows:

- Alejandro Rodriguez is a lawful permanent resident of the United States who arrived in the country as an infant. He is the brother and son of U.S. Citizens, a dental assistant who has been detained for over three years without a custody hearing and separated from his child while challenging the government's efforts to deport him. Abel Perez Ruelas is a stepfather to U.S. Citizens, the husband of a U.S. Citizen and a nurse at a senior-living facility. He is the recipient of an approved application to adjust his status, however is unable to do so due to his ongoing detention. Abel and Yusuf represent themselves as well as others detained under 8 U.S.C. § 1226(a).
- Abdirizak Aden Farah is a Somali refugee who faced persecution since childhood as a member of the Marehan minority in his country, and was almost killed as an adult after having his wrists slashed by members of the militant group al-Shabaab. He has been detained in the U.S. for over eight months without a hearing, or without any contact with his wife and baby daughter. Yussuf Abdikadir is a Somali refugee and survivor of war who (at age 11) lost his two brothers, father, and grandmother. He is a husband, and father of four, who has been detained for over seven months without a custody hearing, and without an attorney or the ability to represent himself due to not speaking English. Abdirizak and Yussuf represent themselves and those in subclass 8 U.S.C. § 1225(b).
- Jose Farias Cornejo is a Lawful Permanent Resident of the U.S. who was brought to the country as an infant and has never left. He is the brother of four U.S. Citizens, eligible for cancellation of removal and has been detained for over a year without a hearing to determine whether his detention remains justified. As Cornejo says, "[t]he time that I have spent in detention has been very hard on my family. It has been very difficult to be separated from my mother, siblings, and fiancé. I feel guilty that I cannot be there to help support them. I also have found it very difficult to fight my removal case while in detention. I struggled to find an attorney to help me while I've been in detention, which has delayed my case several months. I wish I could fight my case outside of detention, where I could be with my family and maintain better contact with my attorney." J.A., at 292, *Jennings*, 138 S. Ct. 830 (No. 15-1204). He represents himself as well as the others detained under §8 U.S.C. 1226(e).

Additional class members who are eligible for relief and are subject to mandatory detention include individuals from El Salvador, Ethiopia, Israel, Cambodia, and Senegal; an individual who missed the birth of his second child while detained; small business owners; and, an individual who was the primary caretaker for his seriously ill mother before she passed away during her son's 438 days of detention. *See, e.g.,* Declaration of Ahilan T. Arulanatham, J.A., at 202, 229–35; *Jennings*, 138 S. Ct. 830 (No. 15-1204). Each of the subclasses and class members are represented by an individual, constituted by many. Beyond the walls of detention, each individual class member represents not just others similarly situated, but also an impacted family and community.

As Petitioners describe, detention of many class members is initiated by agents "simply ... checking a box on a form that contains no specific explanation and reflects no individualized deliberation." Petitioners' Notice of Motion and Motion for Summary Judgment at 9, *Rodriguez v. Holder*, No. CV 07-3239 TJH (RNBx) 2013 WL 5229795 (C.D. Cal. Aug. 6, 2013), *rev'd sub nom. Jennings v. Rodriguez*, 138 S. Ct. 830 (No. 15-1204). This is unfortunately in keeping with the way detained immigrants often have their individuality stripped away by the various administrative systems with which they are forced to engage. As Justice Sotomayor noted during oral arguments in an exchange about the similarities between immigration and criminal detention, in both cases, "they," the individuals detained, "are referred to by number, not by name." Transcript of Oral Reargument at 7–8, *Jennings*, 138 S. Ct. 830 (No. 15-1204).

Fair treatment of those detained requires that we reject a pro forma finding and instead depend on a consideration of the intricacies of each immigrant's past experience, current situation, and future access to relief. FEMINIST JUDGMENTS: REWRITTEN OPINIONS OF THE UNITED STATES SUPREME COURT 15 (Kathryn M. Stanchi, Linda L. Berger, & Bridget J. Crawford eds., 2016) ("Feminist practical reasoning recognizes that what counts as a problem and effective resolutions of that problem will depend on 'the *intricacies of each specific* factual context.' It brings together the voices and stories of *individual* women's lived experiences with the broader historical, cultural, economic, and social context described in historical and social science research. Feminist practical reasoning rejects the notion that there is a *monolithic* source for reason, values, and justifications ....") (emphasis added).

At oral argument, attorneys for the petitioners reminded us of the individuals who live the consequences of the interpretation of these statutory provisions. In referencing the "need for an inquiry, that is, the need for a hearing that is *individualized* rather than a categorical presumption that someone is a danger and flight risk," Mr. Arulanantham, counsel for the Petitioners, spoke as Mr. Rodriguez, saying, "*I came here at the age of one. I don't know anybody in the place I'm from, so I'm not a flight risk. Or I'm going to win my case because I'm eligible for cancellation of removal.*" Transcript of Oral Argument at 32, 48, *Jennings*, 138 S. Ct. 830 (No. 15-1204).

The use of individual narrative has a powerful history. "Critical race theorists use storytelling as a methodological tool for giving voice to marginalized persons and their communities. They tell stories that challenge the majority's stories in which it constructs for itself 'a form of shared reality in which its own superior position is seen as natural.' As a result, critical race theorists focus on giving voice to marginalized persons and communities because they are suppressed in the majority's stories." Adalberto Aguirre, *Academic Storytelling: A Critical Race Theory Story of Affirmative Action*, 43 Sociological Perspectives 319, 321 (2000), *citing* Richard Delgado *Storytelling for Oppositionists and Others: A Plea for Narrative*, 87 Mich. L. Rev. 2411, 2412 (1989).

An individual involved in any class action litigation is often required to lay bare their individual story and vulnerabilities, while also fitting into a pattern or structure of what is common and familiar, in order to make claims for individualized consideration. This case presents a question that appears to be part of a larger and more sinister attack on the notion of the due process class action claim. It is clear to us that the government may have been tempted to take this one step further toward the conclusion that class actions are an inappropriate avenue for individual liberty as required by the Due Process Clause; this Court rejects this path of inquiry.

CONCLUSION

Because the Court of Appeals correctly concluded that periodic bond hearings are required, we affirm the decision of the Ninth Circuit Court of Appeals. The Constitution mandates that bail proceedings, where detention continues for longer than six months, are required. Should there be any doubt, we also affirm that similarly situated respondents can litigate similar cases as a class, moving forward.

Finally, this Court recognizes that the right to periodic, individualized review does not guarantee release and that notwithstanding such review, many noncitizens may remain detained despite this ruling. One question not presented here, but which the Court invites future parties to raise, is the constitutionality of immigration detention itself, a practice which has grown more and more widespread, often with devastating, and even deadly, consequences. This Court is hard pressed to continue justifying the detention of noncitizens facing deportation; Abel, Alejandro, Yusuf, Jose, and Abdirizak, and their families and those like them, deserve better.

15

Commentary on *Department of Homeland Security v. Regents of the University of California*, 140 S. Ct. 1891 (2020)

Kevin R. Johnson

For years, debate has raged in the United States over immigration reform. Democrats and Republicans in Congress simply cannot agree on how to best fix what both concede to be a "broken" immigration system. A major stumbling block to reform has been the inability to compromise on whether Congress should create a pathway to citizenship for undocumented immigrants.[1]

Absent immigration reform, undocumented immigrants necessarily explore available relief under existing law. In deciding which noncitizens to seek to remove from the United States, the U.S. government has historically exercised some form of prosecutorial discretion. Through what is known as deferred action, the government may decline to enforce the immigration laws against certain noncitizens subject to removal under the immigration laws.[2] Deferred action allows the U.S. government to focus scarce enforcement resources on the removal of noncitizens who pose the greatest risk to public safety, such as serious criminals and terrorists.

With Congress failing to pass immigration reform during his first term, President Obama in 2012 unveiled the Deferred Action for Childhood Arrivals (DACA) policy.[3] It provided relief, including authorization to lawfully work, to undocumented

---

[1] *See generally* MICHAEL A. OLIVAS, PERCHANCE TO DREAM: A LEGAL AND POLITICAL HISTORY OF THE DREAM ACT AND DACA (2020) (providing a detailed account of various versions of the Development, Relief, and Education for Alien Minors (DREAM) Act, which would provide a durable legal status to young undocumented immigrants).

[2] *See generally* SHOBA SIVAPRASAD WADHIA, BEYOND DEPORTATION: THE ROLE OF PROSECUTORIAL DISCRETION IN IMMIGRATION CASES (2015).

[3] Janet Napolitano, Sec'y of Homeland Sec., Memorandum on Exercising Prosecutorial Discretion with Respect to Individuals Who Came to the United States as Children (June 15, 2012). The Obama administration later announced Deferred Action for Parents of Americans (DAPA). Pol'y Directive 044-02, Jeh C. Johnson, Sec'y of Homeland Sec., Memorandum on Exercising Prosecutorial Discretion with Respect to Individuals Who Came to the United States as Children and with Respect to Certain Individuals Who Are the Parents of U.S. Citizens or Permanent Residents (Nov. 20, 2014). A court enjoined the implementation of DAPA and it never went into effect. *See* United States v. Texas, 579 U.S. 547 (2016).

immigrants who arrived in the United States as children.[4] DACA benefited close to 800,000 undocumented immigrants.[5]

Some critics decried DACA as an unlawful "amnesty."[6] In pursuit of an aggressive immigration enforcement agenda, the Trump administration attempted to rescind DACA, which would have stripped DACA recipients of relief and subjected them to possible removal from the United States. The Supreme Court addressed challenges to the attempted rescission in the much-awaited decision in *Department of Homeland Security v. Regents of the University of California*.[7]

Recognizing the basic humanity of immigrants, Professor Jennifer Lee Koh's rewrite of the *Regents* decision expands the constitutional protections available to them. Besides exemplifying the best of feminist methodology, Koh directly addresses a critical issue that the Supreme Court failed to decide – the lawfulness of DACA.

THE SUPREME COURT OPINION

Writing for the 5-4 majority, Chief Justice John Roberts held that the Trump administration's effort to rescind DACA was "arbitrary and capricious" in violation of the Administrative Procedure Act (APA). Courts also have found that other Trump administration immigration-related policies violated the APA.[8] These rulings appear to have been influenced in no small part by the general assessment that the Trump administration routinely relied on raw political power, not reasoned policy analysis, in its immigration decisions.

The Court in *Regents* specifically concluded that the Trump administration had failed to satisfy the APA's basic procedural requirements for reasoned decision-making. Most fundamentally, the administration neglected to consider the weighty reliance interests of the DACA recipients at stake with rescission of the policy. As the Court specifically observed:

> Respondents ... stress that, since 2012, DACA recipients have "enrolled in degree programs, embarked on careers, started businesses, purchased homes, and even married and had children, all in reliance" on the DACA program. The consequences of the rescission, respondents emphasize, would "radiate outward" to DACA recipients' families, including their 200,000 U.S.-citizen children, to the schools where DACA recipients study and teach, and to the employers who have invested time and money in training them.[9]

---

4   Napolitano, *supra* note 3.
5   Jens Manuel Krogstad, *DACA Has Shielded Nearly 790,000 Young Unauthorized Immigrants from Deportation*, Pew Rsch. Ctr. (Sept. 1, 2017).
6   *See* Kevin R. Johnson, *Lessons About the Future of Immigration Law from the Rise and Fall of DACA*, 52 U.C. Davis L. Rev. 343, 365–70 (2018).
7   140 S. Ct. 1891 (2020).
8   *See, e.g.*, Dep't of Commerce v. New York, 139 S. Ct. 2551, 2575 (2019) (holding that the addition of a U.S. citizenship question to the 2020 Census had been done in violation of the Administrative Procedure Act).
9   140 S. Ct. at 1914 (citations omitted).

The Court further highlighted the evidence that DACA's rescission would have significant adverse impacts on the U.S. economy, which the Trump administration also had failed to consider. "[E]xcluding DACA recipients from the lawful labor force, may ... result in the loss of $215 billion in economic activity and an associated $60 billion in federal tax revenue over the next 10 years. Meanwhile, states and local governments could lose $1.25 billion in tax revenue each year."[10]

At the same time, Part IV of Chief Justice Roberts' opinion, which Justice Sotomayor did not join, concluded that plaintiffs had failed to plead facts sufficient to support a plausible inference that anti-Latinx racial animus motivated the Trump administration's rescission of DACA and thus violated the Equal Protection guarantee. The opinion expressed concern about opening the proverbial floodgates to Equal Protection challenges to immigration laws and policies:

> [B]ecause Latinos make up a large share of the unauthorized alien population, one would expect them to make up an outsized share of recipients of any cross-cutting immigration relief program. *Were this fact sufficient enough to state a claim, virtually any generally applicable immigration policy could be challenged on equal protection grounds.*[11]

That grudging analysis, if applied to future cases, ultimately would make it difficult to plead – much less prove – claims that provisions of the immigration laws and policies discriminate on the basis of race.

Chief Justice Roberts rejected the Equal Protection claim to the rescission of DACA despite the fact that nearly ninety percent of DACA recipients, who stood to lose their legal status with the dismantling of the policy, were Latinx[12] and President Trump had repeatedly vilified Latinx immigrants.[13] The cavalier treatment of the Equal Protection challenge to DACA's rescission holds significance because of the well-known impacts of the U.S. immigration laws on noncitizens of color from the developing world, impacts that the Chief Justice acknowledged in his opinion.[14] Given those racially disparate effects, Latinx people, U.S. citizens as well as immigrants, widely perceive the immigration laws and their enforcement as racially discriminatory. In turn, supporters of the President, as well as President Trump himself, no doubt understood the one-sided racial consequences of his immigration policies.

Dissenting from Part IV of Chief Justice Roberts' opinion, Justice Sonia Sotomayor cogently explained that "[t]he complaints each set forth particularized facts that

---

[10]   *Id.* (citation omitted).
[11]   *Id.* at 1915–16 (citation omitted) (emphasis added).
[12]   *See Top Countries of Origin for DACA Recipients*, Pew Rsch. Ctr. (Sept. 25, 2017).
[13]   *See, e.g.,* Eli Watkins & Abby Phillip, *Trump Decried Immigrants from "Shithole Countries" Coming to US*, CNN (Jan. 12, 2018); *"Drug Dealers, Criminals, and Rapists": What Trump Thinks of Mexicans*, BBC News (Aug. 31, 2016).
[14]   *See generally* Kevin R. Johnson, *Systemic Racism in the U.S. Immigration Laws*, 97 Ind. L.J. (forthcoming 2022).

plausibly allege discriminatory animus."[15] In making that assessment, she relied on the President's anti-Latinx statements, the overwhelming disparate impacts of DACA's rescission on Latinx persons, and the abrupt reversal of the policy.

THE FEMINIST JUDGMENT

Writing as Justice Koh, Professor Jennifer Lee Koh's revisiting of *Regents* places at the forefront the constitutional challenge to the rescission of DACA. By so doing, she engages in meaningful constitutional review of the policy's attempted dismantling. The rewritten opinion's discussion of the Supreme Court's 1982 decision in *Plyler v. Doe*,[16] which transformed the public schools by holding that Texas could not constitutionally deny undocumented children a K-12 education, powerfully demonstrates the benefits to noncitizens of constitutional review.

Candidly acknowledging that "[t]he nation's immigration laws have a long history of racism and discrimination," Koh rejects the miserly approach of Chief Justice Roberts to the pleading requirements for an Equal Protection challenge to the rescission of DACA. In line with Justice Sotomayor's dissent, Koh holds that the Board of Regents of the University of California can proceed on its claim that the plaintiffs plausibly alleged that the Trump administration's attempt to rescind DACA was racially motivated and therefore violated the Equal Protection guarantee.

Historically, successful constitutional challenges to the immigration laws and policies have been few and far between. Such challenges long have been, in many instances, barred outright. For example, upholding the discriminatory Chinese Exclusion Act of 1882,[17] the Supreme Court in *Chae Chan Ping v. United States* (*The Chinese Exclusion Case*), held that, if Congress "considers the presence of foreigners of a different race in this country, who will not assimilate with us, to be dangerous to its peace and security, ... *its determination is conclusive upon the judiciary*."[18] Rather than overruling *The Chinese Exclusion Case*, the Court continues to invoke what is known as the plenary power doctrine – the idea that Congress has absolute, denominated plenary power over the immigration laws – to immunize the U.S. immigration laws and policies from constitutional review.[19] Indeed, just days after it rejected the Trump administration's attempt to end DACA, the Court upheld application of a statutory provision allowing for the removal without due process of a Sri Lankan asylum seeker who was apprehended on U.S. soil, invoking

---

[15] . 140 S. Ct. at 1917 (Sotomayor, J. concurring in part, concurring in the judgment in part, and dissenting in part).

[16]   457 U.S. 202 (1982).

[17]   Ch. 126, 22 Stat. 58 (1882).

[18]   130 U.S. 581, 606 (1889) (emphasis added).

[19]   *See generally* Gabriel J. Chin, *Segregation's Last Stronghold: Race Discrimination and the Constitutional Law of Immigration*, 46 UCLA L. REV. 1 (1998).

with vigor an unvarnished version of the plenary power doctrine.[20] Similarly, the Supreme Court in 2018 relied on plenary power precedent to apply a toothless standard of review and uphold President Trump's ban on the admission of noncitizens into the United States from a group of predominantly Muslim nations.[21] Despite Donald Trump's many anti-Muslim statements, the Court accepted at face value the national security justification offered by the administration for the Muslim ban.

Even if a court finds that the pleading of an Equal Protection challenge satisfies the basic pleading standard, a plaintiff still must establish a discriminatory intent by the U.S. government to prevail.[22] Proving such an intent is incredibly difficult, especially with respect to challenging the generally color blind, race neutral modern U.S. immigration laws; it, however, is not impossible.[23] President Trump's inflammatory attacks on Latinx noncitizens provide potent evidence of a discriminatory intent in the decision to rescind DACA.[24]

As a majority of the Supreme Court did, Koh finds that DACA's rescission was arbitrary and capricious and violated the APA. She relies on *Heckler v. Chaney*[25] to refine the Court's analysis to generally limit review of discretionary decisions to enforce, rather than *not* enforce, the immigration laws. However, by bringing to the forefront stories of DACA recipients Yazmin, Sana, and Maricruz, Koh formidably strengthens the force of the majority's argument that the Trump administration failed to consider the full impacts of DACA's rescission on the beneficiaries of the policy. Emphasizing the devastating human costs of DACA's rescission in a way that the Supreme Court failed to do, Koh's opinion thus goes well beyond the Court's identification of the failure to meet the APA's technical procedural requirements.

Koh's rewritten decision does one last important thing. Responding to the policy's critics and the Trump administration accusation that DACA amounted to an unlawful "amnesty," she finds that DACA's rescission was arbitrary and capricious because it rested on the flawed assertion that DACA was unlawful. In so doing, Koh demonstrates that deferred action has long been "a feature of our immigration system" and "has been recognized as a practical reality by both Congress and the courts." By expressly holding that DACA was lawful, Koh addressed a central issue of the case that the Supreme Court studiously avoided.

Because the majority did not address DACA's lawfulness, it left open the door to the possibility that, if proper procedures were followed and relevant interests and factors were appropriately considered, a presidential administration hostile to

---

[20]   *See* Department of Homeland Security v. Thuraissigiam, 140 S. Ct. 1959, 1982–83 (2020).
[21]   *See* Trump v. Hawaii, 138 S. Ct. 2392, 2418–23 (2018).
[22]   *See, e.g.*, Washington v. Davis, 426 U.S. 229, 239–48 (1976).
[23]   *See, e.g.*, United States v. Carrillo-Lopez, 555 F.Supp. 3d 996 (D. Nev. 2021) (holding that, because Congress passed a law prohibiting illegal reentry into the United States after removal with a discriminatory intent against Mexican citizens, the law violates Equal Protection).
[24]   *See supra* note 13 and accompanying text.
[25]   470 U.S. 821 (1985).

immigration (like the Trump administration) could dismantle DACA. In fact, after the *Regents* decision, the Department of Homeland Security (DHS) continued to stridently dispute DACA's lawfulness. In an extraordinary press statement, it proclaimed that DACA was created "out of thin air and implemented illegally," and that the Court's decision "merely delays the President's lawful ability to end the illegal amnesty program."[26] That conclusory statement failed to acknowledge that the Supreme Court in *Regents* emphatically did not decide the lawfulness of DACA. Adamantly refusing to fully comply with the Court's decision, the Trump administration announced that it would not accept new DACA applications but would only review renewal requests from current DACA recipients.[27]

In her rewritten opinion, Koh rejects the Supreme Court's juiceless administrative law approach to reject DACA's rescission. Her feminist perspective adds measurably to the analysis. Koh firmly rejects the view that a facially neutral immigration policy cannot be racially discriminatory, which draws on foundational teachings of feminist legal theory.[28] Moreover, exemplifying feminist methodology that advocates bringing outsider perspectives to the forefront,[29] she tells the stories of DACA recipients to bring to life the true human impacts on real people of DACA's rescission. Although the majority opinion in *Regents* likely will have few lasting legal impacts, and certainly will not bring the nation meaningful immigration reform or in any way diminish the systemic racism embedded in contemporary U.S. immigration law and policy, Koh's analysis would allow future courts to squarely challenge and remove that racism.

IMMIGRATION REIMAGINED

Despite the Supreme Court's decision in *Regents*, DACA's turbulent journey is far from over. The Trump administration only partially complied with the decision by allowing current recipients to renew DACA relief but refusing to accept any new applications. After the Biden administration announced that it would accept new DACA applications, a district court in a case brought by DACA opponents enjoined the policy change.[30] The administration next proposed a rule authorizing DACA.[31]

---

[26] Press Release, Dep't of Homeland Sec., DHS Statement on Supreme Court Decision on DACA (June 18, 2020).

[27] *See* Vidal v. Wolf, No. 16-CV-4756 (NGG) (VMS), 2020 U.S. Dist. LEXIS 228328, at *23 (E.D.N.Y. Dec. 4, 2020) (ordering the Trump administration to accept new DACA applications).

[28] *See* Katherine T. Bartlett, *Feminist Legal Methods*, 103 HARV. L. REV. 829, 879 (1990) ("The postmodern critique of foundationalism is persuasive to many feminists, whose experiences affirm that rules and principles asserted as universal truths reflect particular, contingent realities that reinforce their subordination.").

[29] *See generally* Kathryn Abrams, *Hearing the Call of Stories*, 79 CAL. L. REV. 971 (1991) (articulating the need for outsider stories to be integrated into the critical analysis of the law).

[30] *See* Texas v. United States, 549 F. Supp. 3d 572 (S.D. Tex., 2021).

[31] Deferred Action for Childhood Arrivals, 86 Fed. Reg. 53,736 (Sept. 28, 2021).

Koh's rewritten decision reveals the influence of partisan politics on the Trump administration's decision to rescind DACA. Political skirmishing over DACA will likely continue. But DACA addressed simply one problem among many in the current U.S. immigration system. Perhaps the most contentious issue in the rancorous debate is whether the nation should regularize the immigration status of the roughly eleven million undocumented immigrants living in the United States. A political stalemate has made permanent relief for undocumented immigrants politically unattainable for the time being.

Interestingly, the Supreme Court's finding that the Trump administration's rescission of DACA violated the Administrative Procedure Act has had something of a boomerang effect. When the Biden administration attempted to walk back some of the Trump administration's more extreme immigration measures, courts relied on *Regents* to hold that such efforts were arbitrary and capricious.[32]

In the end, DACA is simply one battle in the larger war over comprehensive immigration reform. Ultimately, a congressional solution offering a durable immigration status to undocumented immigrants is necessary. Congress could pass a version of a bill that might, for example, create a path to lawful immigration status, and ultimately citizenship, for young undocumented immigrants as well as other groups of undocumented noncitizens. Other possibilities for immigration reform include relaxing the rules for legal immigration (and thus reducing the incentives under current law for undocumented immigration), decreasing the use of detention in immigration enforcement, reforming and restructuring the immigration court system, and changing the rules for applying for asylum. Unfortunately, immigration, with all its racial overtones, has become such a polarizing partisan issue that meaningful compromise in Congress to this point has proven to be impossible.

Put simply, DACA is the tip of the proverbial iceberg when it comes to the many problems that need to be addressed in contemporary immigration law and policy, a characteristic that makes the policy a somewhat unlikely lightning rod for the debate over immigration reform. That the debate about DACA stands for much more than DACA is evident from the damning claim that the policy amounts to an unlawful "amnesty" for undocumented immigrants, which is anathema to those who steadfastly oppose any kind of path to legalization for undocumented immigrants and, more generally, comprehensive immigration reform.

Whatever its ultimate impacts, DACA helped galvanize a generation engaged in a political movement seeking no less than full justice for immigrants.[33] The contemporary immigrant rights movement is active politically. Immigrants, including

---

[32] *See, e.g., Texas*, 549 F. Supp. 3d at 580–82, 622–24.
[33] *See* Kevin R. Johnson, *Bringing Racial Justice to Immigration Law*, 116 Nw. U.L. Rev. Online 1, 11–15 (2021) (discussing the impacts of the recent increase in immigrant activism in the United States and how it might help bring about immigration reform).

undocumented immigrants, openly participate in the political process in ways unlike immigrants – especially undocumented ones – of past eras. Life in the shadows of social life has been firmly rejected for strident advocacy. The growth in immigrant rights activism appears here to stay and at some point in time may help pressure Congress to pass immigration reform. By establishing meaningful constitutional limits on immigration law and policy and ensuring judicial review of constitutional challenges to the immigration laws, Koh's rewritten opinion in *Regents* would facilitate such reform by requiring a dialogue between the Courts, Congress, and the Executive Branch.

DEPARTMENT OF HOMELAND SECURITY v. REGENTS OF THE UNIVERSITY OF CALIFORNIA, 140 S. ct. 1891 (2020)

Justice Jennifer Lee Koh delivered the opinion of the Court:

This country has long struggled to reconcile its commitment to equality and liberty with its treatment of young people who came to the United States as children and call the United States home, but whose presence is not authorized by federal immigration authorities. *See, e.g., Plyler v. Doe*, 457 U.S. 202, 219–20 (1982). This case involves the federal government's recent approach to the unique considerations associated with this population, the exercise of executive discretion with respect to immigration law, and the principles that govern how the government deploys that discretion.

In the summer of 2012, the Department of Homeland Security (DHS) implemented an immigration program known as Deferred Action for Childhood Arrivals, or DACA. DACA allows certain immigrants who entered the United States as children, and who lack authorized immigration status, to apply for and receive DACA for periods of two years at a time. Being granted DACA means that recipients could receive some safety from deportation, become eligible to receive work authorization, and receive certain limited federal benefits. DACA does not, however, provide them either with lawful status or with most of the benefits that typically come with fully authorized immigration status. Some 700,000 people nonetheless availed themselves of this opportunity, which has allowed them to secure jobs, pursue professional career paths, support their families, serve their communities, and plan their lives with minimized fear of deportation.

DACA recipients include people who have pursued professional degrees and careers, like attorney Dulce G., who came to the country at age four, struggled through financial hardship, and received scholarships to attend law school. *Regents v. Dep't of Homeland Sec.*, 908 F.3d 476, 485–86 (9th Cir. 2018). So, too, with Yazmin I., a medical student pursuing surgical oncology, whose own mother left behind a career as a physician to provide opportunities to her children. DACA holders are entrepreneurs, like Sana A., a Lead Innovation Designer at a major multinational company; are breadwinners for their families, like Angelica V. who is a mother of five; and are public servants, like Maricruz R., a schoolteacher and member of the Oregon DACA Coalition. The list is long, extending to a diverse array of careers, institutions, companies, and communities. Amicus Br. of United We Dream & 50 Orgs. 3–36.

Five years after the creation of DACA, the Attorney General under a new President advised DHS to rescind DACA, based on his conclusion that it was unlawful. The Department's Acting Secretary issued a memorandum terminating the program, citing the reasons given by the Attorney General. The termination was challenged by DACA recipients and a wide range of parties who alleged, among other things, that racial animus motivating the decision was a violation of the Equal Protection Clause of the U.S. Constitution and that the Acting Secretary had violated the APA by failing to adequately consider the reliance interests of DACA holders and premising the rescission on a flawed legal premise. For the reasons that follow, we conclude that the equal protection claims should proceed in the lower courts, and that the Acting Secretary did violate the APA, such that the rescission must be vacated on that basis.

I

A

Congress enacts the immigration statutes governing who can enter and remain in the country with lawful status, as well as who is subject to deportation, through the Immigration and Nationality Act ("INA"). 8 U.S.C. §§ 1101–1537. But despite Congress' central role in developing the immigration laws, the executive branch must exercise prosecutorial discretion with respect to the implementation of those laws. Indeed, "[a] principal feature of the removal system is the broad discretion exercised by immigration officials." *Arizona v. United States*, 567 U.S. 387, 396 (2012). In any given case, immigration officials "must decide whether it makes sense to pursue removal at all." *Id.* And at each stage of the removal process, they have "discretion to abandon the endeavor." *Reno v. American-Arab Anti-Discrimination Comm.* (AADC), 525 U.S. 471, 483 (1999). Many forms of prosecutorial discretion exist, such as deferred action, parole, temporary protected status, deferred enforced departure, or extended voluntary departure. *See generally* Shoba Sivaprasad Wadhia, *Beyond Deportation: The Role of Prosecutorial Discretion in Immigration Cases* (2015).

This case involves the federal government's exercise of deferred action. By the time of the creation of DACA, deferred action was already a well-accepted feature of the executive's enforcement of the immigration laws. Although deferred action began "without express statutory authorization," *AADC*, 525 U.S. at 484 (citing Charles Gordon et al., *Immigration Law and Procedure* § 72.03[2][h] (Matthew Bender, ed. 1998)), it has since been recognized by the Supreme Court as a "regular practice." *Id.* Congress, too, has since explicitly recognized deferred action in the INA, 8 U.S.C. § 1227(d)(2); *see also* REAL ID Act of 2005, Pub. L. No. 109-13, div. B, 119 Stat. 231 § 202(c)(2)(B)(viii). Pursuant to federal statutory acknowledgement of deferred action, regulations promulgated in the 1980s allowed recipients of deferred action to apply for work authorization if they could demonstrate an "economic necessity for employment." Control of Employment of Aliens, 52 Fed. Reg. 16,216, 16,228 (May 1, 1987) (codified at 8 C.F.R. § 274a.12(c)(14)). Regulations promulgated under the George W. Bush Administration provided that deferred action recipients would not accrue "unlawful presence" for purposes of the INA's bars on re-entry. Eligibility for "U" Nonimmigrant Status, 72 Fed. Reg. 53,014, 53,039 (Sept. 17, 2007) (codified at 8 C.F.R. § 214.14(d)(3)). No law requires that deferred action be granted on an individualized basis. Nonetheless, numerous presidents have engaged in some form of deferral of deportation. Amicus Br. of Immigr. L. Scholars 9–12.

B

In June 2012, the Secretary of Homeland Security created a program to provide deferred action to "certain young people who were brought to this country as children." Janet Napolitano, Sec'y of Homeland Sec., Memorandum on Exercising Prosecutorial Discretion with Respect to Individuals Who Came to the U. S. as Children (June 15, 2012). Known as DACA and created by a memorandum issued by the Secretary, the program is available to noncitizens who were under age thirty-one as of June 15, 2012; came to the United States while under the age of sixteen; have continuously resided in the United States since June 15, 2007; are current students, have completed high school, or are honorably discharged veterans; have not been convicted of certain crimes identified by DHS; and are deemed by DHS to not threaten national security or public safety. *Id.* at 1.

The 2012 DACA Memorandum instructs the three primary immigration agencies, Immigration and Customs Enforcement (ICE), Customs and Border Protection (CBP), and Citizenship and Immigration Services (USCIS) to "immediately exercise their discretion, on an individual basis, in order to prevent low priority individuals from being placed into removal proceedings or removed from the United States." *Id.* at 2. It specifically directs ICE to exercise prosecutorial discretion and grant deferred action in two-year periods for persons in removal proceedings. *Id.* It also instructs USCIS to establish a process for applicants to request DACA, and to "accept applications to determine whether these individuals qualify for work authorization during this period of deferred action." *Id.* at 3. Deferred action has provided benefits to certain immigrants under regulations long predating DACA's creation, 52 Fed. Reg. at 16228; 72 Fed. Reg. at 53,039, so that recipients are eligible to receive Social Security and Medicare benefits, 8 C.F.R. § 1.3(a)(4)(vi); 42 C.F.R. § 417.422(h).

In November 2014, DHS issued a memorandum announcing expansions to DACA and the creation of another deferred action program. With respect to DACA, the memorandum sought to expand DACA eligibility by making more persons eligible for its benefits based on age and date of entry. The 2014 DACA expansions also increased the deferred action and work authorization period to three years, compared to the original two years in the 2012 program. Pol'y Directive 044-02, Jeh C. Johnson, Sec'y of Homeland Sec., Memorandum on Exercising Prosecutorial Discretion with Respect to Individuals Who Came to the United States as Children and with Respect to Certain Individuals Who Are the Parents of U.S. Citizens or Permanent Residents (Nov. 20, 2014). DHS also created a program, which came to be known as Deferred Action for Parents of Americans and Lawful Permanent Residents, or DAPA, which was designed to grant deferred action to certain parents whose children were U.S. citizens or lawful permanent residents. As the memorandum noted, "[c]ase-by-case exercises of deferred action for children and long-standing members of American society who are not enforcement priorities are in this Nation's security and economic interests and make common sense, because they encourage these people to come out of the shadows, submit to background checks, pay fees, apply for work authorization[,] ... and be counted." *Id.* at 3. It is estimated that over four million people would have benefited from DAPA. *Texas v. United States*, 809 F.3d 134, 148 (5th Cir. 2015).

Before DHS could implement the November 2014 Memorandum, twenty-six states, led by Texas, filed a lawsuit in the Southern District of Texas. *Texas v. United States*, 86 F. Supp. 3d 591, 604 (S.D. Tex. 2015), raising claims under the procedural requirements of the APA, substantive provisions of the Immigration and Nationality Act (INA), and the Constitution's Take Care Clause. *Id.* at 607, 614, 647. Finding the States likely to succeed on at least one of the claims, Judge Hanen entered a nationwide preliminary injunction that prohibited DHS from implementing both DAPA and the DACA expansion. However, the District Court order left the original 2012 DACA program in place. *Id.* at 677–78.

On appeal before the Court of Appeals for the Fifth Circuit, a divided panel affirmed the preliminary injunction. *Texas v. United States*, 809 F.3d 134, 187–88 (5th Cir. 2015). The majority upheld the injunction on two grounds, with a dissent from Judge King. First, the panel concluded that the States were likely to succeed on their procedural APA claim that the program should have been promulgated through notice-and-comment rulemaking. *Id.* at 177. Second, it held that DAPA conflicted with the INA, given that the INA already contained a process by which undocumented parents could derive lawful immigration status – referring to lawful permanent resident status – through their children's U.S. citizenship or lawful permanent resident status. But DAPA, by providing the limited immigration benefits of deferred action "solely on account of their children's immigration status," was inconsistent with this statutory scheme. *Id.* at 179–80, 186. The Fifth Circuit's holding was also based on its observation that "the INA does not grant the Secretary discretion to grant deferred action and lawful presence on a class-wide basis to 4.3 million otherwise removable aliens." *Id.* at 186 n.202. The Fifth Circuit did not reach the constitutional claims. The decision was later affirmed without opinion by an equally divided Supreme Court. *United States v. Texas,* – U.S. –, 136 S. Ct. 2271, 2272 (2016) (per curiam). After the Supreme Court's affirmance, litigation over DAPA and the DACA expansion continued in the District Court. And while DHS's implementation of those policies remained enjoined, the original 2012 DACA program continued.

C

In the months leading up to the November 2016 presidential election, then-candidate Donald Trump campaigned on a platform that promised to "Make America Great Again." This platform included vows to build a wall between the United States and Mexico and enhance security at U.S borders. The campaign frequently identified immigrants and immigration as the causes of multiple societal ills in the United States. When discussing immigration, then-candidate Trump made numerous statements regarding race and ethnicity, statements that were widely perceived to denigrate people and communities that identify – or are perceived – as racial and ethnic minorities. In November 2016, the U.S. Electoral College voting process resulted in the election of Trump. After his inauguration in January 2017, President Trump enacted a multitude of executive-level immigration policies, one of which included securing federal funding for the construction of a physical barrier along the U.S.-Mexico border.

Despite its general antagonism toward immigrants, the Trump Administration initially showed signs of support for DACA. A memorandum issued by then-DHS Secretary John Kelly in February 2017 explained that the Administration would immediately rescind all previously issued "directives, memoranda or field guidance" regarding immigration enforcement priorities – with the exception of the 2012 DACA and 2014 DAPA policies, which it did not revoke. In March 2017, then-Secretary Kelly stated that DACA shows the government's "commitment … toward … Dreamer[s];" Compl. ¶ 46, *Garcia v. United States,* No. 3:17-cv-05380 (N.D. Cal. Sept. 18, 2017). And in April 2017, the President stated that DACA recipients should "rest easy" because his policy would be to "allow the [D]reamers to stay." *Id.* ¶ 47. Finally, in June 2017, when the 2014 DAPA memo was rescinded (along with the expansions of DACA that took place in 2014), the Administration continued to leave the original 2012 DACA policy in place. John F. Kelly, Sec'y of Homeland Sec., Rescission of Memorandum Providing for Deferred Action for Parents of Americans and Lawful Permanent Residents ("DAPA") (June 15, 2017).[34]

---

[34] During that same month, ten of the twenty-six plaintiffs from the DAPA litigation wrote to Attorney General Jeff Sessions to demand rescission of the 2012 DACA memo by September 5. If so, they would dismiss the still-pending DAPA litigation or otherwise amend their complaint to additionally challenge the legality of DACA.

But several months later, on September 4, 2017, the Attorney General advised Acting Secretary of Homeland Security Elaine Duke via a short letter to rescind DACA. That letter stated as follows:

DACA was effectuated by the previous administration through executive action, without proper statutory authority and with no established end-date, after Congress' repeated rejection of proposed legislation that would have accomplished a similar result. Such an open-ended circumvention of immigration laws was an unconstitutional exercise of authority by the Executive Branch.

The Attorney General cited the Fifth Circuit's opinion and this Court's 4-4 affirmance to conclude that DACA shared the "same legal … defects that the courts recognized as to DAPA" and was therefore "likely" to meet a similar fate. Letter from Jefferson B. Sessions III, U.S. Att'y Gen., to Elaine Duke, Acting Sec'y of Homeland Sec. (Sept. 4, 2017).

The next day, on September 5, 2017, Duke issued a memorandum that implemented the advice of the Attorney General. That memo described the background of DACA and DAPA, the outcomes of the litigation in the appeals court and this Court, and the Attorney General's letter, and concluded that the "DACA program should be terminated." Elaine C. Duke, Acting Sec'y of Homeland Sec., Memorandum on Rescission of DACA (Sept. 5, 2017). The memo did not engage in independent analysis of the Attorney General's claims as to DACA's unlawfulness. While the Duke memo described how DHS would wind down the program, the memo did not discuss how the rescission of DACA would impact the over 700,000 individuals who had relied on the program for the prior five years.

Later that same day, President Trump announced on Twitter that he might "revisit" the rescission of DACA. See Donald J. Trump (@realDonaldTrump), Twitter (Sept. 5, 2017, 8:38 PM). In the months following the issuance of the Duke Memo, President Trump continued to issue public statements about DACA, which suggested that DHS rescinded the program in order to increase the Administration's political leverage with Congress in its negotiations over funding the border wall and other immigration measures. On October 8, 2017, for example, President Trump sent a letter to congressional leaders setting out "Immigration Principles and Policies" that "must be included as part of any legislation addressing the status of [DACA] recipients." Letter from Donald J. Trump to Congressional Leaders (Oct. 8, 2017). These "Principles and Policies" included funding for a border wall. *Id.* In subsequent statements, the President explicitly linked the continuation of DACA with the border wall. See Donald J. Trump (@realDonaldTrump), Twitter (Dec. 29, 2017, 8:16 AM) ("The Democrats have been told, and fully understand, that there can be no DACA without the desperately needed WALL at the Southern Border and an END to the horrible Chain Migration & ridiculous Lottery System of Immigration etc."); Donald J. Trump (@realDonaldTrump), Twitter (Jan. 23, 2018, 11:07 PM) ("[I]f there is no Wall, there is no DACA."); Donald J. Trump

(@realDonaldTrump), Twitter (Feb. 5, 2018, 9:36 AM) ("Any deal on DACA that does not include STRONG border security and the desperately needed WALL is a total waste of time.").

D

After Acting Secretary Duke's rescission announcement, various plaintiffs ranging from individual DACA recipients and states to the Regents of the University of California and the National Association for the Advancement of Colored People challenged the rescission of DACA in the U.S. District Courts for the Northern District of California (*Regents of the Univ. of Cal. v. United States Dep't of Homeland Sec.*), the Eastern District of New York (*Batalla Vidal v. Duke*), and the District of Columbia (*NAACP v. Trump*). The claims that the rescission violated the Equal Protection Clause and amounted to arbitrary and capricious agency action in violation of the APA are relevant here.[35]

All three District Courts ruled for the plaintiffs on at least one claim at different stages of the litigation. The equal protection claims were found to have been adequately alleged in both *Regents* and *Batalla Vidal*, in light of President Trump's statements as candidate and in office, the disproportionate impact of the DACA rescission on Latinx communities, and the timing of the rescission. 298 F. Supp. 3d 1304, 1315 (N.D. Cal. 2018); 291 F. Supp. 3d 260, 279 (E.D.N.Y. 2018). The *Regents* and *Batalla Vidal* courts also found that the plaintiffs were likely to succeed on the merits of their arbitrary and capricious claims, and entered coextensive nationwide preliminary injunctions. 279 F. Supp. 3d 1011, 1046–48 (N.D. Cal. 2018); 279 F. Supp. 3d 401, 436–47 (E.D.N.Y. 2018). In NAACP, the D.C. District Court granted partial summary judgment to the plaintiffs on their APA claim, while deferring a ruling on the equal protection claim. 298 F. Supp. 3d 209, 246, 249 (D.D.C. 2018). The District Court stayed its order for ninety days to permit DHS to "reissue a memorandum rescinding DACA, this time providing a fuller explanation for the determination that the program lacks statutory and constitutional authority." *Id.* at 245.

In response to the D.C. District Court's order, Duke's successor, Secretary Kirstjen M. Nielsen, issued another memorandum to elaborate upon the reasons for rescinding DACA. Kirstjen M. Nielsen, Sec'y of Homeland Sec., Memorandum on the Rescission of DACA (June 22, 2018). First, Secretary Nielsen reiterated the Attorney General's position as to DACA's unlawfulness. Second, she added that the agency sought to avoid "legally questionable" policies. Third, she identified policy reasons for rescinding DACA. The final paragraph of the memorandum noted the "asserted reliance interests" associated with continuing DACA but determined that they did

---

[35] Plaintiffs also raised notice and comment claims, which failed below, and assorted due process challenges, some of which survived motions to dismiss. Those claims are not before us.

not "outweigh the questionable legality of the DACA policy and other reasons" for the rescission. The D.C. District Court declined to revise its prior order in light of Secretary Nielsen's memo, finding that it did not provide sufficient elaboration and explanation for either the agency's claims that DACA was unlawful or of the need for the rescission. *NAACP v. Trump*, 315 F. Supp. 3d 457, 460–61, 473–74 (D.D.C. 2018).

While appeals before the Second, Ninth, and D.C. Circuits were still pending, the Government filed three simultaneous petitions for certiorari before judgment. The case comes to us in an unusual procedural posture, insofar as it was after the Ninth Circuit affirmed the nationwide injunction in *Regents*, 908 F.3d 476 (2018), but before the other two Circuits issued rulings. We nonetheless granted the petitions and consolidated the cases. 139 S. Ct. 2779 (2019). We note the concerns raised by the district and appeals courts in *Regents* and *Vidal* that the administrative record before the courts was incomplete. We nonetheless evaluate the claims raised here.

II

The Government Invokes Two Jurisdictional Provisions of the INA as Independent Bars to Review. Neither Applies

Section 1252(b)(9) bars review of claims arising from "action[s]" or "proceeding[s] brought to remove an alien." 8 U.S.C. § 1252(b)(9). That targeted language is not aimed at this sort of case. As we have said before, § 1252(b)(9) "does not present a jurisdictional bar" where those bringing suit "are not asking for review of an order of removal," "are not challenging the decision … to seek removal," or "are not even challenging the process by which … removability will be determined." *Jennings* v. *Rodriguez*, 138 S. Ct. 830, 841 (2018) (plurality opinion); *id.* at 876 (Breyer, J., dissenting). And it is certainly not a bar where, as here, the parties are not challenging any removal proceedings.

Section 1252(g) is similarly narrow. That provision limits review of cases "arising from" decisions "to commence proceedings, adjudicate cases, or execute removal orders." 8 U.S.C. § 1252(g). We have previously rejected as "implausible" the Government's suggestion that § 1252(g) covers "all claims arising from deportation proceedings" or imposes "a general jurisdictional limitation." *AADC*, 525 U.S. at 482. The rescission, which revokes a deferred action program with associated benefits, is not a decision to "commence proceedings," much less to "adjudicate" a case or "execute" a removal order.

III

We first address Respondents' equal protection challenges. These claims come to us in a preliminary posture. All that respondents needed to do at this stage of the litigation was state sufficient facts that would "allo[w a] court to draw the reasonable inference that [a] defendant is liable for the misconduct alleged." *Ashcroft v. Iqbal*, 556 U.S. 662, 678 (2009).[36] Facially neutral actions can run afoul of the Equal Protection Clause where the enactment was motivated by a discriminatory purpose and results in a disproportionate impact on racial and ethnic minorities. *Arlington Heights v. Metropolitan Housing Development Corp.*, 429 U.S. 252, 264–66 (1977). A showing of racially disproportionate impact, alone, is not sufficient for an equal protection finding. *Washington v. Davis*, 426 U.S. 229, 242 (1976). But assessing discrimination "demands a sensitive inquiry," including both "circumstantial and direct evidence of intent," for which impact may provide a "starting point." *Arlington Heights*, 429 U.S. at 266. In evaluating equal protection claims, courts should assess the historical context and background of the governmental action, the specific events preceding the decision, the extent to which normal procedures were followed, and the contemporary statements of the decision-makers. *Id.* at 267–68.

Moreover, although the executive enjoys broad discretion to implement immigration policy, that discretion is not so broad as to permit the executive to engage in government-sponsored discrimination. And when it comes to the unique population of young people who came to the United States as children, this Court has recognized value in "the abolition of governmental barriers presenting unreasonable obstacles to advancement on the basis of individual merit." *Plyler v. Doe*, 457 U.S. 202, 222 (1982).

Respondents' claims should be permitted to proceed on remand. The complaints each set forth particularized facts that plausibly allege discriminatory animus.

First, President Trump made statements both before and after he assumed office sufficient to suggest that racial animus motivated the decision to rescind DACA. As the underlying complaints detailed, then-candidate Trump declared, for instance, that Mexican immigrants are "the bad ones," and "criminals, drug dealers, [and] rapists," and that individuals protesting at his campaign rally were "thugs who were flying the Mexican flag." *Batalla Vidal*, 291 F. Supp. 3d at 276 (internal quotation marks omitted). Before and after the inauguration, Trump described Latinx immigrants as "animals" and "bad hombres." *Id.* As President, Trump claimed that undocumented immigrants were responsible for "the drugs, the gangs, the cartels, the crisis of smuggling and trafficking, [and] MS 13." *Regents*, 298 F. Supp. 3d at 1314 (internal quotation marks omitted).

The Government urges us to treat these statements as divorced in time and context from the decision to rescind DACA. This Court recently chose to minimize the significance of the President's statements in evaluating Proclamation

---

[36] The Government contends that the equal protection claim is foreclosed by *AADC*, 525 U.S. at 488. But the challenge today is not raised "as a defense against [] deportation," and is not a claim of "selective enforcement." *Id.* Rather, it is a freestanding claim that the Executive Branch was motivated by racial animus to end a program that overwhelmingly benefits a certain ethnic group.

No. 9645, 82 Fed. Reg. 45,161 (Sept. 24, 2017), which barred entry of individuals from several Muslim-majority countries, *Trump* v. *Hawaii*, 138 S. Ct. 2392 (2018). There, we rationalized that foreign policy and national security concerns justified rejecting the equal protection claims raised. We leave it to future generations to pass judgment on the wisdom of our decision in *Hawaii*. For present purposes, DACA recipients do not implicate the same concerns as *Hawaii*. The President's statements reveal how the Administration views the recipients of DACA and those most impacted by migration from Mexico. According to respondents, the President's belief and encouragement of the view that DACA recipients and their communities were less than fully human because of their race and association with Mexico were an animating force behind the rescission of DACA. Taken together, "the words of the President," even more so here than in *Hawaii*, help to "create the strong perception" that the rescission decision was "contaminated by impermissible discriminatory animus." *Id.* at 2440 (Sotomayor, J., dissenting). This perception provides respondents with grounds to litigate their equal protection claims further.

The Government also argues that the decision to rescind DACA belonged to Secretary Duke, not the President. But a President generally has tremendous influence over his cabinet. *See Humphrey's Executor v. United States*, 295 U.S. 602, 627–28 (1935) (citing *Myers v. United States*, 272 U.S. 52 (1926)). With the DACA rescission, President Trump specifically issued statements over Twitter to suggest that he was a driving force behind the rescission. The President is certainly free to make whatever statements he wishes. What he cannot do is issue statement after statement evincing, encouraging, and fomenting racial animus toward immigrants, direct the creation of policies consistent with that animus, and insulate his actions from constitutional scrutiny by disclaiming responsibility over those actions altogether simply because a member of his cabinet carries out the action.

Second, the impact of the policy decision on Latinx persons is extraordinary, with approximately ninety-three percent of current DACA recipients belonging to Latinx communities. Compl. ¶ 9, *Cty. of Santa Clara v. Trump*, No. 3:17-cv-05813 (N.D. Cal. Oct. 10, 2017). This disproportionate impact must be viewed in the context of the President's public statements on and off the campaign trail. At the motion-to-dismiss stage, further consideration is merited for an allegation that an executive decision disproportionately harms the same racial group that the President branded as undesirable mere months earlier.

We recognize that a number of immigration policies have an acute impact on racial and ethnic minorities in the United States. There is a concern that permitting the equal protection claims to go forward regarding the DACA rescission will render a vast array of immigration laws and policies vulnerable to equal protection challenges. But this case does not raise a challenge to the entire immigration scheme. And the possibility of future challenges does not justify wholesale dismissal of the equal protection claims at this early stage in the litigation. The particular impact of the DACA rescission – in combination with the President's statements – makes the equal protection challenges worthy of further development in the lower courts.

The nation's immigration laws have a long history in racism, bigotry, and discrimination dating back to the Chinese Exclusion Acts, and continuing on through laws barring the naturalization of nonwhite people, the national origins quota system, and the targeting of Mexican immigrants for deportation at various points in history. *See generally* Kelly Lyttle Hernandez, *Migra! A History of the U.S. Border Patrol* (2010); Kevin R. Johnson, *The "Huddled Masses" Myth: Immigration and Civil Rights* (2004); Ian Haney Lopez, *White by Law* (2006); Lucy Salyer, *Laws Harsh as Tigers: Chinese Immigrants and the Shaping of Modern Immigration Law* (1995). As the NAACP stated, "when the Government is motivated by racial discrimination in publicly canceling a program that protects hundreds of thousands of people from removal, it sends an unmistakable message of racial hierarchy to society as a whole." Amicus Br. of NAACP Legal Def. & Educ. Fund, Inc. & LatinoJustice PRLDEF, at 15. Whether other immigration laws are vulnerable to equal protection concerns in the future remains to be considered in a future case. By allowing the claims to proceed at the current stage, we permit the courts to at least evaluate the merits of those claims.

The facts in respondents' complaints create more than a "sheer possibility that a defendant has acted unlawfully." *Iqbal*, 556 U.S. at 678. Whether they ultimately amount to actionable discrimination should be determined only after factual development on remand. We do not have the benefit of a fully developed administrative record in this matter, and it is too early to dismiss the equal protection claims without the benefit of a complete record.

IV

"The APA sets forth the procedures by which federal agencies are accountable to the public and their actions subject to review by the courts." *Franklin v. Massachusetts*, 505 U.S. 788, 796 (1992). It requires agencies to engage in "reasoned decisionmaking," *Michigan v. EPA*, 576 U.S. 743, 750 (2015) (quoting *Allentown Mack Sales & Service, Inc. v. NLRB*, 522 U.S. 359, 374 (1998)), and directs that agency actions be "set aside" if they are "arbitrary" or "capricious," 5 U.S.C. § 706(2)(A). Under this "narrow standard of review, ... a court is not to substitute its judgment for that of the agency," *FCC v. Fox Television Stations, Inc.*, 556 U.S. 502, 513 (2009) (quoting *Motor Vehicle Mfrs. Assn. of United States, Inc. v. State Farm Mut. Automobile Ins. Co.*, 463 U.S. 29, 43 (1983)), but instead to assess only "whether the decision was based on a consideration of the relevant factors and whether there has been a clear error of judgment," *Citizens to Preserve Overton Park, Inc. v. Volpe (Overton Park)*, 401 U.S. 402, 416 (1971).

A

Before turning to the arbitrary and capricious claims, we first address the Government's argument that DHS's decision is unreviewable under the APA and that this Court lacks jurisdiction.

Although the APA establishes a "basic presumption of judicial review [for] one 'suffering legal wrong because of agency action,'" *Abbott Laboratories v. Gardner*, 387 U.S. 136, 140 (1967) (quoting 5 U.S.C. § 702), the Government argues that the presumption is rebutted because the DACA rescission amounts to "agency action [that] is committed to agency discretion by law," § 701(a)(2).

To "honor the presumption of review, we have read the exception in § 701(a) (2) quite narrowly," *Weyerhaeuser Co. v. United States Fish and Wildlife Serv.*, 139 S. Ct. 361, 370 (2018), and have limited it to those rare "administrative decision[s] traditionally left to agency discretion," *Lincoln v. Vigil*, 508 U.S. 182, 191 (1993). This narrow category of unreviewable actions includes an agency's decision not to institute enforcement proceedings, *Heckler v. Chaney*, 470 U.S. 821, 831–32 (1985). The Government primarily relies on this exception.

In *Chaney*, the Court held that the Food and Drug Administration (FDA)'s denial of a petition by several death row inmates, requesting that the FDA take enforcement action, was presumptively unreviewable. We emphasized the well-established tradition that "an agency's decision not to prosecute or enforce" is "generally committed to an agency's absolute discretion." *Id.* at 831. *Chaney* identified a number of factors leading to this presumption, reasons that generally have to do with an agency's decision not to enforce the law. The Government contends that the rescission of DACA is equivalent to the individual nonenforcement decision at issue in *Chaney*, arguing that the rescission of DACA as a nonenforcement policy is no different – for purposes of reviewability – from the initial adoption of that policy.

However, *Chaney* recognized "a critical distinction between enforcement decisions and *non*-enforcement decisions," Br. for Regents 23–24, because "when an agency refuses to act it generally does not exercise its *coercive* power over an individual's liberty or property rights." 470 U.S. at 832. The DACA rescission is not simply an act of nonenforcement. For a DACA recipient to lose the protection from deportation offered by DACA means increased vulnerability to the possibility of deportation and detention, along with the family separation, alienation, physical isolation and loss of home that come with immigration enforcement. Thus, "[b]y *eliminating* a non-enforcement policy, the government paves the way for the subsequent exercise of coercive power over individuals, including arrest and deportation." Br. for Regents 24. *Chaney* permits review in situations where the government's coercive power over its subjects is enhanced by the agency action.

Not only does the rescission of DACA impact the government's coercive power over people by eliminating protection from deportation, it comes nowhere close to resembling the one-time enforcement decision at issue in *Chaney* in terms of scope and impact. The DACA rescission here affects nearly 700,000 people, with widespread impact on multiple industries, communities, and families.

The benefits attendant to and process for instituting deferred action provide further confirmation that DACA is more than simply a nonenforcement policy. By virtue of receiving deferred action, the 700,000 DACA recipients may request work authorization and are eligible for Social Security and Medicare. Unlike an agency's refusal to take requested enforcement action, access to such benefits is an interest "courts often are called upon to protect." *Chaney*, 470 U.S. at 832.

Because the rescission of the DACA program involves a different set of factors from a nonenforcement policy, its rescission is subject to review under the APA and is not covered by the narrow exception to judicial review at 5 U.S.C. § 701(a)(2).

B

We now turn to the claim that the rescission of DACA was arbitrary and capricious. The DACA rescission fails for at least two reasons: first, because the Secretary failed to adequately weigh the significant reliance interests of the over 700,000 DACA recipients; and second, because the rescission rested on a flawed legal premise regarding the legality of DACA. The Secretary's actions might also be invalid under the APA for a third reason, that the reasons for the decision were pretextual in nature, but the sparse administrative record does not permit us to draw that conclusion here.

Since 2012, DACA recipients have "enrolled in degree programs, embarked on careers, started businesses, purchased homes, and even married and had children, all in reliance" on the DACA program. Br. for Regents 41. Indeed, ninety-six percent of DACA recipients are employed or enrolled in school, more than seventy percent pursued educational opportunities not previously available to them, and nearly sixty percent entered the workforce for the first time. Amicus Br. of United We Dream 7. DACA recipients as a whole own 59,000 homes, making $613.8 million in mortgage payments. Their spending power is about $24.1 billion. Excluding DACA recipients from the lawful labor force may result in the loss of $215 billion in economic activity and an associated $60 billion in federal tax revenue over the next ten years. Br. for Regents 6. Meanwhile, states and local governments could lose $1.25 billion in tax revenue each year. *Id.* Some DACA recipients, such as members of LGBT communities, have relied on DACA for safety and security that they might not enjoy in their countries of origin. Amicus Br. of United We Dream 33–36. The consequences of the rescission would "radiate outward" to DACA recipients' families (including their 200,000 U.S.-citizen children), to the schools where DACA recipients study and teach, to the employers who have invested time and money in training them, and to the communities that they serve. Br. for Regents 41–42; Br. for Resp't State of N.Y. et al. 42; *see also* Amicus Br. of 143 Bus. Ass'ns & Cos. 17 (estimating that hiring and training replacements would cost employers $6.3 billion). Indeed, DACA recipients are part of the fabric of the United States. It is worth acknowledging that their value does not arrive from their degrees, professional accomplishments, or economic contributions, but because they are 700,000 different human beings and members of the national community.

To date, Attorney General Sessions has issued one letter (the September 2017 letter), and two Secretaries of Homeland Security have issued two memoranda purporting to explain the justification for the DACA rescission: Acting Secretary Duke's September 2017 memo and Secretary Nielsen's June 2018 memo.

The Attorney General's letter was the first explanation for the rescission, based on his conclusion that the original creation of DACA lacked statutory authority, was created despite Congressional rejection of legislation that would have benefitted the DACA recipient population, and that the program was unconstitutional. The letter is one page long, and hardly reflects an explanation to match the scale and scope of the decision to rescind DACA. Sessions, *supra*.

The next day, Acting Secretary Duke issued the official memorandum rescinding DACA. Duke, *supra*. The Duke Memorandum, while lengthier than the Sessions letter, merely echoed the reasons given by the Attorney General. The Duke Memorandum stated that "[t]aking into consideration" the Fifth Circuit's conclusion that DAPA was unlawful because it conferred benefits in violation of the INA, and the Attorney General's conclusion that DACA was unlawful for the same reason, she concluded – without elaboration – that the "DACA program should be terminated."

As a result of the litigation, in June 2018, Secretary Nielsen issued a memorandum months later purporting to justify the DACA rescission. Nielsen, *supra*. That memo also included the argument that DACA was not lawfully issued and reflected some acknowledgement of the impact of the decision on DACA recipients' lives. For reasons explained in the next section, we do not consider that memorandum. If we did consider that memorandum, we would note that while the Nielsen Memo does include a reference to weighing reliance interests, that reference is shallow.

When an agency changes course, as DHS did here, it must "be cognizant that longstanding policies may have 'engendered serious reliance interests that must be taken into account.'" *Encino Motorcars, LLC v. Navarro*, 136 S. Ct. 2117, 2126 (2016) (quoting *Fox Television*, 556 U.S. at 515, finding it "arbitrary and capricious to ignore such matters"). Indeed, where "serious reliance interests [are] at stake," the government must provide more than "conclusory statements." *Id.* at 2127.

Both the Attorney General and Duke also failed to address whether there was "legitimate reliance" on the DACA Memorandum. "Not tak[ing] account of legitimate reliance on prior interpretation" can indicate that a policy change is arbitrary and capricious. *Smiley v. Citibank (South Dakota), N. A.*, 517 U.S. 735, 742 (1996). The Government suggests that the DACA rescission was not required to consider these reliance interests, given the relatively short length of the DACA grants (two years) and that the original DACA program stated that it conferred "no substantive rights." App. to Pet. for Cert. 101a. As a practical matter, it is obvious that hundreds of thousands of DACA recipients and those close to them planned their lives around the program. DHS' authority to terminate DACA does not render those reliance interests as lacking in seriousness or substance. Similarly, the contingent, discretionary nature of DACA benefits does not diminish the legally cognizable reliance interests that existed with DACA.

Indeed, substantive rights to immigration status are not the same thing as reliance interests. As in *Encino Motorcars*, a car dealer may not have a Fifth Amendment entitlement to the Department of Labor's hewing to a particular interpretation of the Fair Labor Standards Act. But the absence of the constitutional right does not empower the Department to disregard reliance interests engendered by the longstanding interpretation of the Act when it alters its regulations. *See Encino Motorcars*, 136 S. Ct. at 2126. Given the wide impact of the DACA program, not just on individual recipients but on nearly every sector of U.S. society, the government should have at least considered the broader reliance interests associated with terminating the program with a level of thoroughness and consideration that matches the scale of the program. While it is not up to this Court to dictate the specific policy outcome that full consideration of the reliance interests at stake would be, it is clear that the Attorney General and Secretary's treatment of those interests was woefully inadequate.

The rescission of DACA also violates the APA due to its misconception regarding DACA's supposed illegality. While administrative agencies enjoy considerable flexibility to enact policy judgments without judicial intervention, a minimum expectation is that the government avoid making decisions based on incorrect legal positions. We have long stated that governmental action "may not stand if the agency has misconceived the law." *SEC v. Chenery Corp.*, 318 U.S. 80, 94 (1943). The central reason provided by the Attorney General, later repeated by the Secretary, was that the initial DACA program was unlawful. This rationale was not legally sufficient.

The reality is (and always has been) that the executive agencies charged with immigration enforcement do not have the resources required to deport every single person present in this country without authorization. Hiroshi Motomura, *Immigration Outside the Law* 26 (2014) ("The letter of the law creates a large removable population, but whether an individual is actually targeted for removal has long depended on government discretion and bad luck."). Recognizing this state of affairs, Congress has explicitly charged the Secretary of Homeland Security with "[e]stablishing national immigration enforcement policies and priorities." 6 U.S.C. § 202(5).

It is therefore no surprise that deferred action has been a feature of our immigration system – albeit one of executive invention – for decades; has been employed categorically on numerous occasions; and has been recognized as a practical reality by both Congress and the courts. In a world where the government can remove only a small percentage of the undocumented noncitizens present in this country in any year, deferred action programs like DACA enable DHS to devote much-needed resources to make necessary enforcement choices. Change is common in immigration law and in the statuses that individuals hold. Alas, an undocumented person who is subject to deportation today may well be a lawful resident, even a citizen, tomorrow. *See Plyler v. Doe*, 457 U.S. 202, 226 (1982). The possibility of changes in status anticipated by the statutory scheme thus supports the exercise of prosecutorial discretion by the executive.

Although the issue is not directly before us, we observe that various factors weigh in favor of finding that DACA was a permissible exercise of executive discretion. The history of deferred action, judicial and legislative recognition of its use, and practical need for prosecutorial discretion in the immigration system all weigh in favor of this Court finding that it was a lawful act of government power. *See generally* Amicus Br. of Immigr. L. Scholars.

The Sessions Letter expresses several possible bases for the agency's ultimate conclusion that DACA was unlawful. Sessions, *supra*. First, the Attorney General states that "DACA was effectuated by the previous administration through executive action ... after Congress' repeated rejection of proposed legislation that would have accomplished a similar result." But nonaction by the legislative branch does not provide a basis for assessing legality. Moreover, the proposed DREAM Act and the DACA program, while addressing the needs of a similar population, do not provide the same types of relief. The DREAM Act would have provided a path to lawful permanent resident status, while DACA simply defers removal. Concluding that Congress' failure to provide relief to a particular population thereby precludes the executive branch from enacting different policies designed to benefit that same population implies a legislative power to declare what the law is through inaction – a power that simply does not exist. This argument therefore provides no independent reason to think that DACA is unlawful.

The Attorney General's primary other bases for concluding that DACA was illegal were that the program was "effectuated ... without proper statutory authority" and that it amounted to "an unconstitutional exercise of authority." More specifically, the Attorney General asserted that "the DACA policy has the same legal and constitutional defects that the courts recognized as to DAPA" in the *Texas* litigation.

As the Ninth Circuit observed, "[t]he claim of 'constitutional defects' is a puzzling one because as all the parties recognize, no court has ever held that DAPA is unconstitutional." *Regents*, 908 F.3d at 506. The government makes no attempt in this appeal to defend the Attorney General's assertion that the DACA program is unconstitutional, instead pointing to both Secretaries' lack of reliance on the unconstitutionality argument. We therefore do not address it further.

Regarding DACA's alleged legal defects, the long history of deferred action in immigration enforcement belies the Attorney General's contention. Moreover, the Fifth Circuit's reasons for striking down the related DAPA policy do not directly apply to DACA. The Fifth Circuit concluded that DAPA was unlawful on two grounds: first, that DAPA should have been promulgated through notice-and-comment rulemaking; and second, that DAPA was substantively inconsistent with the INA. See *Texas v. United States*, 809 F.3d 134, 171–78, 179–86 (5th Cir. 2015). It is worth emphasizing that the Fifth Circuit's decision came at the preliminary injunction stage, as a result of which DAPA never went into effect. The *Texas* decision was therefore not a conclusion as to DAPA's legality on the merits, but rather an initial assessment of the likelihood of success.

The Attorney General and Secretary relied on the Fifth Circuit's statutory authority holding. But the Fifth Circuit's conclusion that DAPA lacked statutory authorization relied on reasons that are specific to the undocumented parents of status-holding children, reasons that do not apply to DACA. *Id.* at 179–80 (stating that the INA contains "an intricate process for illegal aliens to derive a lawful immigration classification from their children's immigration status" but that "DAPA would allow illegal aliens to receive the benefits of lawful presence solely on account of their children's immigration status without complying with any of the requirements … that Congress has deliberately imposed.").[37] With respect to DACA holders, the Fifth Circuit did not discuss any similar provisions in the INA that define how undocumented persons who arrived in the United States as children may obtain status.

The Fifth Circuit's injunction also applied to the expanded DACA program, but the lower court failed to analyze those provisions of the program. Instead, one of the key bases for the Fifth Circuit's reasoning – that the INA already contained a provision through which parents could gain immigration status through their children – applies to neither DACA nor its expansion. The *Texas* courts' treatment of DACA thus fails to provide persuasive authority for the Attorney General's claim of DACA's illegality.

The Government also points to the issue of "litigation risk," as opposed to outright illegality, as a basis for the rescission. But the language of the Attorney General's announcement fails to make a distinction between the two, and the record here suggests no meaningful difference between the two concepts.

Finally, agency action may also be set aside where it rests "on a pretextual basis," an analysis that may require delving into extra-record evidence, particularly where "the evidence tells a story that does not match the explanation [given] for [a] decision." *Dep't of Commerce v. New York*, 139 S. Ct. 2551, 2573–75 (2019). Despite the sparse administrative record before us, the reasons given by the Attorney General and Secretary related to the legality of DACA do not appear to tell the whole story. Instead, some of the evidence suggests that the DACA rescission was both motivated

---

[37] We note that the Fifth Circuit's reasoning was flawed on its face, given that the Fifth Circuit relied on INA provisions that allowed U.S. citizen or lawful permanent resident children to petition for the lawful permanent resident status of their parents, thereby raising a series of immigration classifications entirely distinct from the DACA or DAPA-eligible population.

by racial animus and deployed by President Trump as a "bargaining chip" in efforts to secure Congressional funding for the construction of a border wall. The "specific sequence of events leading up to the challenged decision," *Arlington Heights v. Metropolitan Housing Development Corp.*, 429 U.S. 252, 267 (1977), especially the abrupt change in position, plausibly suggests that something other than questions about the legality of DACA motivated the rescission decision. Accordingly, it raises the possibility of a "significant mismatch between the decision … made and the rationale … provided." 139 S. Ct. at 2575. As late as June 2017, DHS insisted it remained committed to the original DACA program, even while rescinding DAPA as well as the 2014 expansions to DACA. But a mere three months later, DHS terminated DACA in its entirety without considering important aspects of the termination.

Unlike *Department of Commerce*, we have a minimal administrative record. But *Department of Commerce* illustrated how the initial administrative record submitted to the Court lacked evidence that ultimately became available as the litigation continued. *Dep't of Commerce*, 139 S. Ct. at 2564, 2574. We therefore remand with the expectation that the administrative record will be supplemented so that resolution of the pretext-based claims of arbitrary and capricious action can take place.

C

The Government urges us to also consider the rationales provided in Secretary Nielsen's June 2018 memo. Nielsen, *supra*. But under traditional administrative law principles, courts may review agency action based only on the reasons given by an agency at the time it took the action. *Michigan*, 576 U.S. at 758. A court can remand to provide an agency with an opportunity to provide a fuller explanation of the agency's reasoning *at the time of the agency action." Pension Benefit Guaranty Corporation v. LTV Corp.*, 496 U.S. 633, 654 (1990) (emphasis added). In providing elaboration for its initial decision, the agency is not free to provide new justifications for its prior action. *Camp v. Pitts*, 411 U.S. 138, 143 (1973) (*per curiam*). An agency can "deal with the problem afresh" by taking *new* agency action. *SEC v. Chenery Corp.*, 332 U.S. 194, 201 (1947) (*Chenery II*), and may offer additional rationales, but in doing so must adhere to the procedural requirements for the new agency action.

The Nielsen Memorandum was by its own terms not a new rule implementing a new policy. Rather than making a new decision, Secretary Nielsen "decline[d] to disturb the Duke memorandum's rescission" and instead "provide[d] further explanation" for that action. Nielsen, *supra*, at 1. In other words, Secretary Nielsen expanded upon the justifications given for the initial rescission of DACA. The Secretary did not take new agency action. Accordingly, the explanations provided by Secretary Nielsen must not amount to impermissible "*post hoc* rationalization." *Overton Park*, 401 U.S. at 420.

But rather than explain the Duke Memorandum's reliance on the argument that the original DACA program was unlawful, *see* Duke, *supra*, Secretary Nielsen instead offers three separate reasons for the rescission. Only one argument addresses DACA's legality. The second argument is that DACA is legally *uncertain,* such that maintaining public trust in the rule of law and avoiding burdensome litigation warrants rescinding the program. But the Duke Memorandum focused on the illegality of DACA, not on the risks associated with its legally questionable status. Third, Secretary Nielsen cites policy reasons as a basis for the rescission, namely that (1) the belief that any class-based immigration relief should come from Congress, not through executive nonenforcement; (2) DHS' preference for exercising prosecutorial discretion on "a truly individualized, case-by-case basis;" and (3) the importance of "project[ing] a message" that immigration laws would be enforced against all classes and categories of aliens. *Id.* at 2–3. But again, neither the Duke Memorandum nor the Attorney General's letter makes any mention of such policy rationales. Given that they amount to *post hoc* rationalizations, they do not change the outcome.

* * *

Debates over immigration have long prompted a range of views. Those debates and ensuing governmental policies have also influenced how racial minorities associated with recent migration are perceived in society. Indeed, the substance of our immigration policies reflects the character of the United States. While this court does not develop the immigration law, where evidence of racial animus appears to have infected a governmental action, then the promise of equal protection should allow discrimination claims to be fully evaluated through the judicial process.

The procedures used to craft those immigration policies matter, too. Irrespective of the multiple views on what immigration policy should be, the government's exercise of discretion is bound by the basic principle that it must adequately consider how its discretionary decisions could impact affected individuals, particularly when the magnitude of those decisions impact hundreds of thousands of people and multiple industries, institutions, and communities. Furthermore, part of the agency avoiding arbitrary and capricious action includes getting the law right when making decisions based on assessments of legality. We recognize that the affected population – young people who came to the United States as children and who have pursued educations, careers, and families here – warrants special consideration. That consideration was absent in the agency's decision here.

All three cases are remanded for further proceedings consistent with this opinion. *It is so ordered.*

Subject Index

Printed in the USA
CPSIA information can be obtained
at www.ICGtesting.com
LVHW021449111123
763672LV00004B/114

9 781009 198943